Forget Me Not

2

ORIGINAL STORY:
Mag Hsu

ART:
Nao Emoto

2

CONTENTS

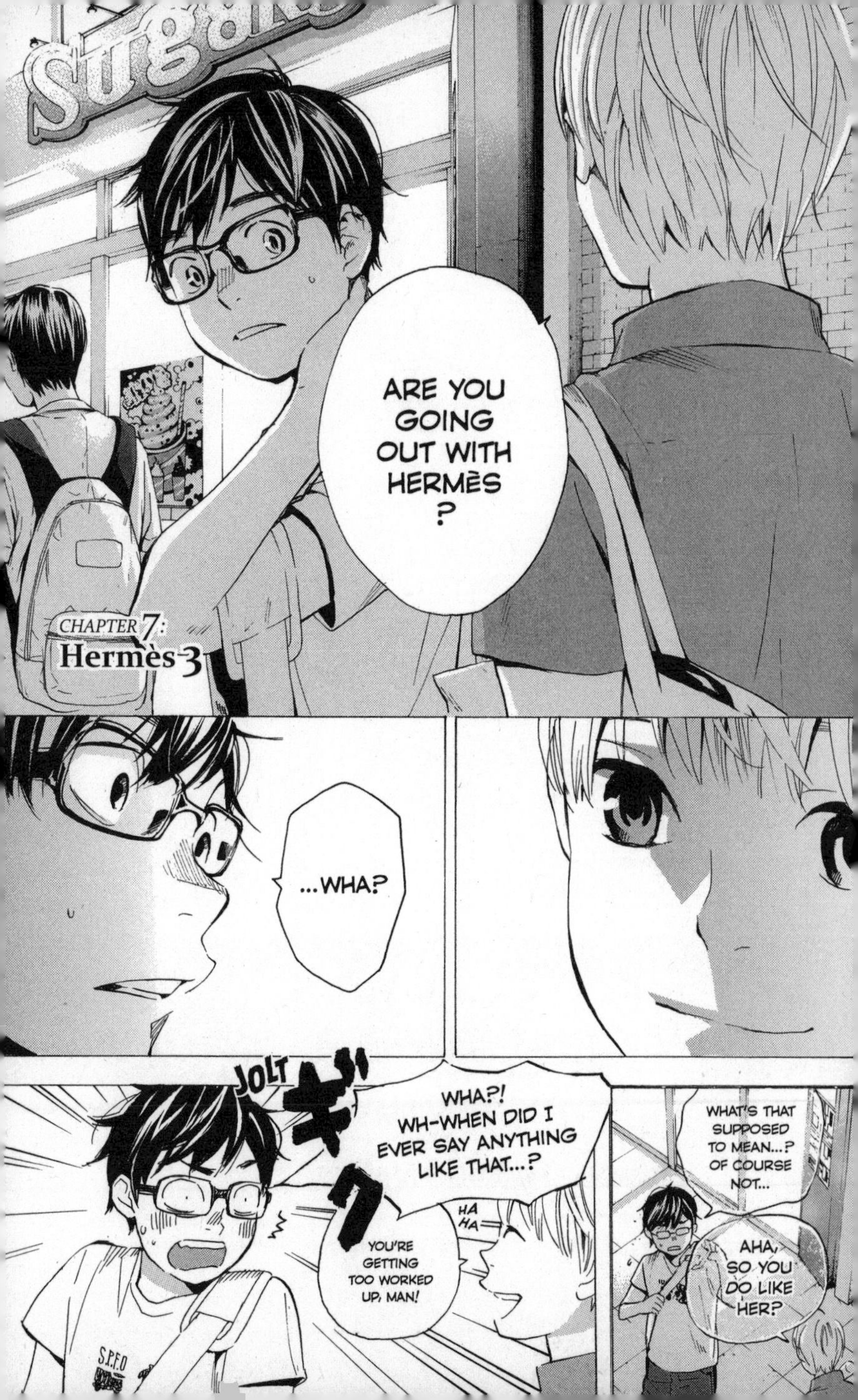
SUGAKO
ARE YOU GOING OUT WITH HERMÈS ?
CHAPTER 7:
Hermès 3
...WHA?
WHAT'S THAT SUPPOSED TO MEAN...? OF COURSE NOT...
AHA, SO YOU DO LIKE HER?
JOLT
WHA?! WH-WHEN DID I EVER SAY ANYTHING LIKE THAT...?
HA HA
YOU'RE GETTING TOO WORKED UP, MAN!
S.P.F.D

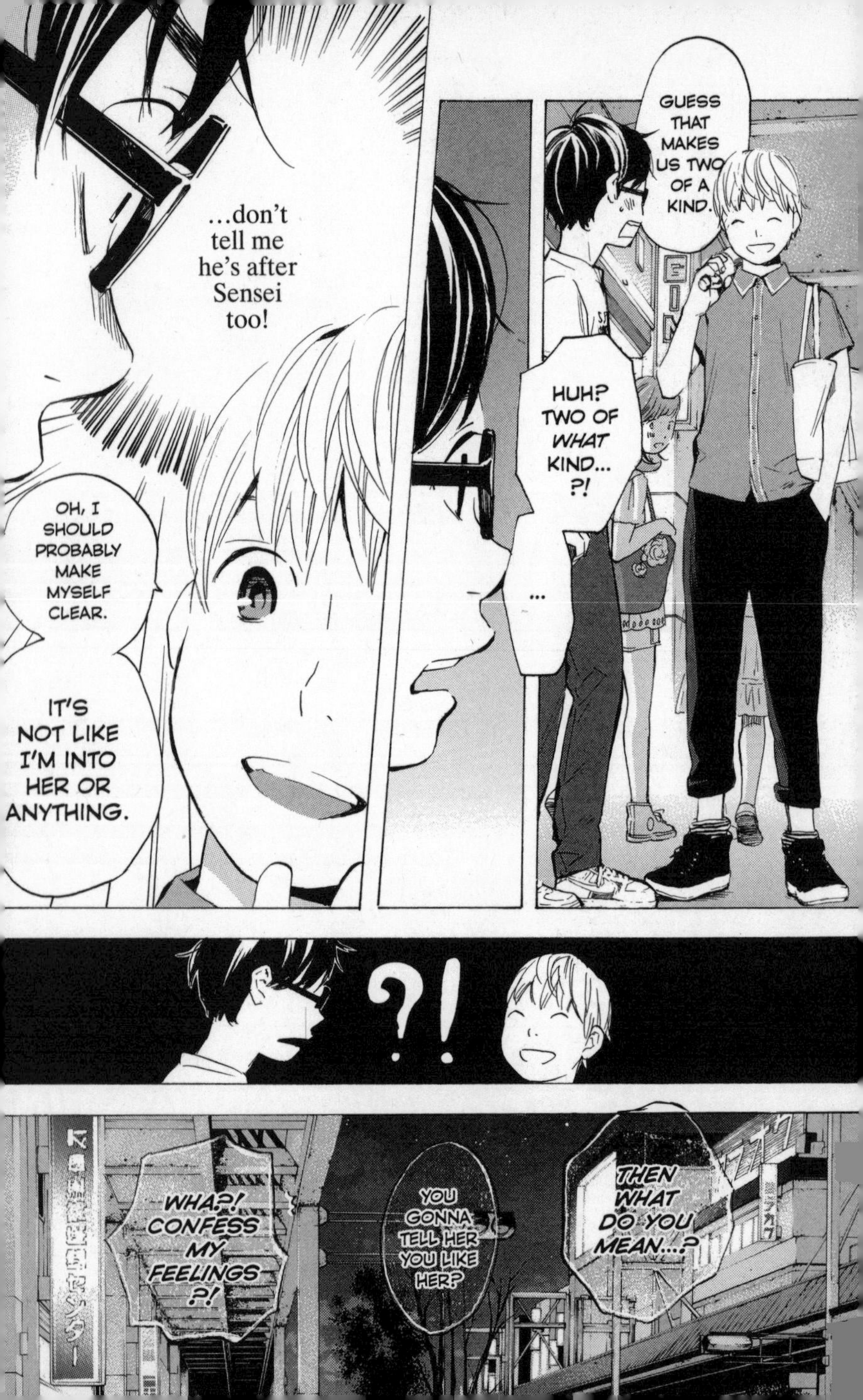
GUESS THAT MAKES US TWO OF A KIND.
HUH? TWO OF *WHAT* KIND...?!
...
...don't tell me he's after Sensei too!
OH, I SHOULD PROBABLY MAKE MYSELF CLEAR.
IT'S NOT LIKE I'M INTO HER OR ANYTHING.
?!
THEN WHAT DO YOU MEAN...?
YOU GONNA TELL HER YOU LIKE HER?
WHA?! CONFESS MY FEELINGS ?!

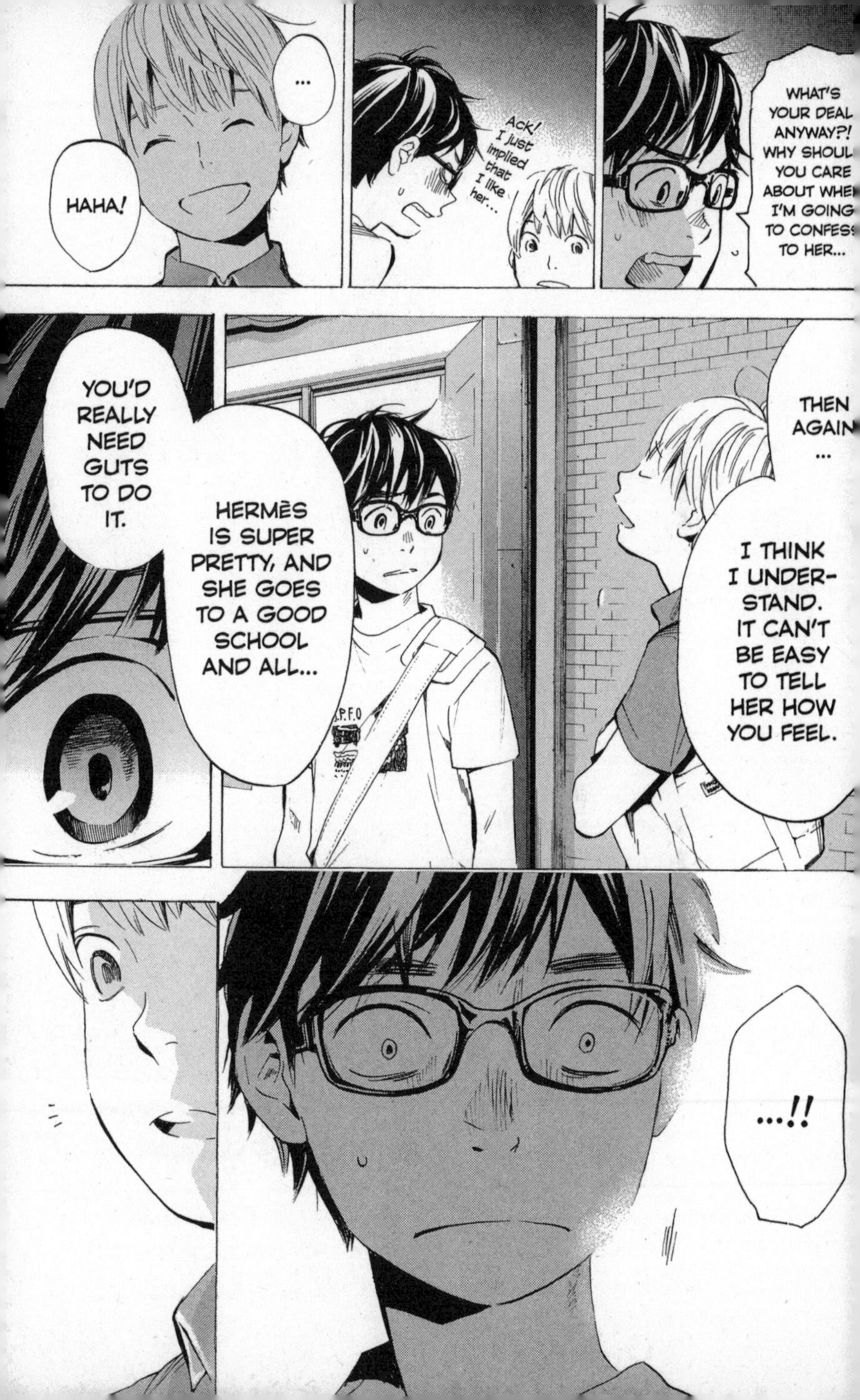
WHAT'S YOUR DEAL ANYWAY?! WHY SHOUL YOU CARE ABOUT WHE I'M GOING TO CONFES TO HER...
Ack! I just implied that I like her...
...
HAHA!
THEN AGAIN ...
I THINK I UNDER-STAND. IT CAN'T BE EASY TO TELL HER HOW YOU FEEL.
HERMÈS IS SUPER PRETTY, AND SHE GOES TO A GOOD SCHOOL AND ALL...
YOU'D REALLY NEED GUTS TO DO IT.
...!!

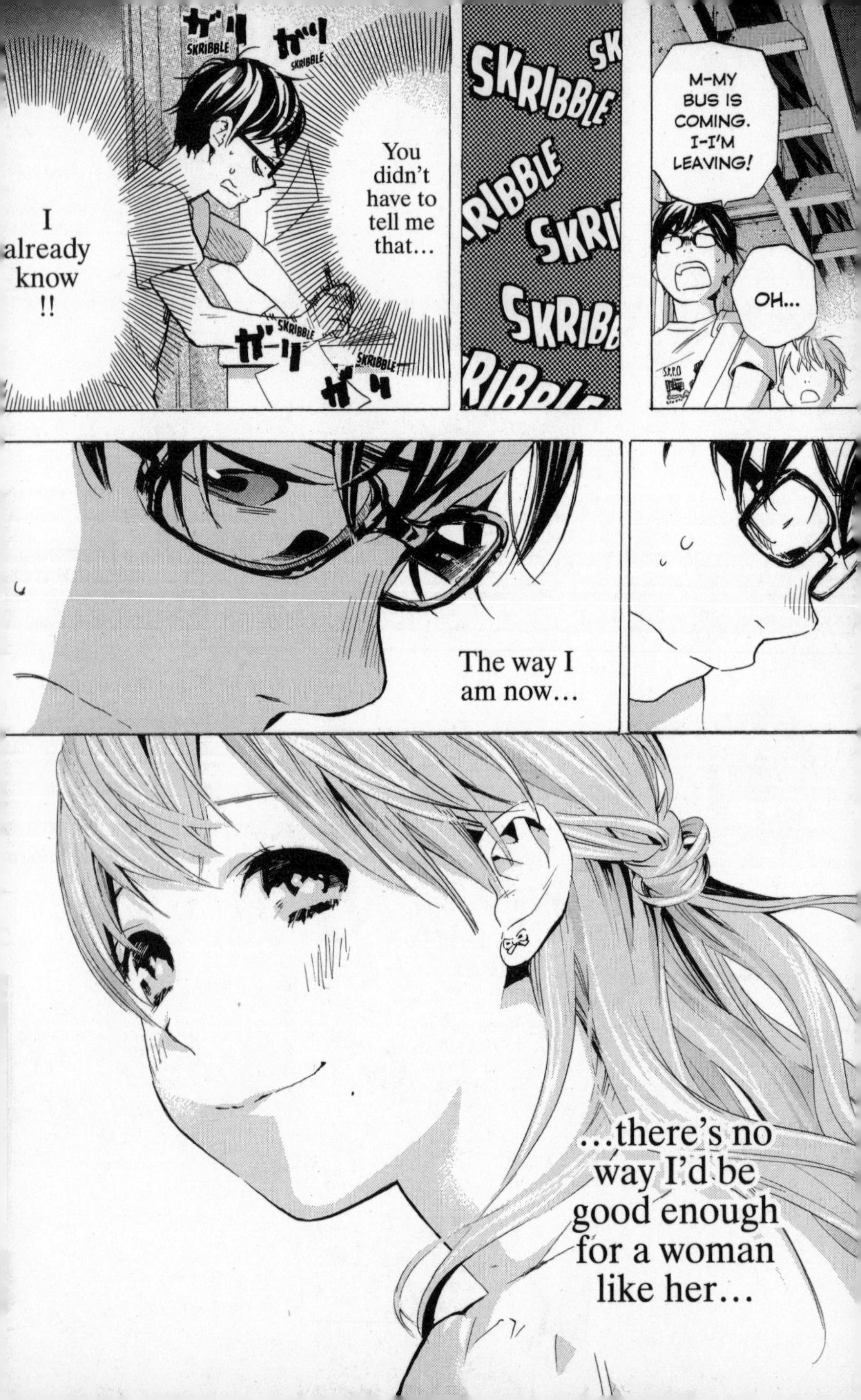
M-MY BUS IS COMING. I-I'M LEAVING!
OH...
SKRIBBLE
SKRIBBLE
SKRIBBLE
SKRIBBLE
SKRIBBLE
You didn't have to tell me that...
I already know !!
SKRIBBLE
SKRIBBLE
The way I am now...
...there's no way I'd be good enough for a woman like her...

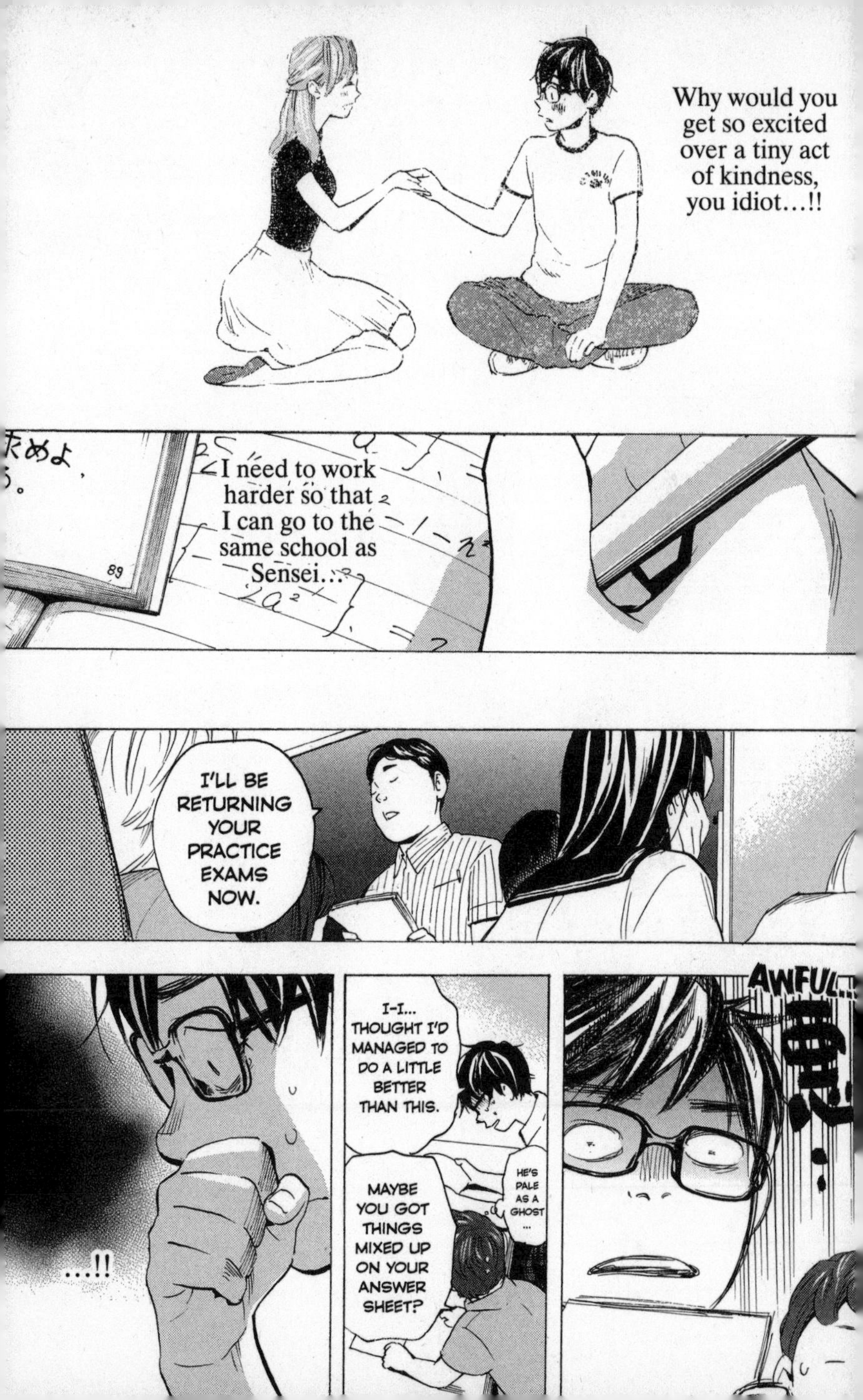
Why would you get so excited over a tiny act of kindness, you idiot…!!
I need to work harder so that I can go to the same school as Sensei…
I'LL BE RETURNING YOUR PRACTICE EXAMS NOW.
AWFUL...
I-I... THOUGHT I'D MANAGED TO DO A LITTLE BETTER THAN THIS.
HE'S PALE AS A GHOST ...
MAYBE YOU GOT THINGS MIXED UP ON YOUR ANSWER SHEET?
...!!

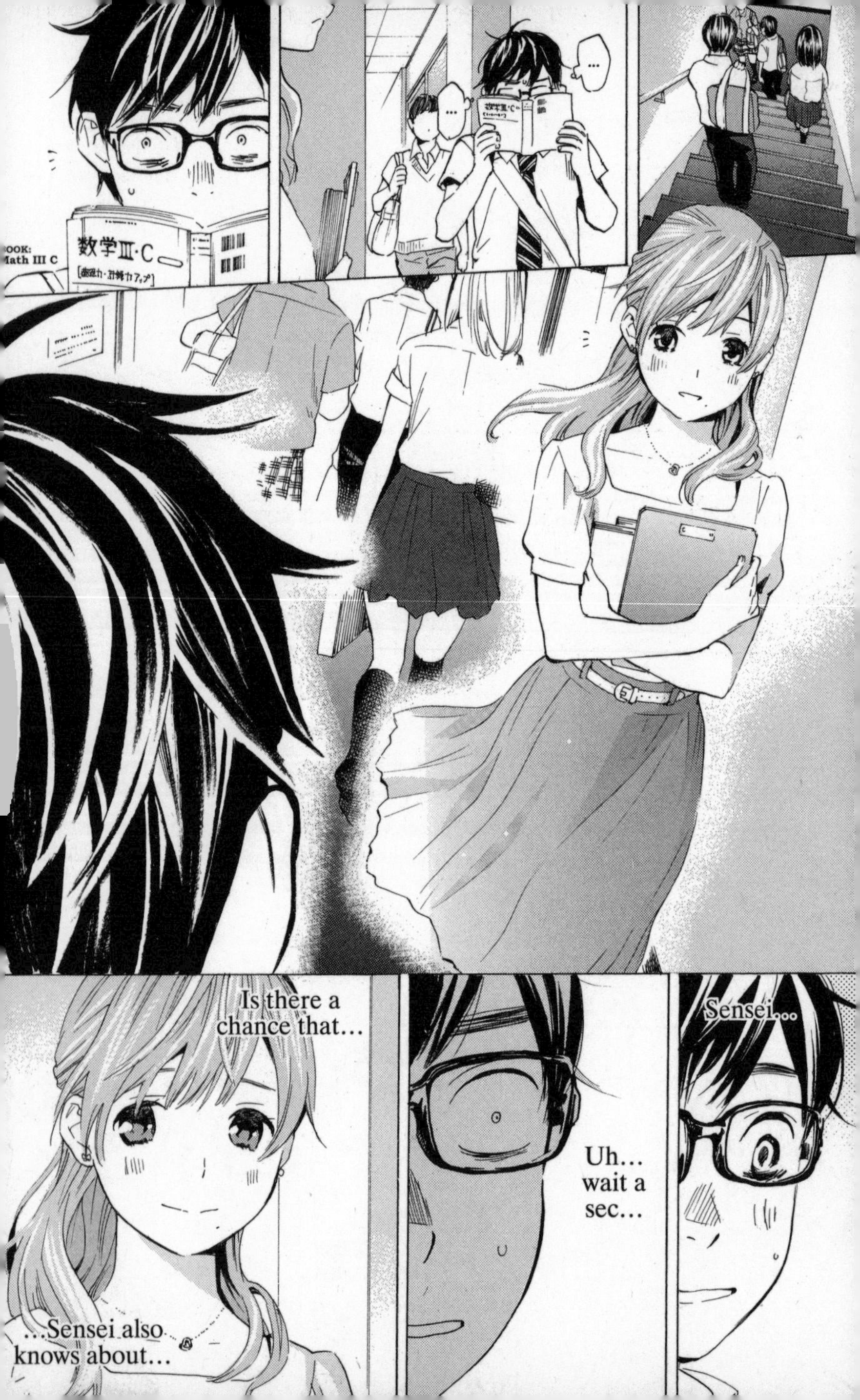
…
…
数学Ⅲ·C
OOK:
Math III C
Sensei…
Uh… wait a sec…
Is there a chance that…
…Sensei also knows about…

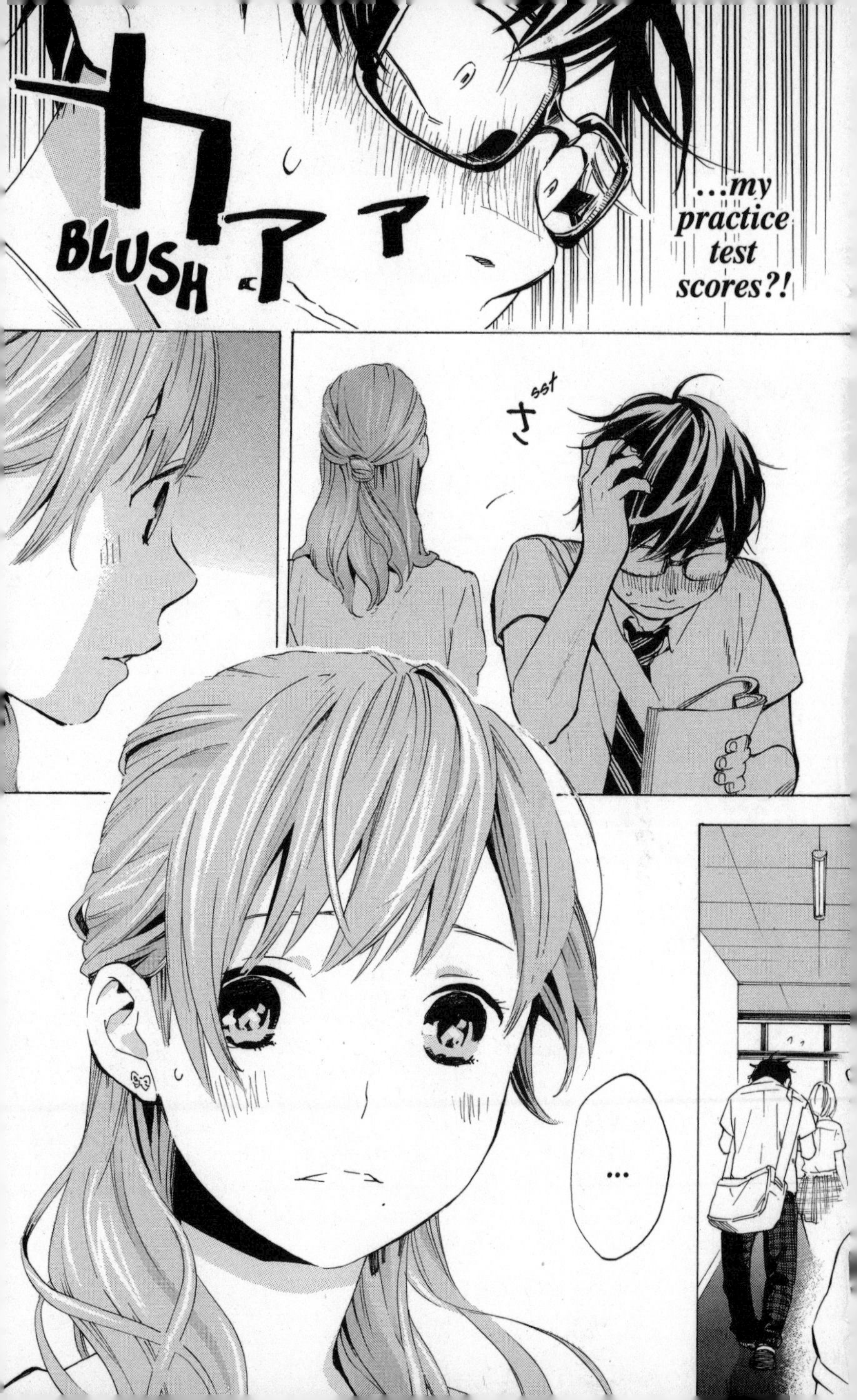

...my practice test scores?!
カァァ
BLUSH
さ
sst
...

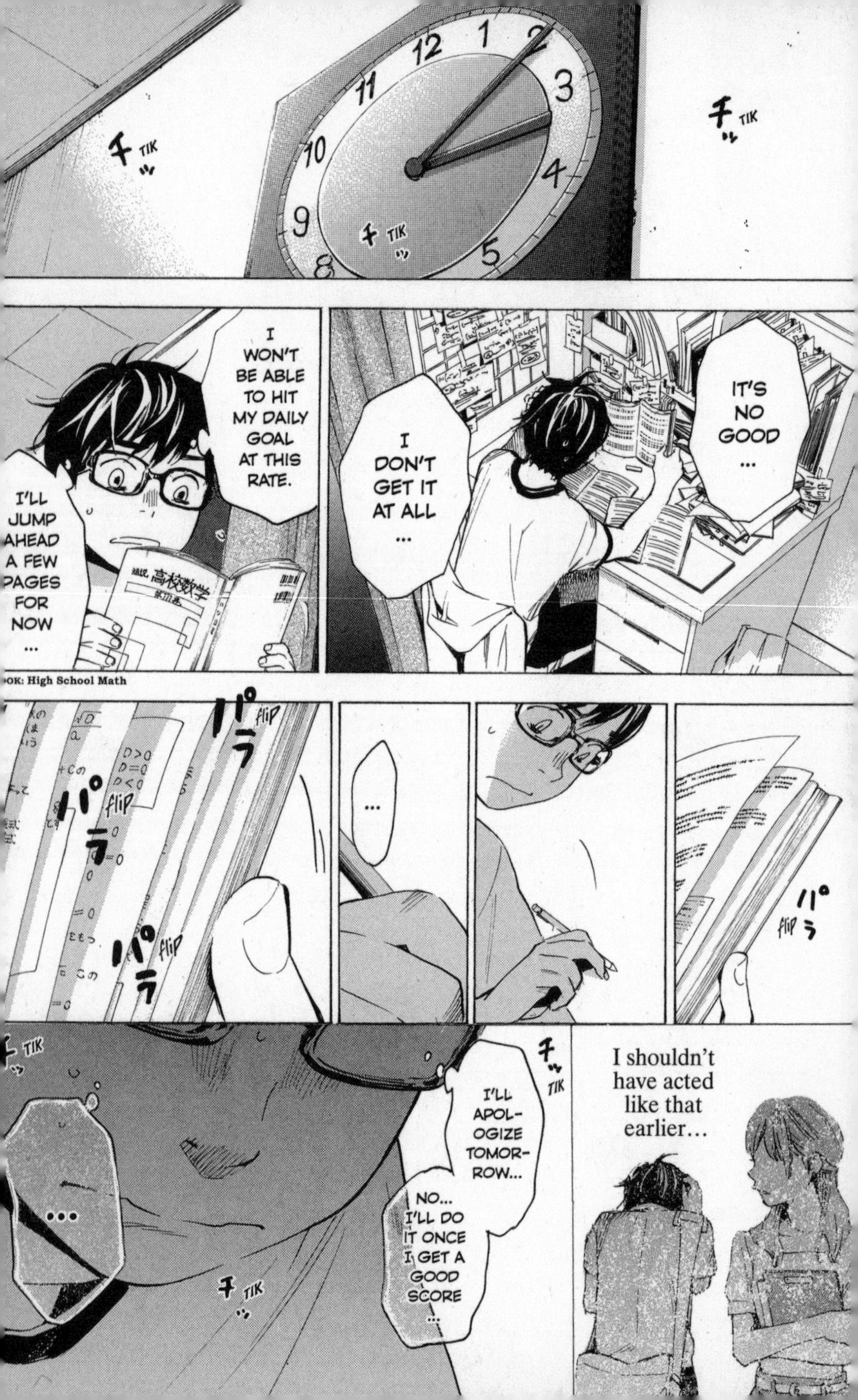
チッ TIK
チッ TIK
チッ TIK
IT'S NO GOOD ...
I DON'T GET IT AT ALL ...
I WON'T BE ABLE TO HIT MY DAILY GOAL AT THIS RATE.
I'LL JUMP AHEAD A FEW PAGES FOR NOW ...
高校数学
パラ flip
...
パラ flip
パラ flip
パラ flip
I shouldn't have acted like that earlier…
チッ TIK
I'LL APOLOGIZE TOMORROW...
NO... I'LL DO IT ONCE I GET A GOOD SCORE ...
チッ TIK
...
チッ TIK

OK: High School Math

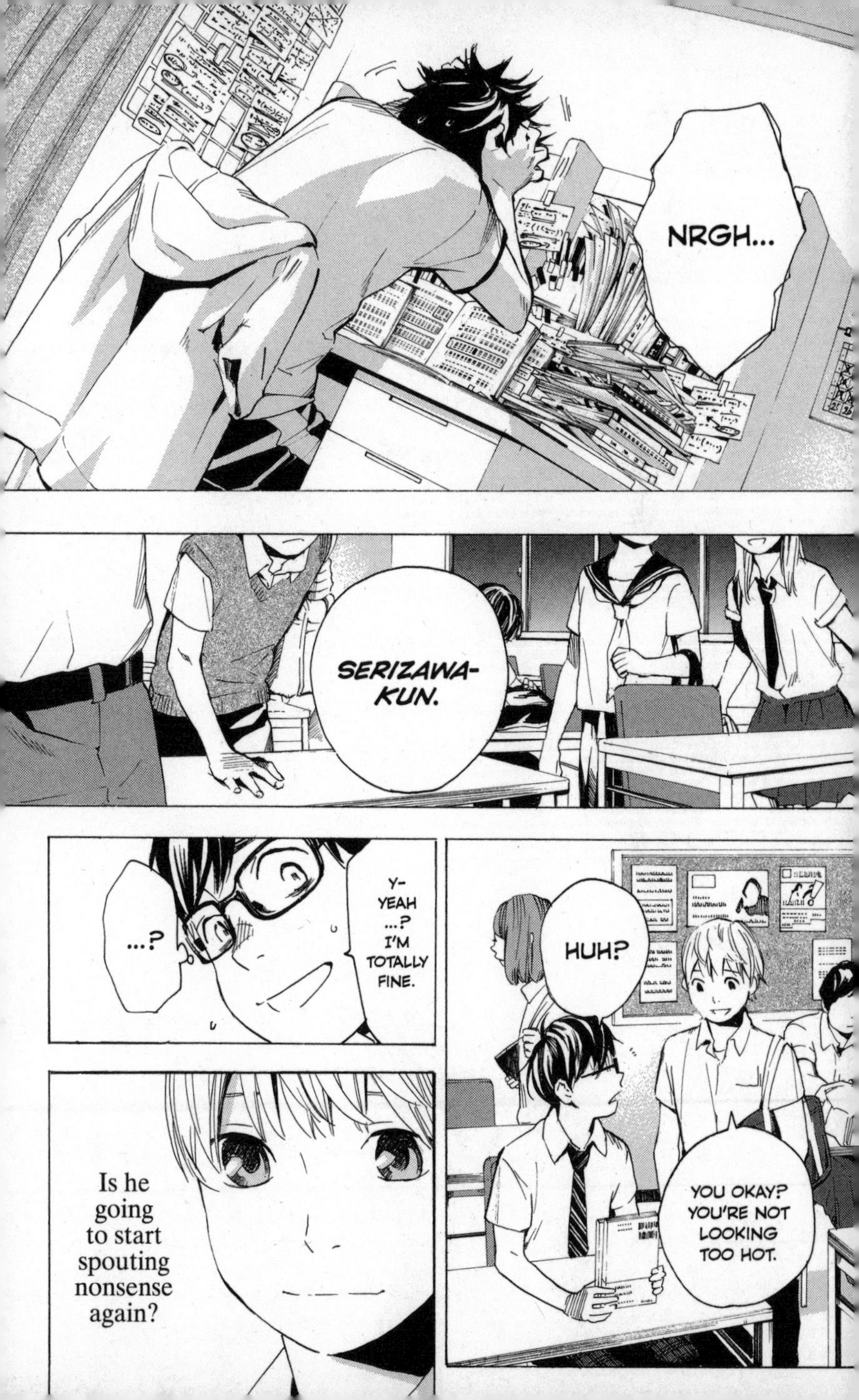
NRGH...
SERIZAWA-KUN.
YOU OKAY? YOU'RE NOT LOOKING TOO HOT.
HUH?
Y-YEAH ...? I'M TOTALLY FINE.
...?
Is he going to start spouting nonsense again?

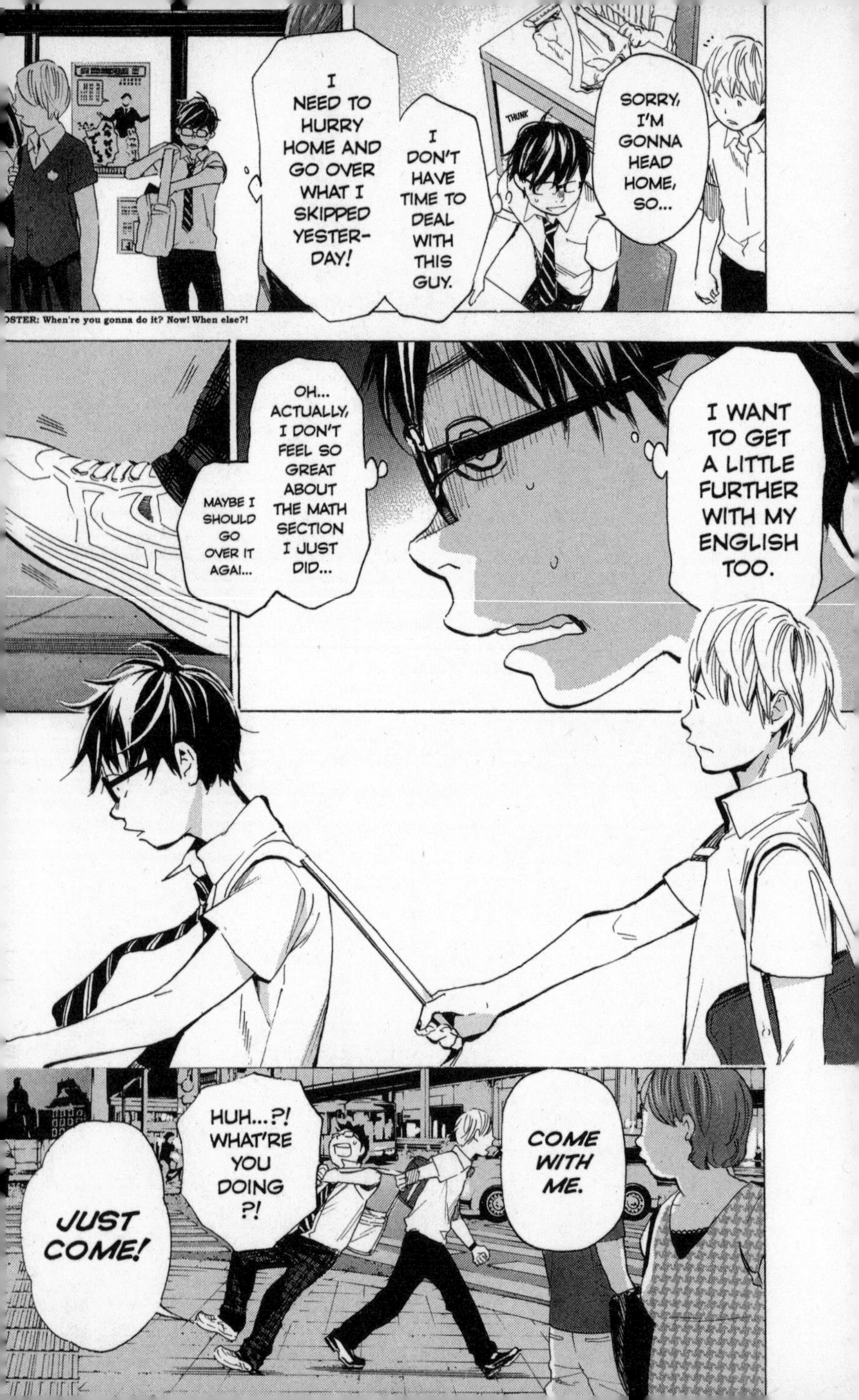
SORRY, I'M GONNA HEAD HOME, SO...
THUNK
I DON'T HAVE TIME TO DEAL WITH THIS GUY.
I NEED TO HURRY HOME AND GO OVER WHAT I SKIPPED YESTER-DAY!
OSTER: When're you gonna do it? Now! When else?!
I WANT TO GET A LITTLE FURTHER WITH MY ENGLISH TOO.
OH... ACTUALLY, I DON'T FEEL SO GREAT ABOUT THE MATH SECTION I JUST DID...
MAYBE I SHOULD GO OVER IT AGAI...
COME WITH ME.
HUH...?! WHAT'RE YOU DOING?!
JUST COME!

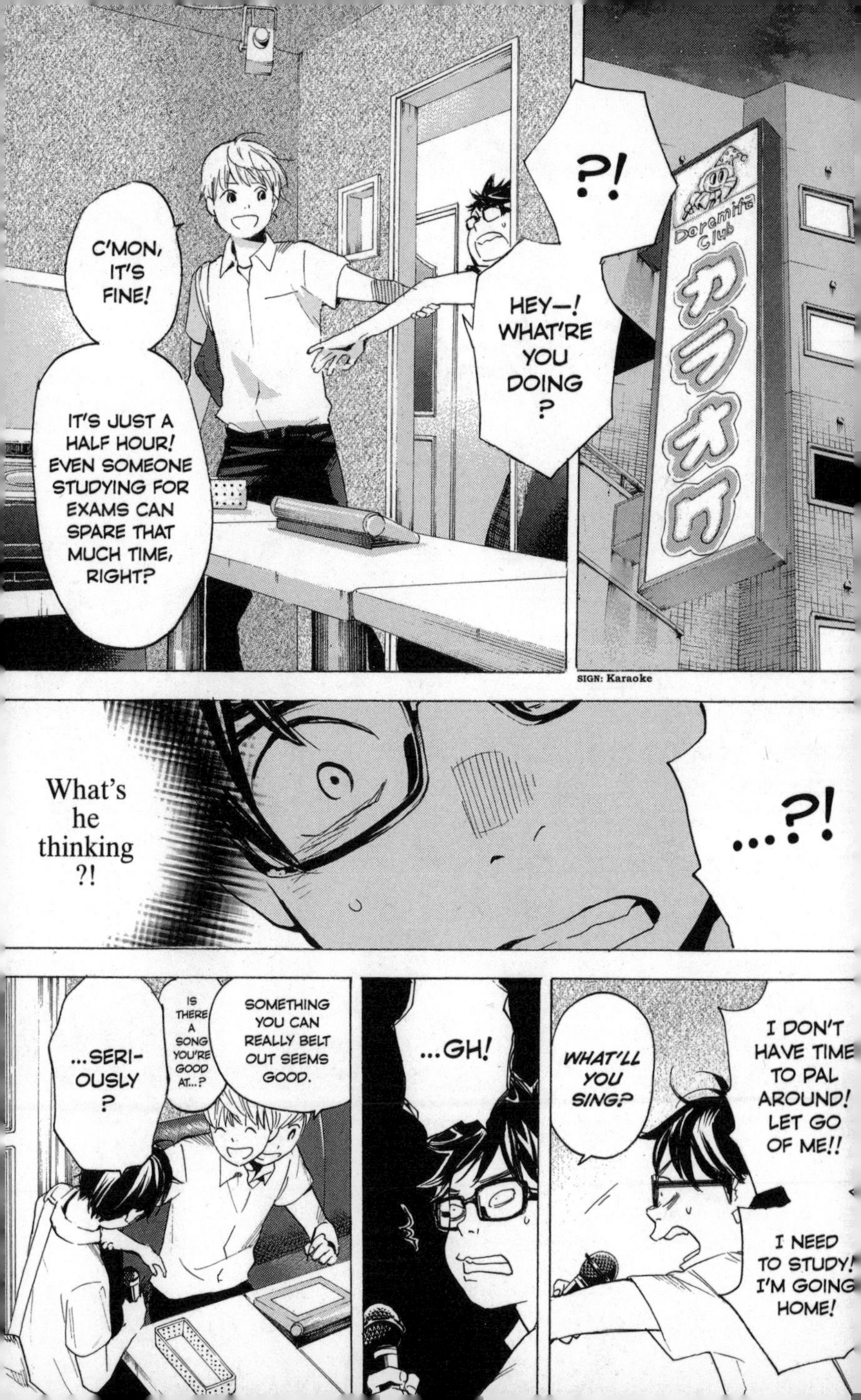
?!
Doremifa Club
カラオケ
HEY—! WHAT'RE YOU DOING?
C'MON, IT'S FINE!
IT'S JUST A HALF HOUR! EVEN SOMEONE STUDYING FOR EXAMS CAN SPARE THAT MUCH TIME, RIGHT?
...?!
What's he thinking?!
I DON'T HAVE TIME TO PAL AROUND! LET GO OF ME!!
WHAT'LL YOU SING?
I NEED TO STUDY! I'M GOING HOME!
...GH!
SOMETHING YOU CAN REALLY BELT OUT SEEMS GOOD.
IS THERE A SONG YOU'RE GOOD AT...?
...SERI-OUSLY?
SIGN: Karaoke

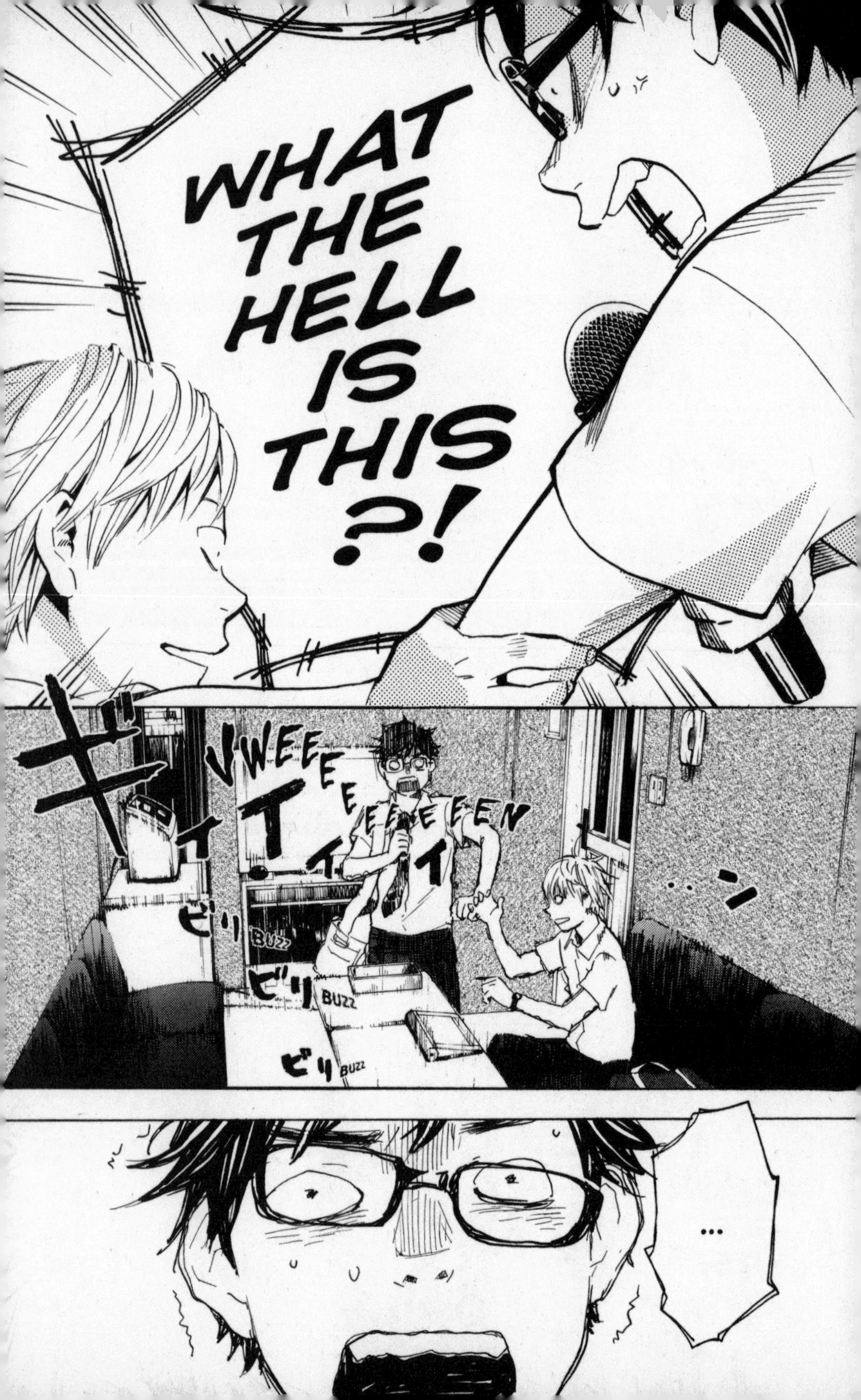

WHAT THE HELL IS THIS?!
ギィイイイ
JWEEEEEEEEEEN
...ン
ビリ BUZZ
ビリ BUZZ
ビリ BUZZ
...

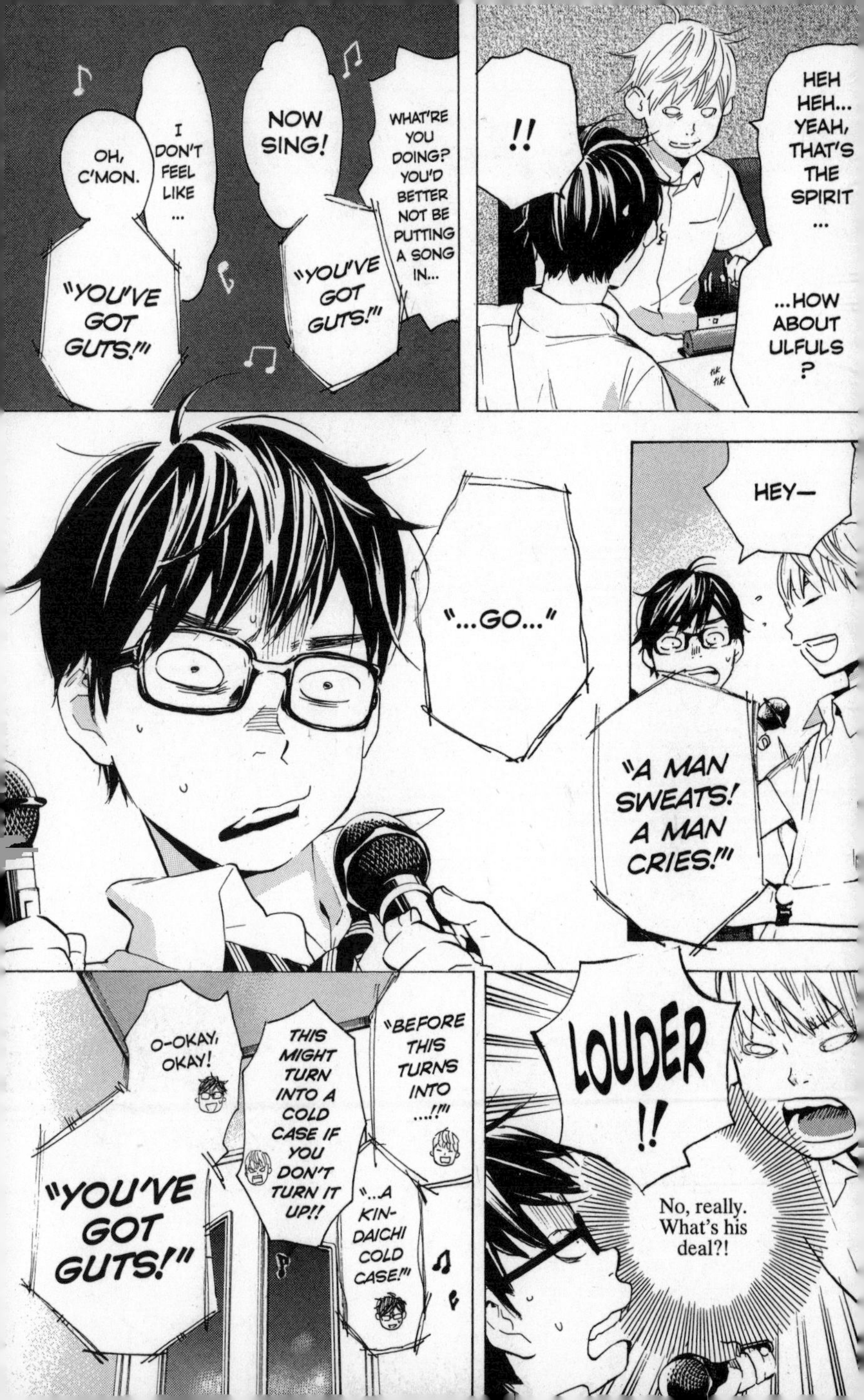
HEH HEH... YEAH, THAT'S THE SPIRIT...
!!
...HOW ABOUT ULFULS?
tik tik
WHAT'RE YOU DOING? YOU'D BETTER NOT BE PUTTING A SONG IN...
NOW SING!
"YOU'VE GOT GUTS!"
I DON'T FEEL LIKE...
OH, C'MON.
"YOU'VE GOT GUTS!"
HEY—
"A MAN SWEATS! A MAN CRIES!"
"...GO..."
LOUDER!!
No, really. What's his deal?!
"BEFORE THIS TURNS INTO ...!"
"...A KIN-DAICHI COLD CASE!"
THIS MIGHT TURN INTO A COLD CASE IF YOU DON'T TURN IT UP!!
O-OKAY, OKAY!
"YOU'VE GOT GUTS!"

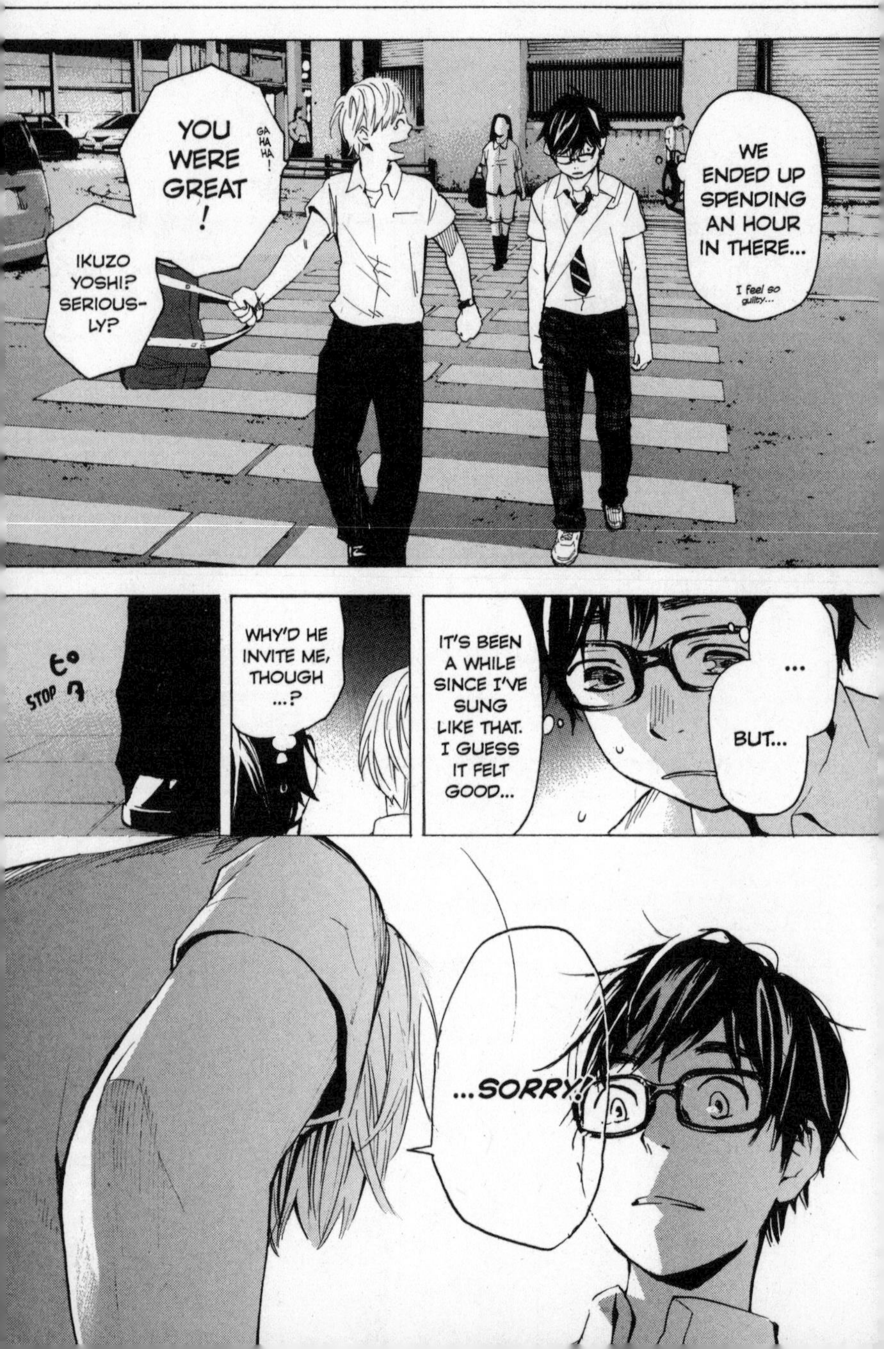
WE ENDED UP SPENDING AN HOUR IN THERE...
I feel so guilty...
GA HA HA!
YOU WERE GREAT!
IKUZO YOSHI? SERIOUSLY?
... BUT...
IT'S BEEN A WHILE SINCE I'VE SUNG LIKE THAT. I GUESS IT FELT GOOD...
WHY'D HE INVITE ME, THOUGH ...?
STOP
...SORRY!

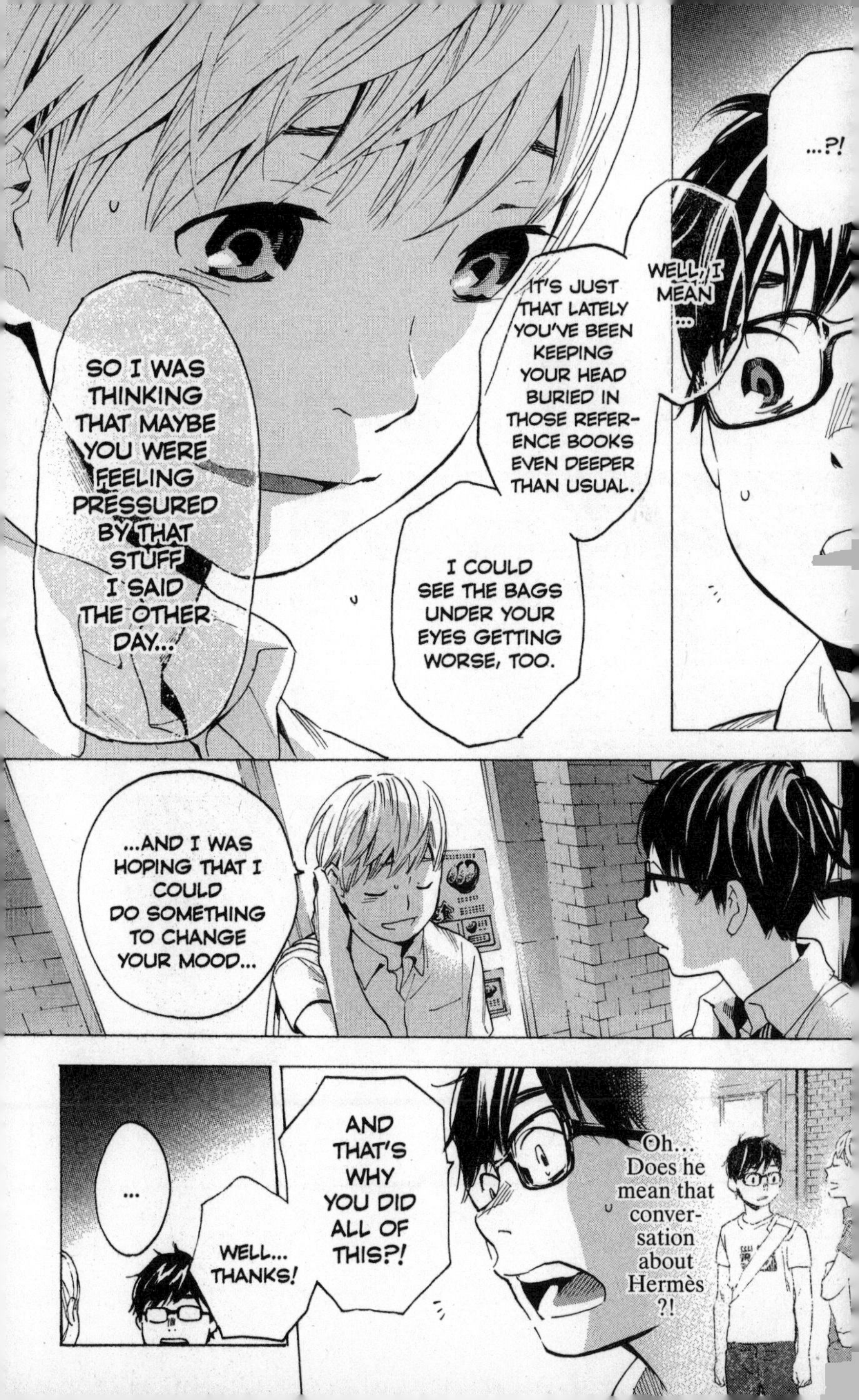
...?!
WELL, I MEAN ...
IT'S JUST THAT LATELY YOU'VE BEEN KEEPING YOUR HEAD BURIED IN THOSE REFERENCE BOOKS EVEN DEEPER THAN USUAL.
I COULD SEE THE BAGS UNDER YOUR EYES GETTING WORSE, TOO.
SO I WAS THINKING THAT MAYBE YOU WERE FEELING PRESSURED BY THAT STUFF I SAID THE OTHER DAY...
...AND I WAS HOPING THAT I COULD DO SOMETHING TO CHANGE YOUR MOOD...
Oh... Does he mean that conversation about Hermès?!
AND THAT'S WHY YOU DID ALL OF THIS?!
...
WELL... THANKS!

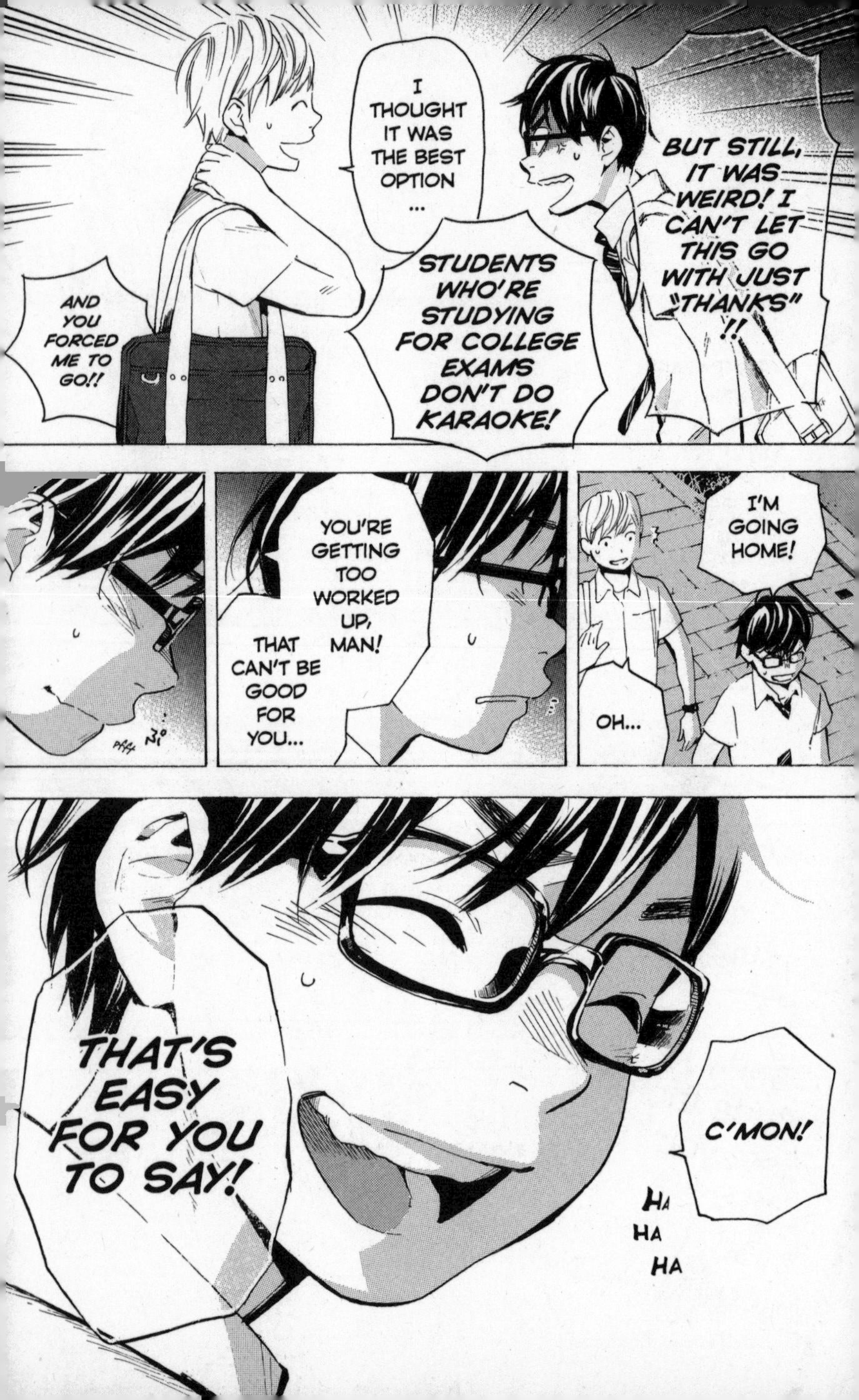
BUT STILL, IT WAS WEIRD! I CAN'T LET THIS GO WITH JUST "THANKS"!!
I THOUGHT IT WAS THE BEST OPTION ...
STUDENTS WHO'RE STUDYING FOR COLLEGE EXAMS DON'T DO KARAOKE!
AND YOU FORCED ME TO GO!!
I'M GOING HOME!
OH...
YOU'RE GETTING TOO WORKED UP, MAN!
THAT CAN'T BE GOOD FOR YOU...
pfff
C'MON!
HA HA HA
THAT'S EASY FOR YOU TO SAY!

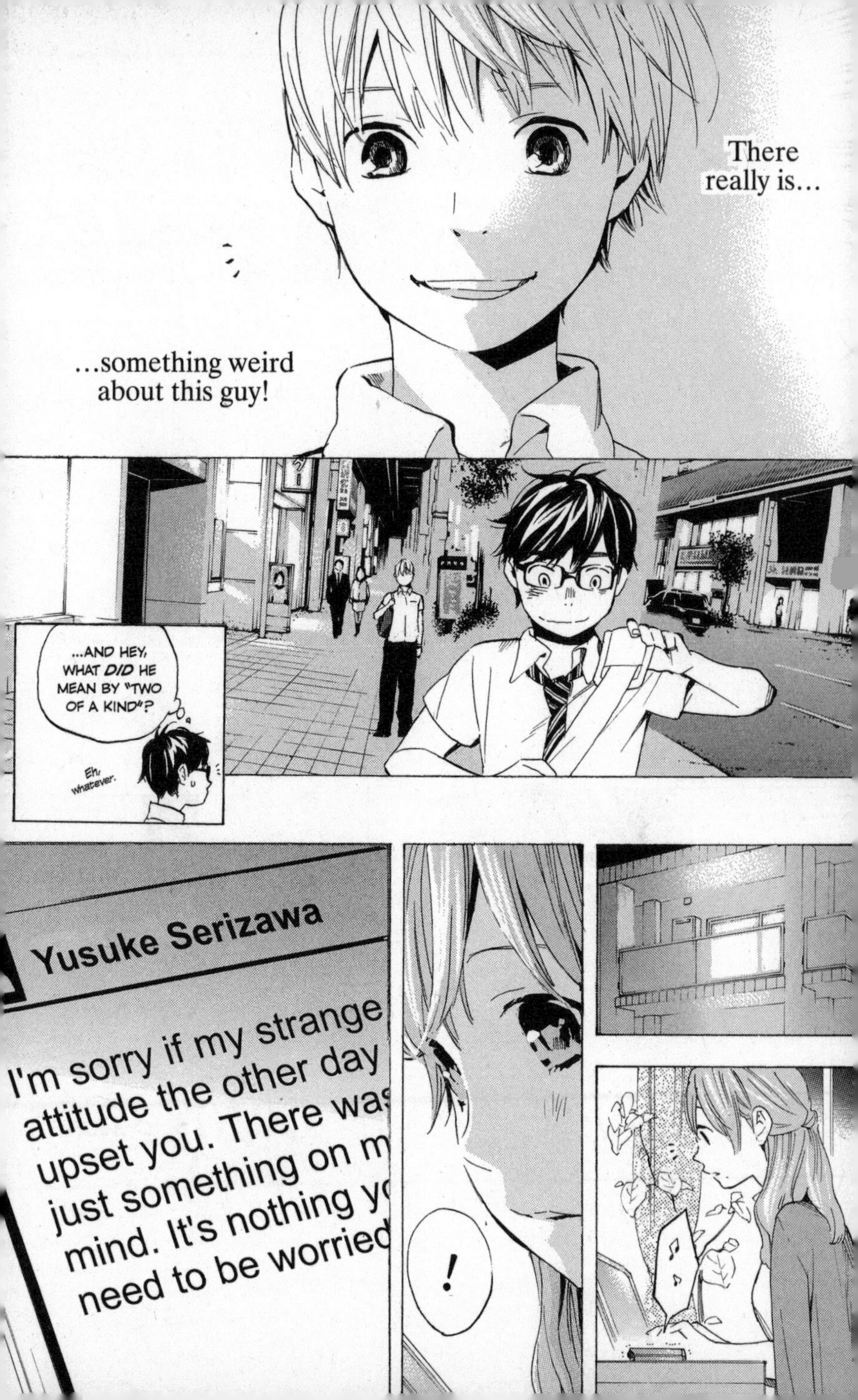
There really is…
…something weird about this guy!
…AND HEY, WHAT *DID* HE MEAN BY "TWO OF A KIND"?
Eh, whatever.
!
Yusuke Serizawa
I'm sorry if my strange attitude the other day upset you. There was just something on m mind. It's nothing y need to be worried

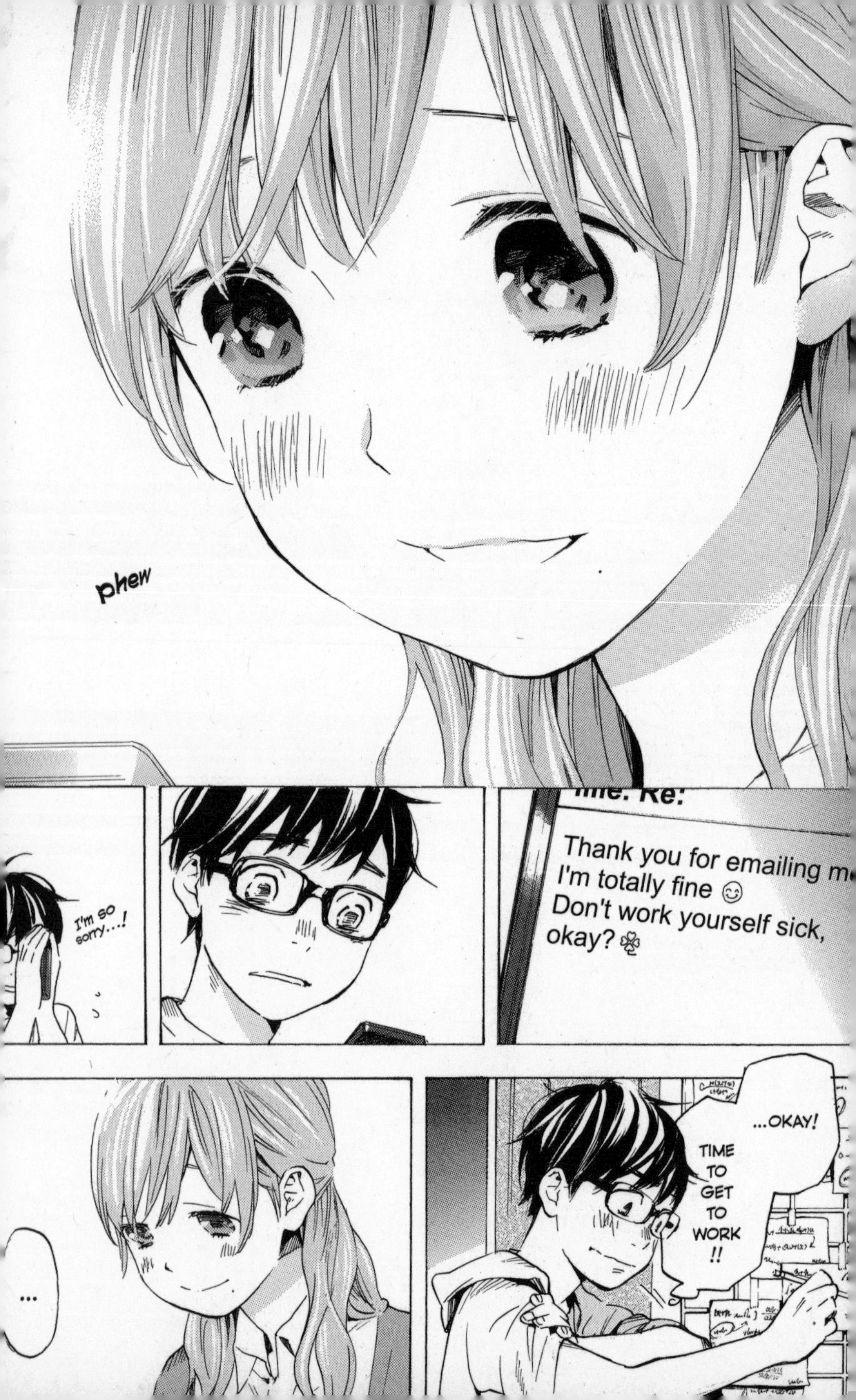
phew
Re:
Thank you for emailing m
I'm totally fine
Don't work yourself sick,
okay?
I'm so sorry...!
...OKAY!
TIME TO GET TO WORK!!
...

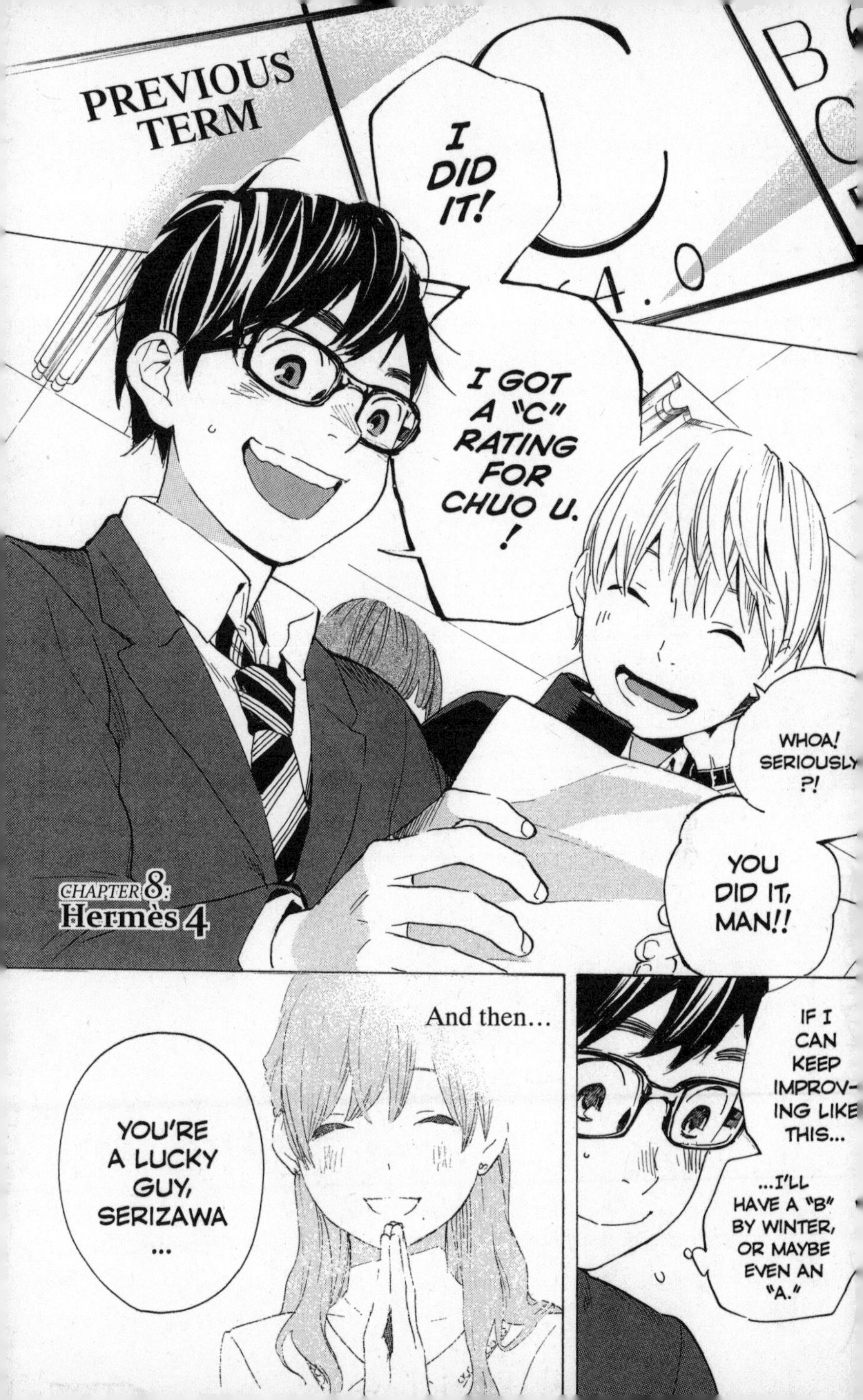
PREVIOUS TERM
I DID IT!
I GOT A "C" RATING FOR CHUO U.!
WHOA! SERIOUSLY?!
YOU DID IT, MAN!!
CHAPTER 8: Hermès 4
IF I CAN KEEP IMPROVING LIKE THIS...
...I'LL HAVE A "B" BY WINTER, OR MAYBE EVEN AN "A."
And then…
YOU'RE A LUCKY GUY, SERIZAWA...

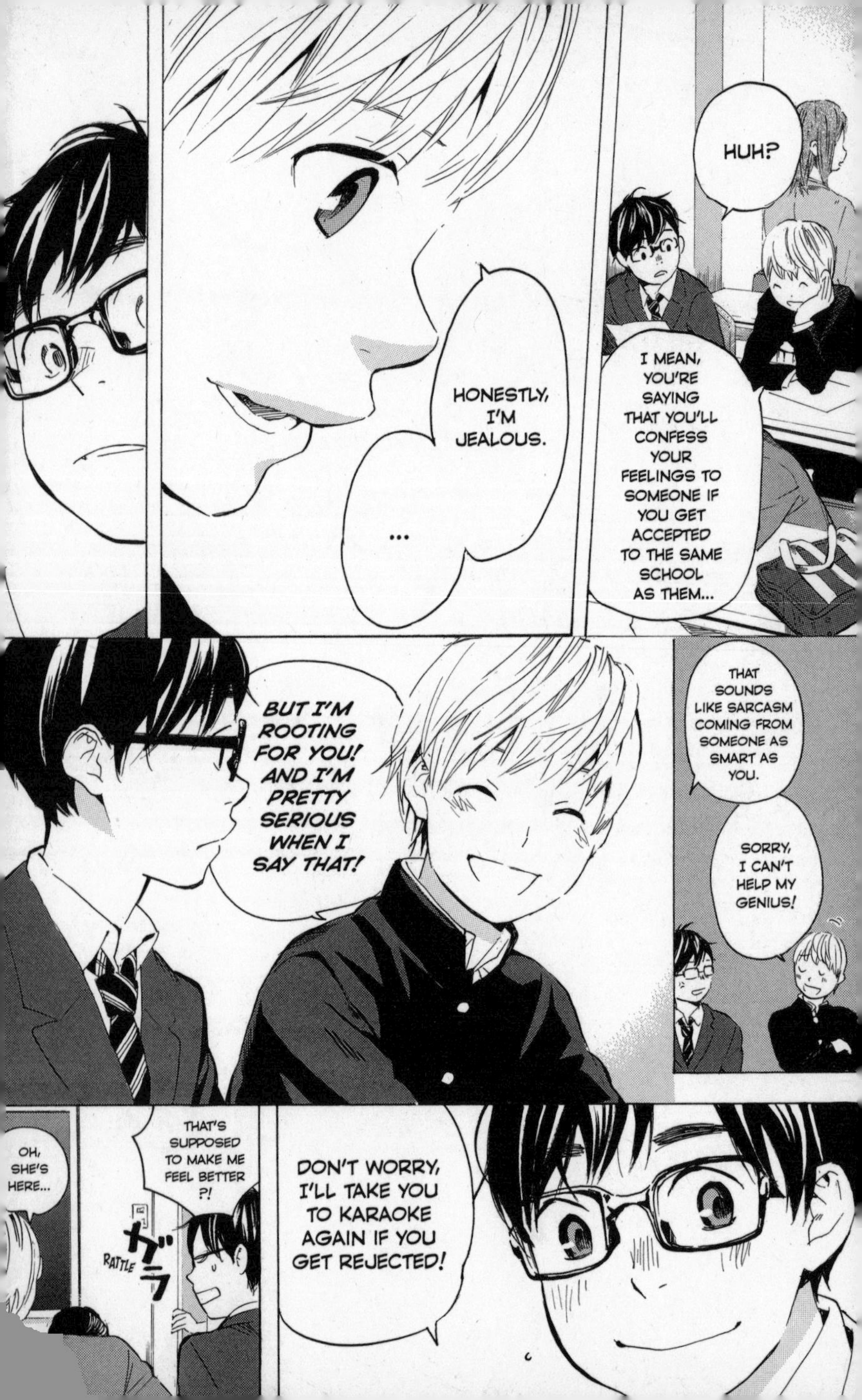
HUH?
I MEAN, YOU'RE SAYING THAT YOU'LL CONFESS YOUR FEELINGS TO SOMEONE IF YOU GET ACCEPTED TO THE SAME SCHOOL AS THEM...
HONESTLY, I'M JEALOUS.
...
THAT SOUNDS LIKE SARCASM COMING FROM SOMEONE AS SMART AS YOU.
SORRY, I CAN'T HELP MY GENIUS!
BUT I'M ROOTING FOR YOU! AND I'M PRETTY SERIOUS WHEN I SAY THAT!
DON'T WORRY, I'LL TAKE YOU TO KARAOKE AGAIN IF YOU GET REJECTED!
THAT'S SUPPOSED TO MAKE ME FEEL BETTER ?!
OH, SHE'S HERE...
ガラ
RATTLE

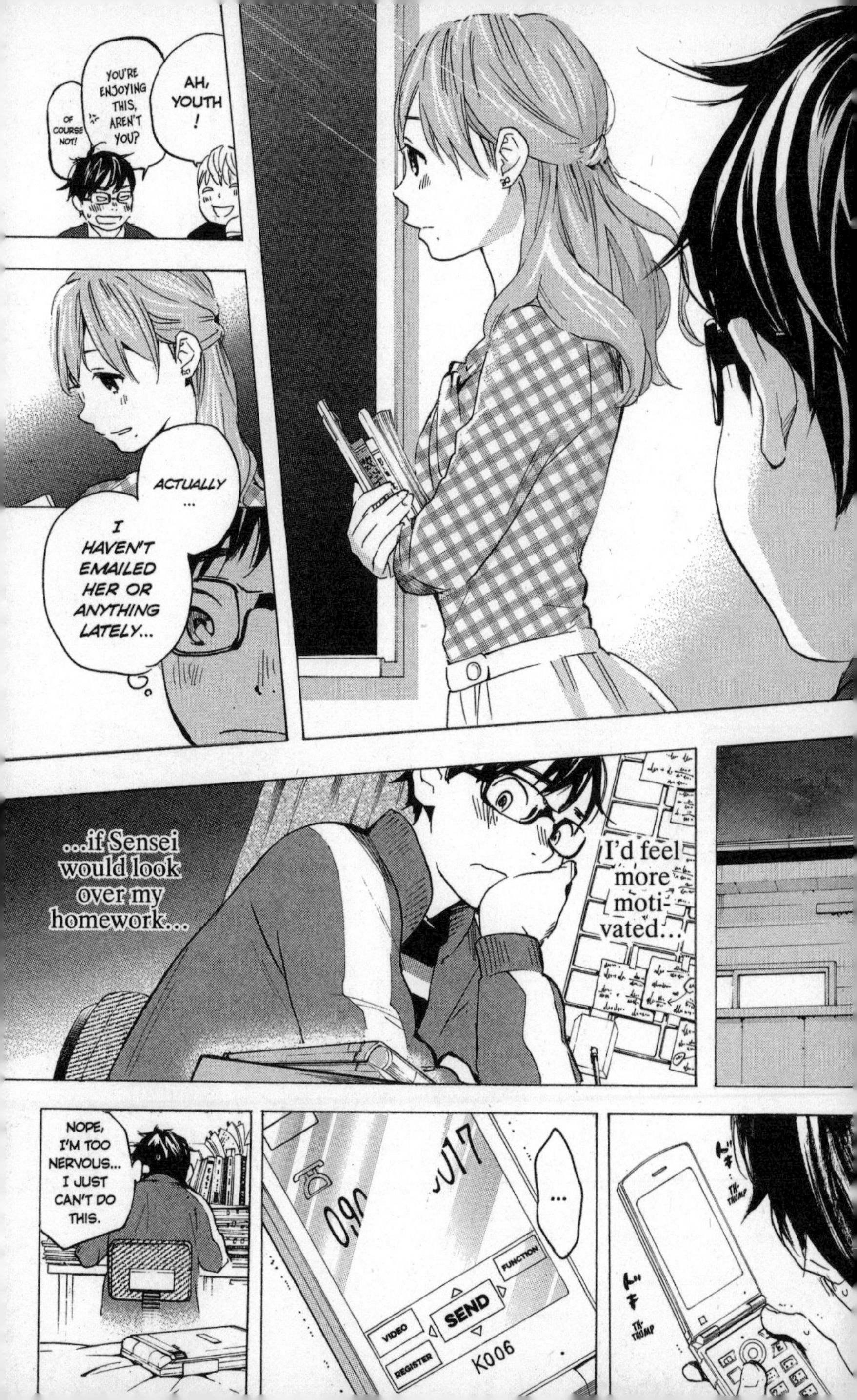
AH, YOUTH!
YOU'RE ENJOYING THIS, AREN'T YOU?
OF COURSE NOT!
ACTUALLY...
I HAVEN'T EMAILED HER OR ANYTHING LATELY...
I'd feel more moti-vated...
...if Sensei would look over my homework...
TH-THUMP
TH-THUMP
...
FUNCTION
SEND
VIDEO
REGISTER
K006
NOPE, I'M TOO NERVOUS... I JUST CAN'T DO THIS.

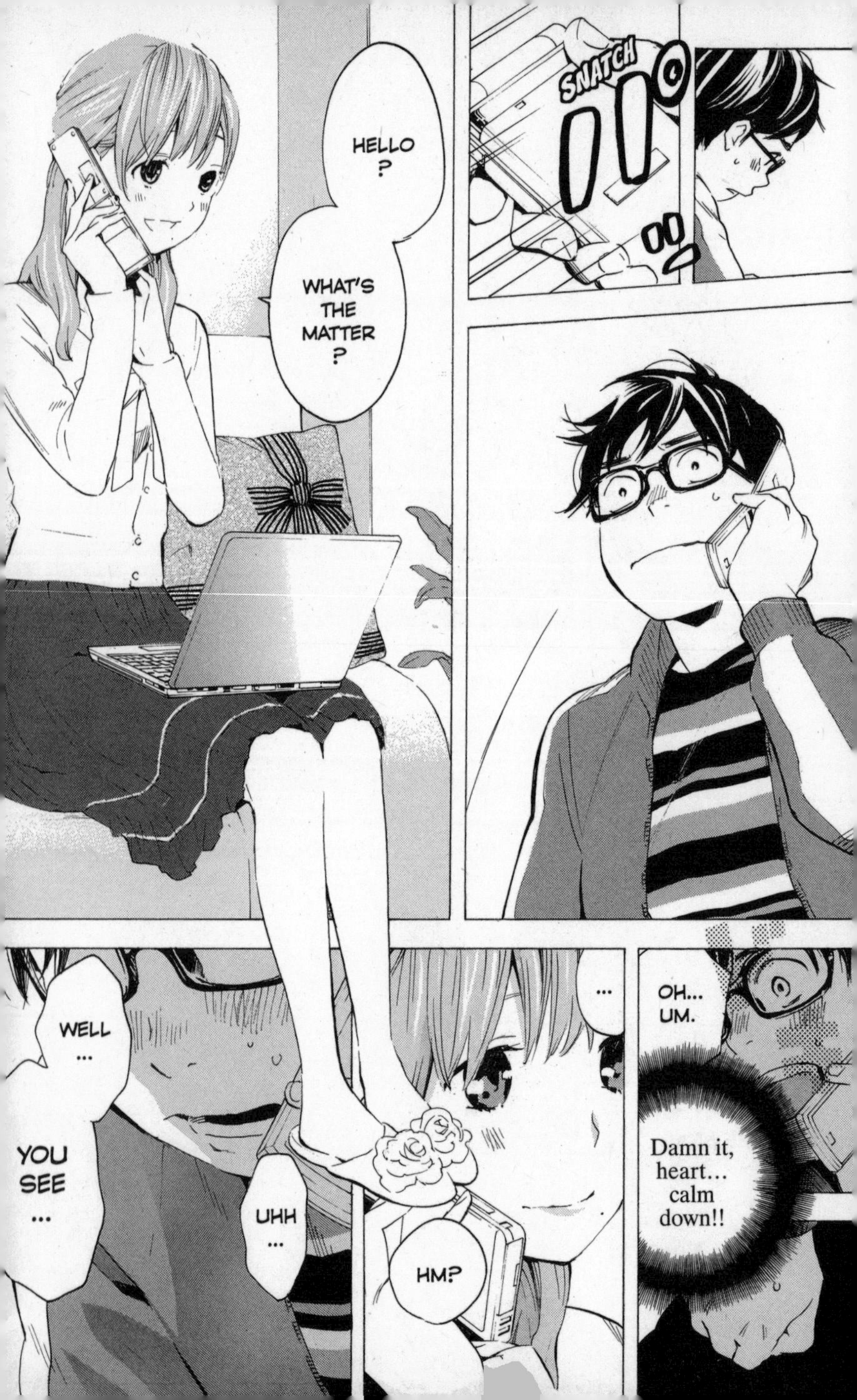
SNATCH
HELLO?
WHAT'S THE MATTER?
OH... UM.
Damn it, heart… calm down!!
...
HM?
WELL...
YOU SEE...
UHH...

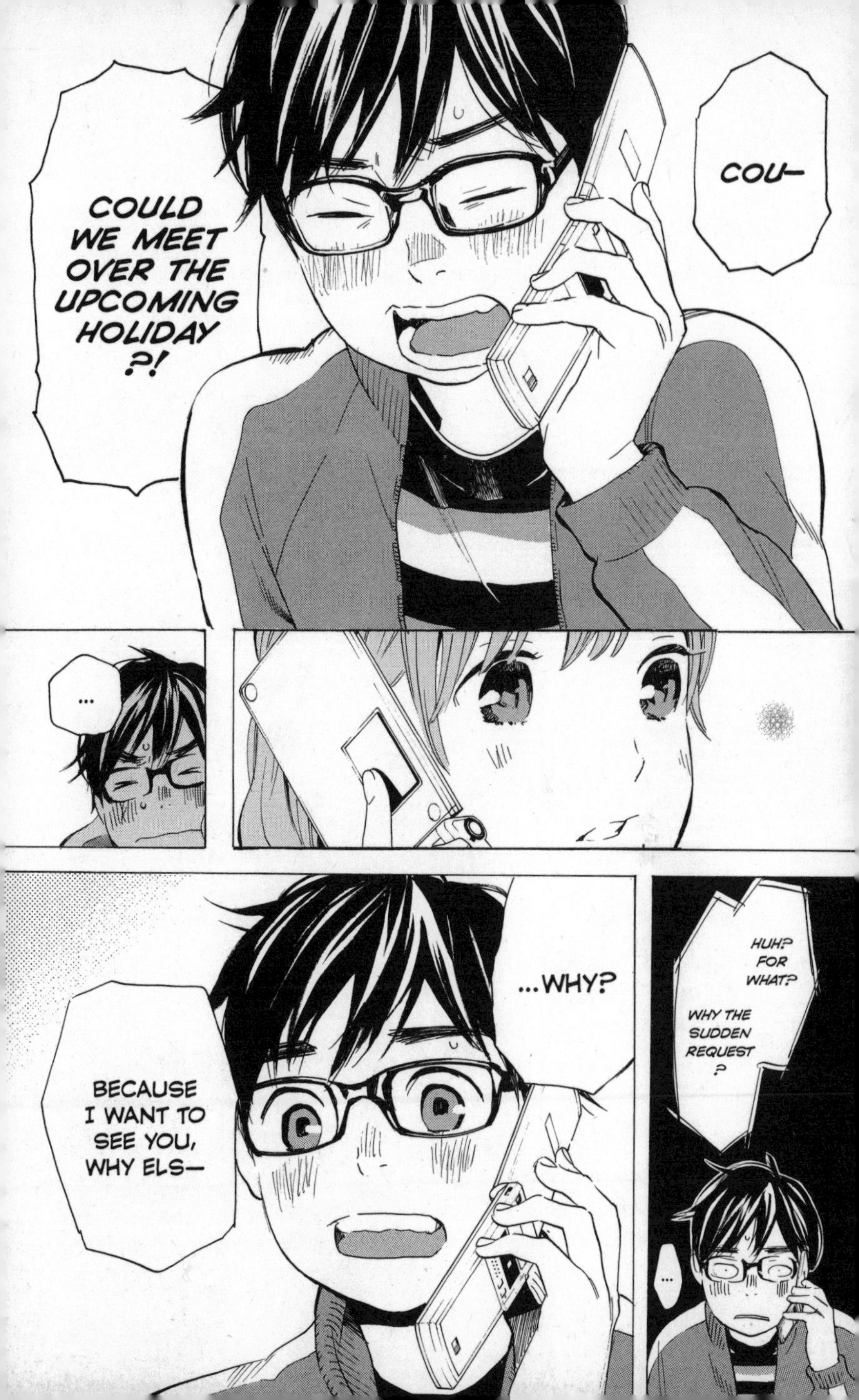
COU—
COULD WE MEET OVER THE UPCOMING HOLIDAY ?!
...
HUH? FOR WHAT?
WHY THE SUDDEN REQUEST ?
...
...WHY?
BECAUSE I WANT TO SEE YOU, WHY ELS—

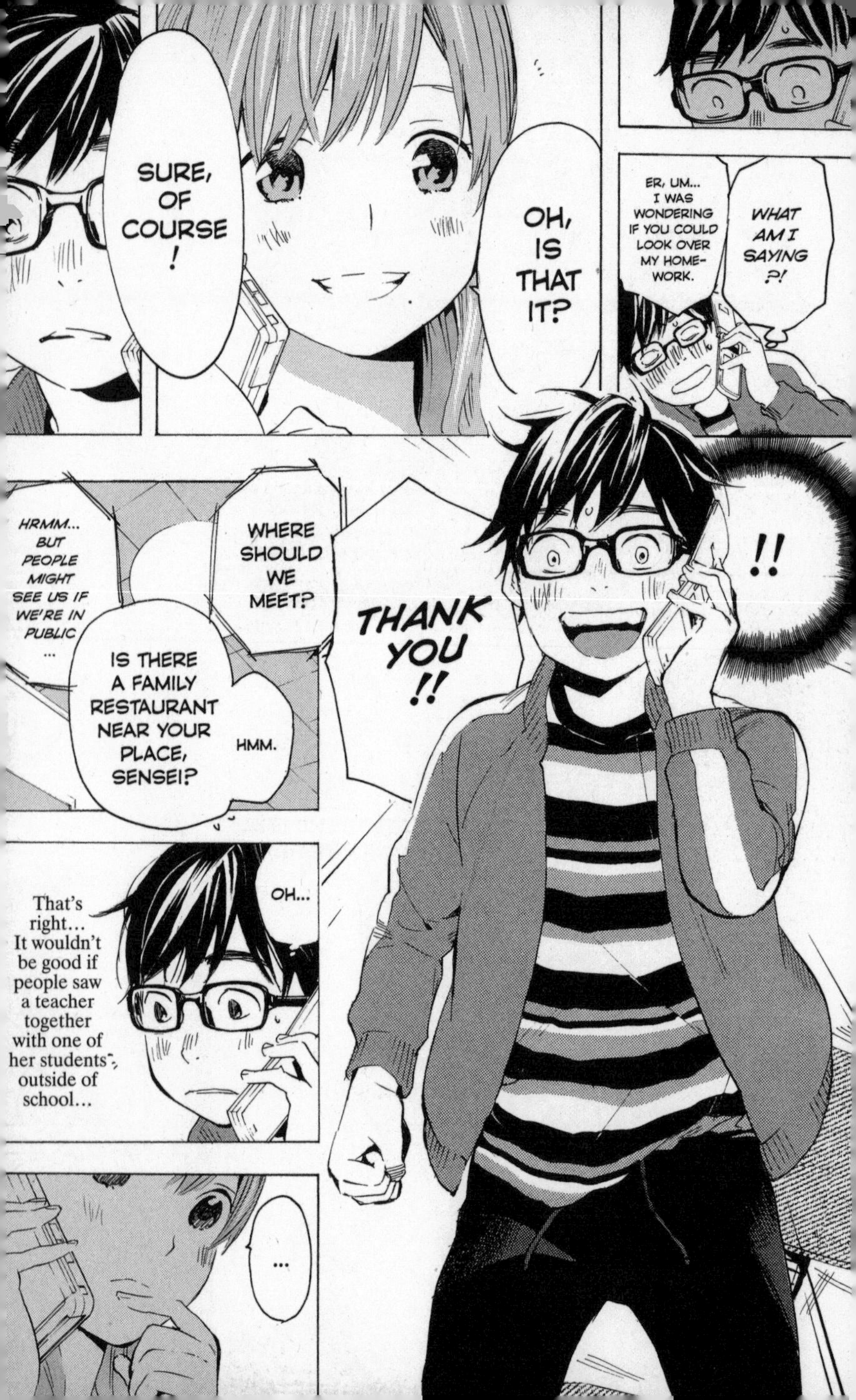
WHAT AM I SAYING ?!
ER, UM... I WAS WONDERING IF YOU COULD LOOK OVER MY HOME-WORK.
OH, IS THAT IT?
SURE, OF COURSE!
!!
THANK YOU!!
WHERE SHOULD WE MEET?
HRMM... BUT PEOPLE MIGHT SEE US IF WE'RE IN PUBLIC...
HMM.
IS THERE A FAMILY RESTAURANT NEAR YOUR PLACE, SENSEI?
OH...
That's right... It wouldn't be good if people saw a teacher together with one of her students outside of school...
...

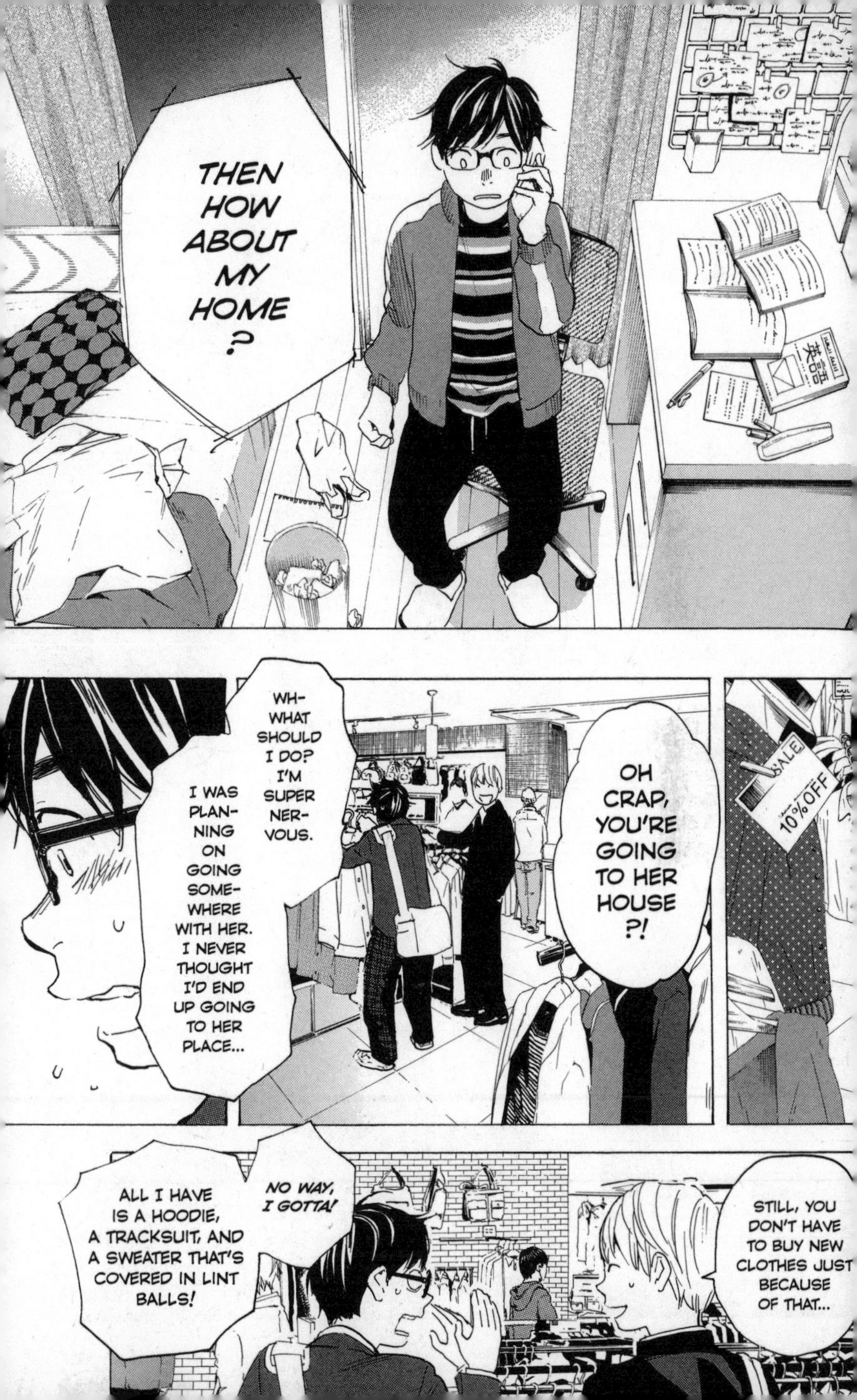
THEN HOW ABOUT MY HOME?
SALE
10%OFF
OH CRAP, YOU'RE GOING TO HER HOUSE?!
WH-WHAT SHOULD I DO? I'M SUPER NER-VOUS.
I WAS PLAN-NING ON GOING SOME-WHERE WITH HER. I NEVER THOUGHT I'D END UP GOING TO HER PLACE...
STILL, YOU DON'T HAVE TO BUY NEW CLOTHES JUST BECAUSE OF THAT...
NO WAY, I GOTTA!
ALL I HAVE IS A HOODIE, A TRACKSUIT, AND A SWEATER THAT'S COVERED IN LINT BALLS!

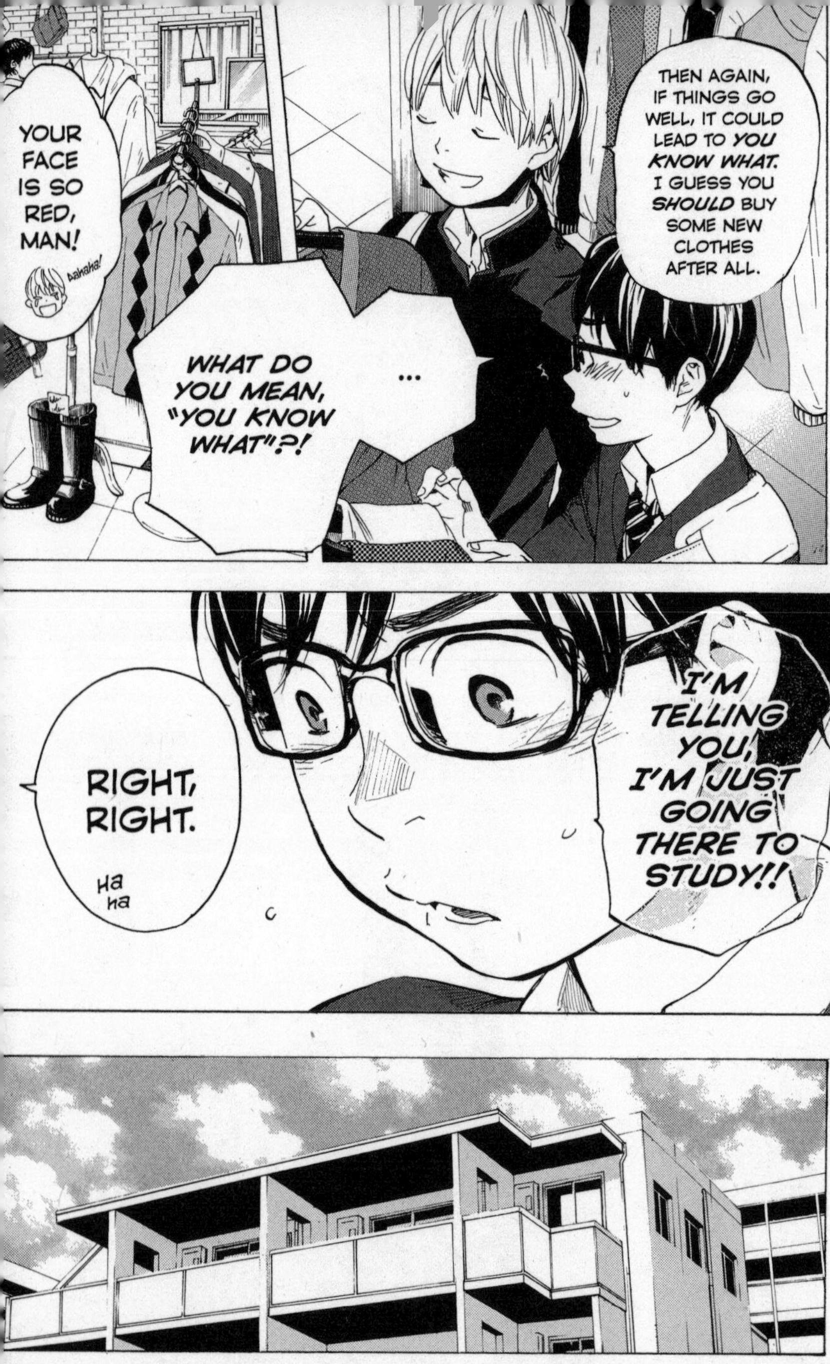
THEN AGAIN, IF THINGS GO WELL, IT COULD LEAD TO *YOU KNOW WHAT.* I GUESS YOU *SHOULD* BUY SOME NEW CLOTHES AFTER ALL.
...
WHAT DO YOU MEAN, "YOU KNOW WHAT"?!
YOUR FACE IS SO RED, MAN!
bahaha!
I'M TELLING YOU, I'M JUST GOING THERE TO STUDY!!
RIGHT, RIGHT.
Ha ha

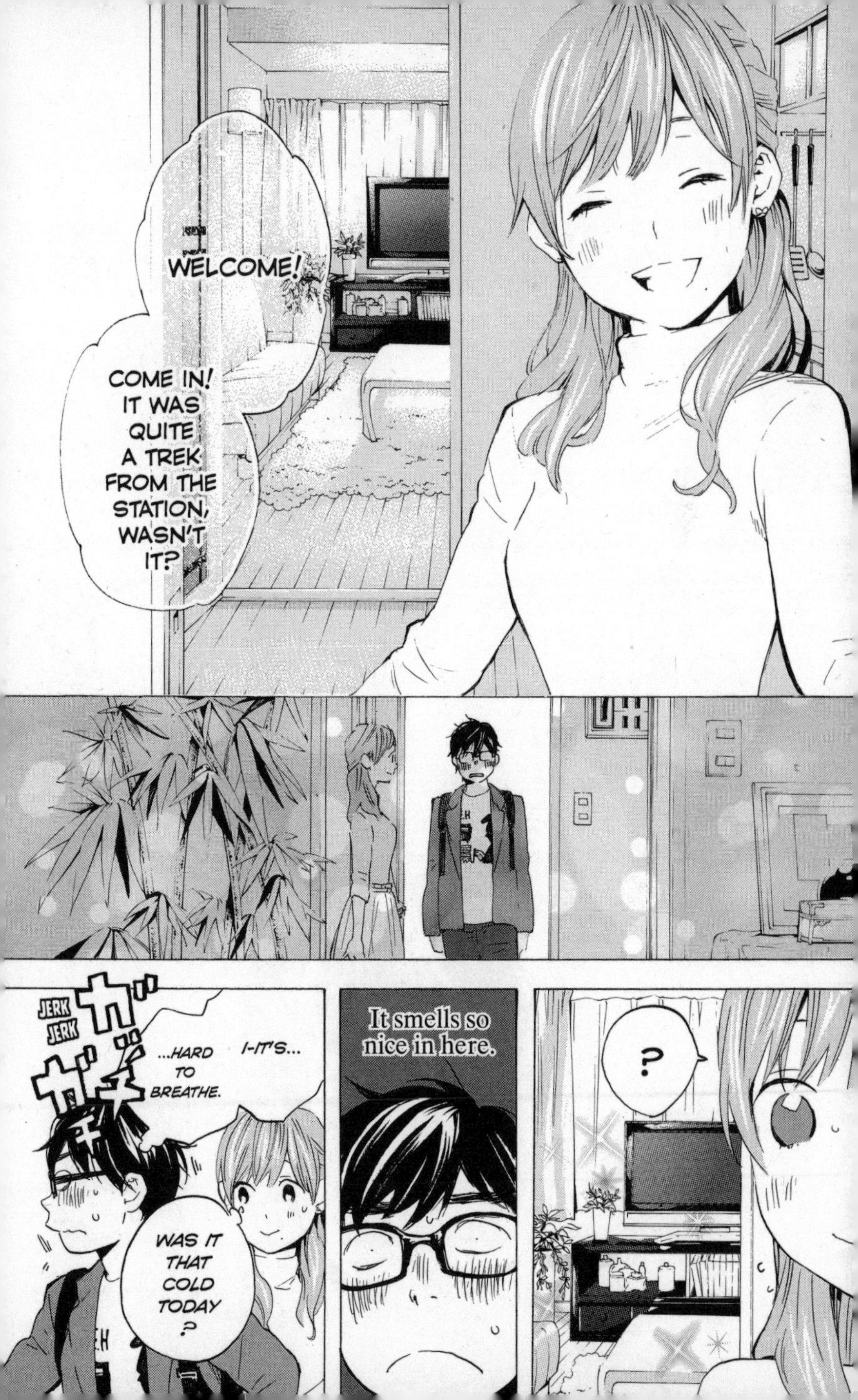
WELCOME!
COME IN! IT WAS QUITE A TREK FROM THE STATION, WASN'T IT?
?
It smells so nice in here.
I-IT'S...
...HARD TO BREATHE.
JERK JERK
WAS IT THAT COLD TODAY?

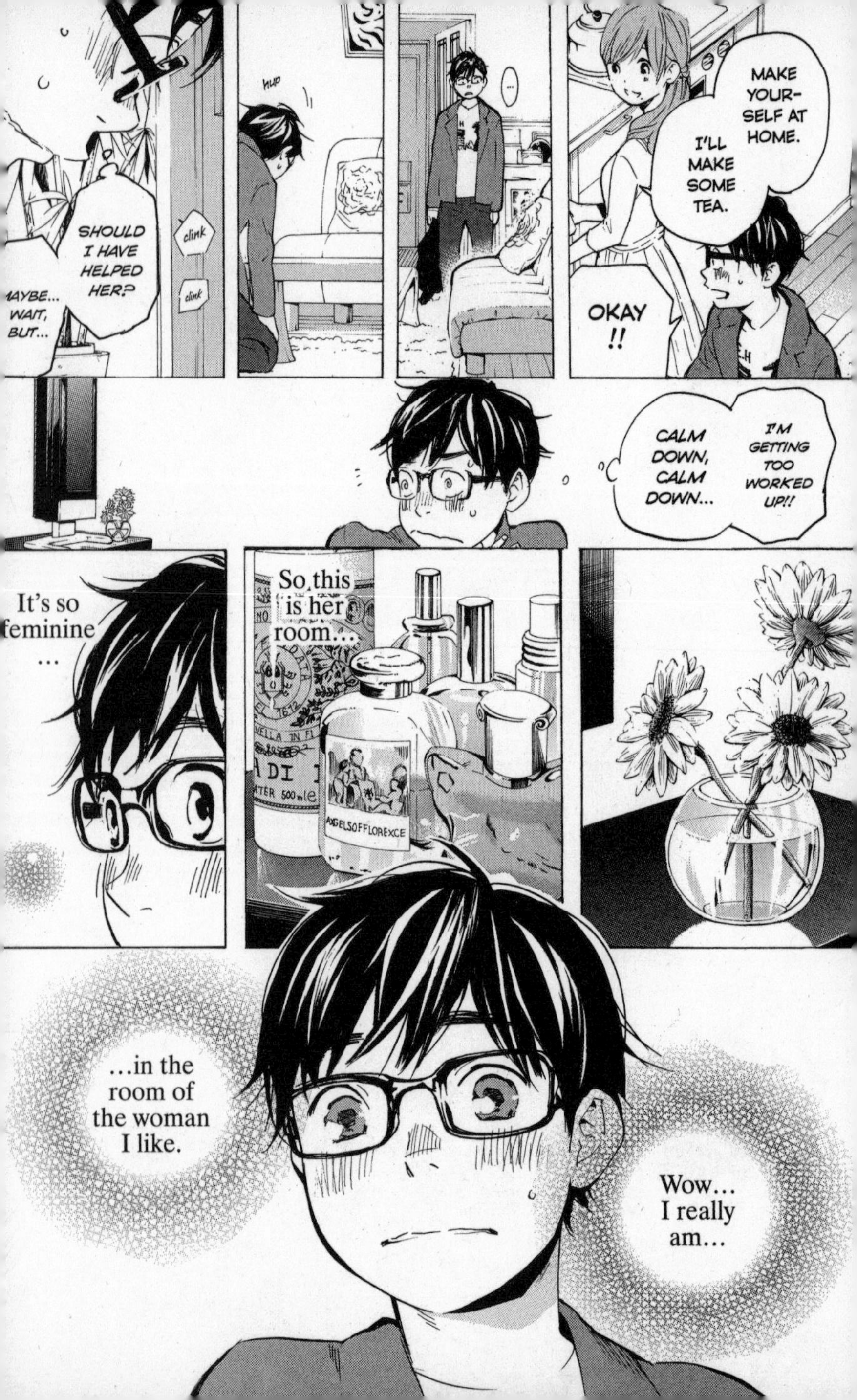
MAKE YOURSELF AT HOME.
I'LL MAKE SOME TEA.
OKAY!!
...
hup
clink
clink
SHOULD I HAVE HELPED HER?
MAYBE... WAIT, BUT...
I'M GETTING TOO WORKED UP!!
CALM DOWN, CALM DOWN...
So this is her room...
It's so feminine...
Wow... I really am...
...in the room of the woman I like.

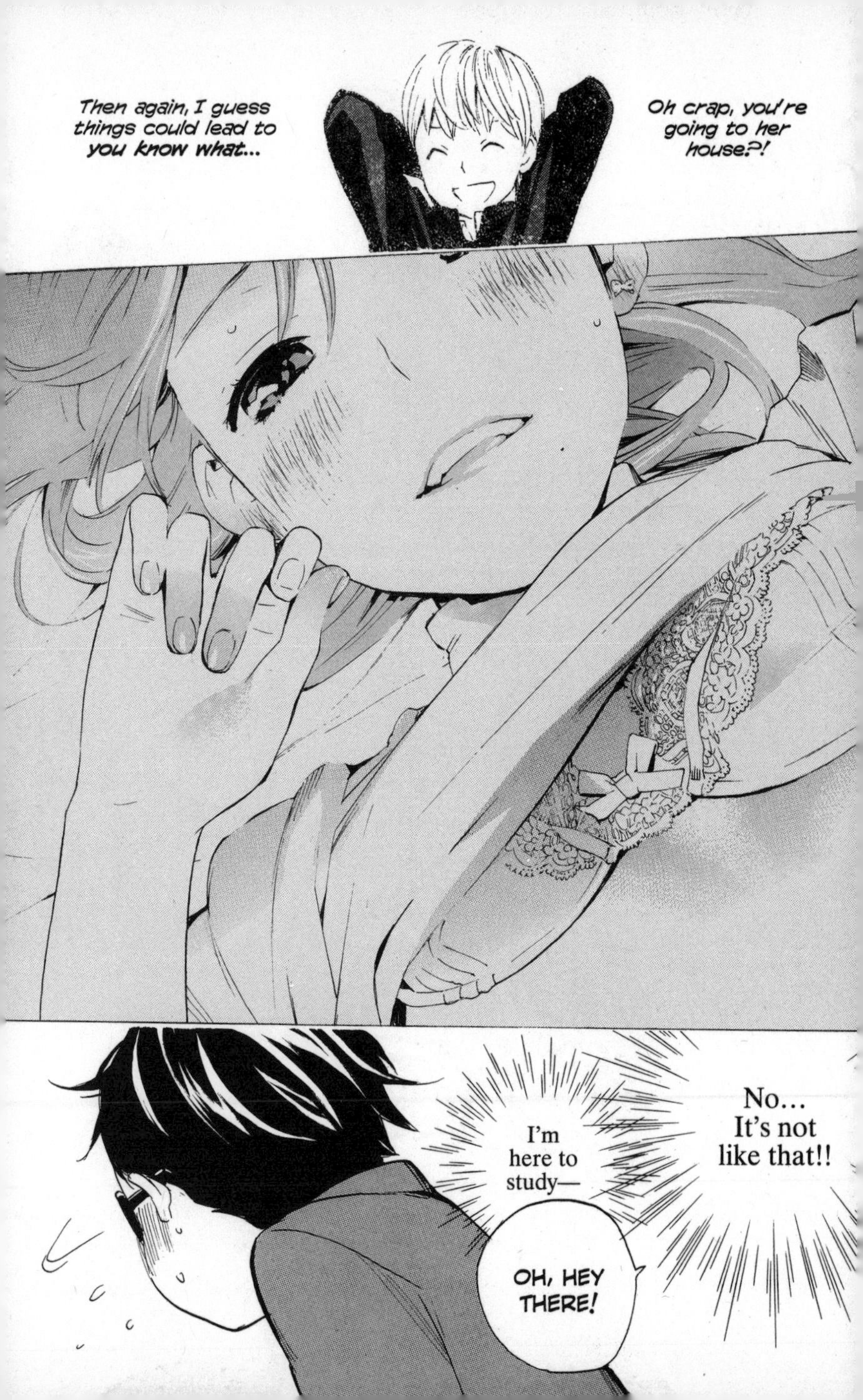
Oh crap, you're going to her house?!
Then again, I guess things could lead to you know what...
No... It's not like that!!
I'm here to study—
OH, HEY THERE!

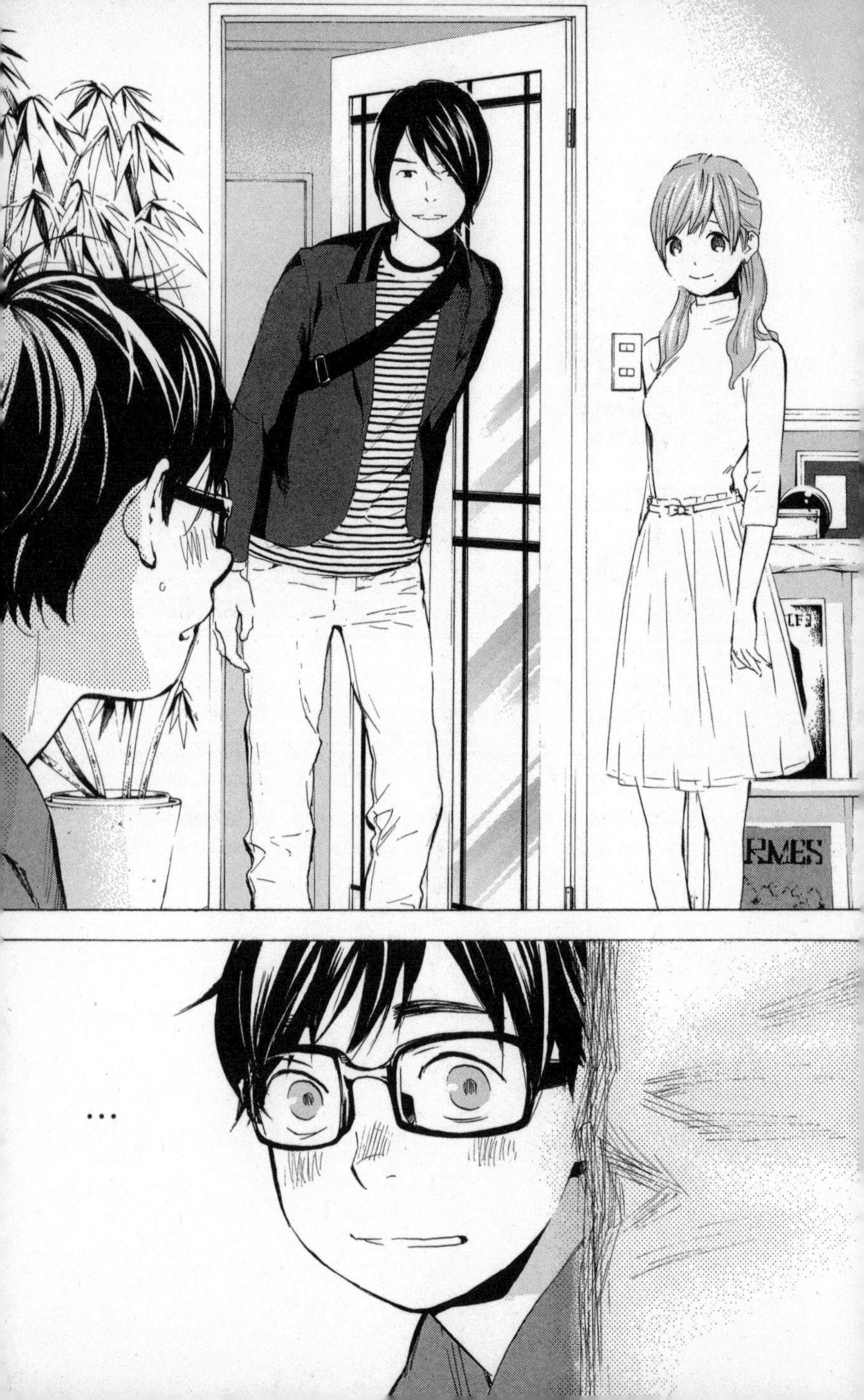
RMES
...

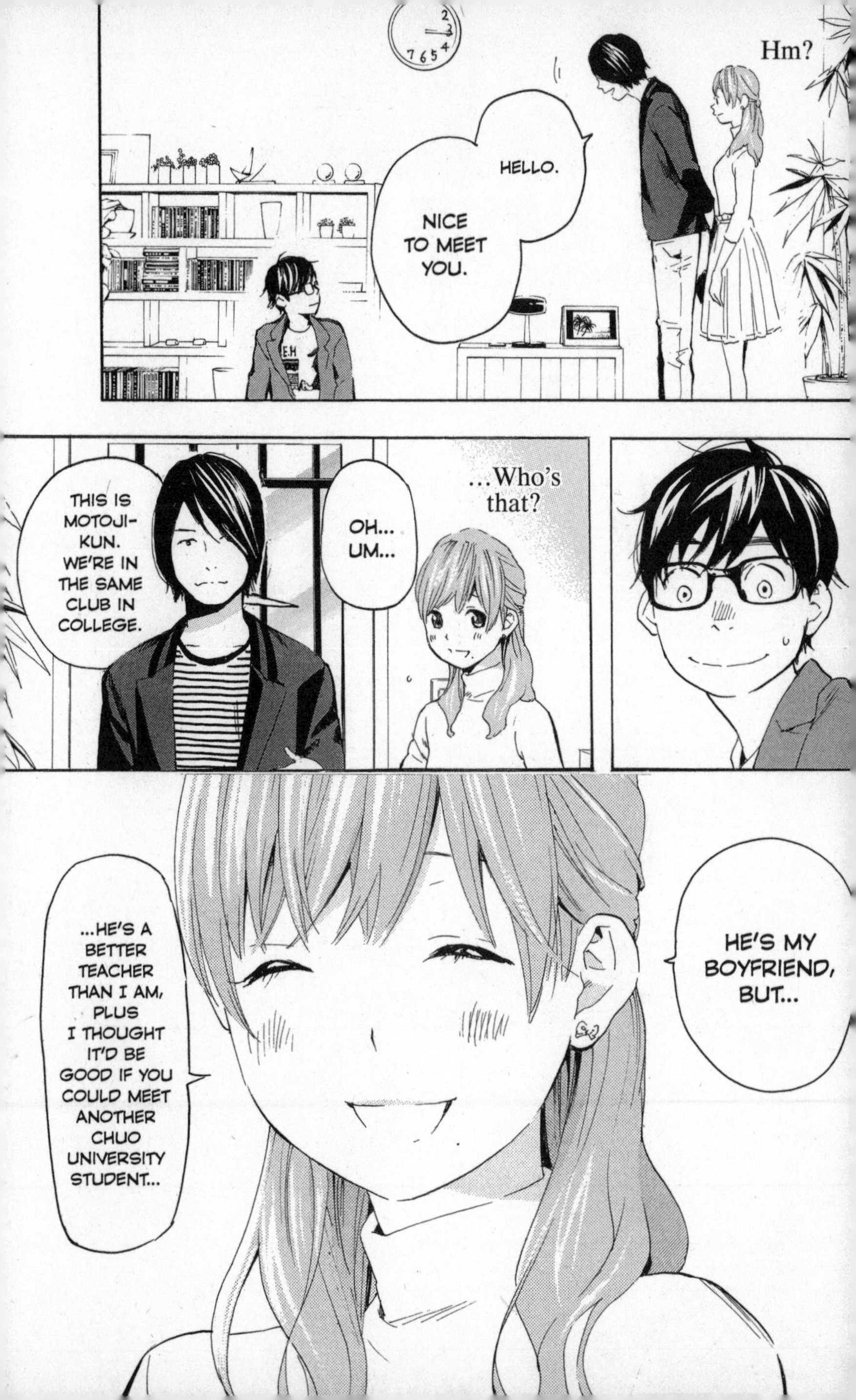
Hm?
HELLO. NICE TO MEET YOU.
…Who's that?
OH... UM...
THIS IS MOTOJI-KUN. WE'RE IN THE SAME CLUB IN COLLEGE.
HE'S MY BOYFRIEND, BUT...
...HE'S A BETTER TEACHER THAN I AM, PLUS I THOUGHT IT'D BE GOOD IF YOU COULD MEET ANOTHER CHUO UNIVERSITY STUDENT...

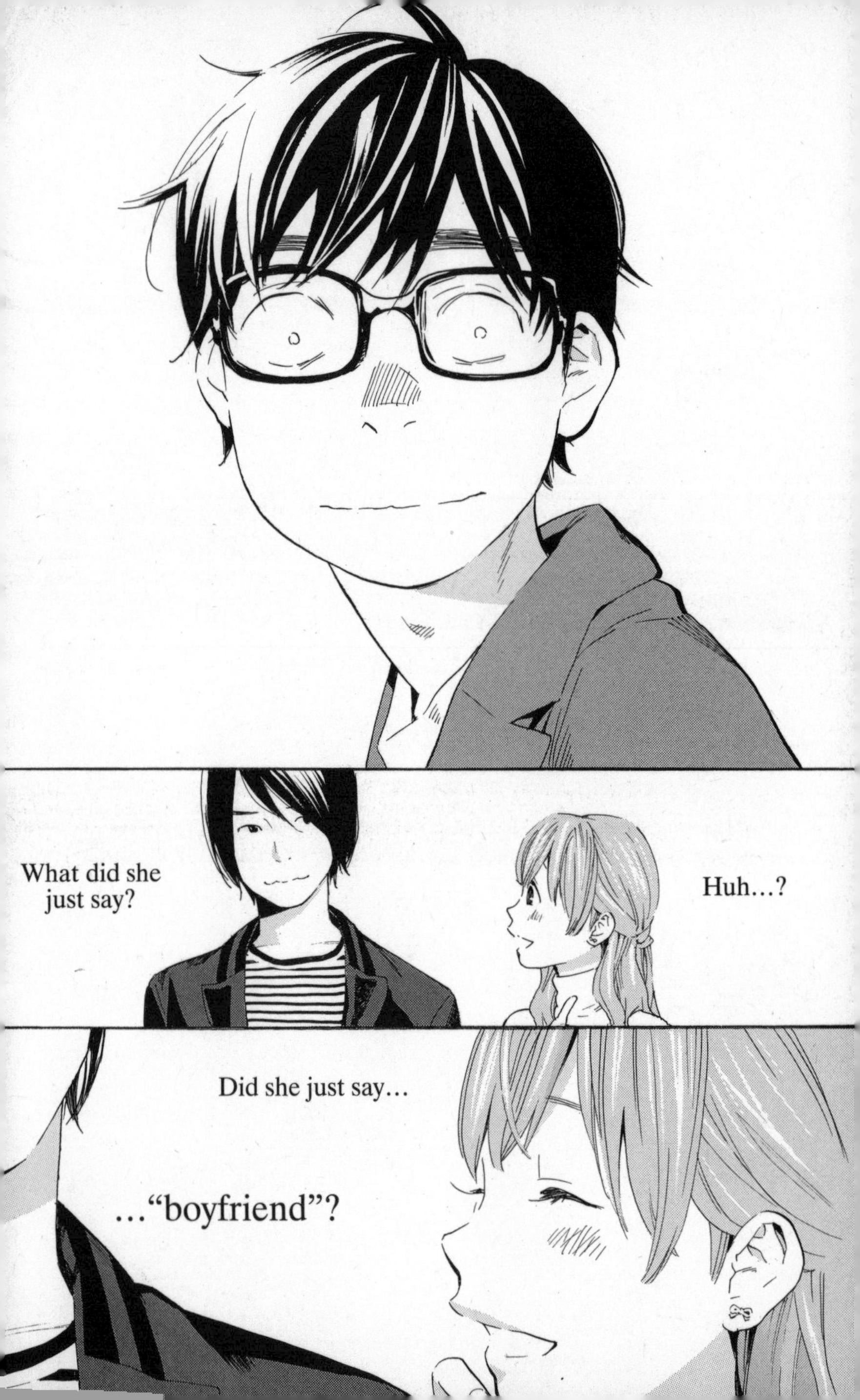
Huh…?
What did she just say?
Did she just say…
…"boyfriend"?

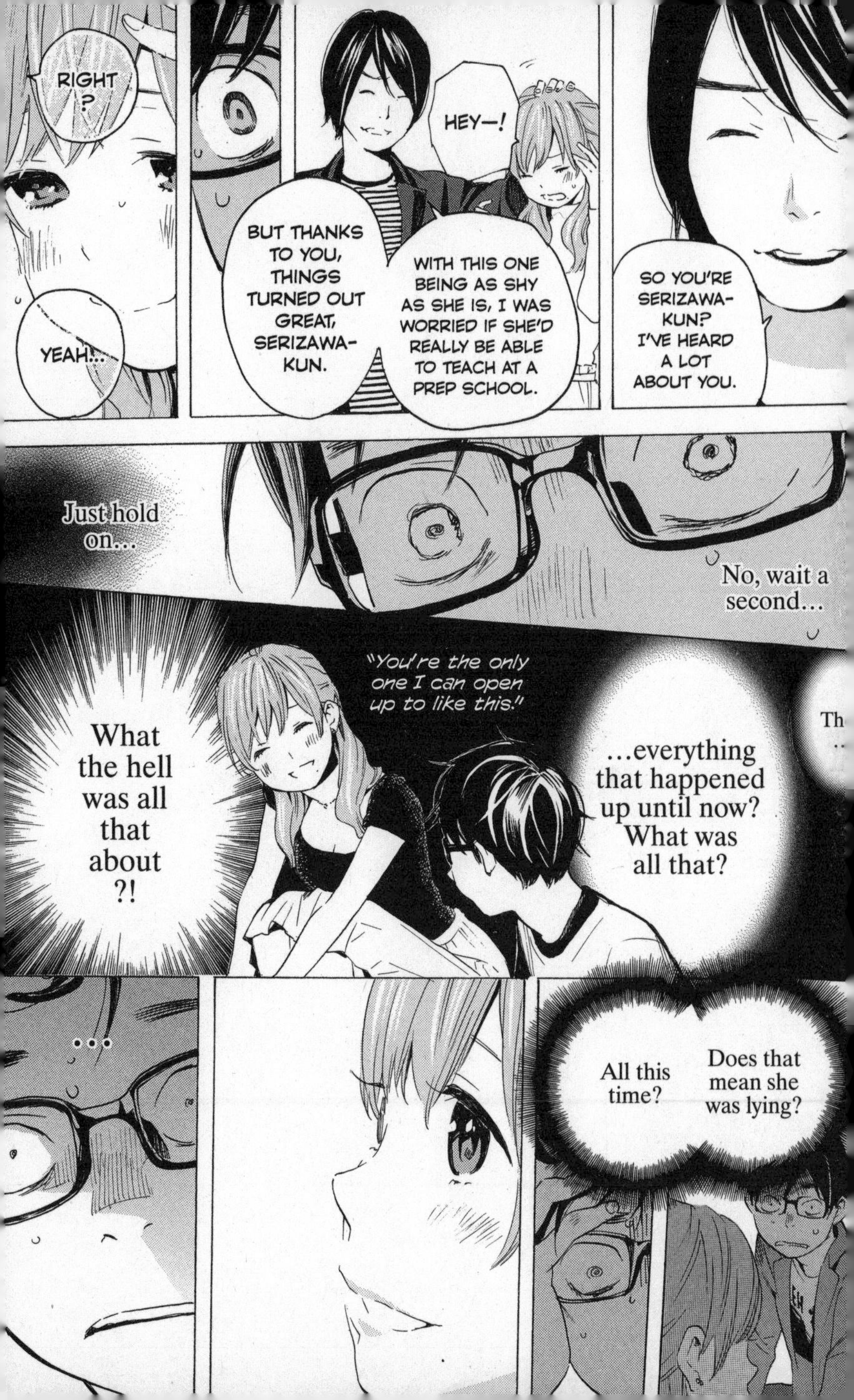
SO YOU'RE SERIZAWA-KUN? I'VE HEARD A LOT ABOUT YOU.
HEY—!
WITH THIS ONE BEING AS SHY AS SHE IS, I WAS WORRIED IF SHE'D REALLY BE ABLE TO TEACH AT A PREP SCHOOL.
BUT THANKS TO YOU, THINGS TURNED OUT GREAT, SERIZAWA-KUN.
RIGHT?
YEAH!...
No, wait a second...
Just hold on...
...everything that happened up until now? What was all that?
"You're the only one I can open up to like this."
What the hell was all that about?!
Does that mean she was lying?
All this time?
...

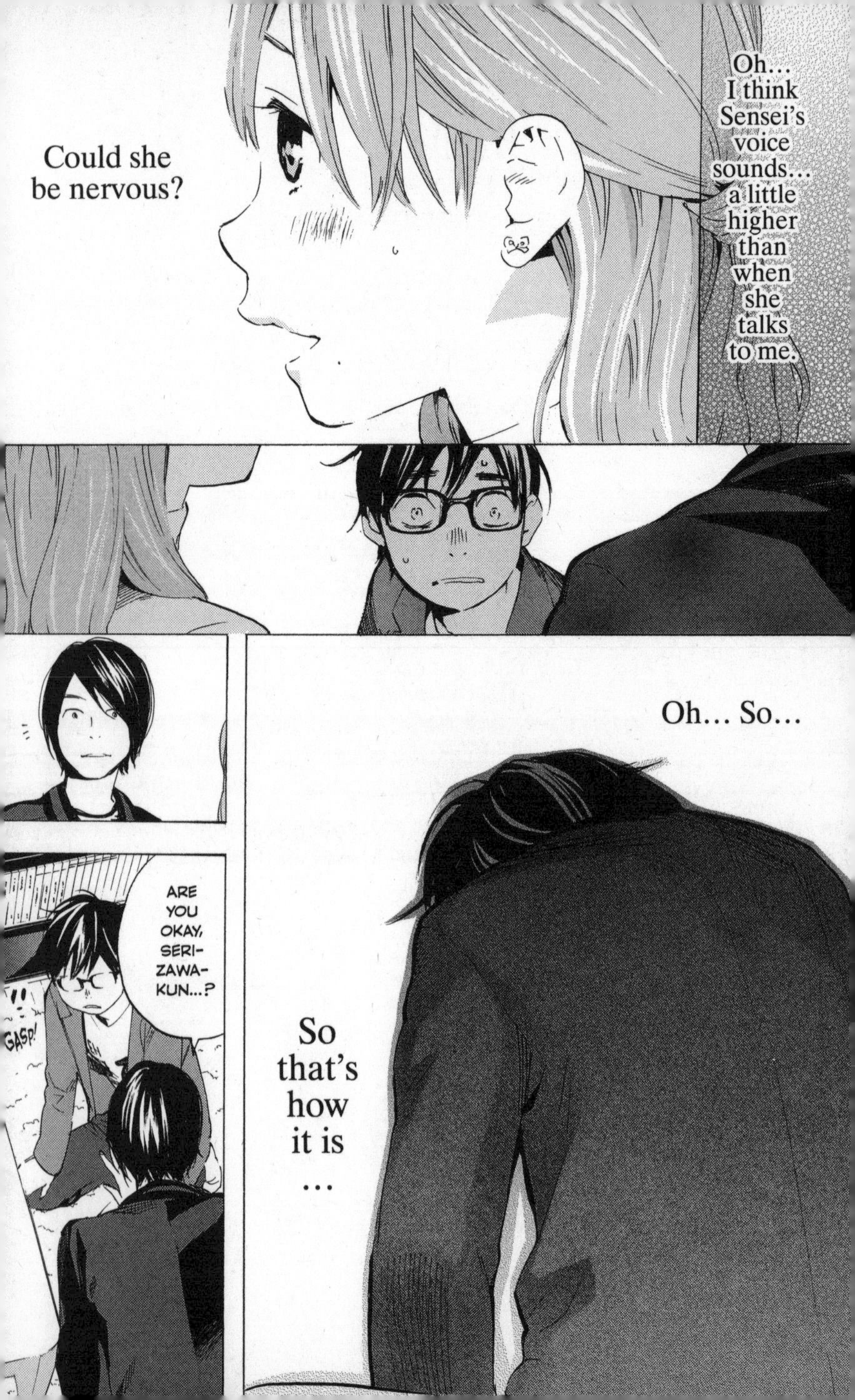
Oh… I think Sensei's voice sounds… a little higher than when she talks to me.
Could she be nervous?
Oh… So…
So that's how it is …
ARE YOU OKAY, SERI-ZAWA-KUN…?
GASP!

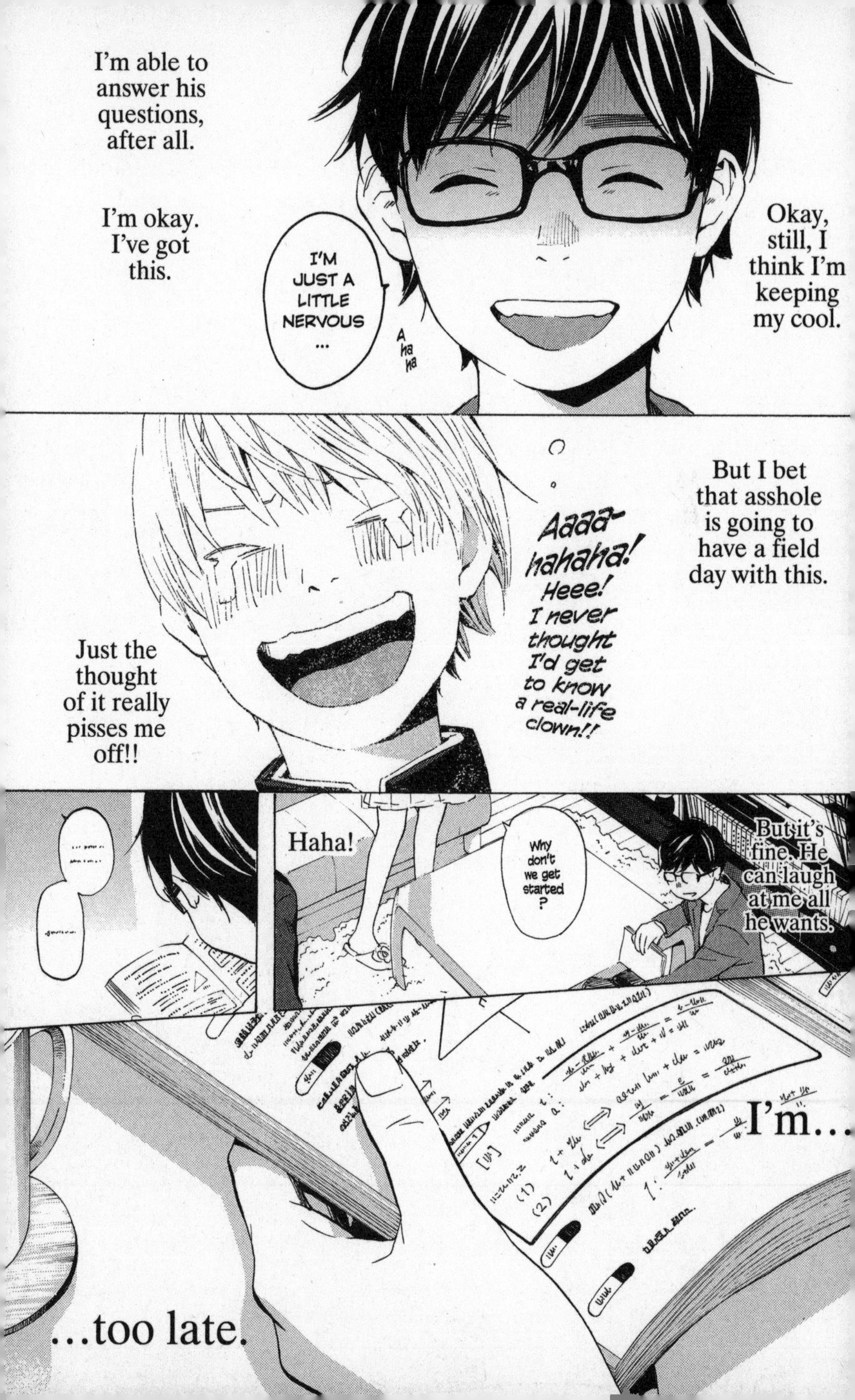
Okay, still, I think I'm keeping my cool.
I'M JUST A LITTLE NERVOUS ...
A ha ha
I'm able to answer his questions, after all.
I'm okay. I've got this.
But I bet that asshole is going to have a field day with this.
Aaaa-hahaha! Heee! I never thought I'd get to know a real-life clown!!
Just the thought of it really pisses me off!!
But it's fine. He can laugh at me all he wants.
Why don't we get started?
Haha!
I'm...
...too late.

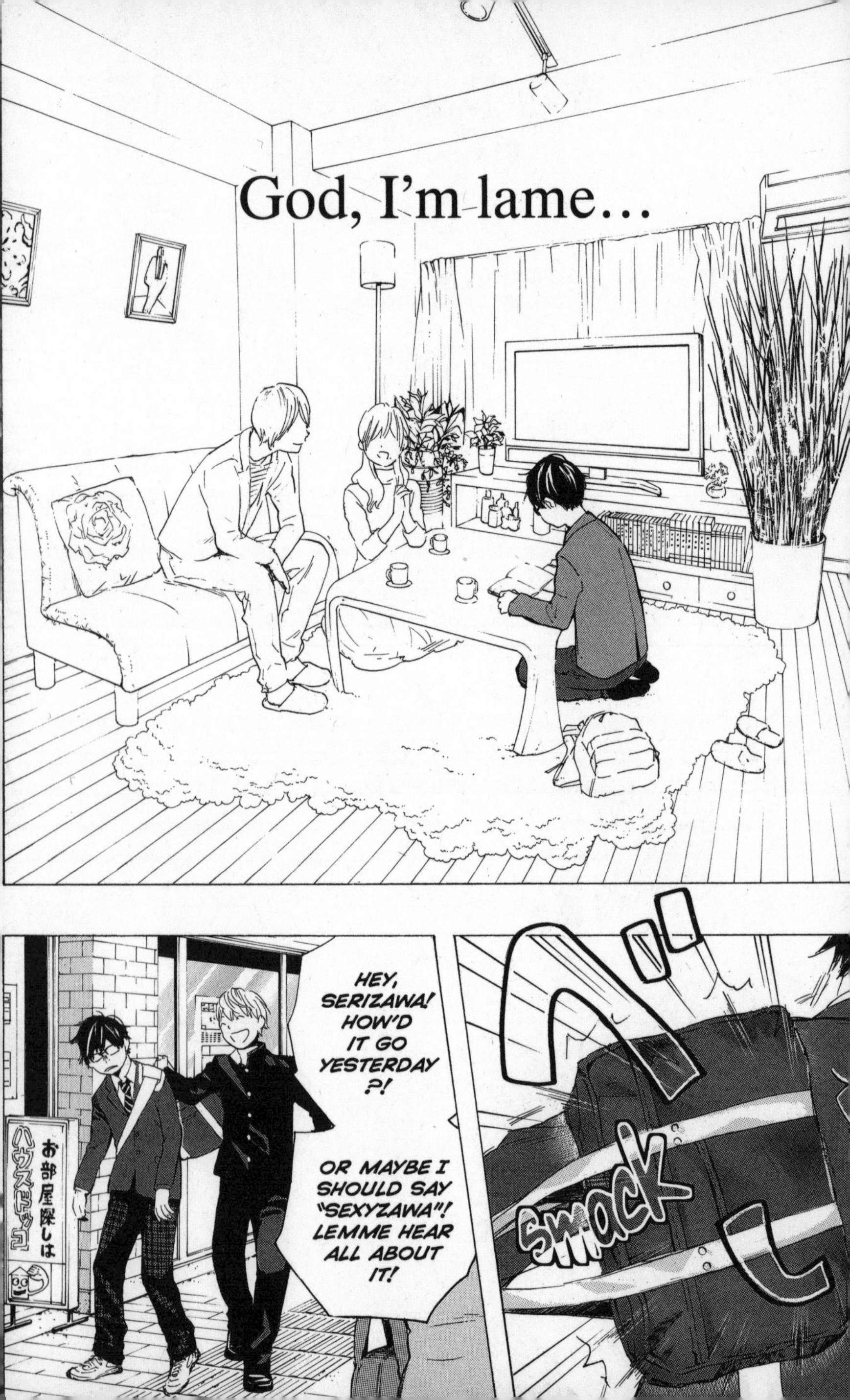
God, I'm lame…
SMACK
HEY, SERIZAWA! HOW'D IT GO YESTERDAY ?!
OR MAYBE I SHOULD SAY "SEXYZAWA"! LEMME HEAR ALL ABOUT IT!
お部屋探しは
ハウスドッコ

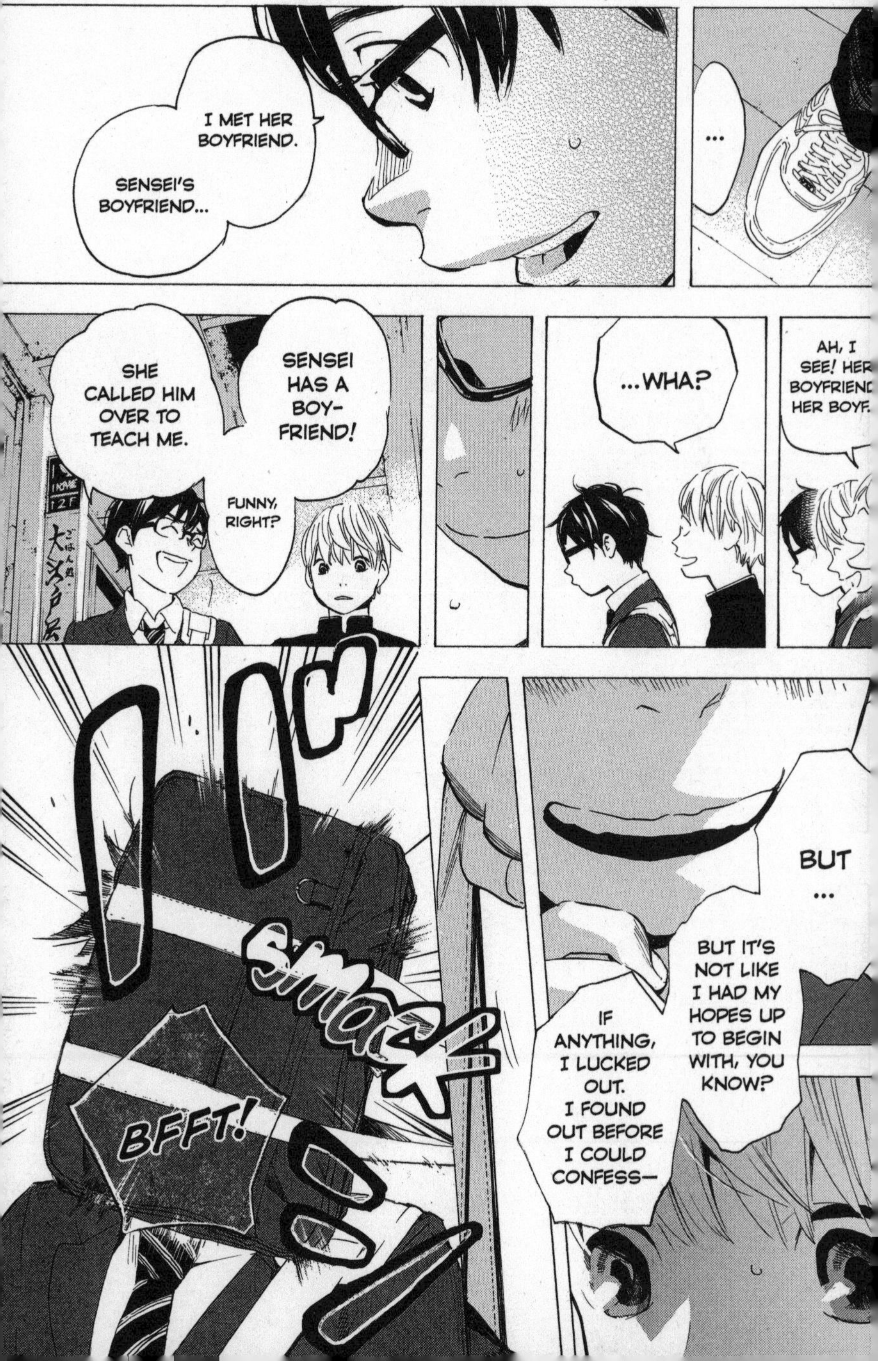
...
I MET HER BOYFRIEND.
SENSEI'S BOYFRIEND...
AH, I SEE! HER BOYFRIEND HER BOYF.
...WHA?
SENSEI HAS A BOY-FRIEND!
SHE CALLED HIM OVER TO TEACH ME.
FUNNY, RIGHT?
BUT ...
BUT IT'S NOT LIKE I HAD MY HOPES UP TO BEGIN WITH, YOU KNOW?
IF ANYTHING, I LUCKED OUT. I FOUND OUT BEFORE I COULD CONFESS—
SMACK!
BFFT!

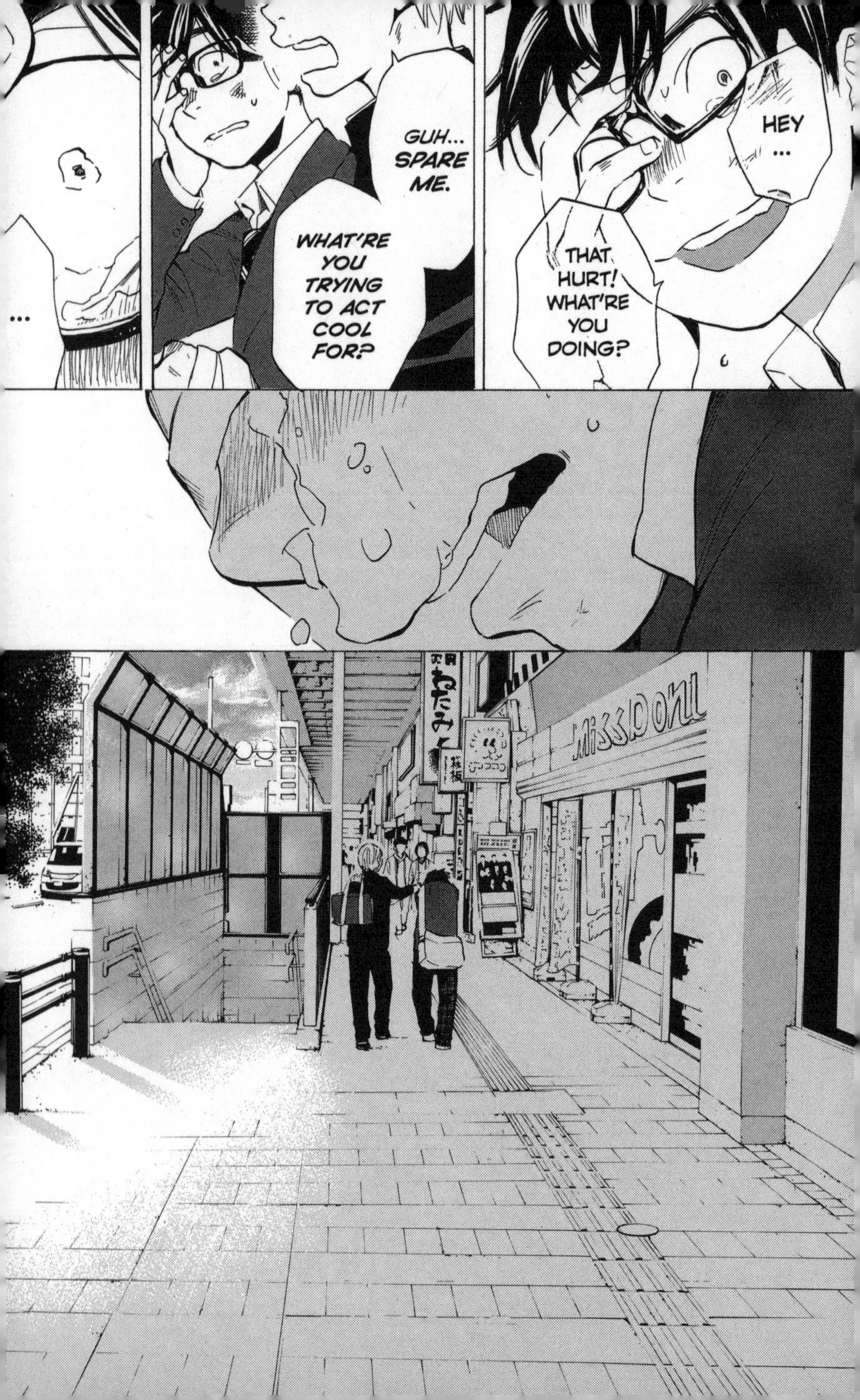
HEY ...
THAT HURT! WHAT'RE YOU DOING?
GUH... SPARE ME.
WHAT'RE YOU TRYING TO ACT COOL FOR?
...

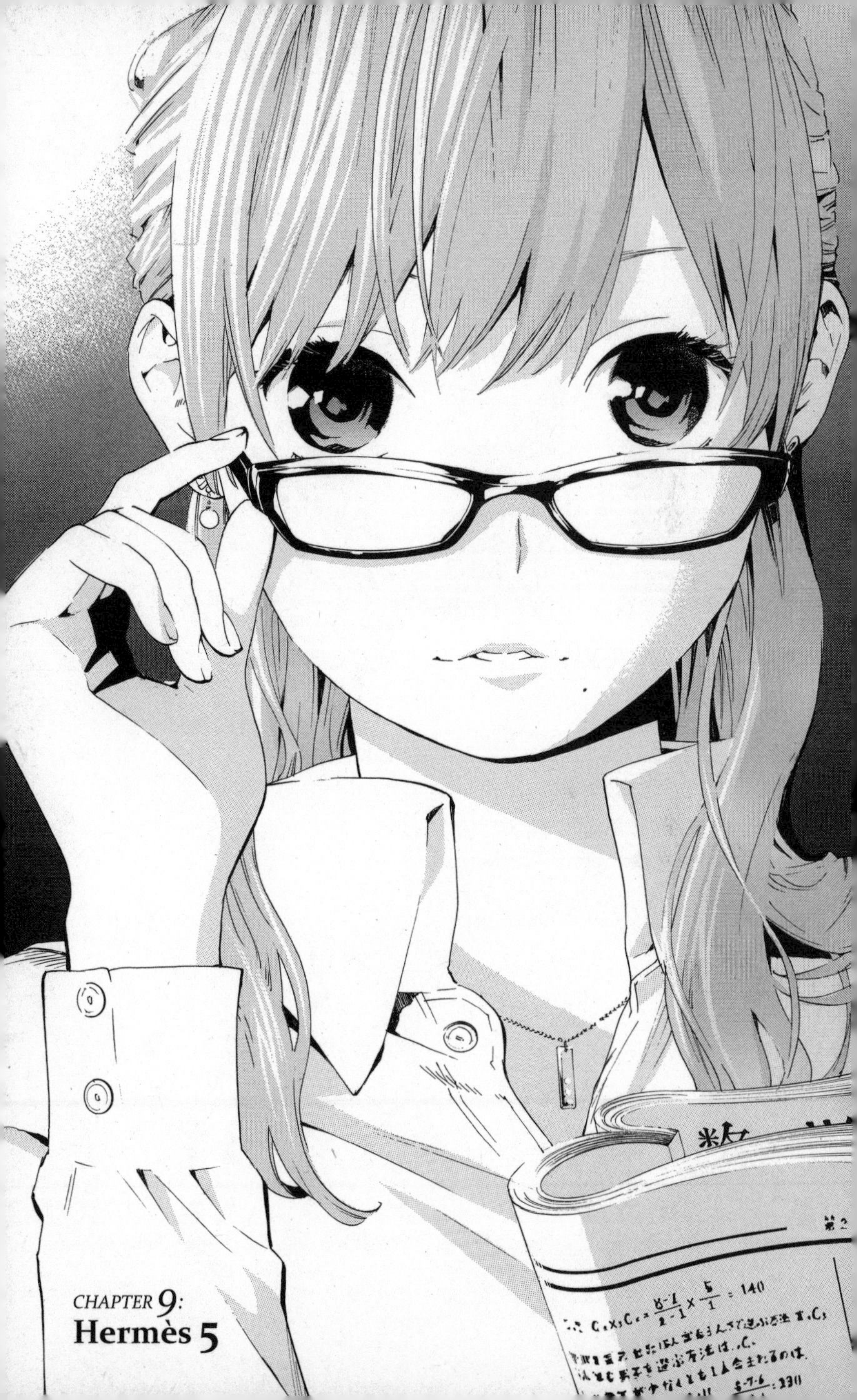

CHAPTER 9: Hermès 5

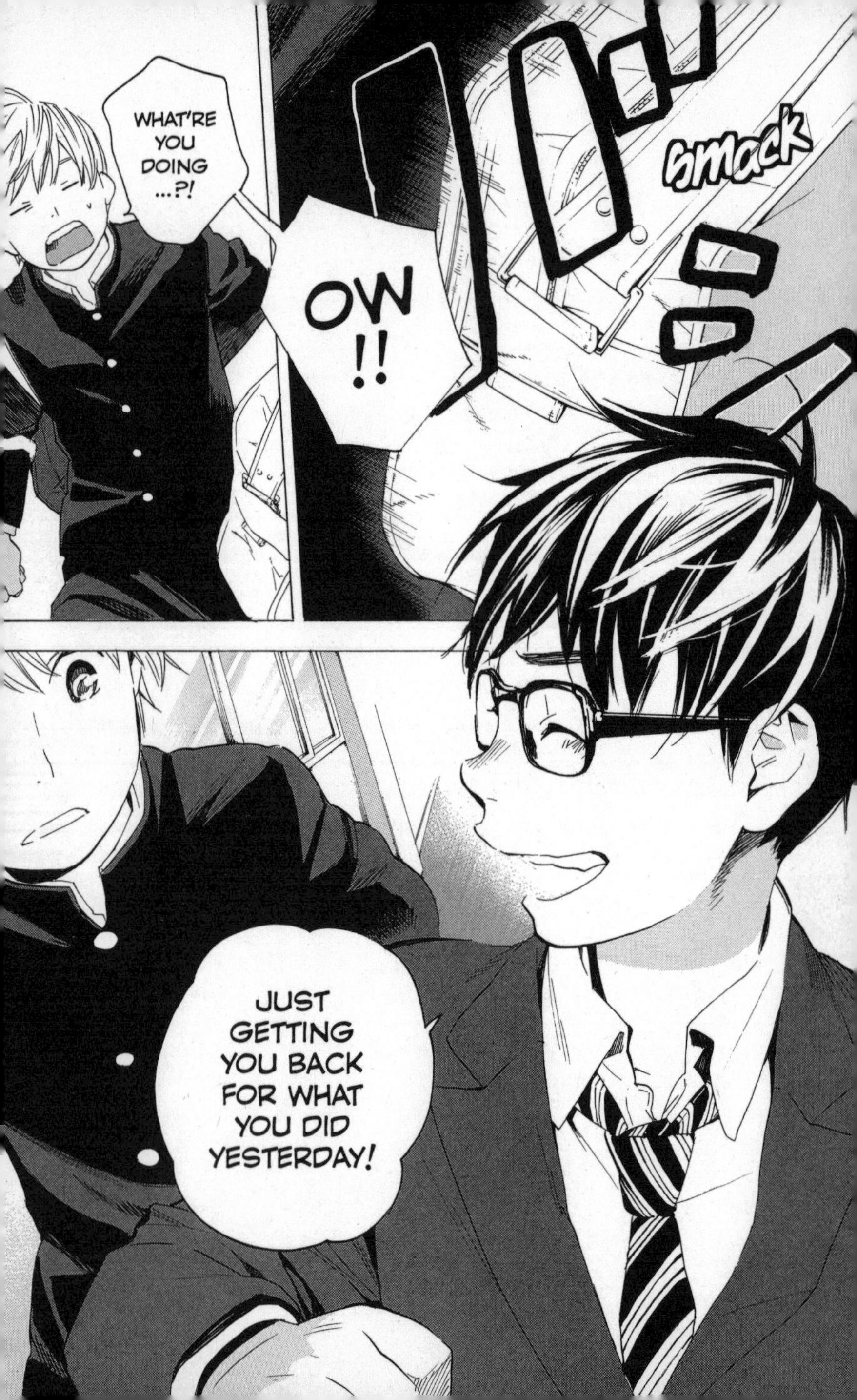
smack
OW!!
WHAT'RE YOU DOING ...?!
JUST GETTING YOU BACK FOR WHAT YOU DID YESTERDAY!

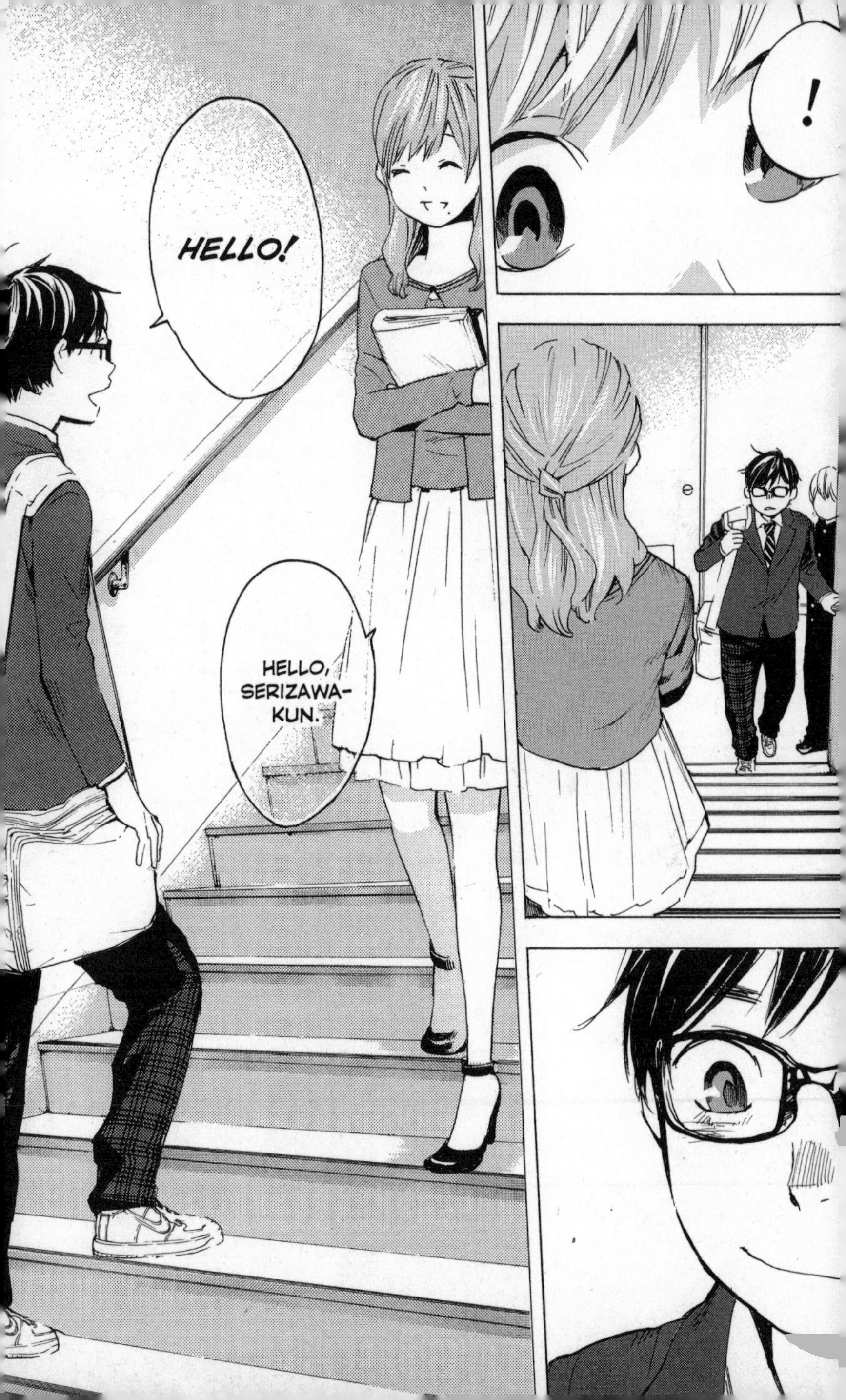
!
HELLO!
HELLO, SERIZAWA-KUN.

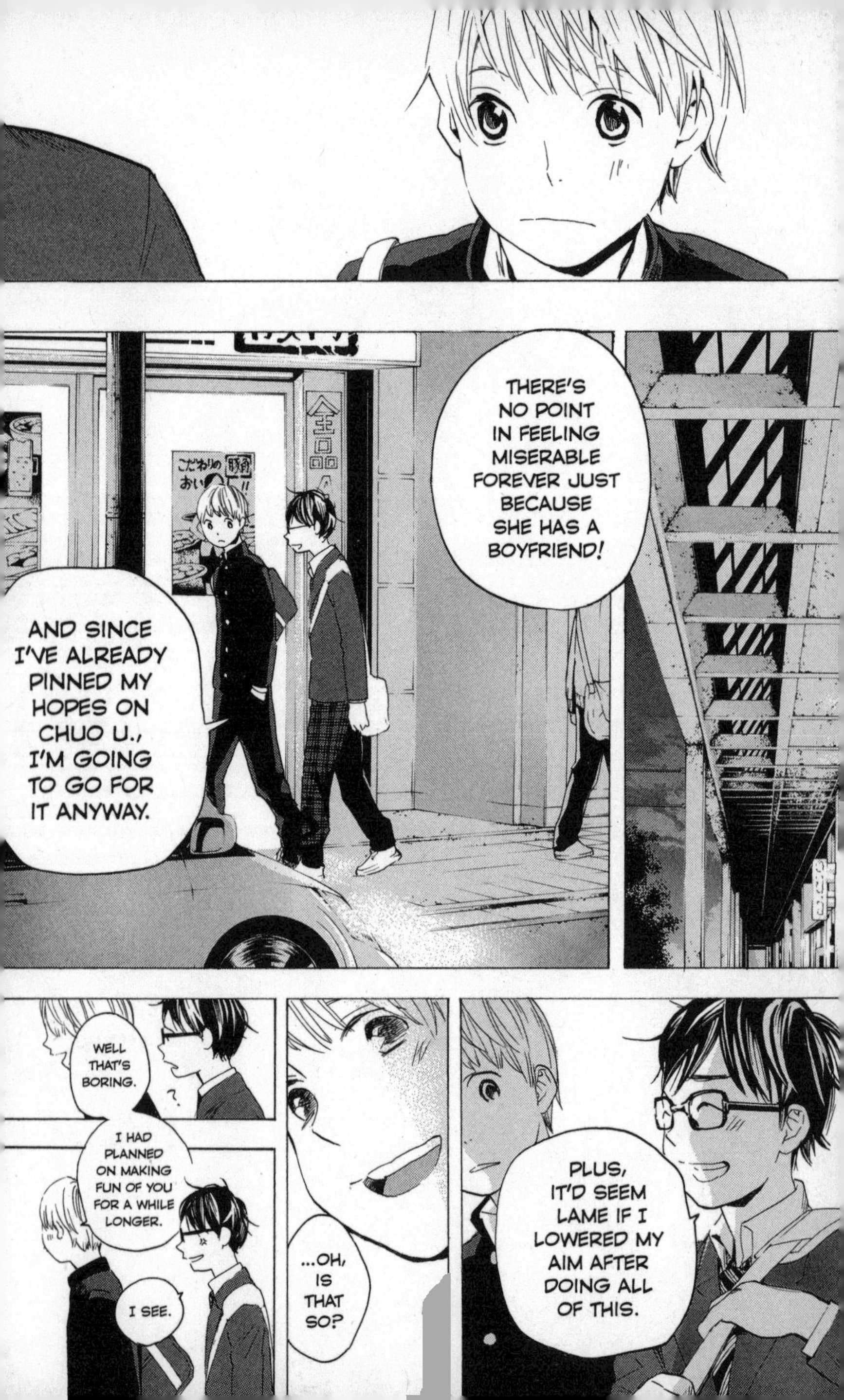
THERE'S NO POINT IN FEELING MISERABLE FOREVER JUST BECAUSE SHE HAS A BOYFRIEND!
AND SINCE I'VE ALREADY PINNED MY HOPES ON CHUO U., I'M GOING TO GO FOR IT ANYWAY.
PLUS, IT'D SEEM LAME IF I LOWERED MY AIM AFTER DOING ALL OF THIS.
...OH, IS THAT SO?
WELL THAT'S BORING.
I HAD PLANNED ON MAKING FUN OF YOU FOR A WHILE LONGER.
I SEE.

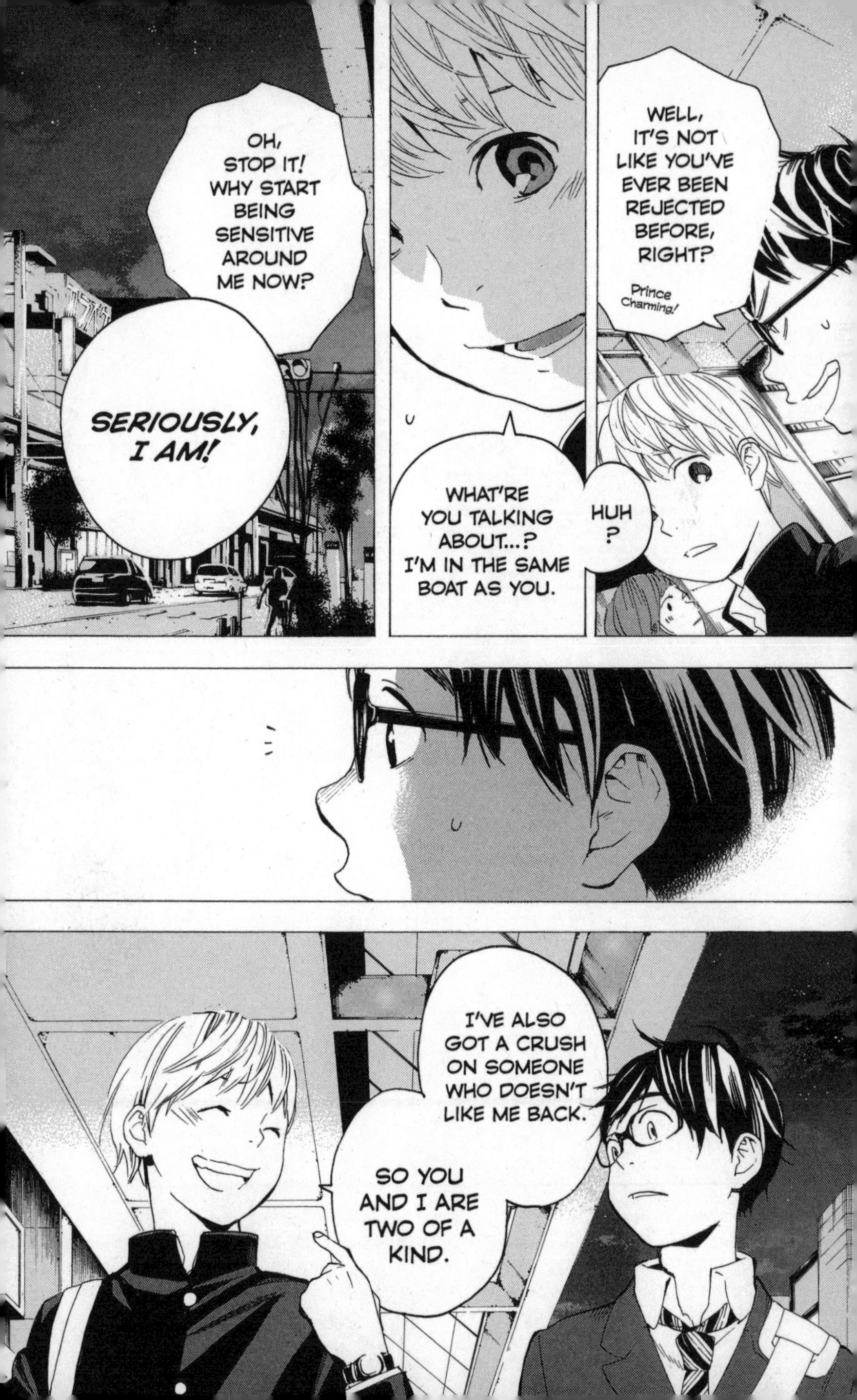
WELL, IT'S NOT LIKE YOU'VE EVER BEEN REJECTED BEFORE, RIGHT?
Prince Charming!
HUH ?
WHAT'RE YOU TALKING ABOUT...? I'M IN THE SAME BOAT AS YOU.
OH, STOP IT! WHY START BEING SENSITIVE AROUND ME NOW?
SERIOUSLY, I AM!
I'VE ALSO GOT A CRUSH ON SOMEONE WHO DOESN'T LIKE ME BACK.
SO YOU AND I ARE TWO OF A KIND.

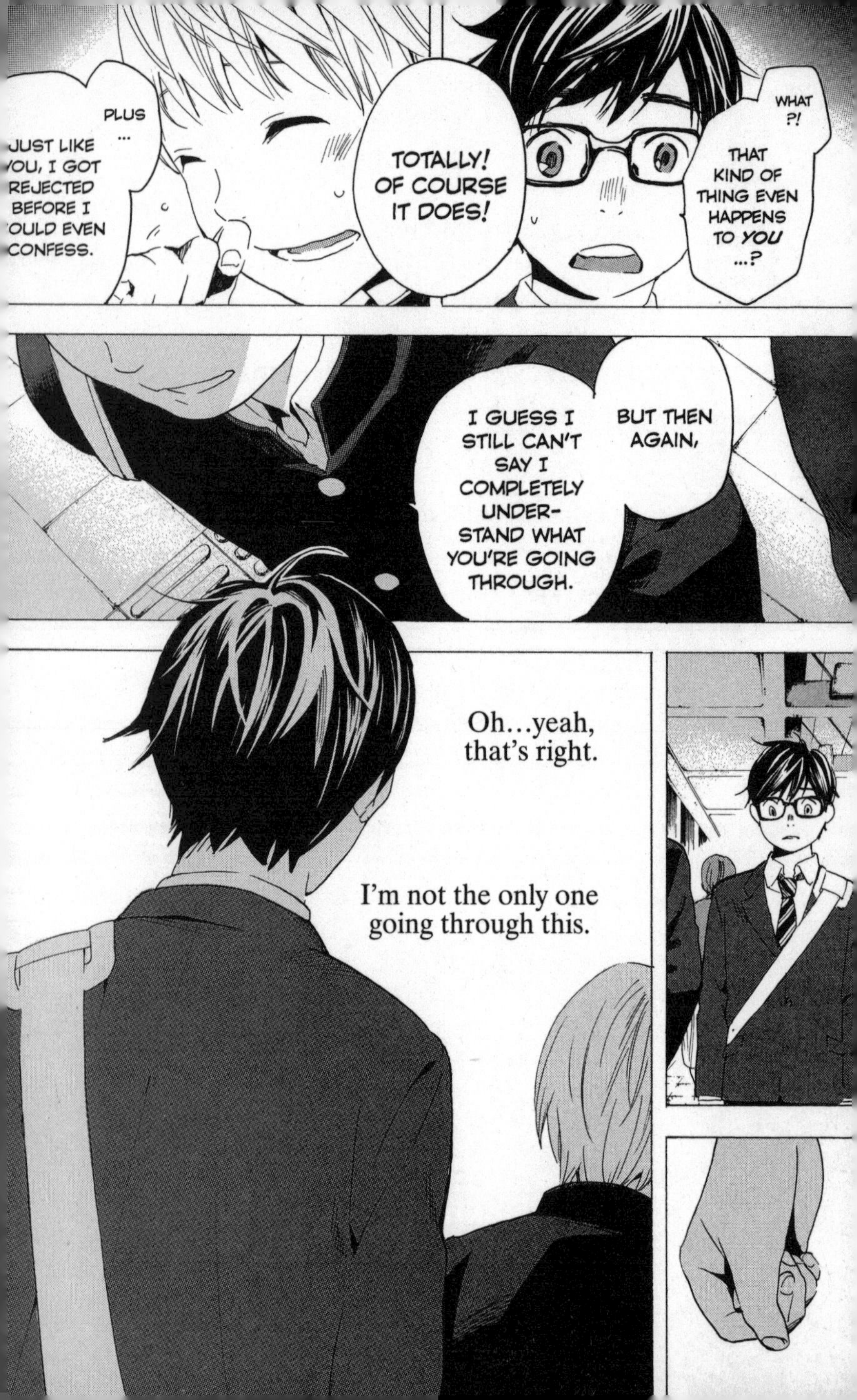
WHAT ?! THAT KIND OF THING EVEN HAPPENS TO *YOU* ...?
TOTALLY! OF COURSE IT DOES!
PLUS ...
JUST LIKE YOU, I GOT REJECTED BEFORE I COULD EVEN CONFESS.
BUT THEN AGAIN,
I GUESS I STILL CAN'T SAY I COMPLETELY UNDER-STAND WHAT YOU'RE GOING THROUGH.
Oh…yeah, that's right.
I'm not the only one going through this.

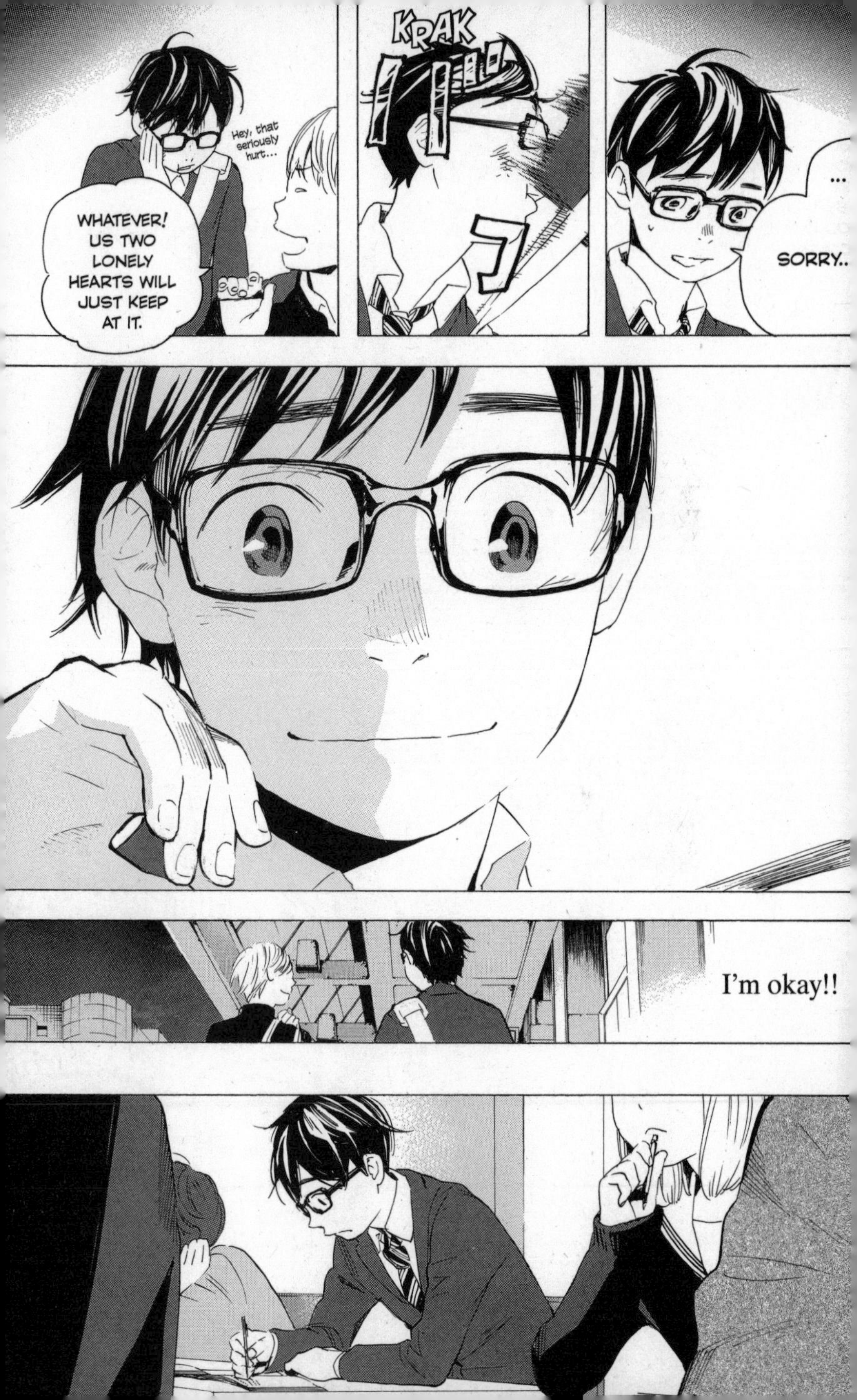
...
SORRY..
KRAK
Hey, that seriously hurt...
WHATEVER! US TWO LONELY HEARTS WILL JUST KEEP AT IT.
I'm okay!!

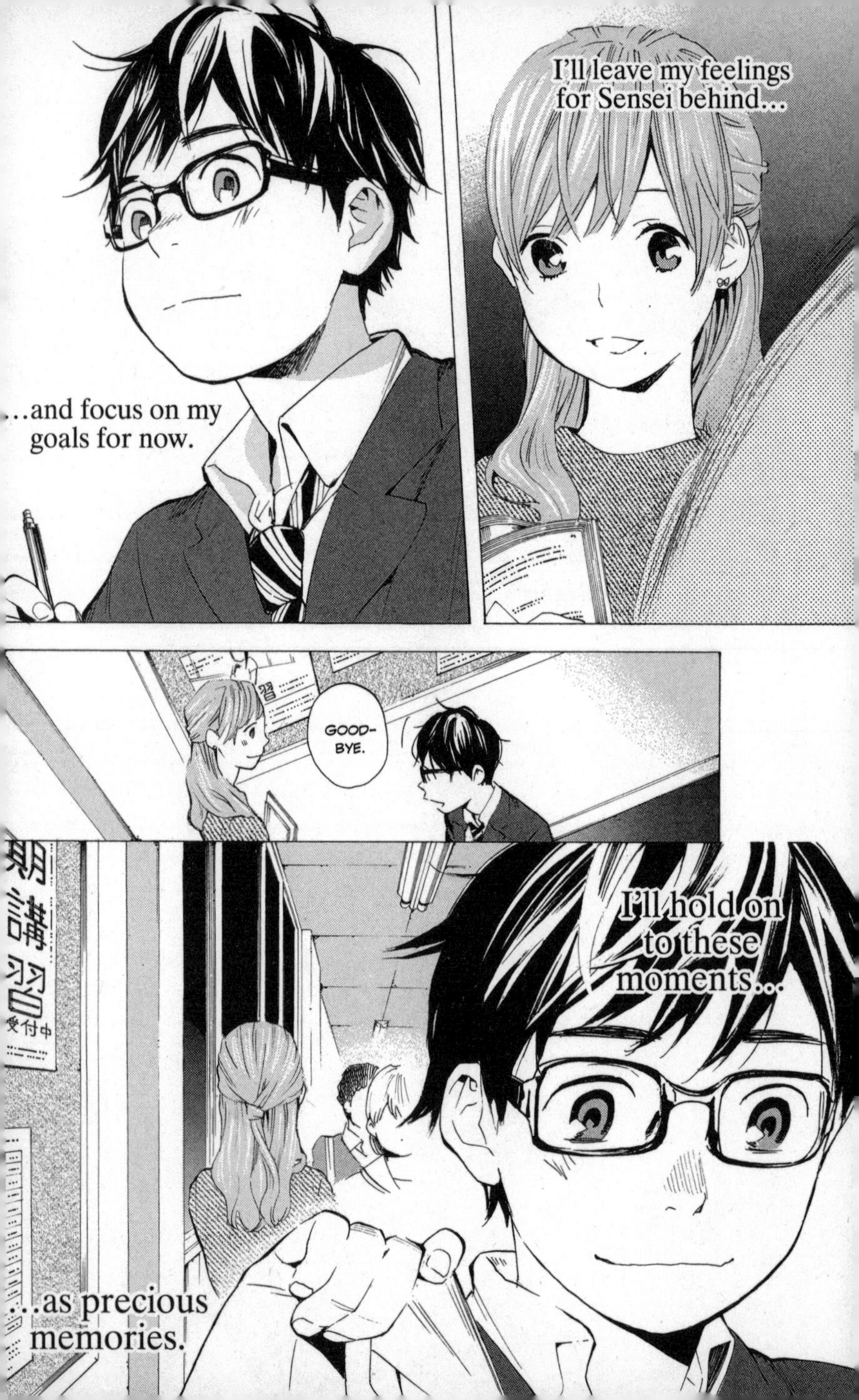
I'll leave my feelings for Sensei behind...
...and focus on my goals for now.
GOOD-BYE.
I'll hold on to these moments...
期講習
受付中
...as precious memories.

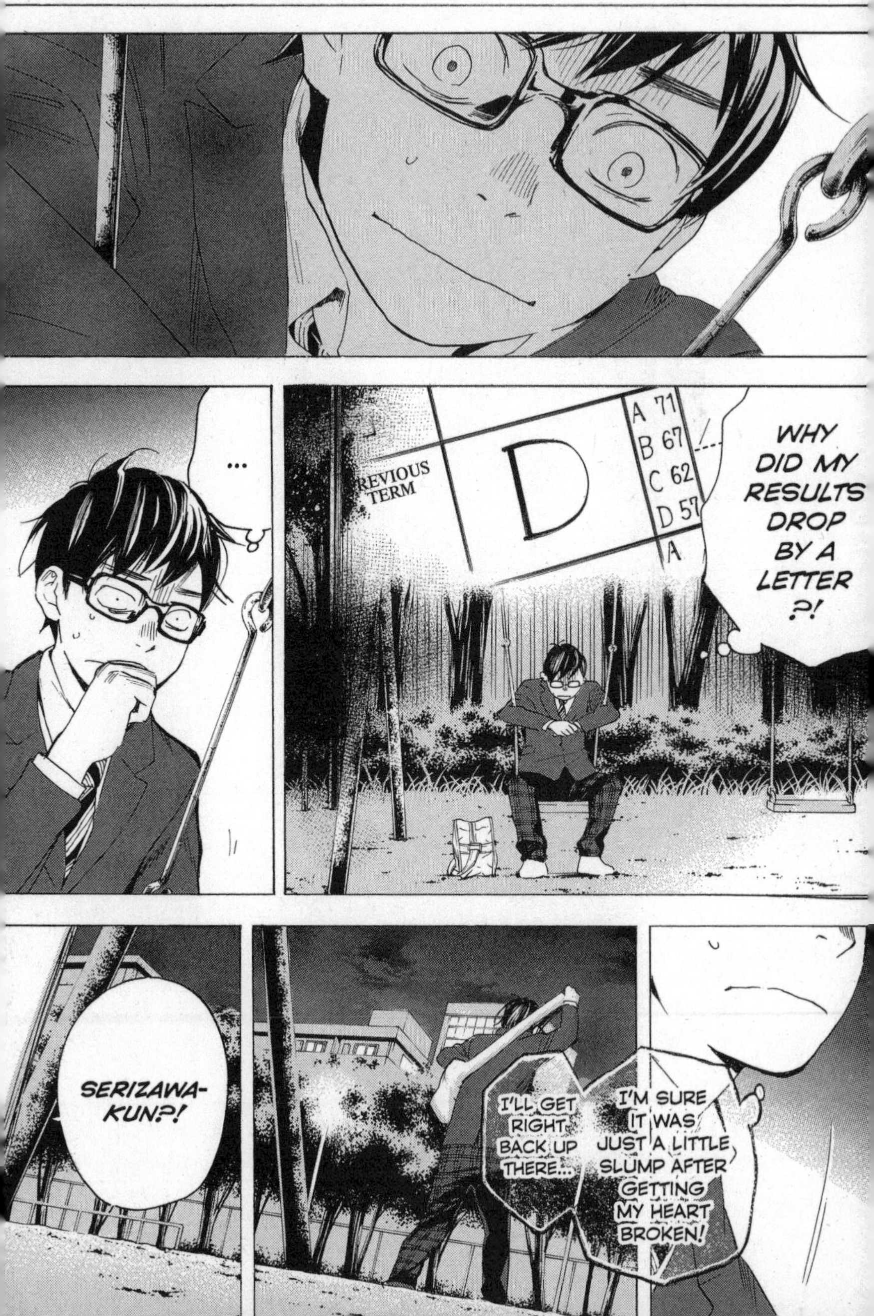
REVIOUS TERM
D
A 71
B 67
C 62
D 57
A
WHY DID MY RESULTS DROP BY A LETTER?!
...
I'M SURE IT WAS JUST A LITTLE SLUMP AFTER GETTING MY HEART BROKEN!
I'LL GET RIGHT BACK UP THERE...
SERIZAWA-KUN?!

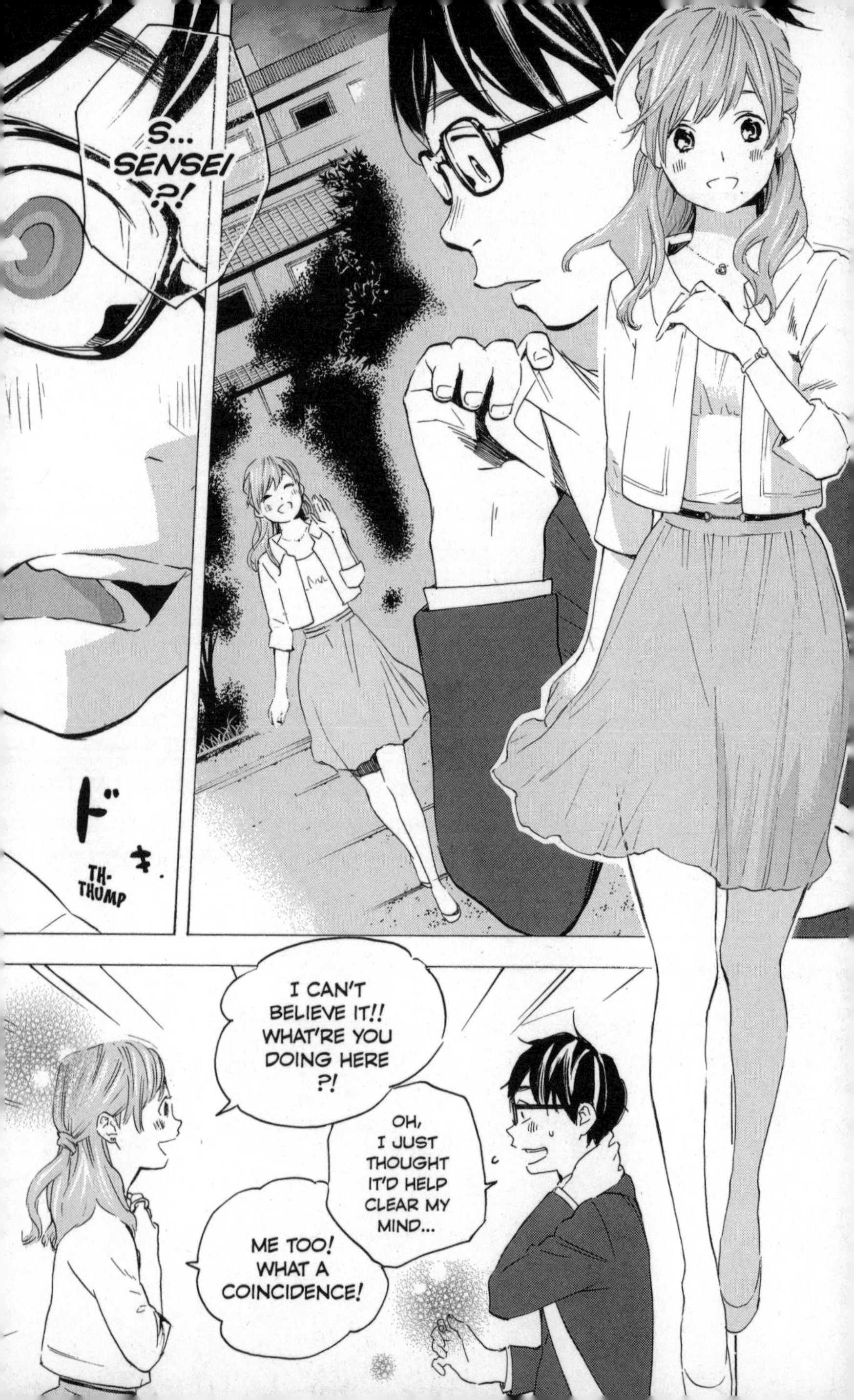
S... SENSEI ?!
ドキ
TH-THUMP
I CAN'T BELIEVE IT!! WHAT'RE YOU DOING HERE ?!
OH, I JUST THOUGHT IT'D HELP CLEAR MY MIND...
ME TOO! WHAT A COINCIDENCE!

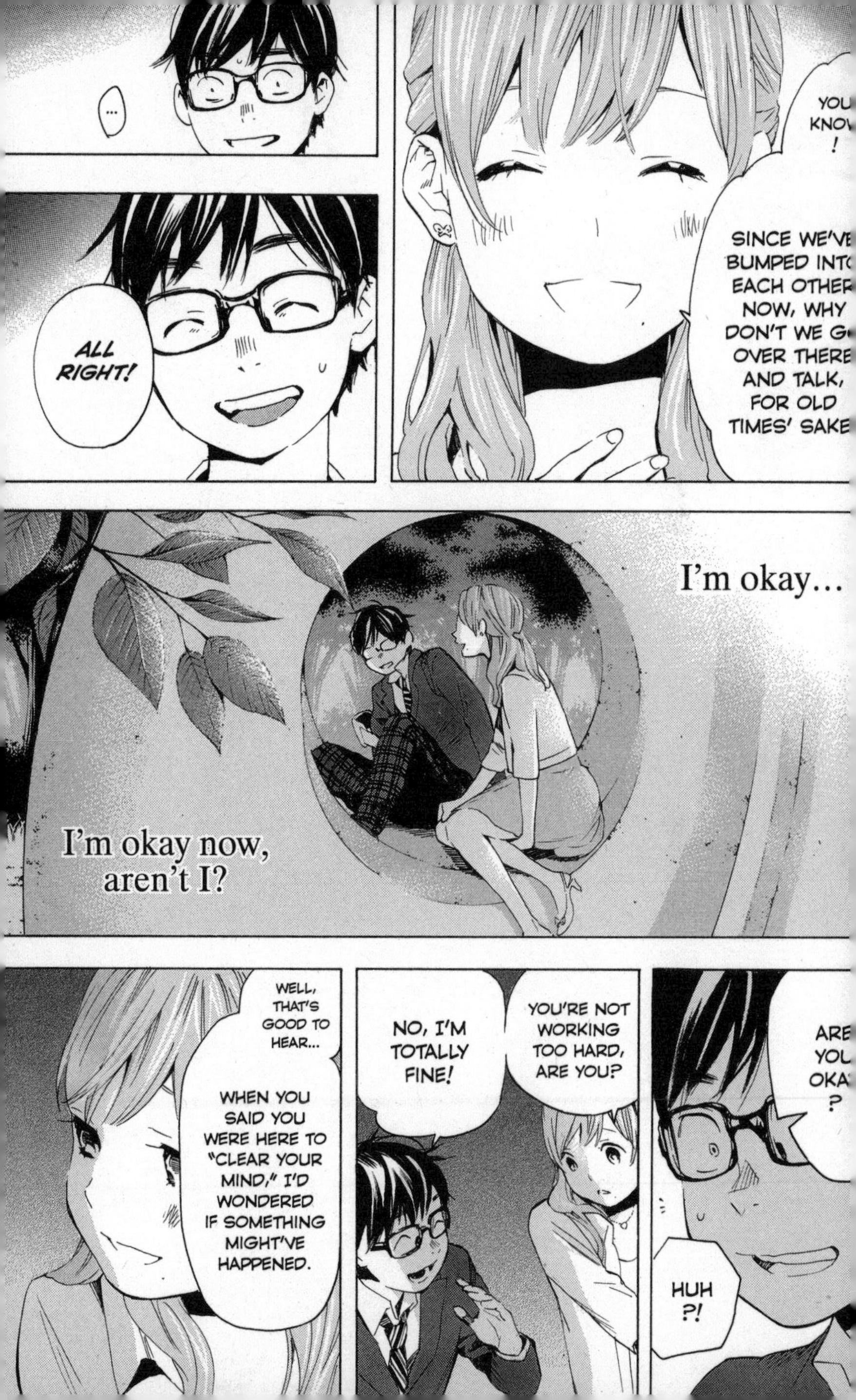
YOU KNOW!
SINCE WE'VE BUMPED INTO EACH OTHER NOW, WHY DON'T WE GO OVER THERE AND TALK, FOR OLD TIMES' SAKE
...
ALL RIGHT!
I'm okay…
I'm okay now, aren't I?
ARE YOU OKAY?
HUH?!
YOU'RE NOT WORKING TOO HARD, ARE YOU?
NO, I'M TOTALLY FINE!
WELL, THAT'S GOOD TO HEAR...
WHEN YOU SAID YOU WERE HERE TO "CLEAR YOUR MIND," I'D WONDERED IF SOMETHING MIGHT'VE HAPPENED.

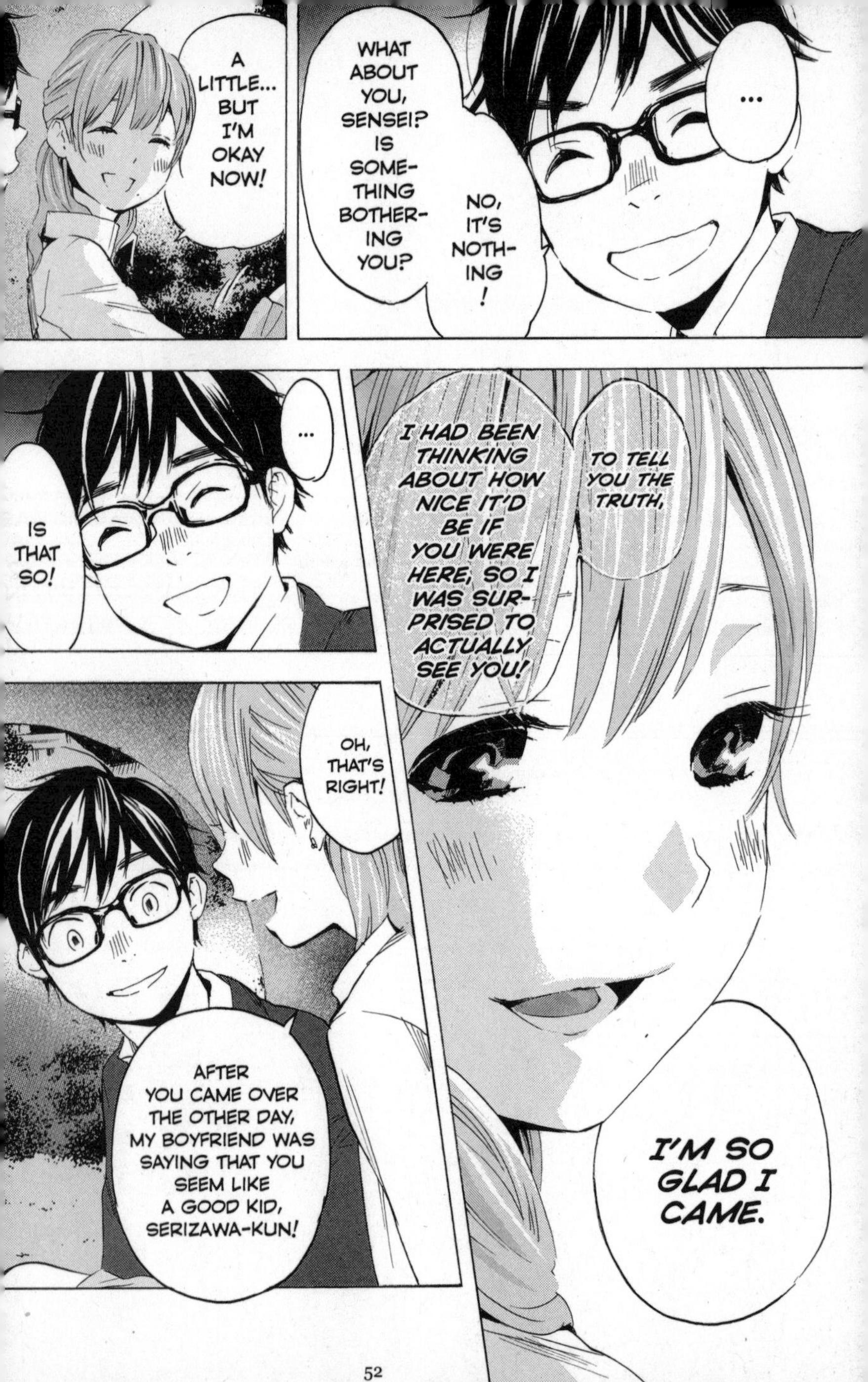
...
WHAT ABOUT YOU, SENSEI? IS SOMETHING BOTHERING YOU?
NO, IT'S NOTHING!
A LITTLE... BUT I'M OKAY NOW!
TO TELL YOU THE TRUTH,
I HAD BEEN THINKING ABOUT HOW NICE IT'D BE IF YOU WERE HERE, SO I WAS SURPRISED TO ACTUALLY SEE YOU!
I'M SO GLAD I CAME.
...
IS THAT SO!
OH, THAT'S RIGHT!
AFTER YOU CAME OVER THE OTHER DAY, MY BOYFRIEND WAS SAYING THAT YOU SEEM LIKE A GOOD KID, SERIZAWA-KUN!

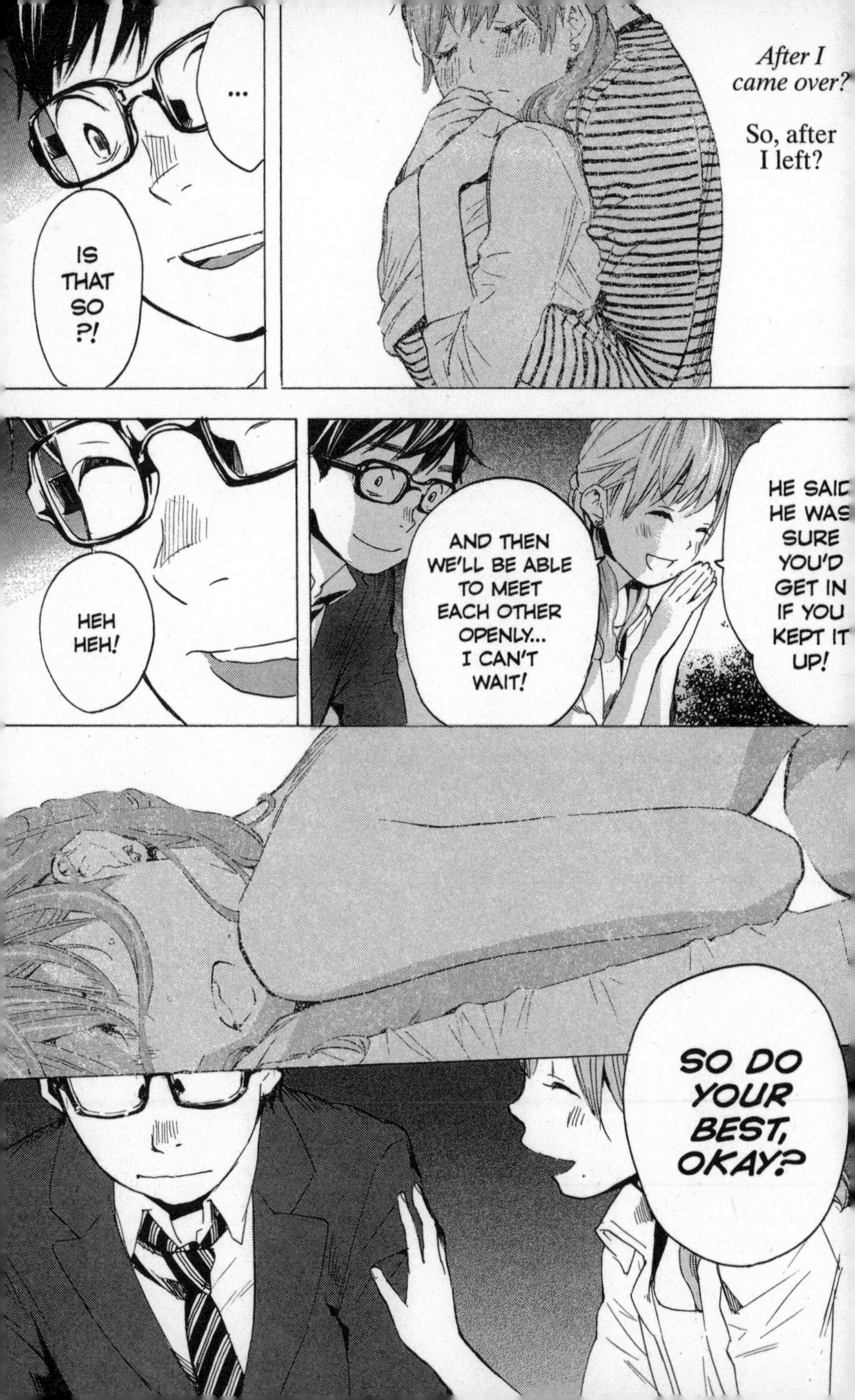
After I came over?
So, after I left?
...
IS THAT SO ?!
HE SAID HE WAS SURE YOU'D GET IN IF YOU KEPT IT UP!
AND THEN WE'LL BE ABLE TO MEET EACH OTHER OPENLY... I CAN'T WAIT!
HEH HEH!
SO DO YOUR BEST, OKAY?

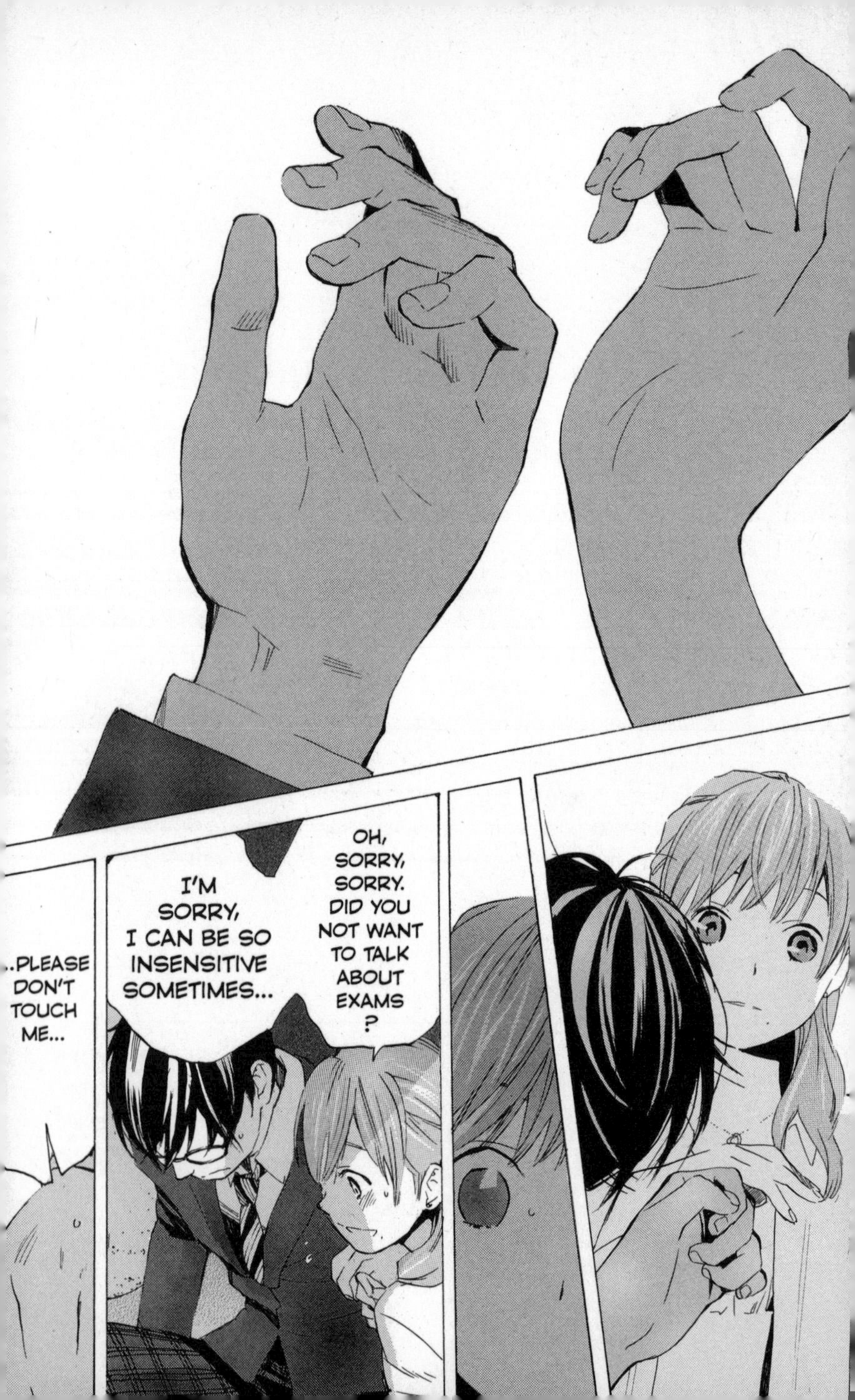
OH, SORRY, SORRY. DID YOU NOT WANT TO TALK ABOUT EXAMS?
I'M SORRY, I CAN BE SO INSENSITIVE SOMETIMES...
..PLEASE DON'T TOUCH ME...

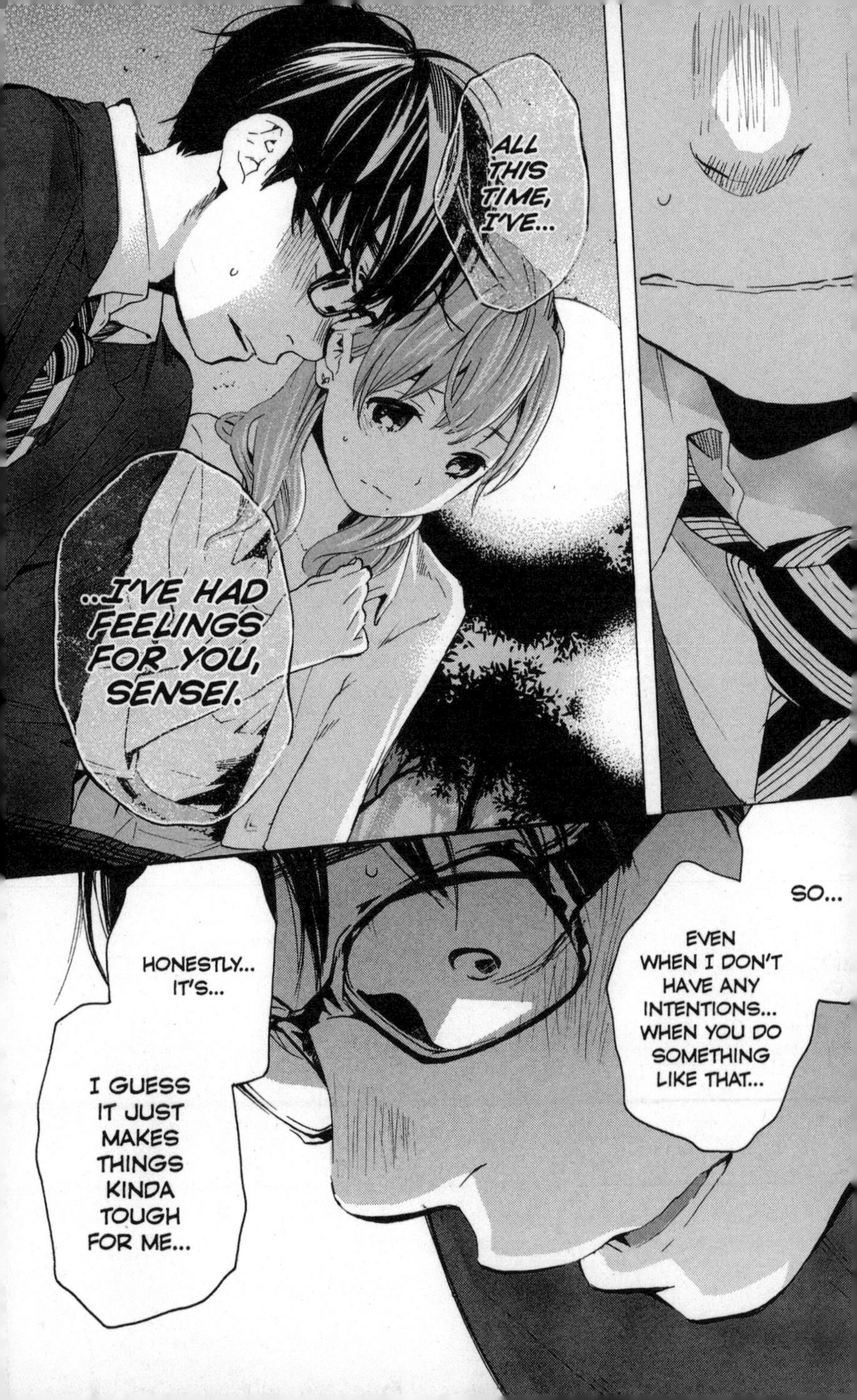
ALL THIS TIME, I'VE...
...I'VE HAD FEELINGS FOR YOU, SENSEI.
SO...
EVEN WHEN I DON'T HAVE ANY INTENTIONS... WHEN YOU DO SOMETHING LIKE THAT...
HONESTLY... IT'S...
I GUESS IT JUST MAKES THINGS KINDA TOUGH FOR ME...

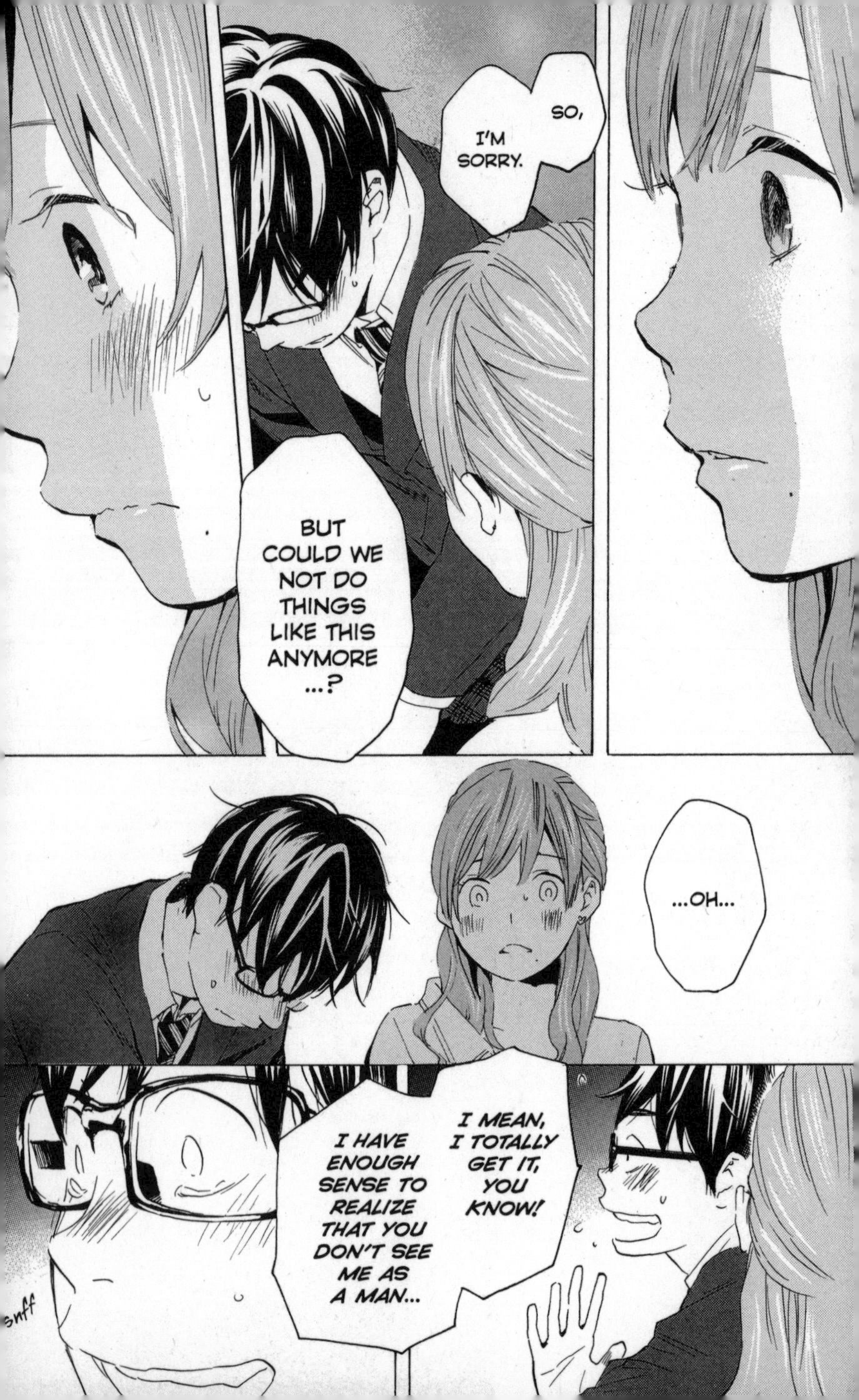
SO, I'M SORRY.
BUT COULD WE NOT DO THINGS LIKE THIS ANYMORE ...?
...OH...
I MEAN, I TOTALLY GET IT, YOU KNOW!
I HAVE ENOUGH SENSE TO REALIZE THAT YOU DON'T SEE ME AS A MAN...
snff

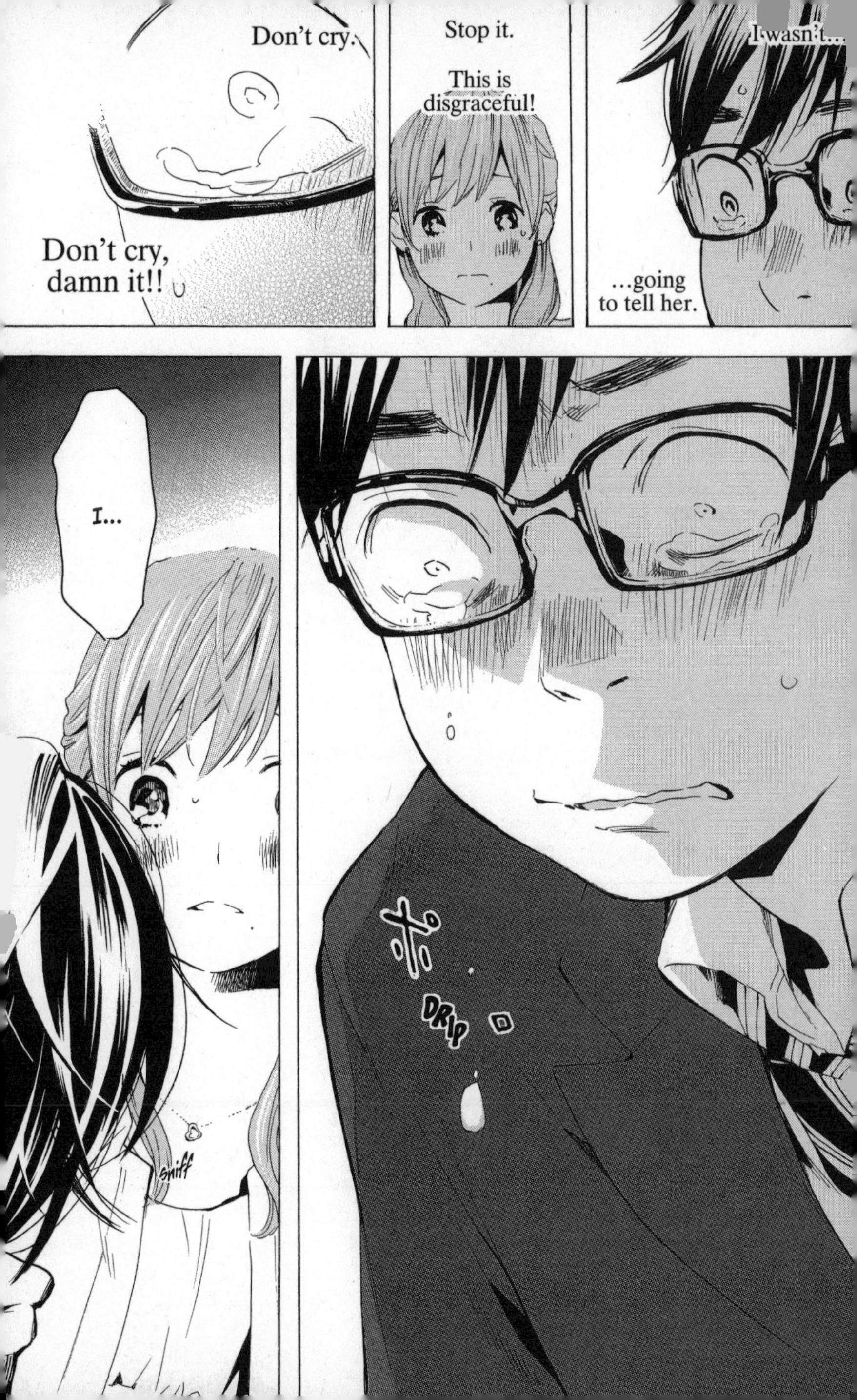
I wasn't...
...going to tell her.
Stop it.
This is disgraceful!
Don't cry.
Don't cry, damn it!!
DRIP
I...
sniff

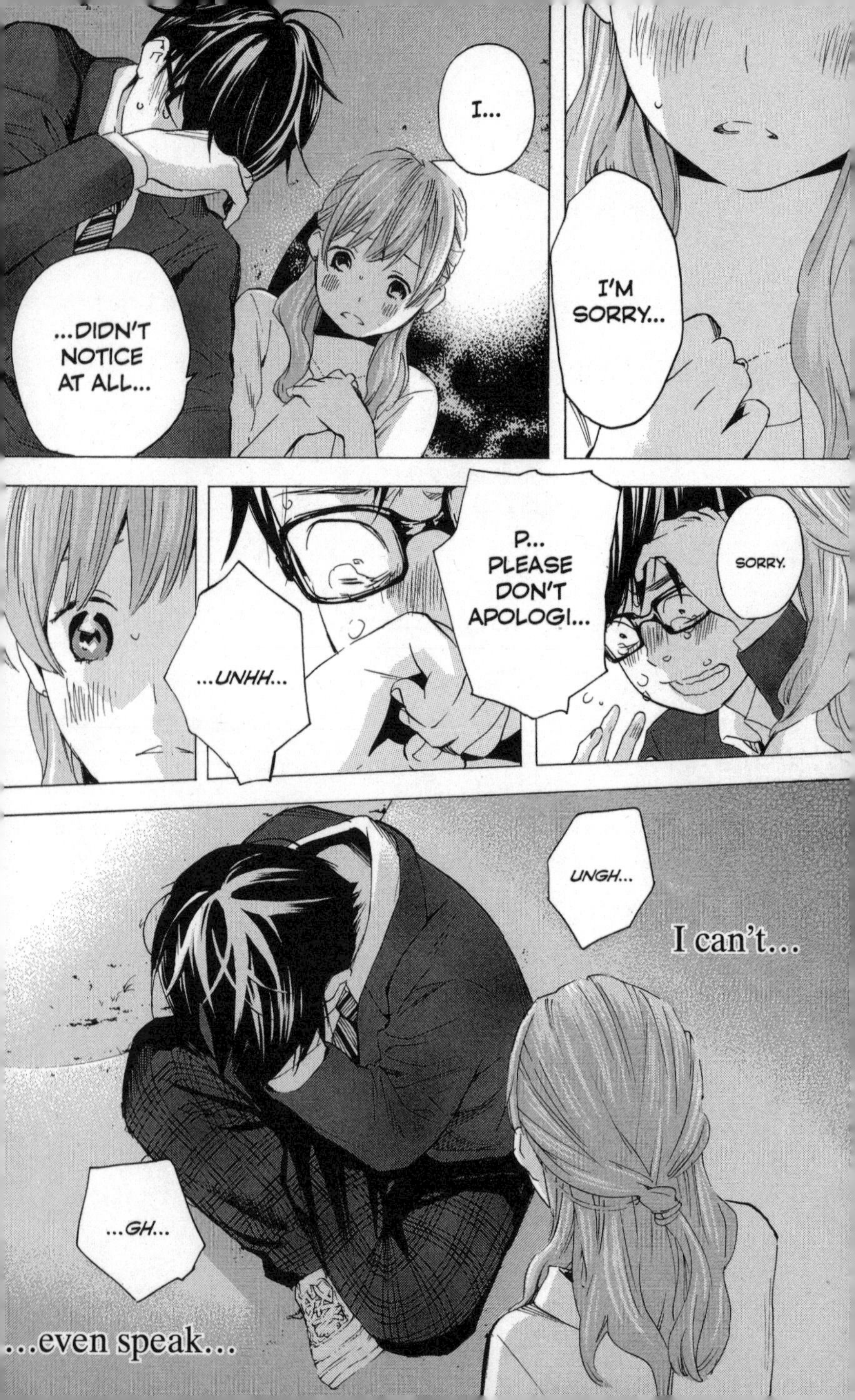
I'M SORRY...
I...
...DIDN'T NOTICE AT ALL...
SORRY.
P... PLEASE DON'T APOLOGI...
...UNHH...
UNGH...
I can't...
...GH...
...even speak...

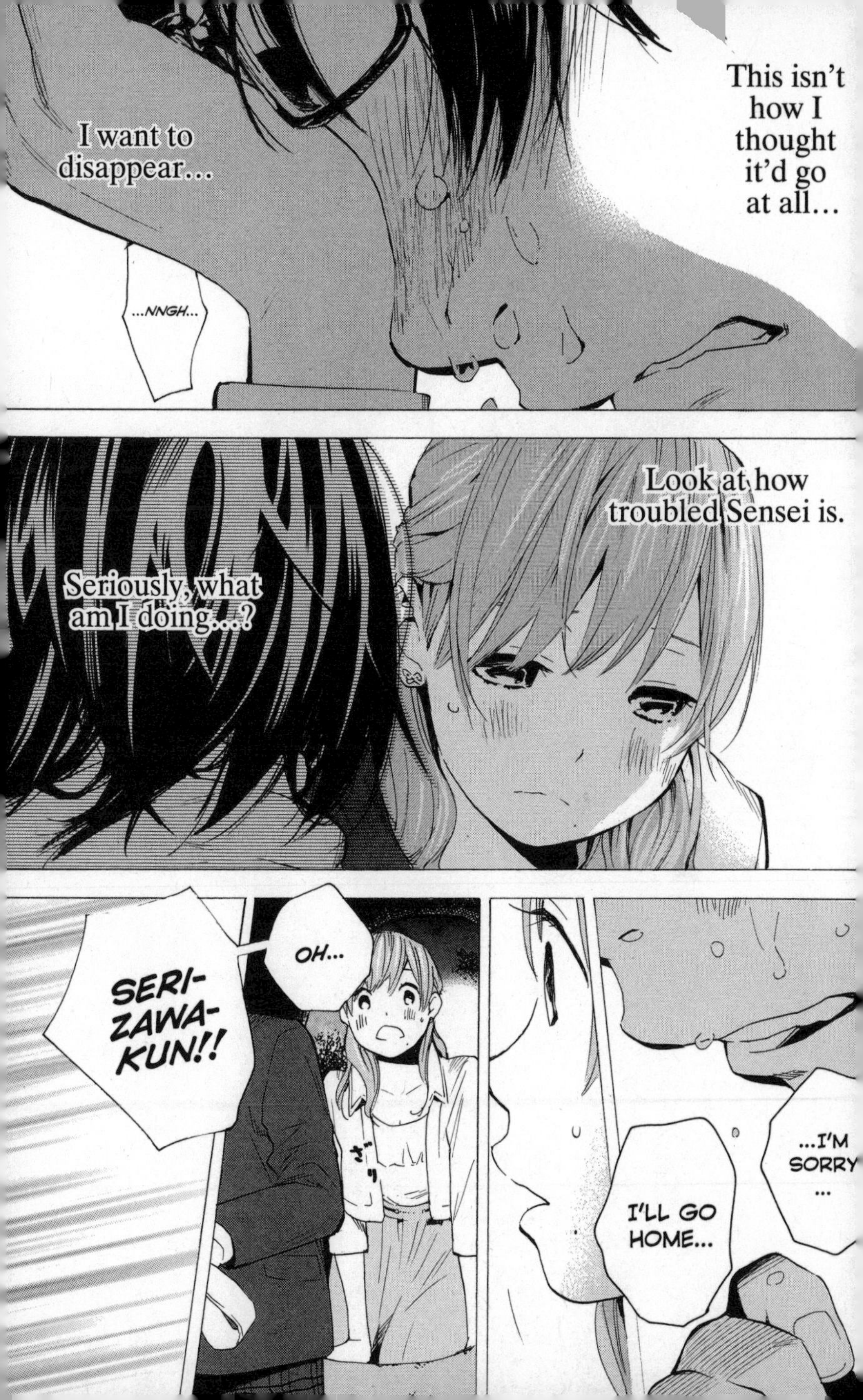
This isn't how I thought it'd go at all…
I want to disappear…
…NNGH…
Look at how troubled Sensei is.
Seriously, what am I doing…?
…I'M SORRY…
I'LL GO HOME…
OH…
SERI-ZAWA-KUN!!

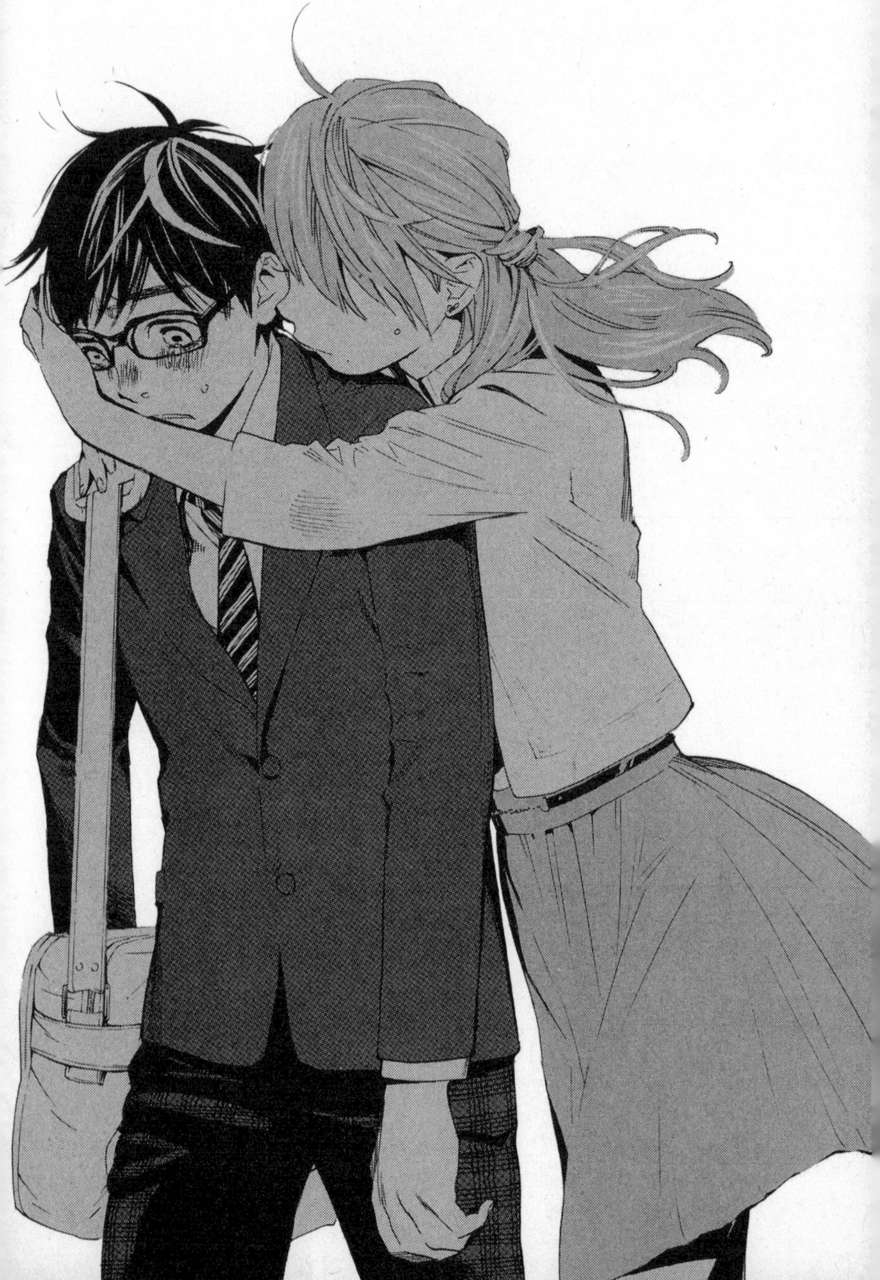

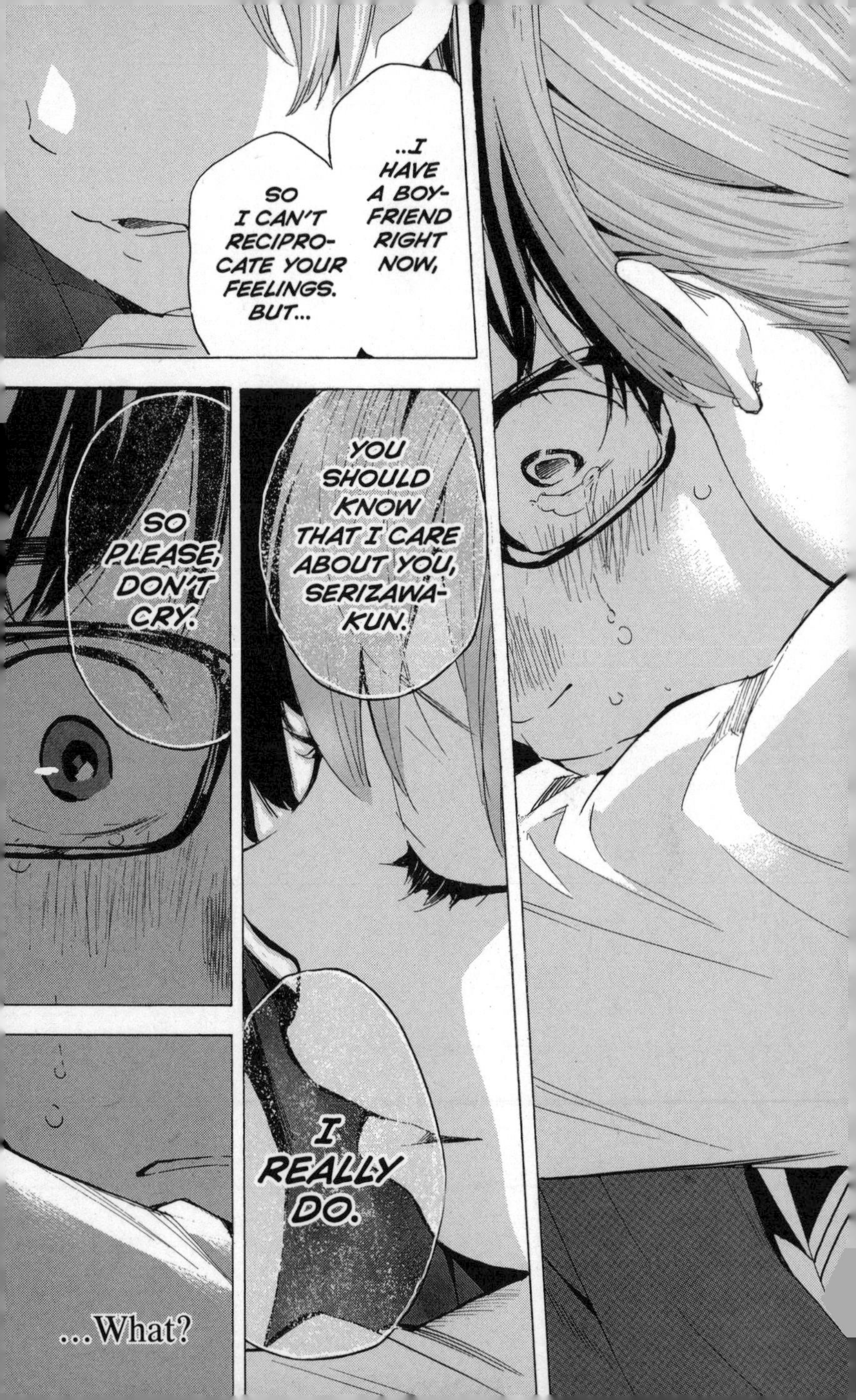
...I HAVE A BOY-FRIEND RIGHT NOW, SO I CAN'T RECIPRO-CATE YOUR FEELINGS. BUT...
YOU SHOULD KNOW THAT I CARE ABOUT YOU, SERIZAWA-KUN.
I REALLY DO.
SO PLEASE, DON'T CRY.
...What?

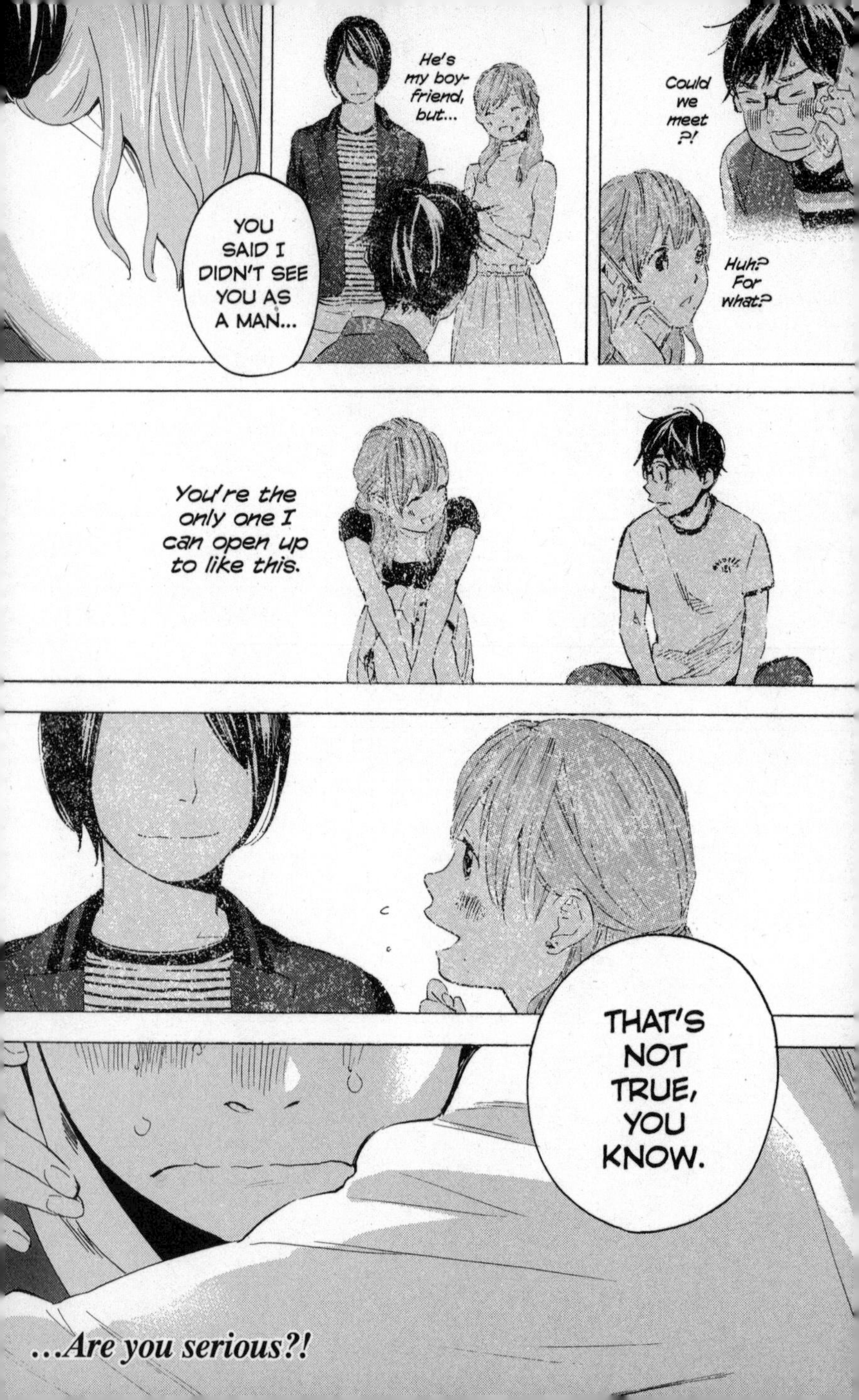
Could we meet?!
Huh? For what?
He's my boy-friend, but...
YOU SAID I DIDN'T SEE YOU AS A MAN...
You're the only one I can open up to like this.
THAT'S NOT TRUE, YOU KNOW.
...Are you serious?!

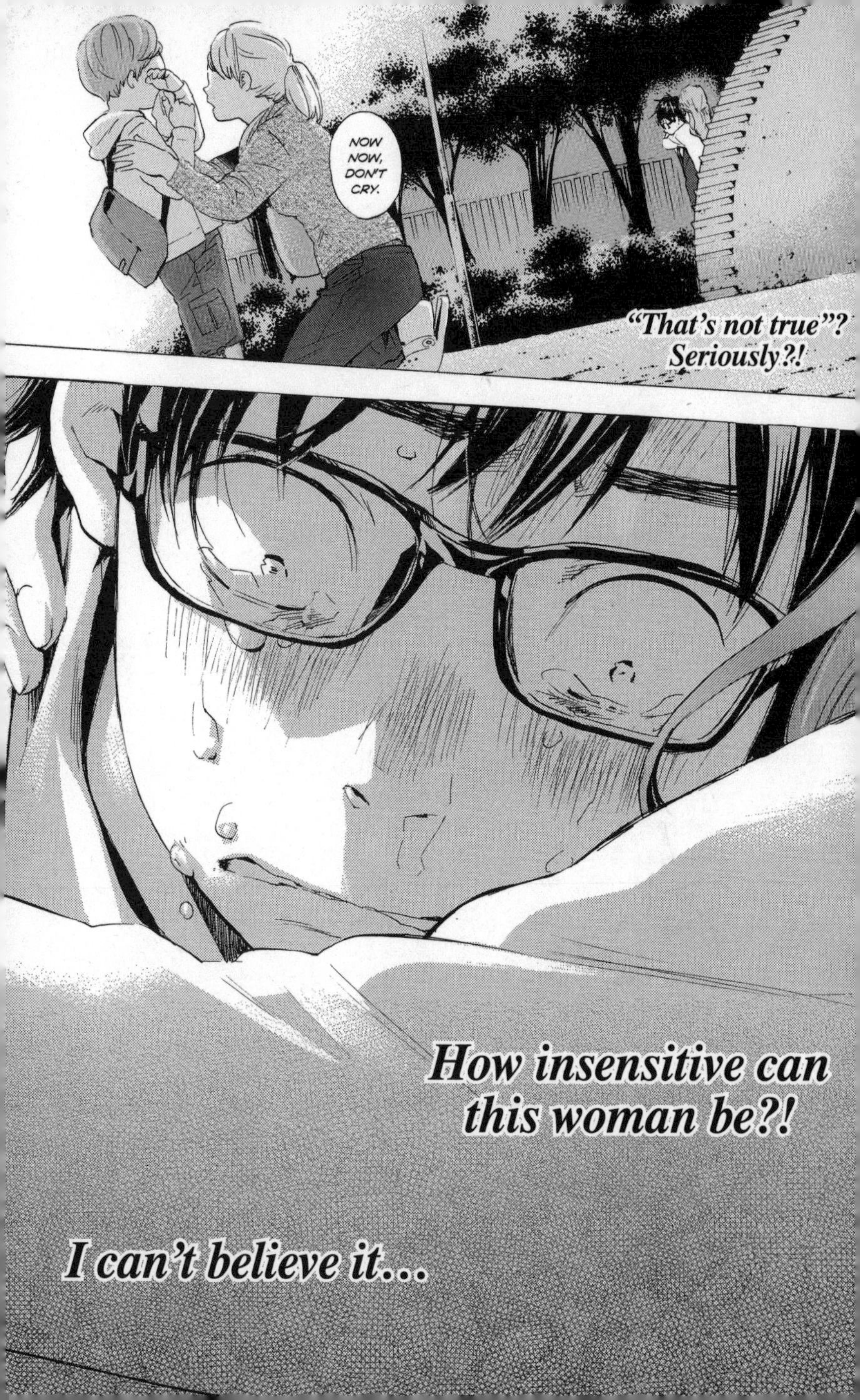
NOW NOW, DON'T CRY.
"That's not true"? Seriously?!
How insensitive can this woman be?!
I can't believe it...

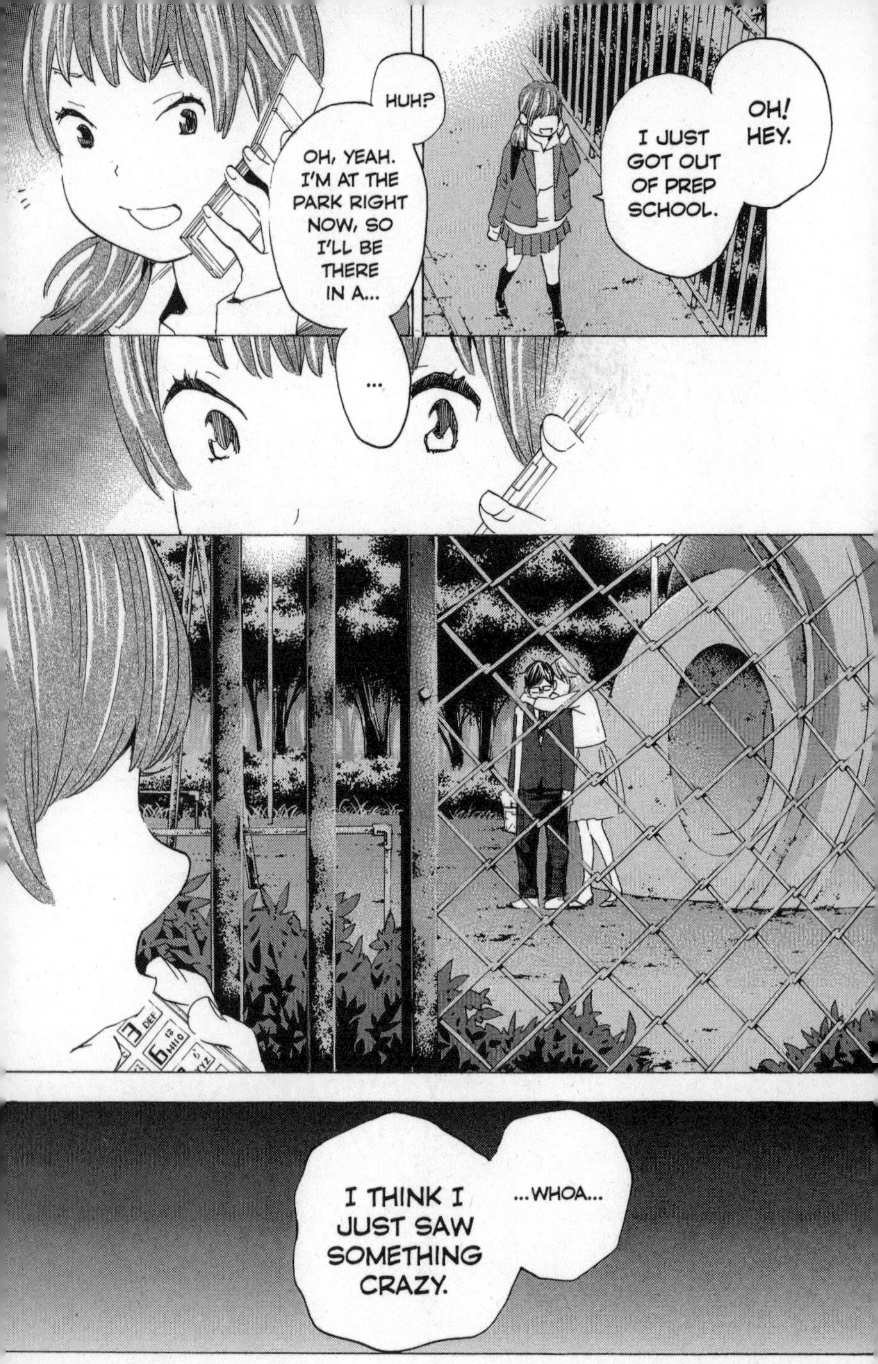
OH! HEY.
I JUST GOT OUT OF PREP SCHOOL.
HUH?
OH, YEAH. I'M AT THE PARK RIGHT NOW, SO I'LL BE THERE IN A...
...
...WHOA...
I THINK I JUST SAW SOMETHING CRAZY.

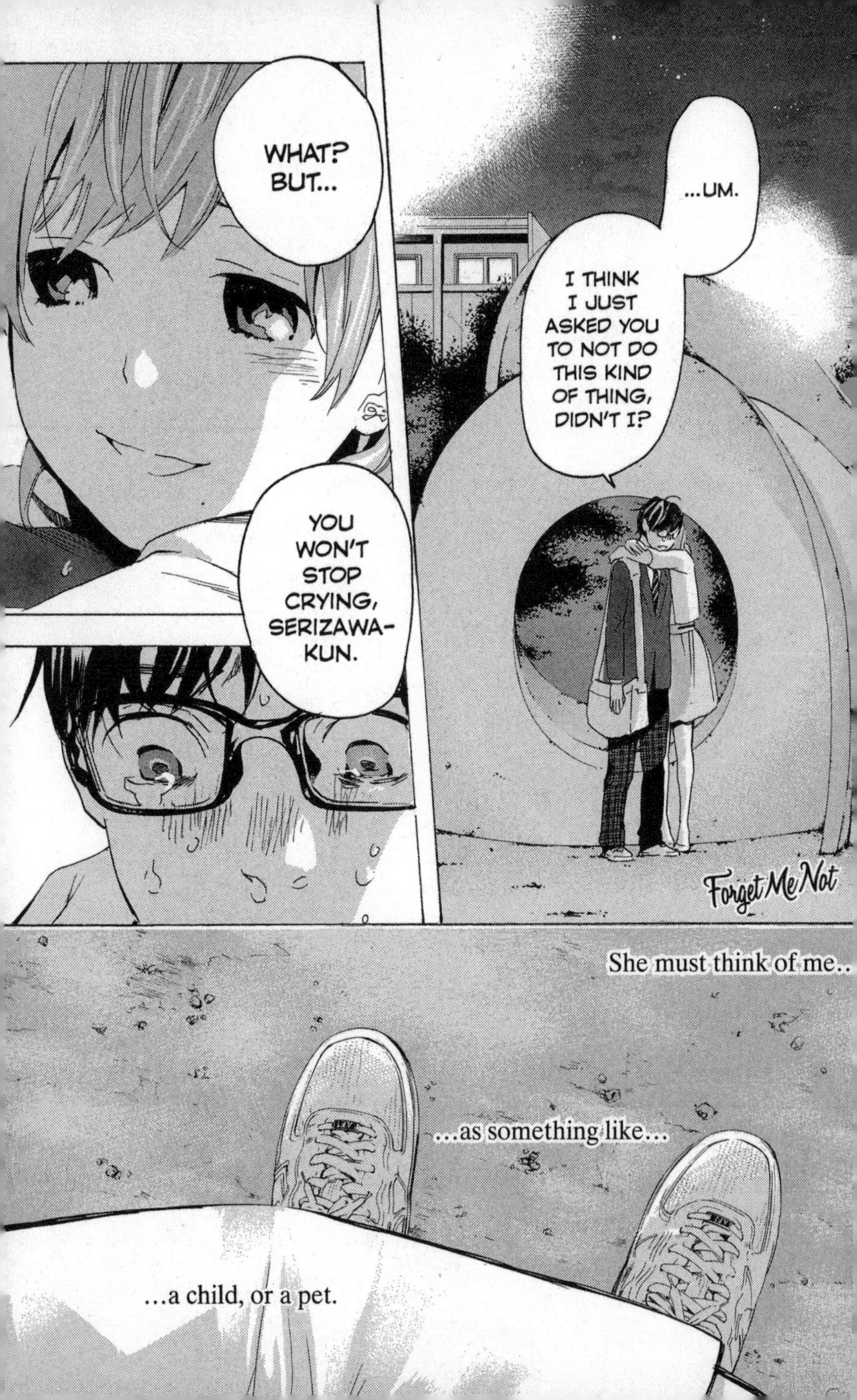
...UM.
I THINK I JUST ASKED YOU TO NOT DO THIS KIND OF THING, DIDN'T I?
Forget Me Not
WHAT? BUT...
YOU WON'T STOP CRYING, SERIZAWA-KUN.
She must think of me...
...as something like...
...a child, or a pet.

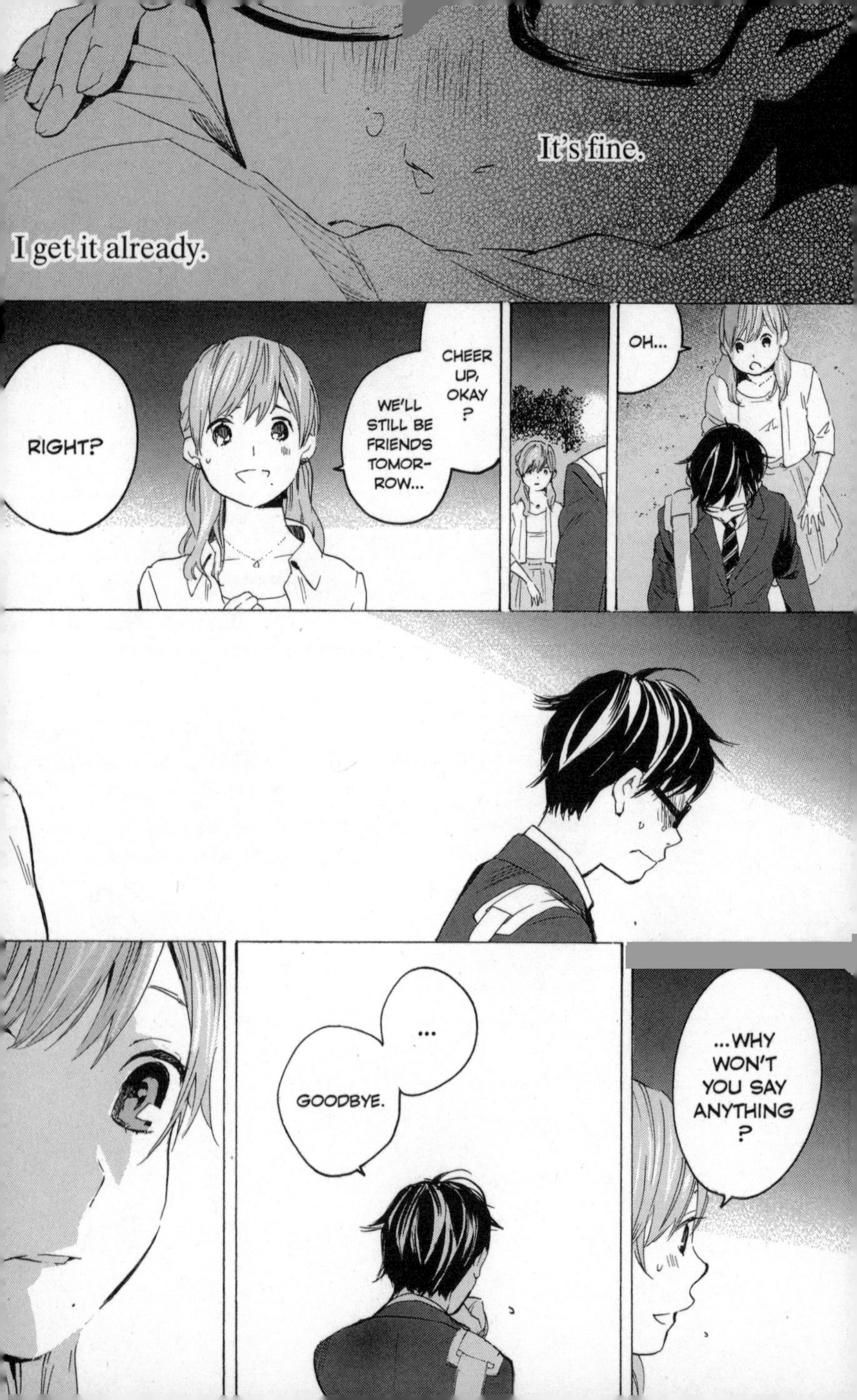
It's fine.
I get it already.
OH...
CHEER UP, OKAY?
WE'LL STILL BE FRIENDS TOMORROW...
RIGHT?
...WHY WON'T YOU SAY ANYTHING?
...
GOODBYE.

CHAPTER 10: Hermès 6

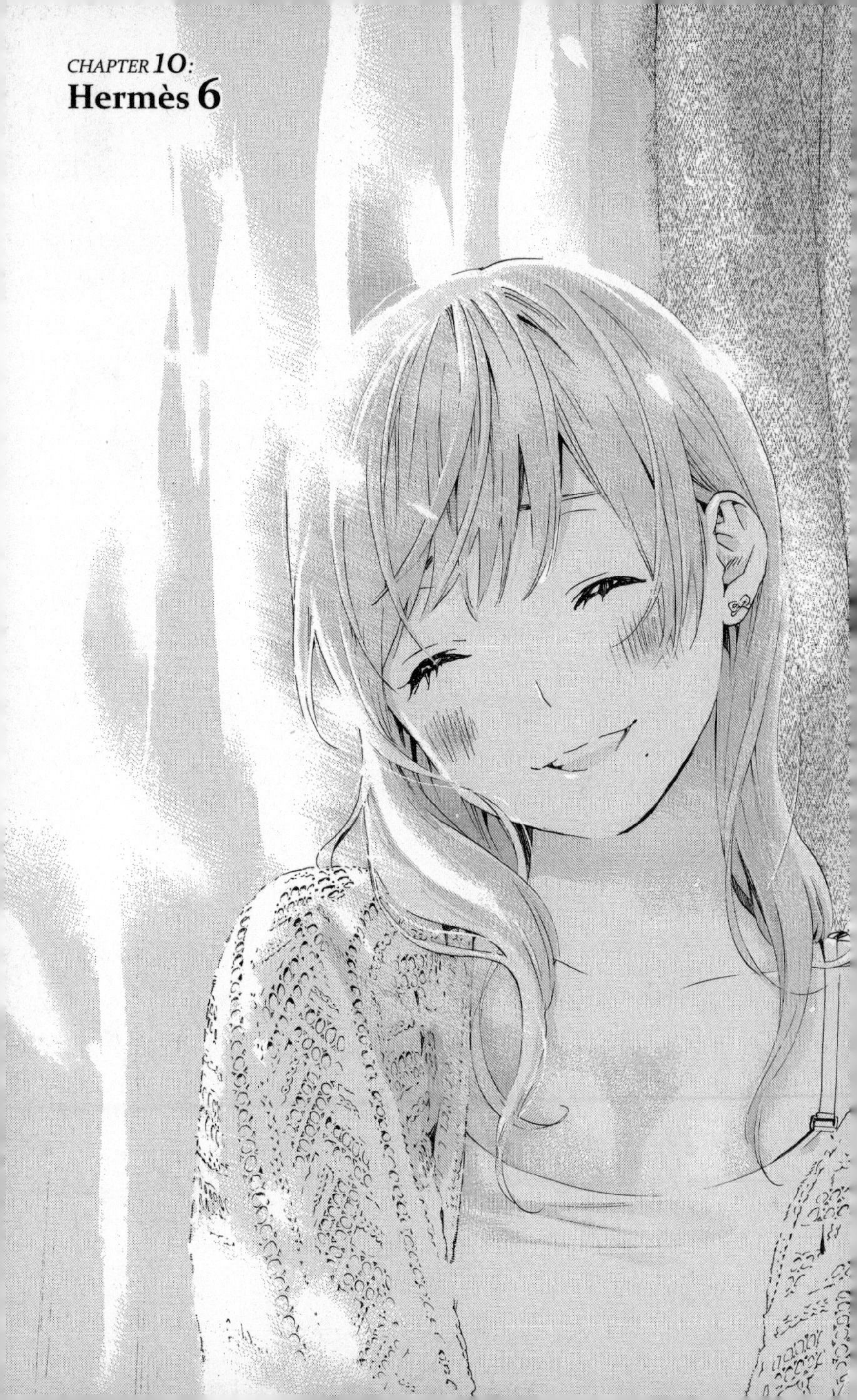

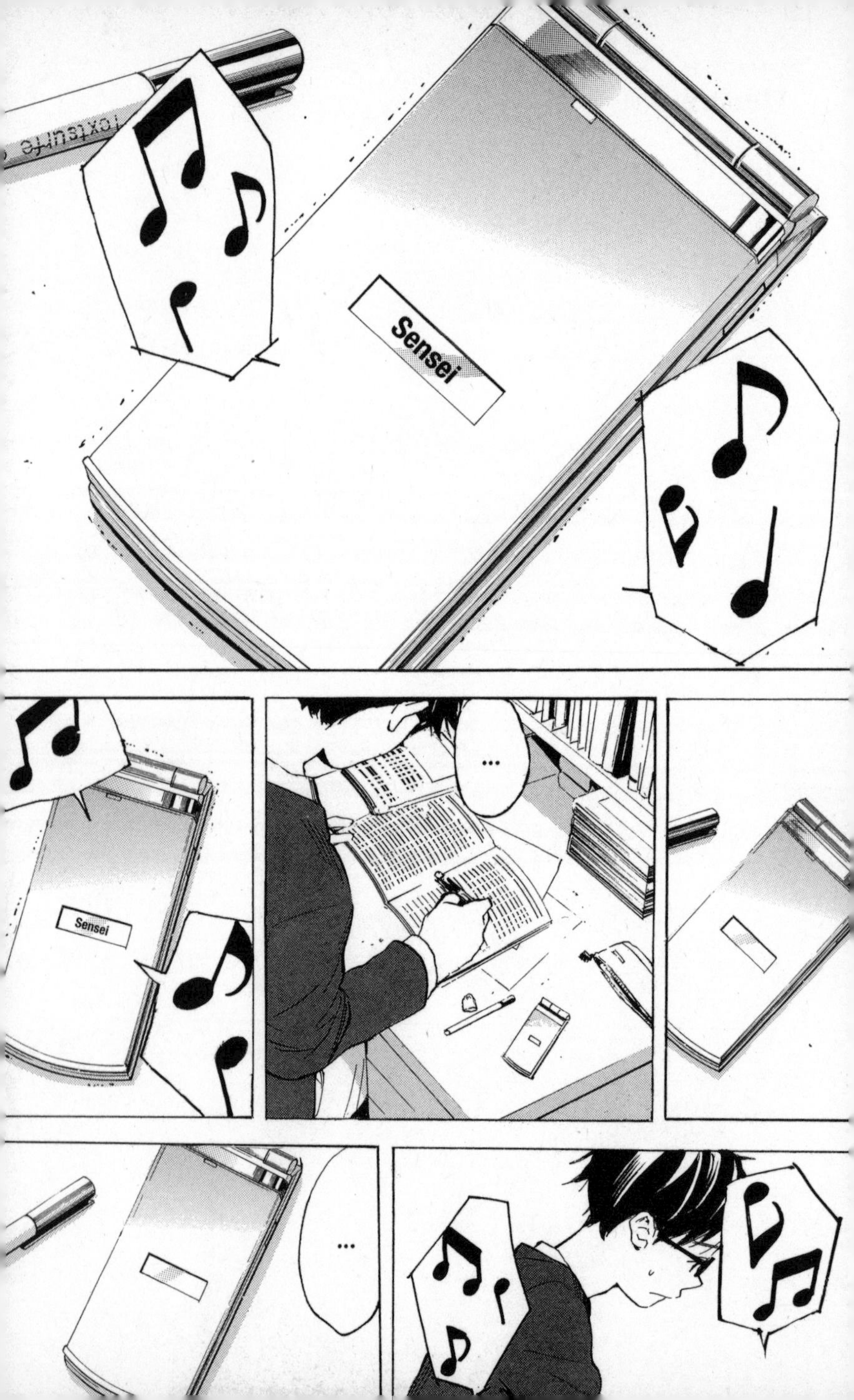
Sensei
...
Sensei
...

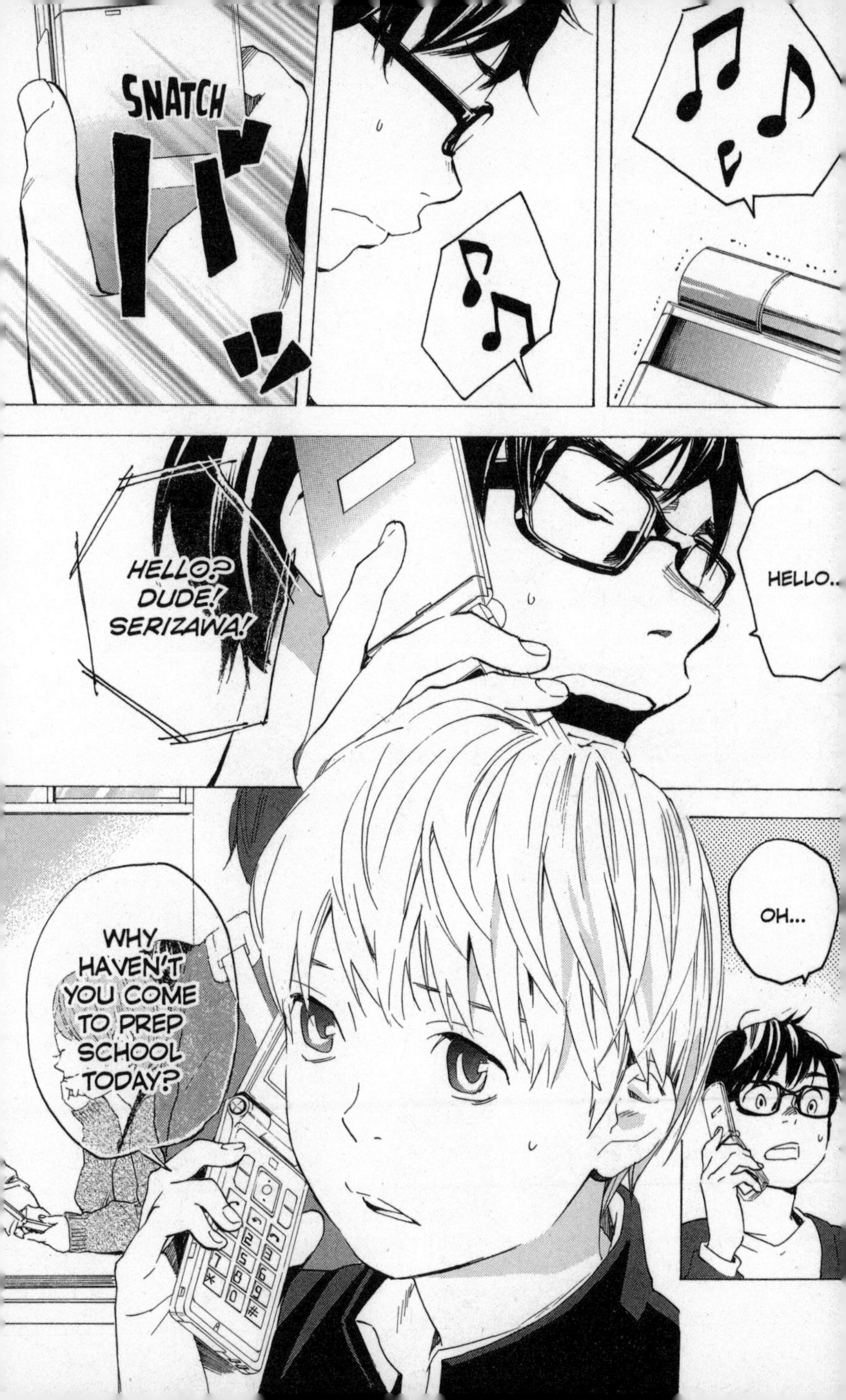
SNATCH
HELLO...
HELLO? DUDE! SERIZAWA!
OH...
WHY HAVEN'T YOU COME TO PREP SCHOOL TODAY?

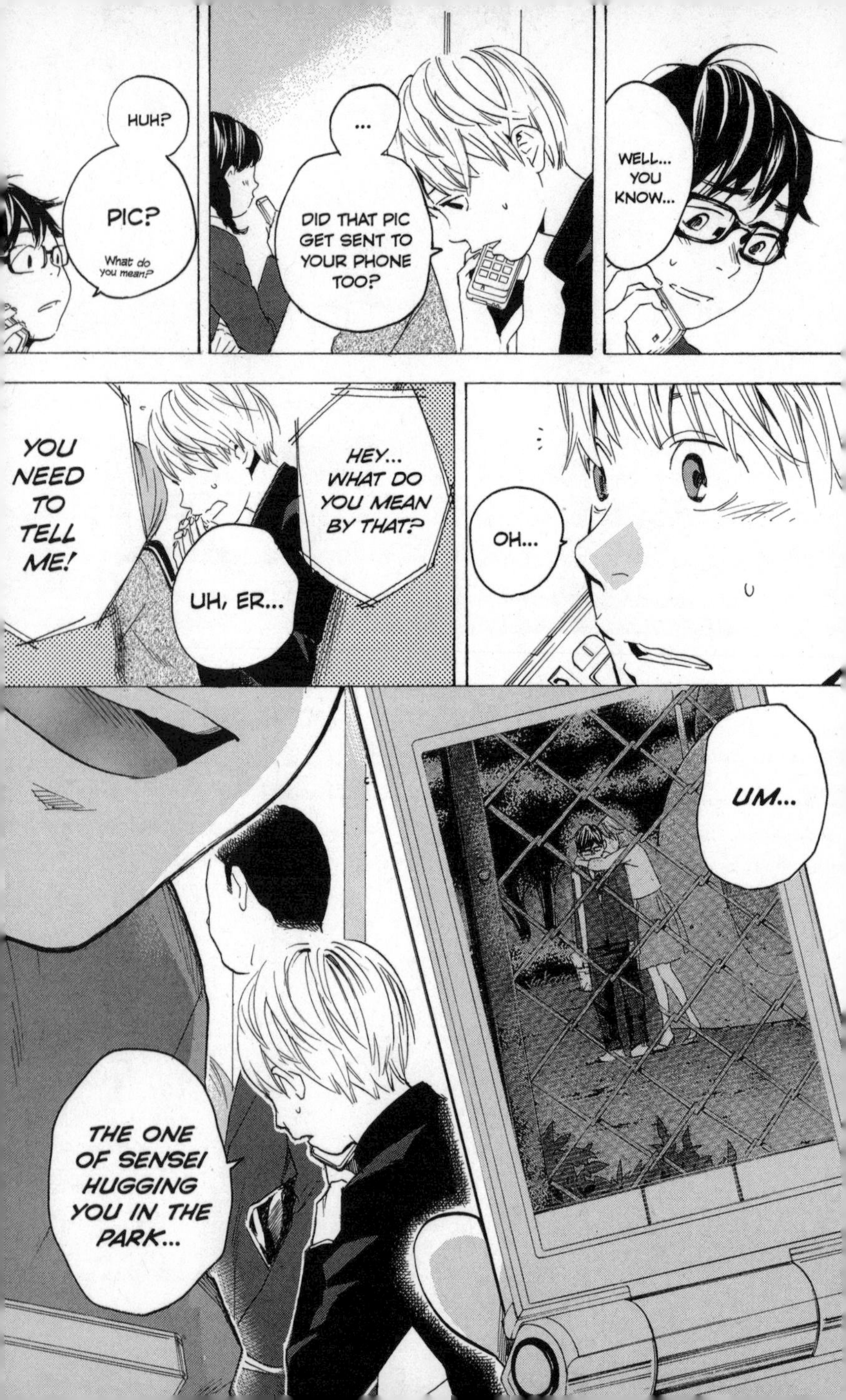
WELL... YOU KNOW...
...
DID THAT PIC GET SENT TO YOUR PHONE TOO?
HUH?
PIC?
What do you mean?
OH...
HEY... WHAT DO YOU MEAN BY THAT?
YOU NEED TO TELL ME!
UH, ER...
UM...
THE ONE OF SENSEI HUGGING YOU IN THE PARK...

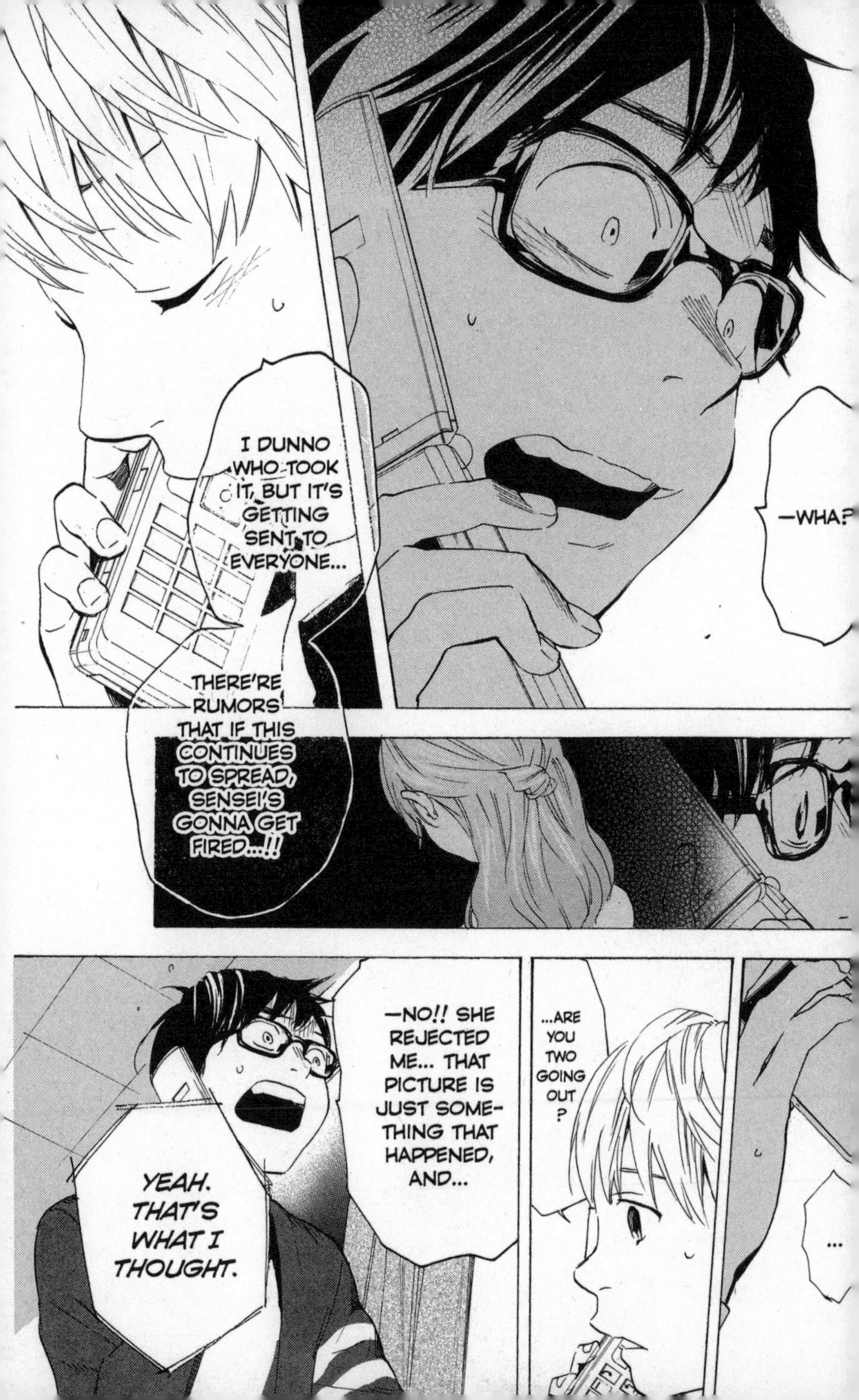
—WHA?
I DUNNO WHO TOOK IT, BUT IT'S GETTING SENT TO EVERYONE...
THERE'RE RUMORS THAT IF THIS CONTINUES TO SPREAD, SENSEI'S GONNA GET FIRED...!!
...
...ARE YOU TWO GOING OUT?
—NO!! SHE REJECTED ME... THAT PICTURE IS JUST SOME-THING THAT HAPPENED, AND...
YEAH. THAT'S WHAT I THOUGHT.

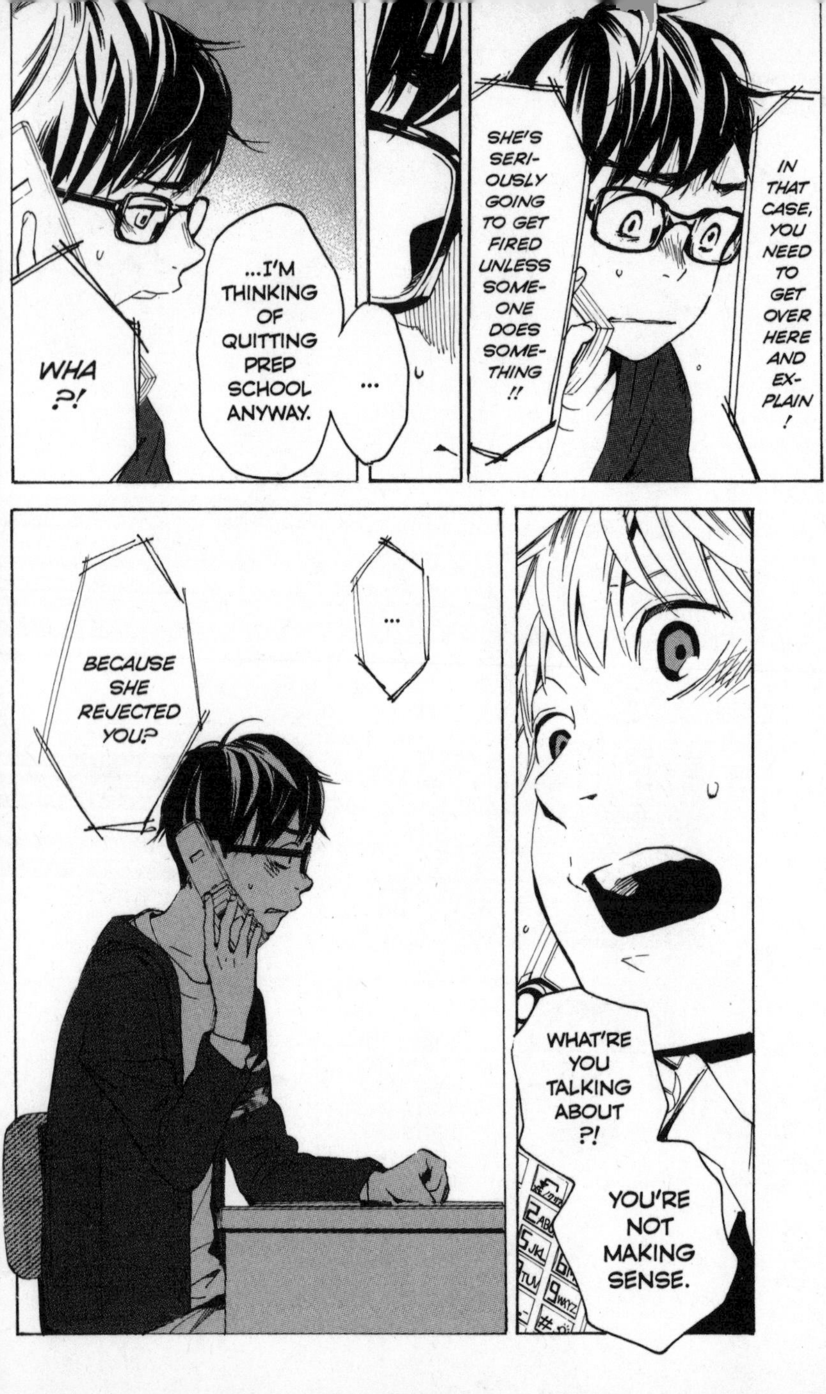
IN THAT CASE, YOU NEED TO GET OVER HERE AND EXPLAIN!
SHE'S SERIOUSLY GOING TO GET FIRED UNLESS SOMEONE DOES SOMETHING!!
...
...I'M THINKING OF QUITTING PREP SCHOOL ANYWAY.
WHA?!
WHAT'RE YOU TALKING ABOUT?!
YOU'RE NOT MAKING SENSE.
...
BECAUSE SHE REJECTED YOU?

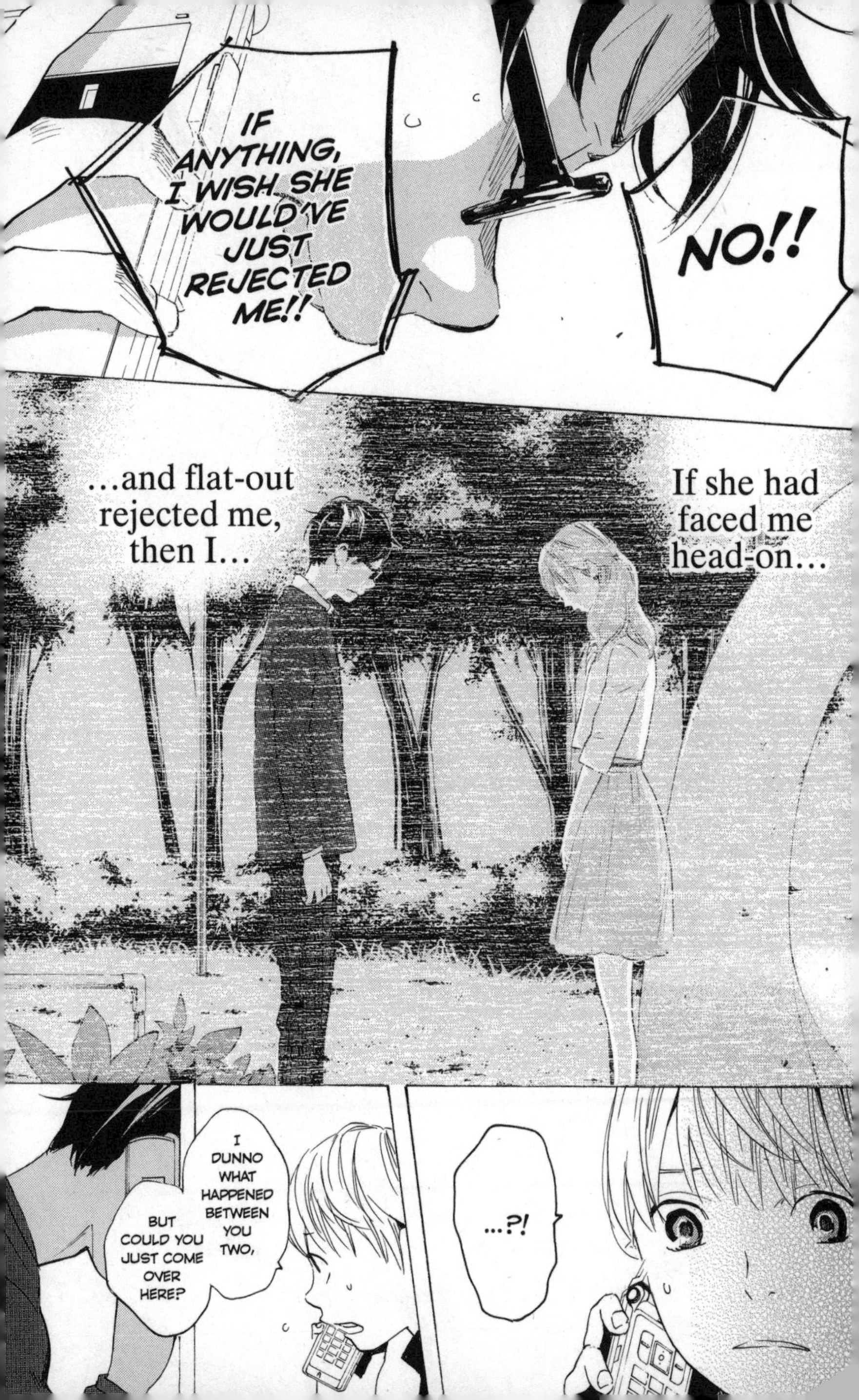
NO!!
IF ANYTHING, I WISH SHE WOULD'VE JUST REJECTED ME!!
If she had faced me head-on…
…and flat-out rejected me, then I…
…?!
I DUNNO WHAT HAPPENED BETWEEN YOU TWO,
BUT COULD YOU JUST COME OVER HERE?

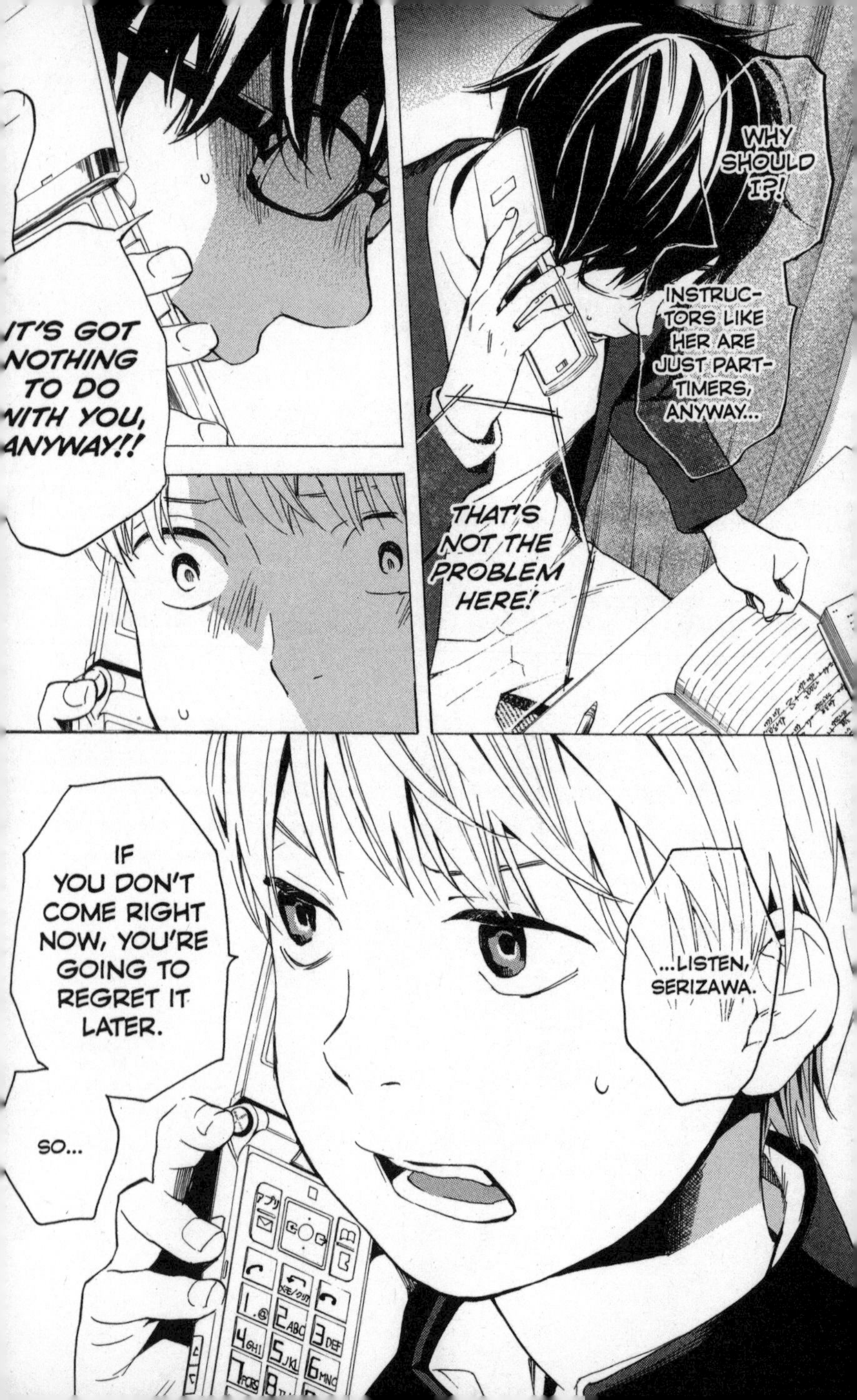
WHY SHOULD I?!
INSTRUCTORS LIKE HER ARE JUST PART-TIMERS, ANYWAY...
THAT'S NOT THE PROBLEM HERE!
IT'S GOT NOTHING TO DO WITH YOU, ANYWAY!!
...LISTEN, SERIZAWA.
IF YOU DON'T COME RIGHT NOW, YOU'RE GOING TO REGRET IT LATER.
SO...

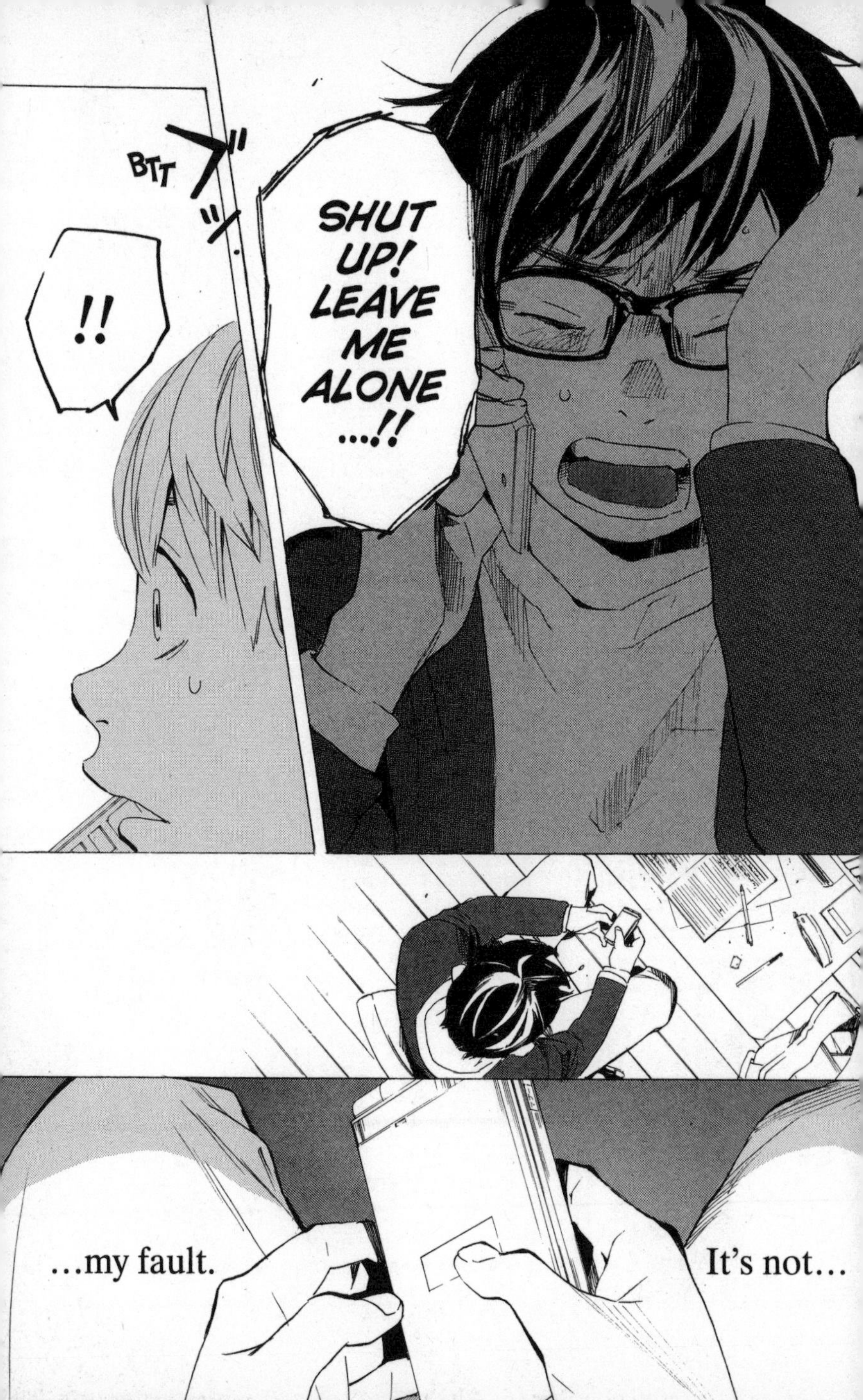
SHUT UP! LEAVE ME ALONE ...!!
BTT
!!
It's not…
…my fault.

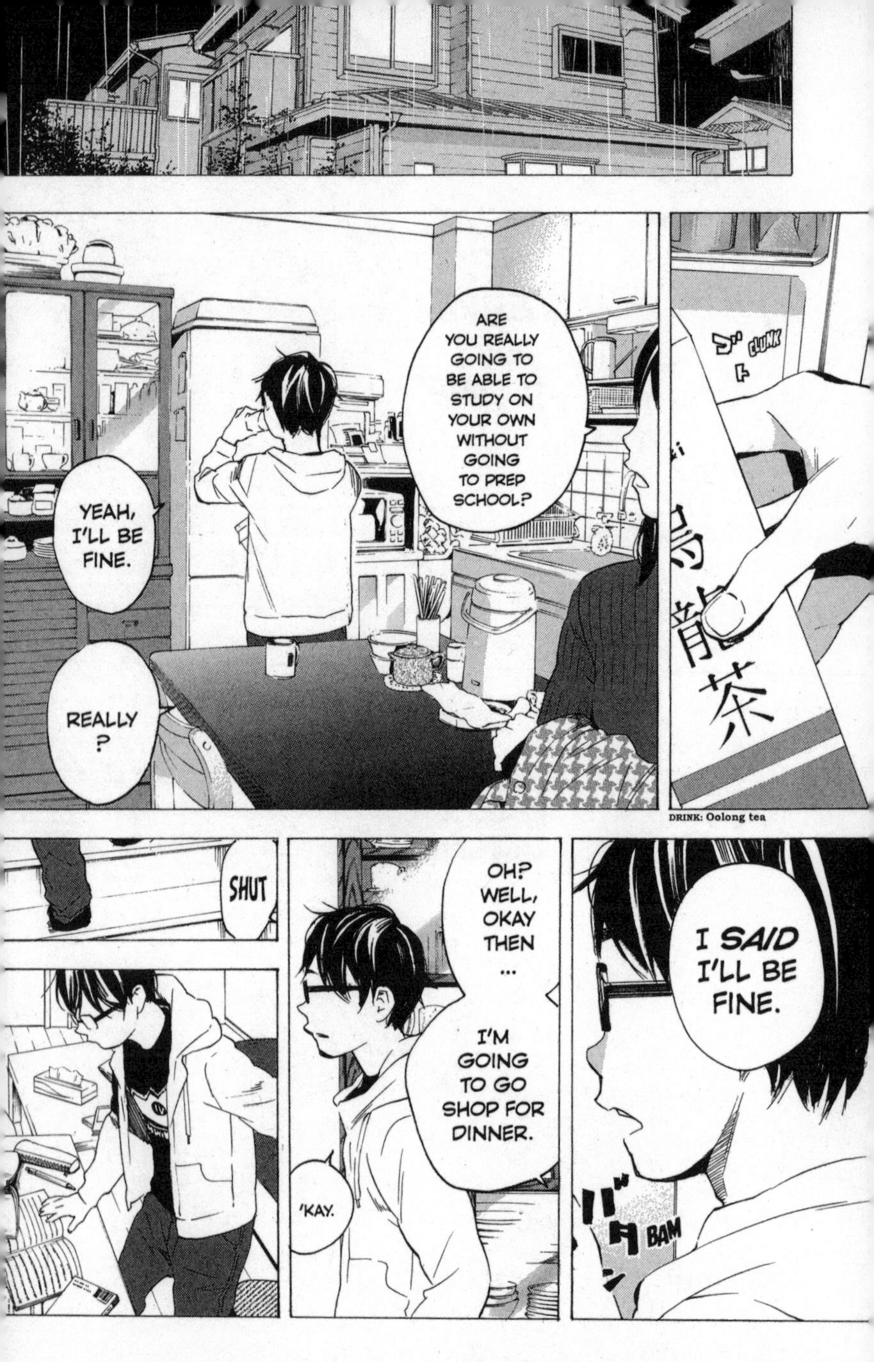
CLUNK
龍茶
DRINK: Oolong tea
ARE YOU REALLY GOING TO BE ABLE TO STUDY ON YOUR OWN WITHOUT GOING TO PREP SCHOOL?
YEAH, I'LL BE FINE.
REALLY?
I SAID I'LL BE FINE.
BAM
OH? WELL, OKAY THEN ...
I'M GOING TO GO SHOP FOR DINNER.
'KAY.
SHUT

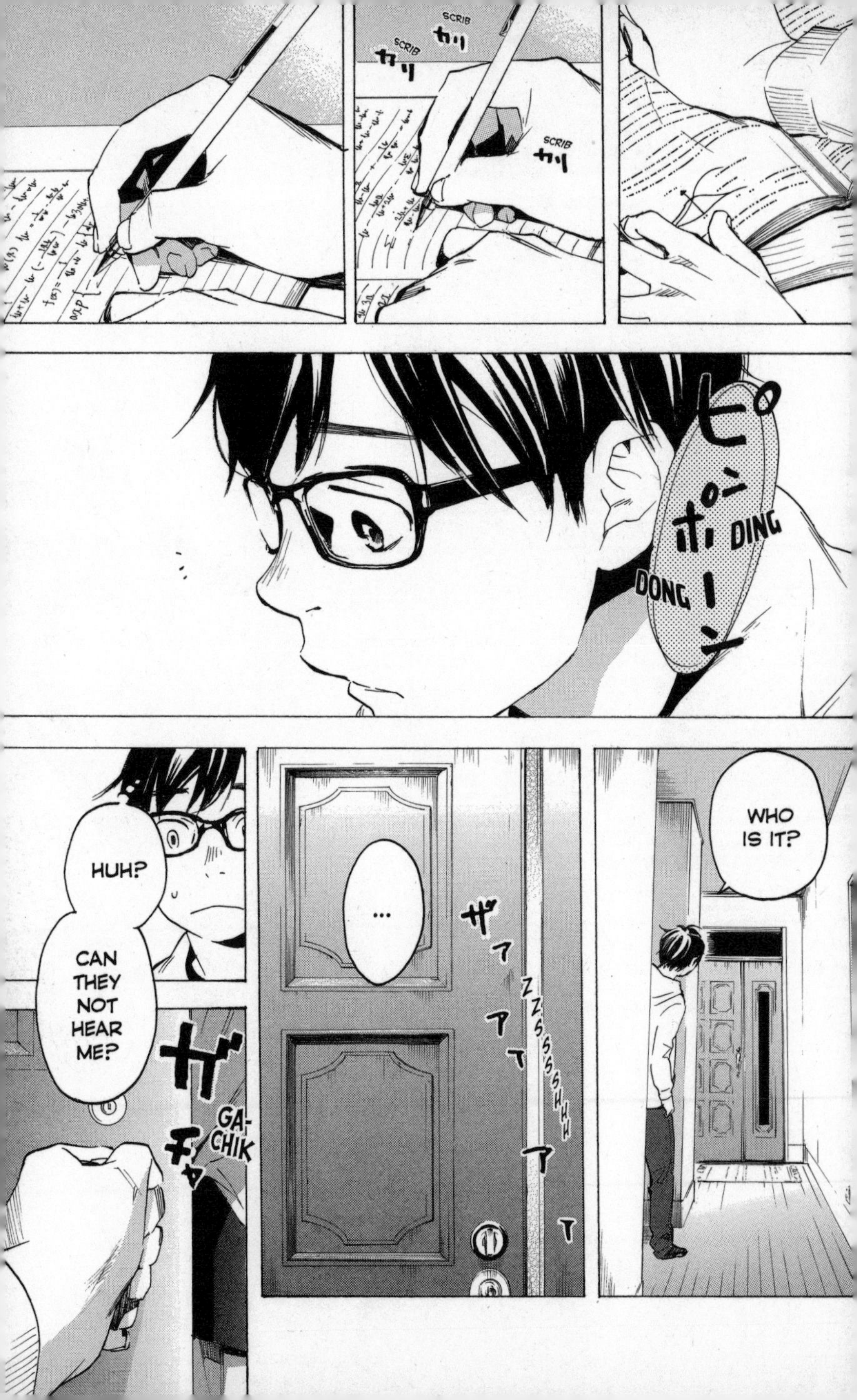
SCRIB
SCRIB
SCRIB
DING DONG
WHO IS IT?
...
ZZSSSSHHH
HUH?
CAN THEY NOT HEAR ME?
GA-CHIK

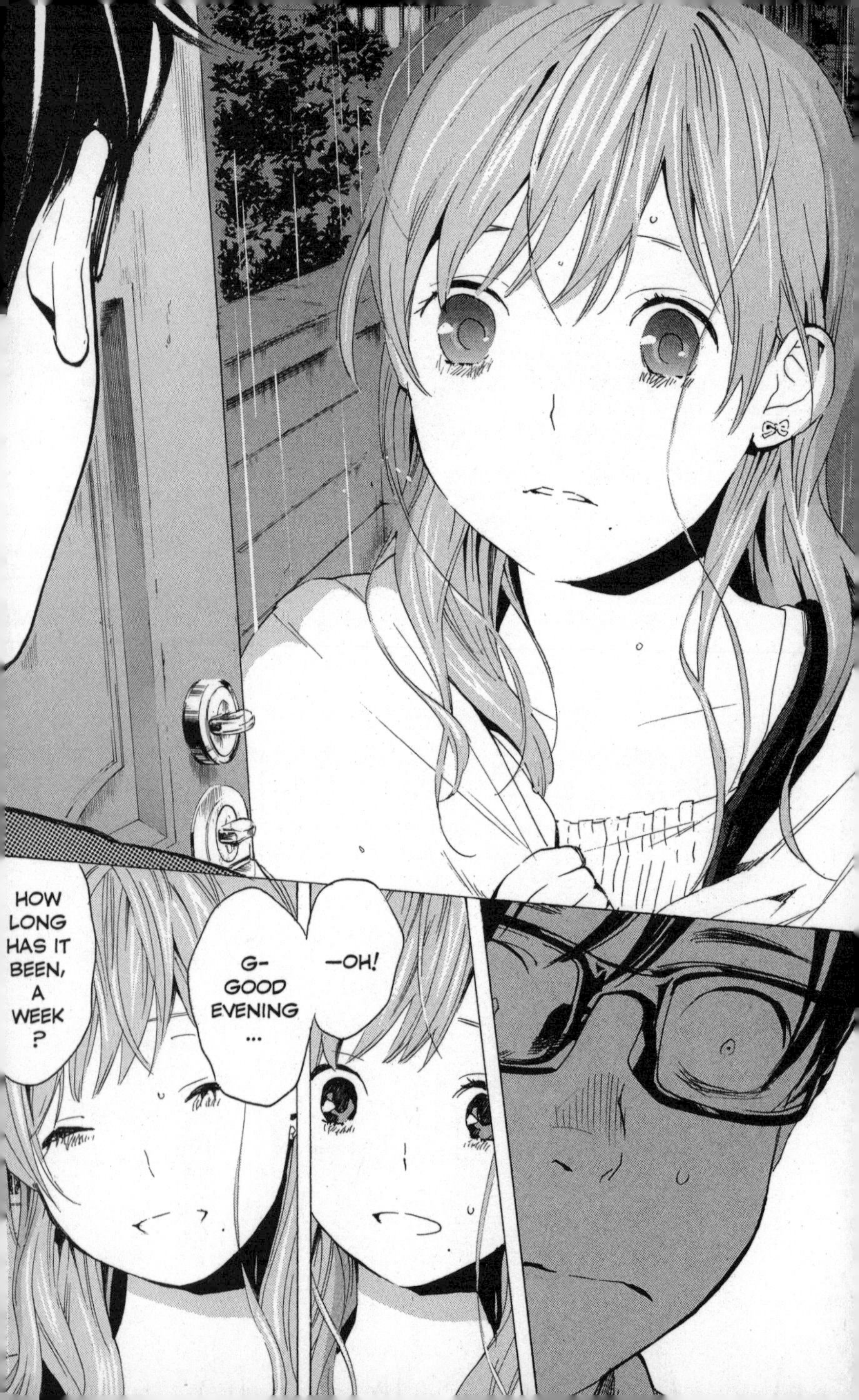
—OH!
G-GOOD EVENING...
HOW LONG HAS IT BEEN, A WEEK?

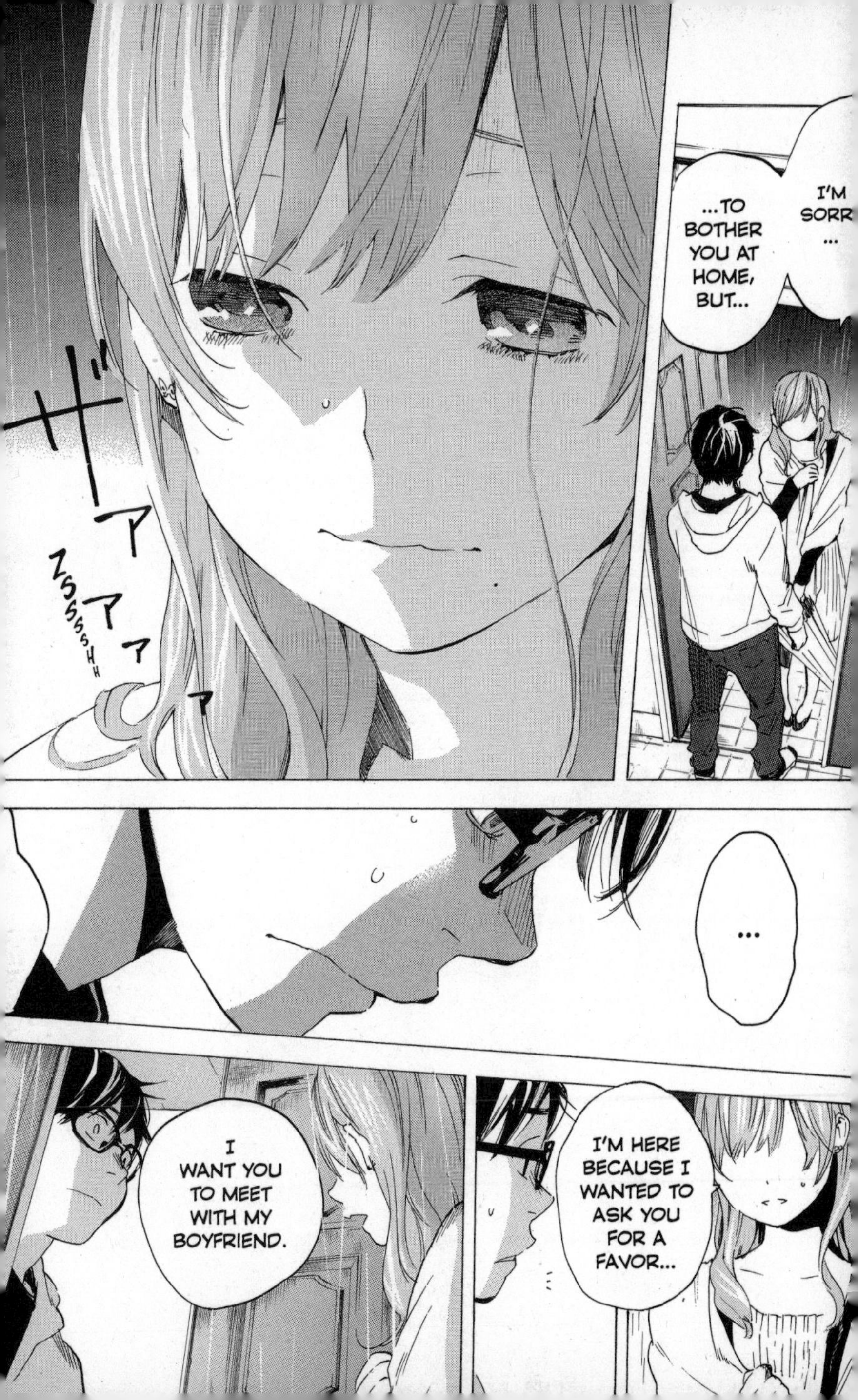
I'M SORR...
...TO BOTHER YOU AT HOME, BUT...
ZSSSSHH
...
I'M HERE BECAUSE I WANTED TO ASK YOU FOR A FAVOR...
I WANT YOU TO MEET WITH MY BOYFRIEND.

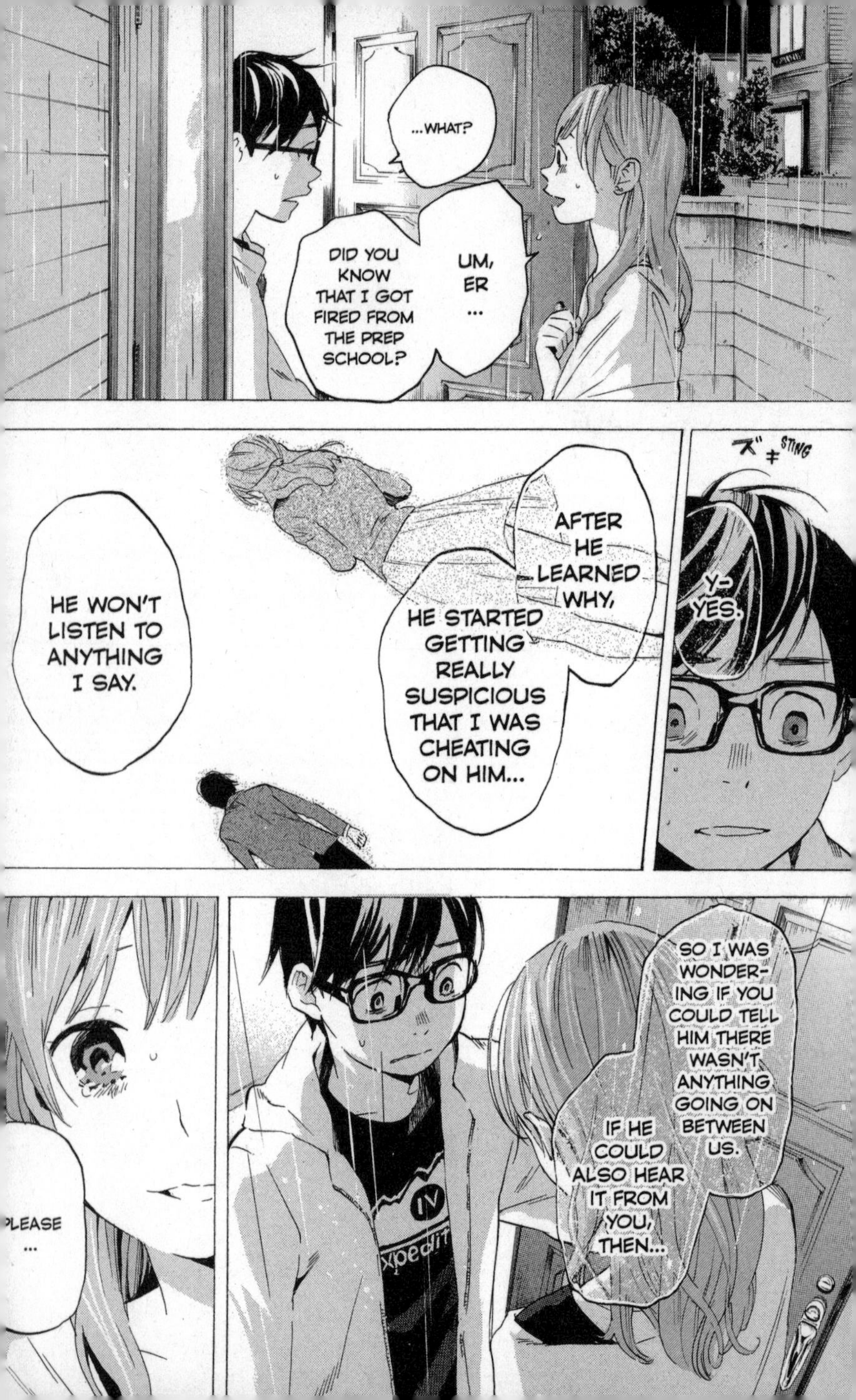
...WHAT?
UM, ER ...
DID YOU KNOW THAT I GOT FIRED FROM THE PREP SCHOOL?
ズキ STING
Y-YES.
AFTER HE LEARNED WHY,
HE STARTED GETTING REALLY SUSPICIOUS THAT I WAS CHEATING ON HIM...
HE WON'T LISTEN TO ANYTHING I SAY.
SO I WAS WONDER-ING IF YOU COULD TELL HIM THERE WASN'T ANYTHING GOING ON BETWEEN US.
IF HE COULD ALSO HEAR IT FROM YOU, THEN...
PLEASE ...

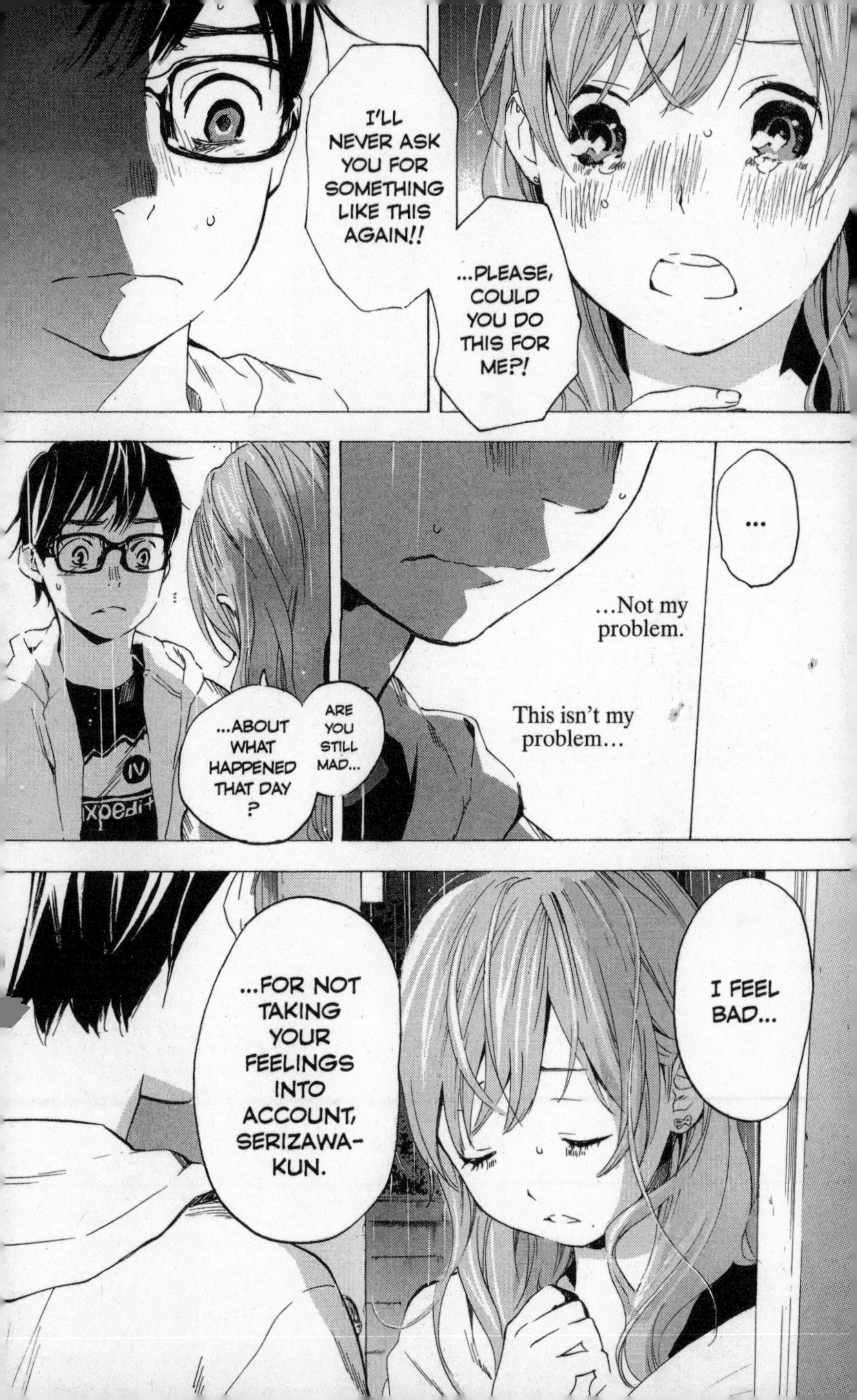
I'LL NEVER ASK YOU FOR SOMETHING LIKE THIS AGAIN!!
...PLEASE, COULD YOU DO THIS FOR ME?!
...
...Not my problem.
This isn't my problem...
ARE YOU STILL MAD...
...ABOUT WHAT HAPPENED THAT DAY?
I FEEL BAD...
...FOR NOT TAKING YOUR FEELINGS INTO ACCOUNT, SERIZAWA-KUN.

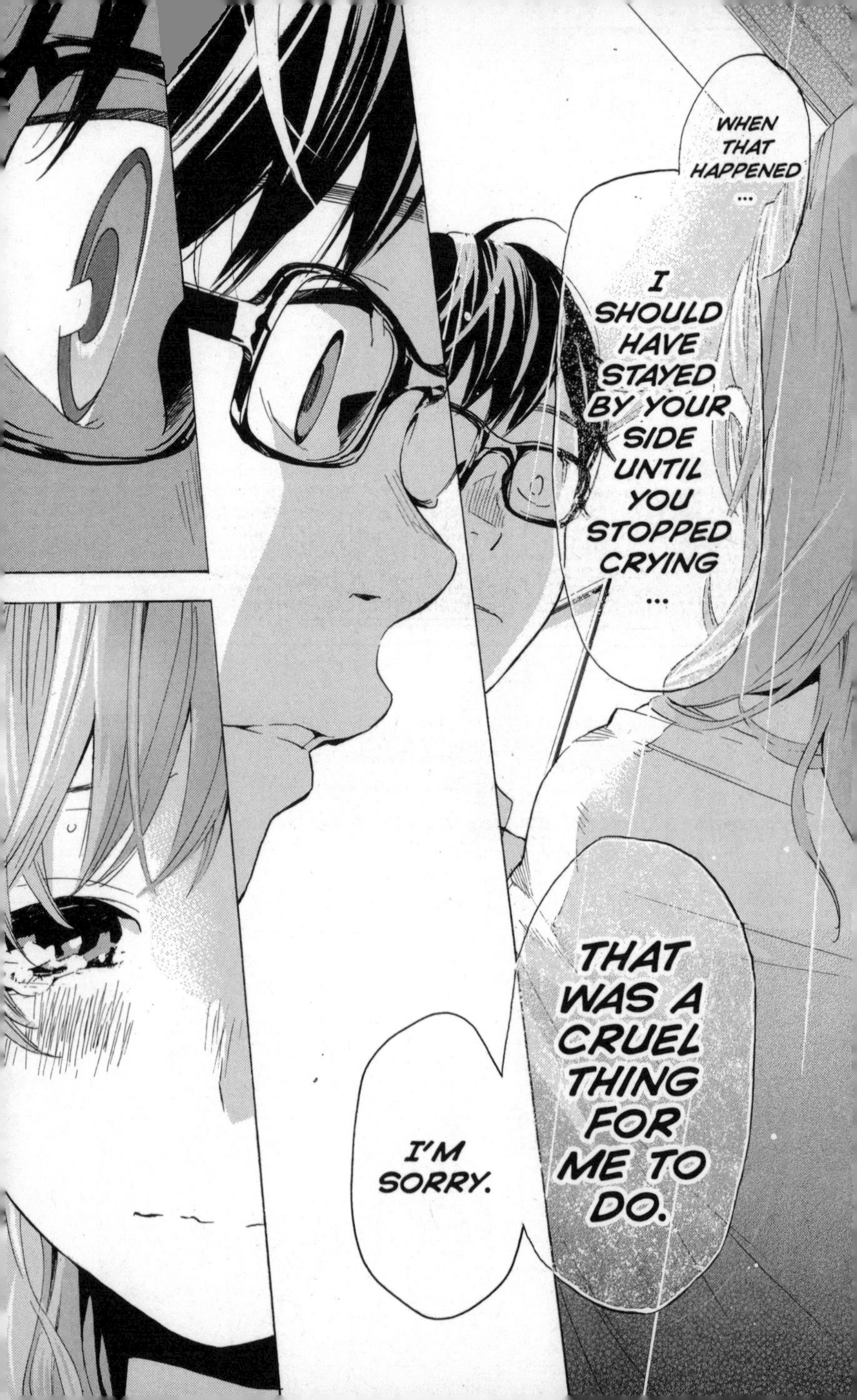
WHEN THAT HAPPENED ...
I SHOULD HAVE STAYED BY YOUR SIDE UNTIL YOU STOPPED CRYING ...
THAT WAS A CRUEL THING FOR ME TO DO.
I'M SORRY.

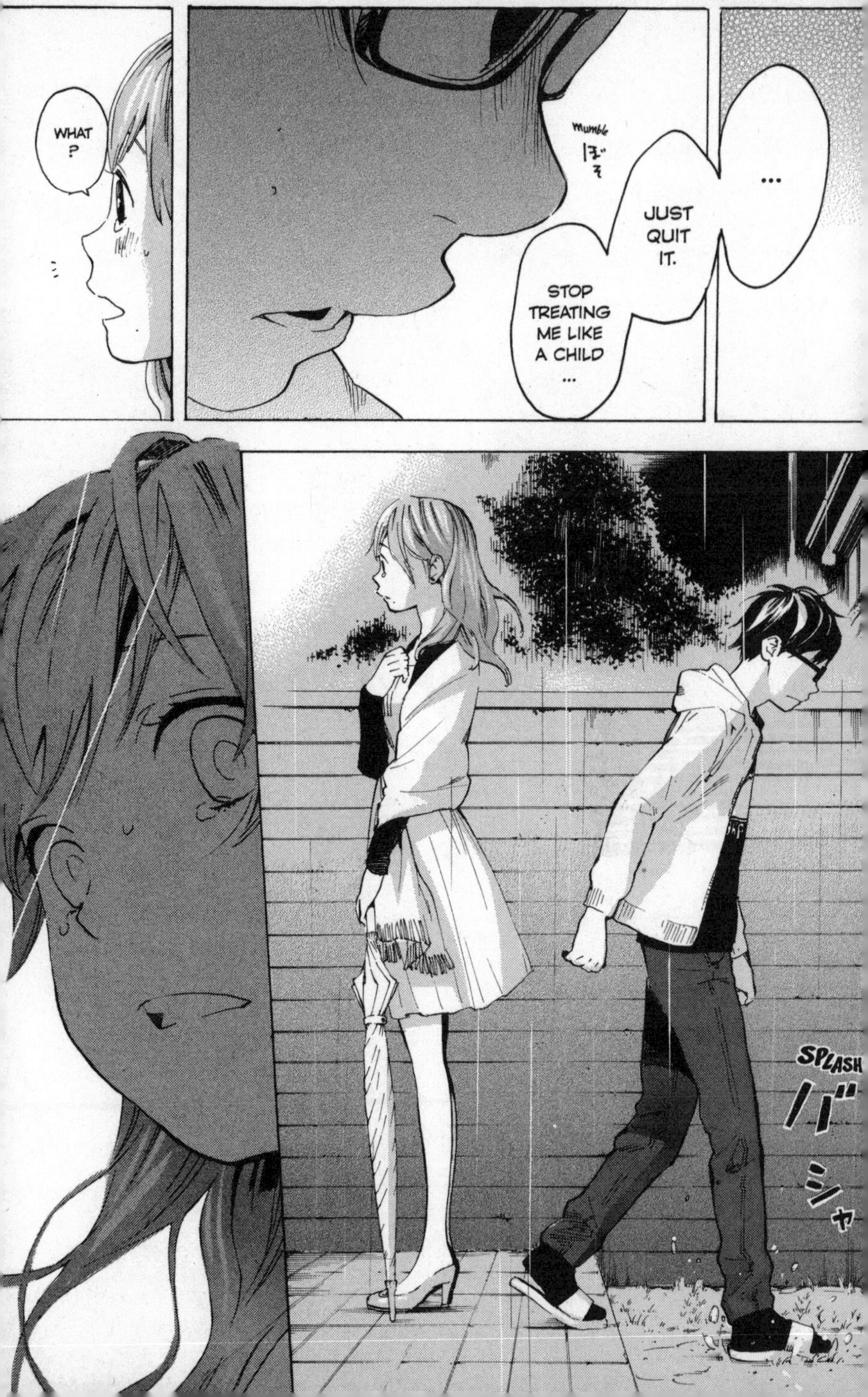
...
mumble
ぼそ
JUST QUIT IT.
STOP TREATING ME LIKE A CHILD ...
WHAT ?
SPLASH
バシャ

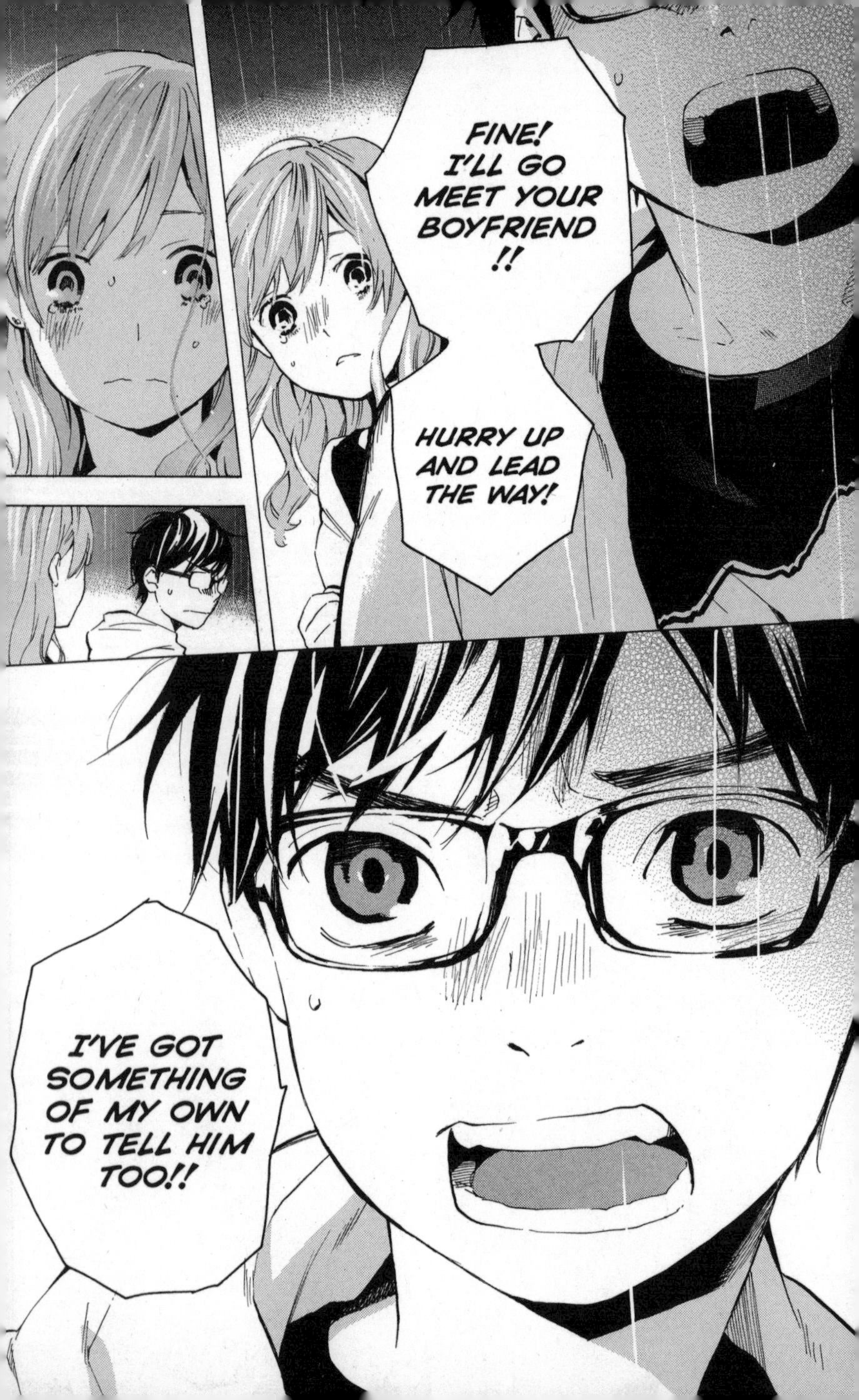
FINE! I'LL GO MEET YOUR BOYFRIEND !!
HURRY UP AND LEAD THE WAY!
I'VE GOT SOMETHING OF MY OWN TO TELL HIM TOO!!

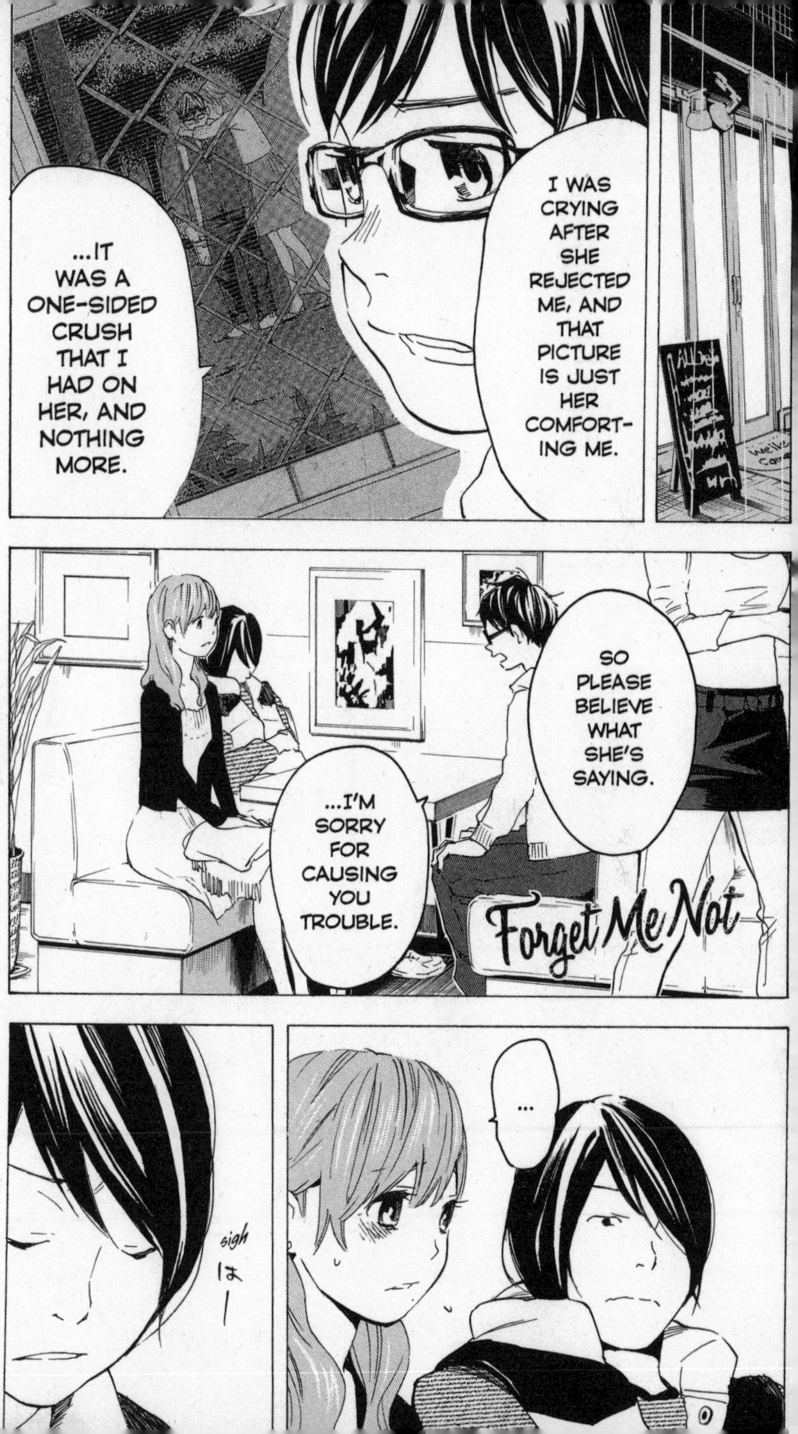
I WAS CRYING AFTER SHE REJECTED ME, AND THAT PICTURE IS JUST HER COMFORTING ME.
...IT WAS A ONE-SIDED CRUSH THAT I HAD ON HER, AND NOTHING MORE.
SO PLEASE BELIEVE WHAT SHE'S SAYING.
...I'M SORRY FOR CAUSING YOU TROUBLE.
Forget Me Not
...
sigh
はー

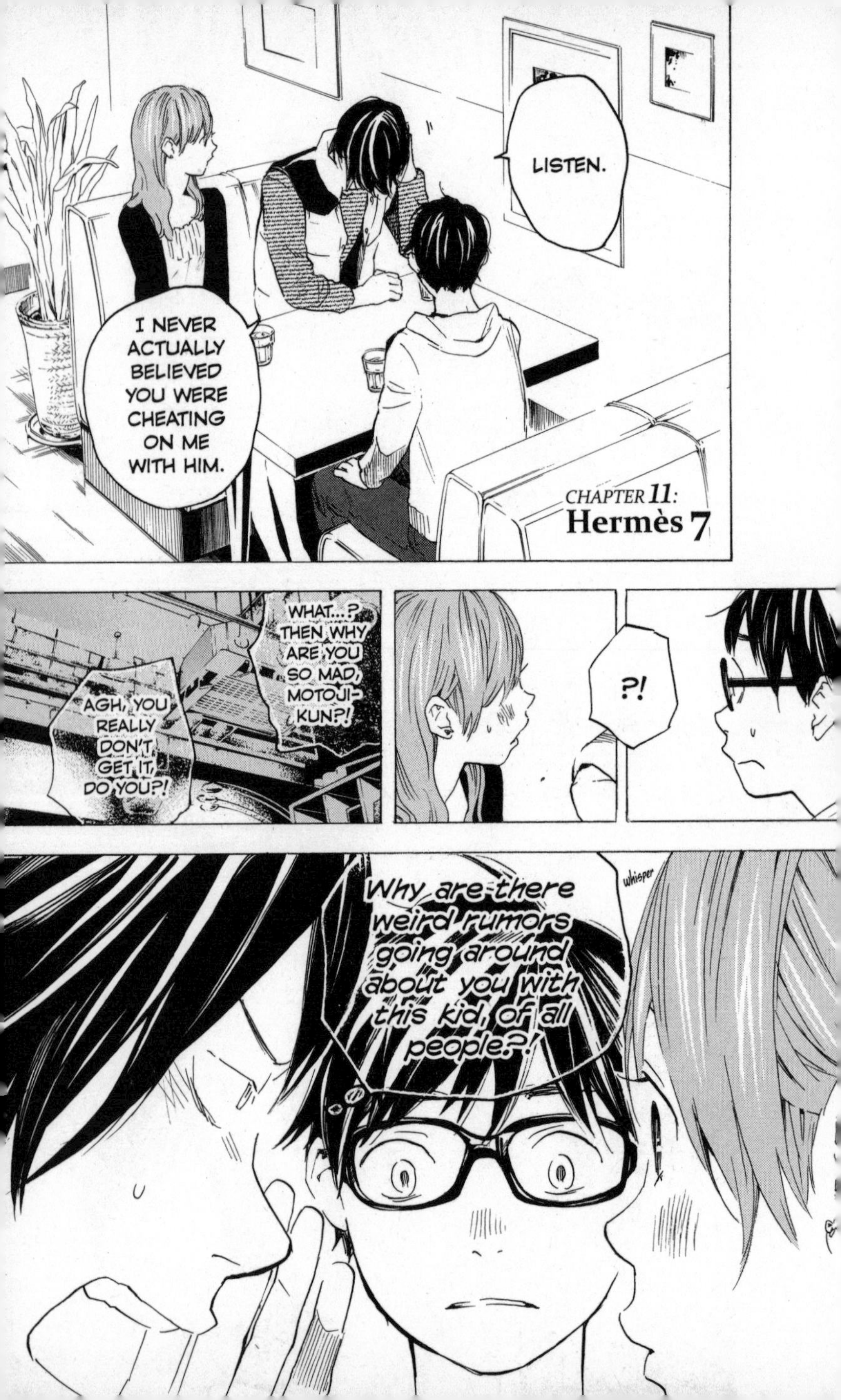
LISTEN.
I NEVER ACTUALLY BELIEVED YOU WERE CHEATING ON ME WITH HIM.
CHAPTER 11: Hermès 7
?!
WHAT...? THEN WHY ARE YOU SO MAD, MOTOJI-KUN?!
AGH, YOU REALLY DON'T GET IT, DO YOU?!
whisper
Why are there weird rumors going around about you with this kid, of all people?!

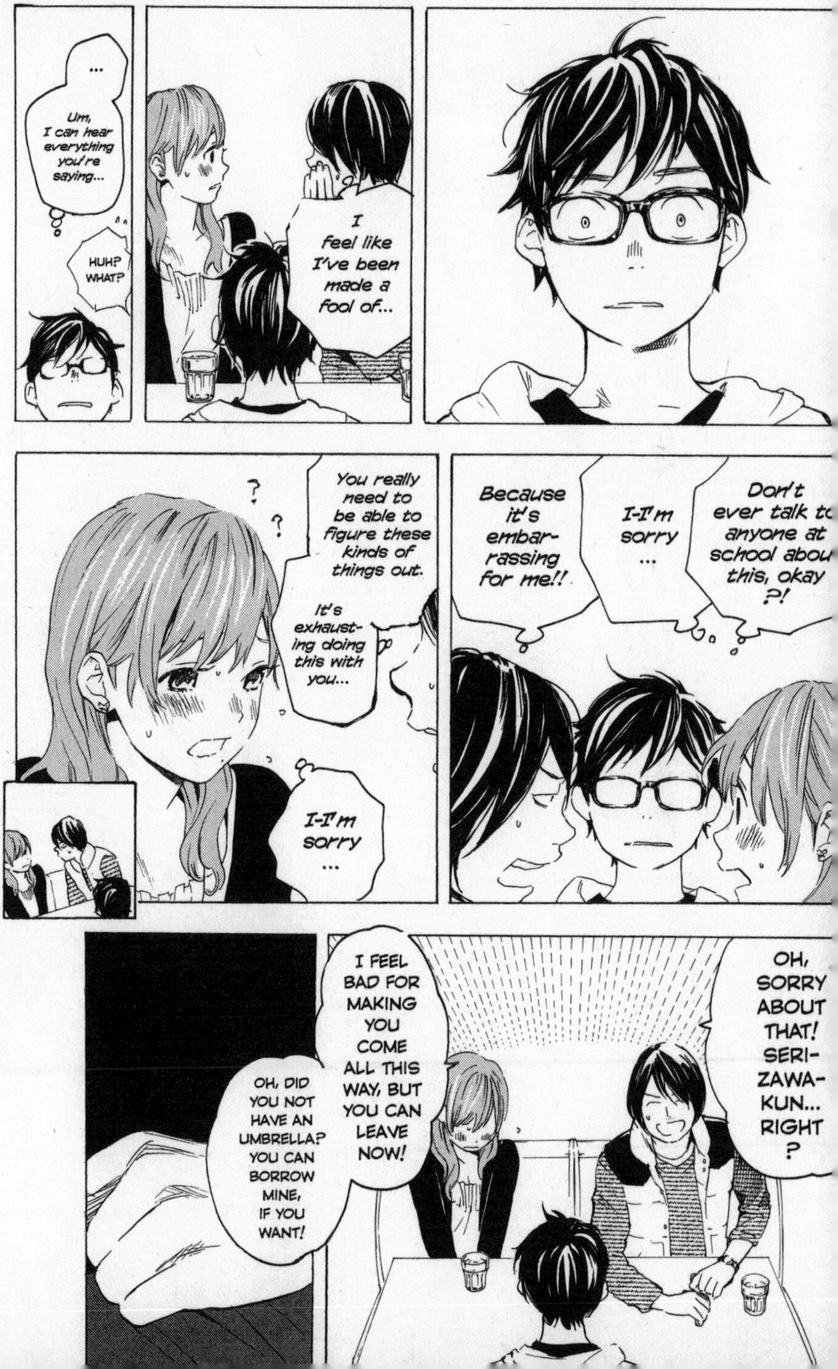

I feel like I've been made a fool of...
...
Um, I can hear everything you're saying...
HUH? WHAT?
Don't ever talk to anyone at school about this, okay ?!
I-I'm sorry ...
Because it's embarrassing for me!!
You really need to be able to figure these kinds of things out.
It's exhausting doing this with you...
I-I'm sorry ...
OH, SORRY ABOUT THAT! SERIZAWA-KUN... RIGHT?
I FEEL BAD FOR MAKING YOU COME ALL THIS WAY, BUT YOU CAN LEAVE NOW!
OH, DID YOU NOT HAVE AN UMBRELLA? YOU CAN BORROW MINE, IF YOU WANT!

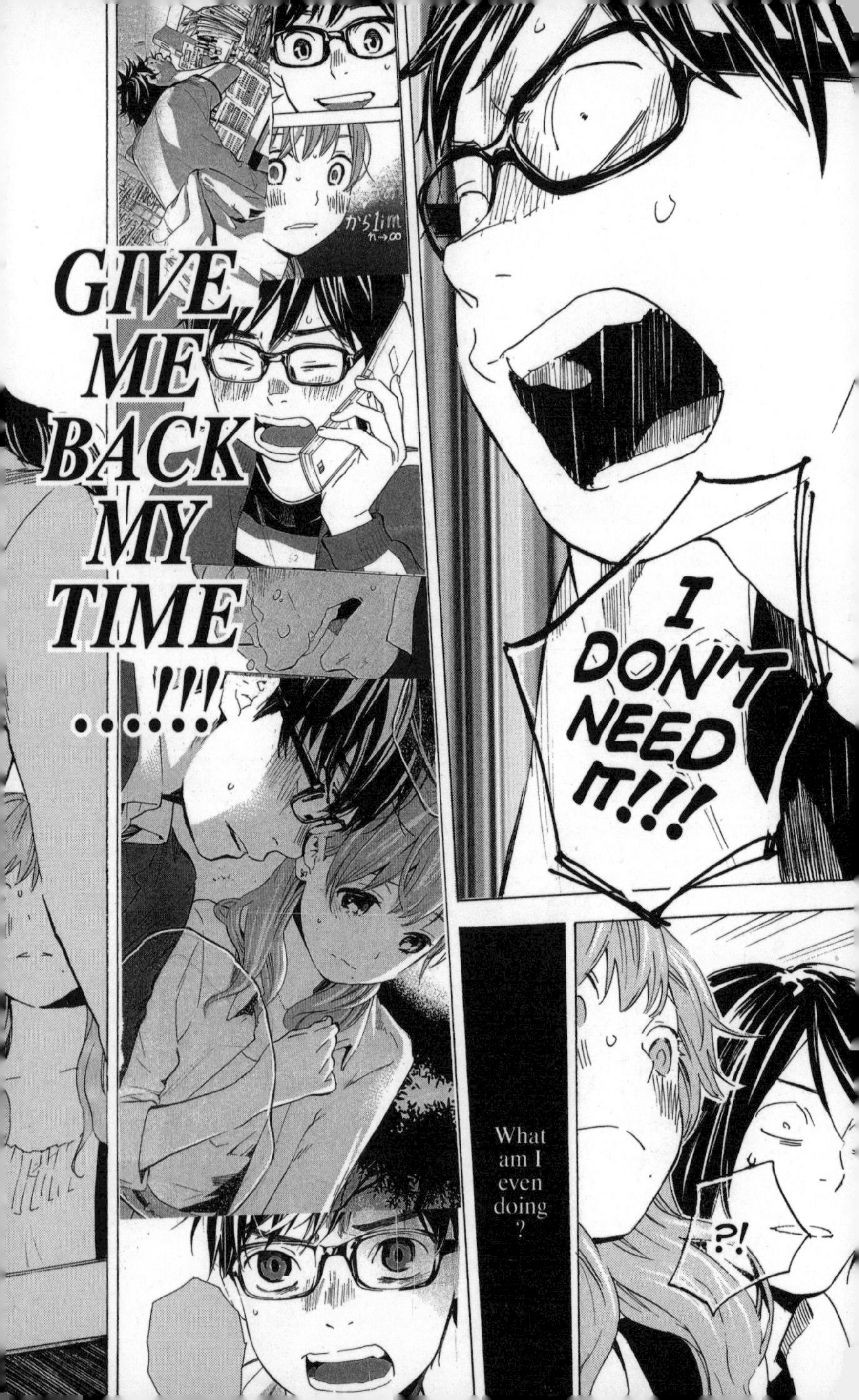
I DON'T NEED IT!!!
What am I even doing?
?!
GIVE ME BACK MY TIME!!!
......

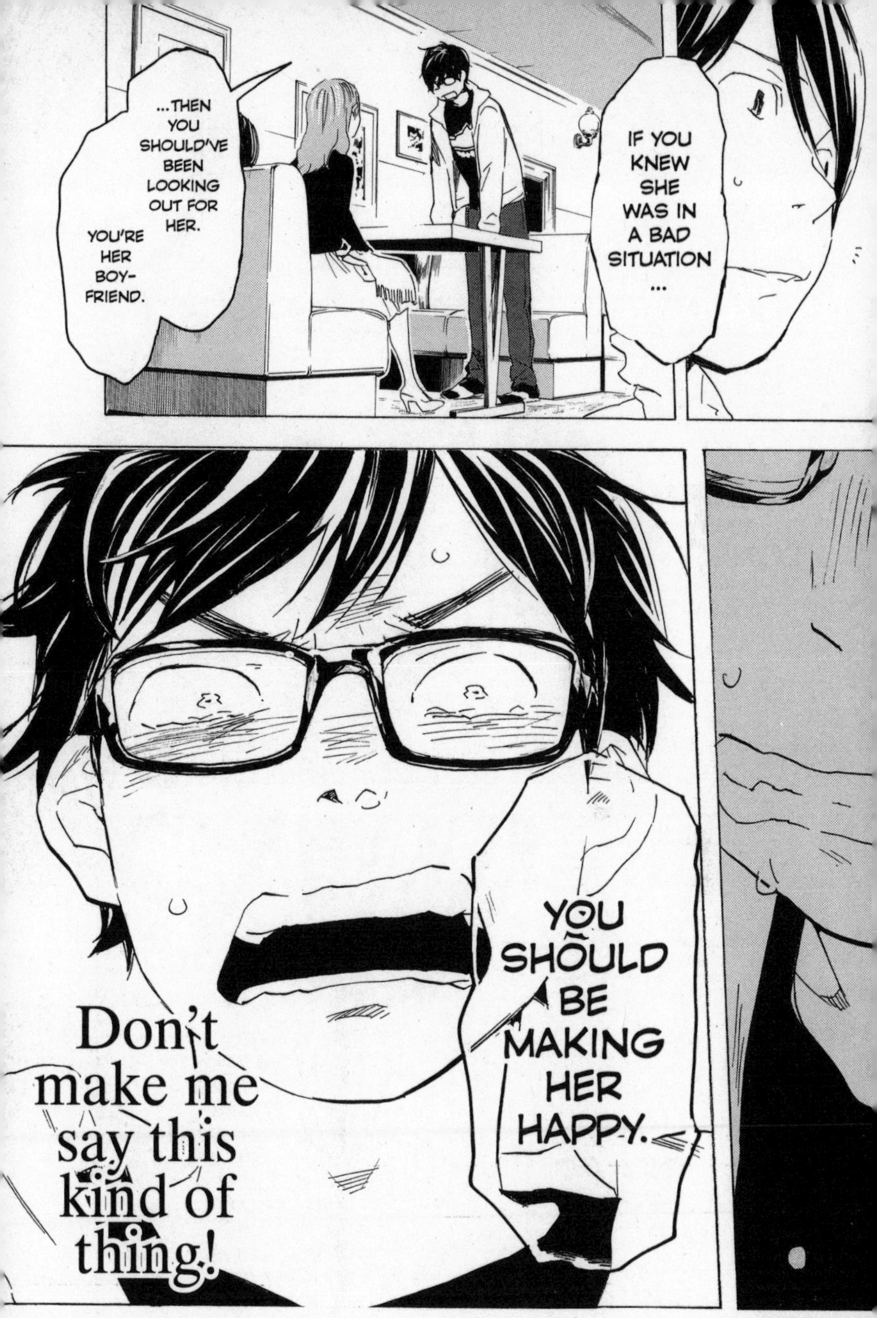
IF YOU KNEW SHE WAS IN A BAD SITUATION ...
...THEN YOU SHOULD'VE BEEN LOOKING OUT FOR HER.
YOU'RE HER BOY-FRIEND.
YOU SHOULD BE MAKING HER HAPPY.
Don't make me say this kind of thing!

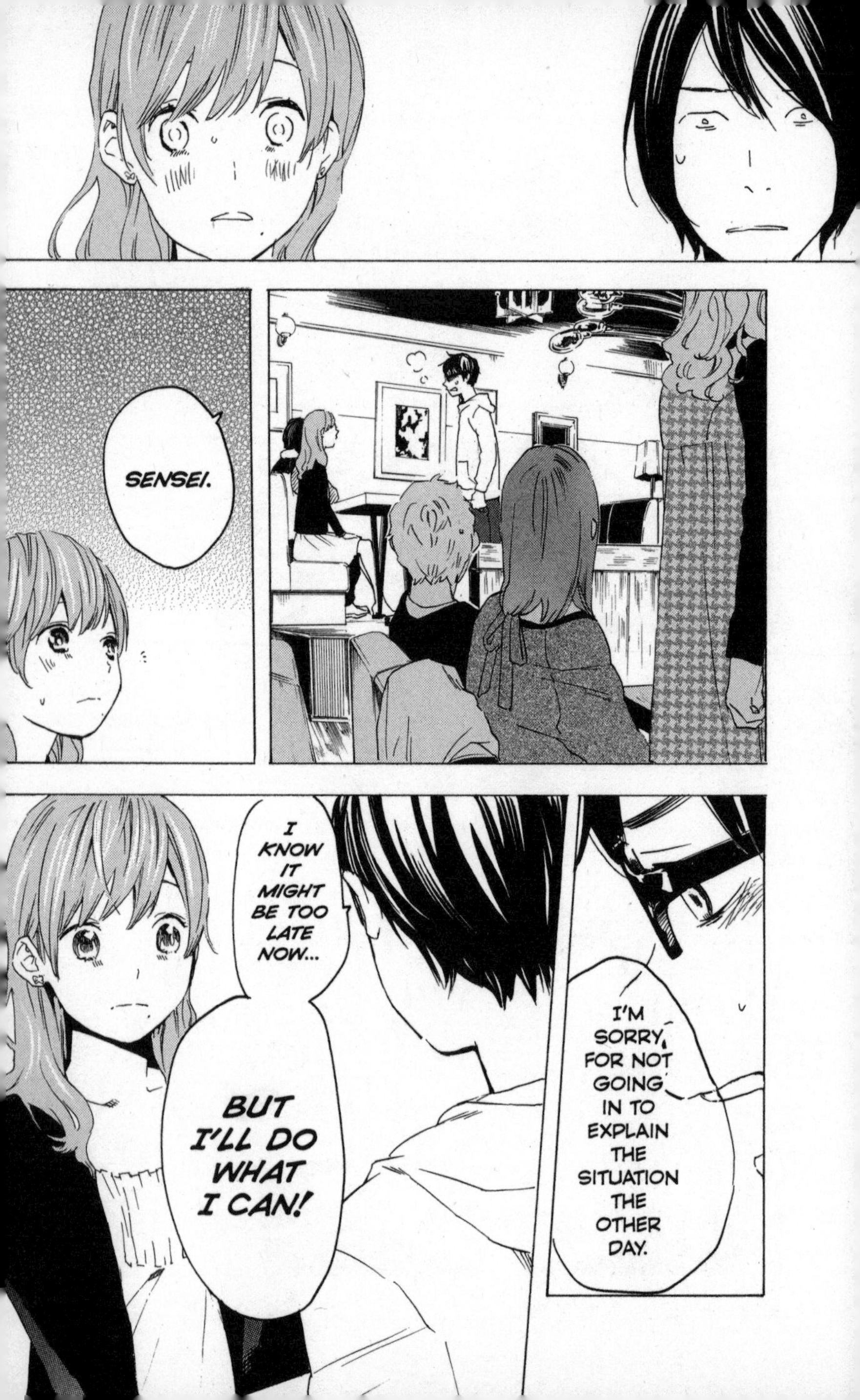
SENSEI.
I'M SORRY, FOR NOT GOING IN TO EXPLAIN THE SITUATION THE OTHER DAY.
I KNOW IT MIGHT BE TOO LATE NOW...
BUT I'LL DO WHAT I CAN!

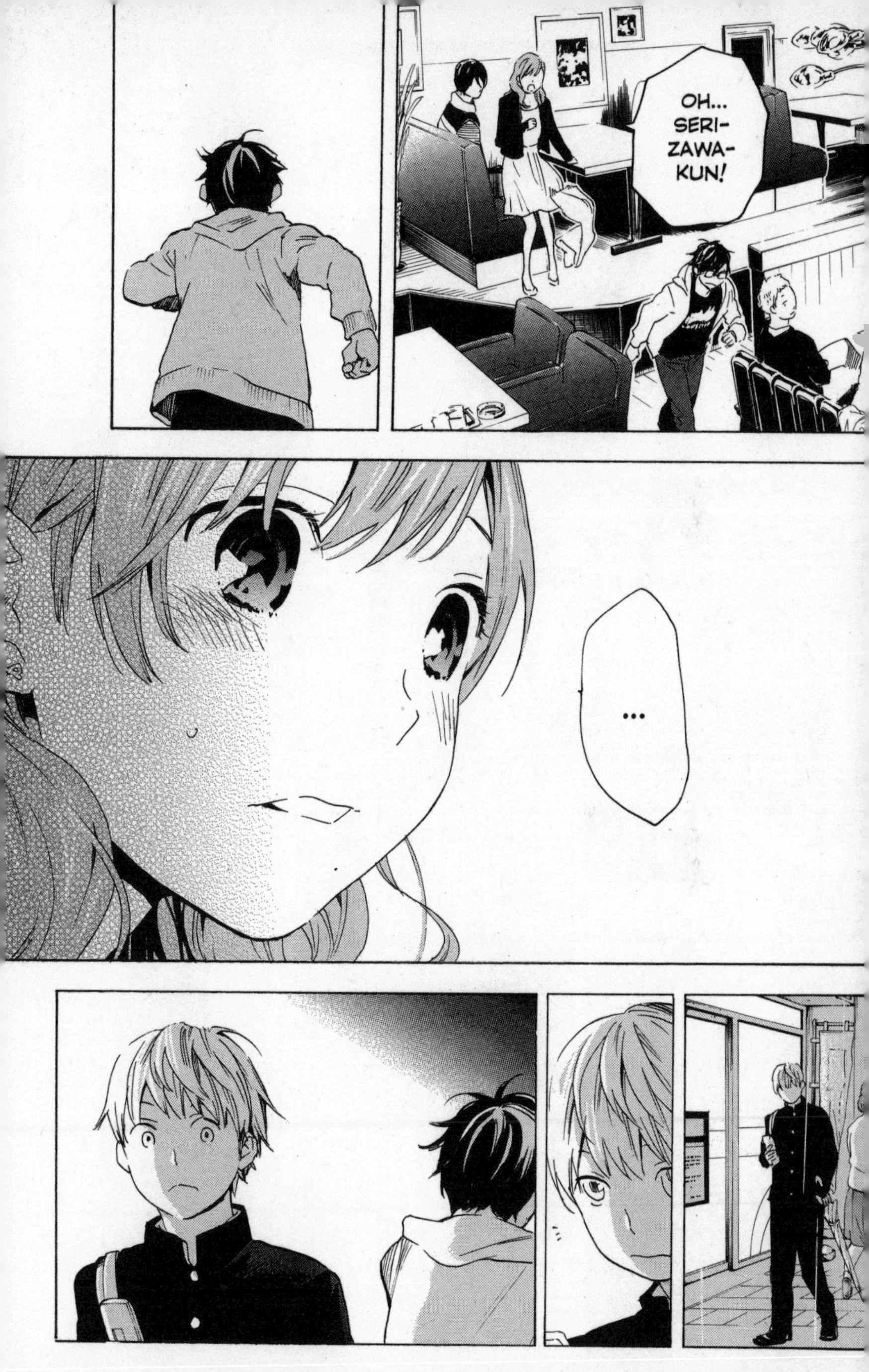
OH... SERI-ZAWA-KUN!
...

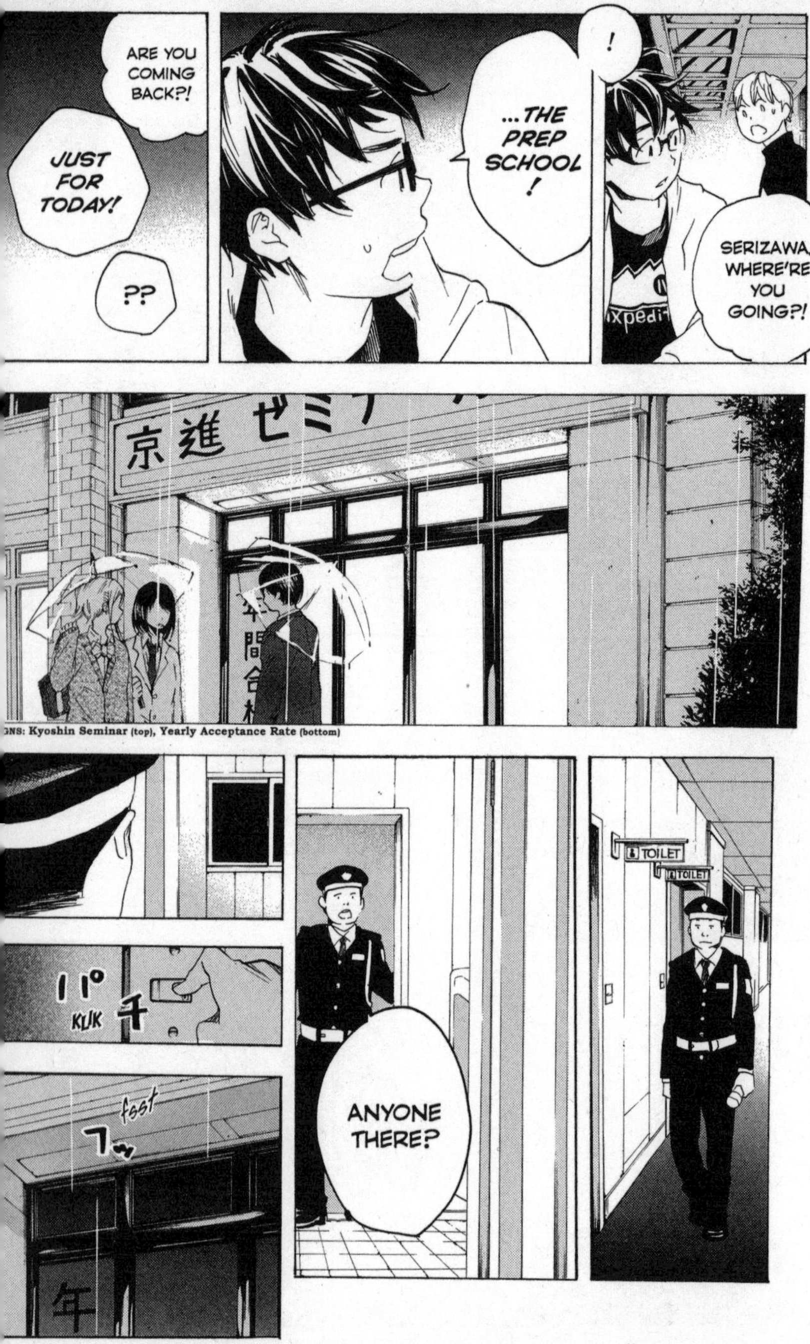
!
SERIZAWA! WHERE'RE YOU GOING?!
...THE PREP SCHOOL!
ARE YOU COMING BACK?!
JUST FOR TODAY!
??
京進ゼミ
TOILET
TOILET
ANYONE THERE?
パチ
KLIK
フッ
fsst

SIGNS: Kyoshin Seminar (top), Yearly Acceptance Rate (bottom)

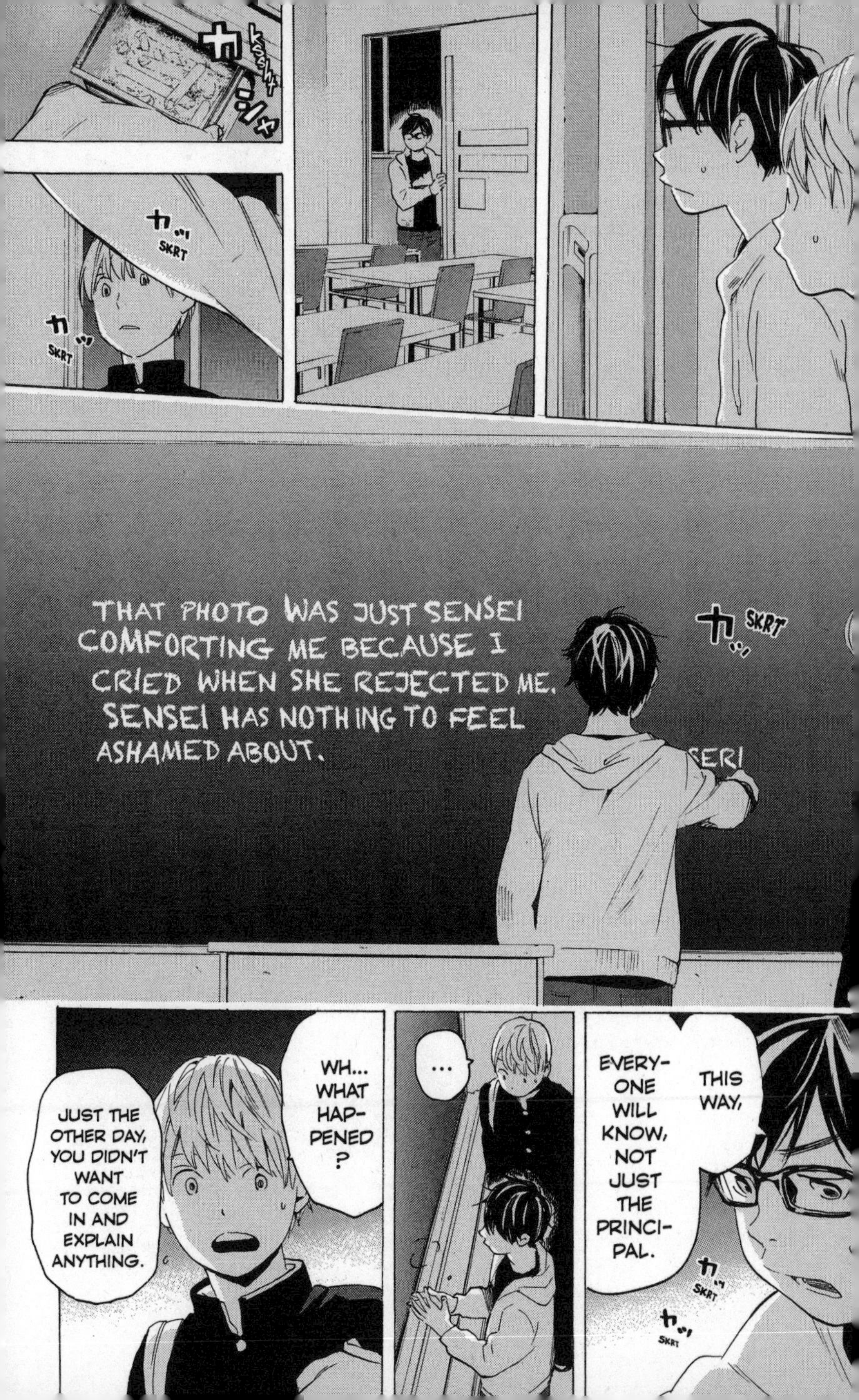
カシャ
kssht
カッ
SKRT
カッ
SKRT
THAT PHOTO WAS JUST SENSEI COMFORTING ME BECAUSE I CRIED WHEN SHE REJECTED ME. SENSEI HAS NOTHING TO FEEL ASHAMED ABOUT.
カッ
SKRT
SERI
THIS WAY,
EVERYONE WILL KNOW, NOT JUST THE PRINCIPAL.
カッ
SKRT
カッ
SKRT
...
WH... WHAT HAPPENED?
JUST THE OTHER DAY, YOU DIDN'T WANT TO COME IN AND EXPLAIN ANYTHING.

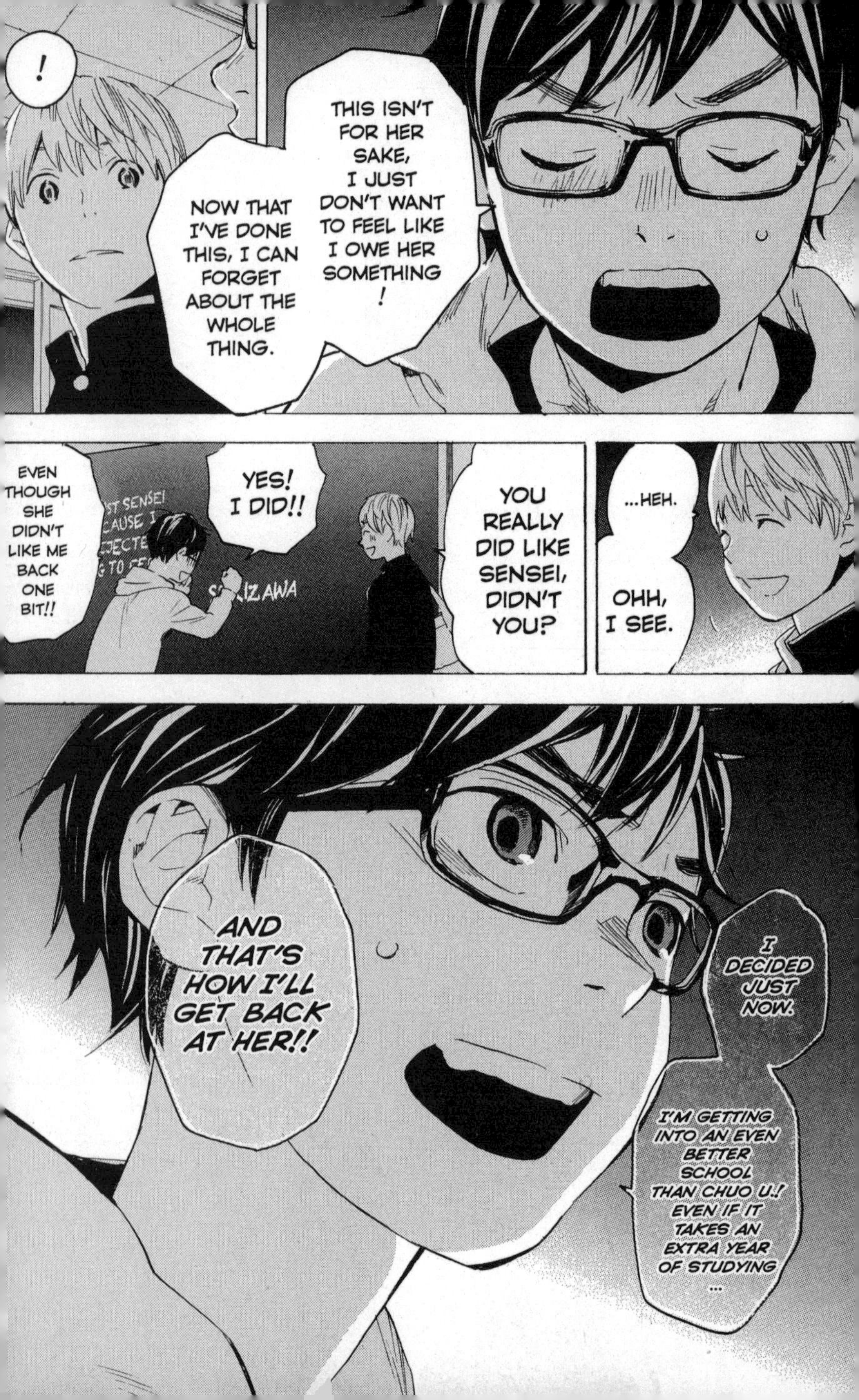

THIS ISN'T FOR HER SAKE, I JUST DON'T WANT TO FEEL LIKE I OWE HER SOMETHING!
NOW THAT I'VE DONE THIS, I CAN FORGET ABOUT THE WHOLE THING.
!
...HEH.
OHH, I SEE.
YOU REALLY DID LIKE SENSEI, DIDN'T YOU?
YES! I DID!!
EVEN THOUGH SHE DIDN'T LIKE ME BACK ONE BIT!!
I DECIDED JUST NOW.
AND THAT'S HOW I'LL GET BACK AT HER!!
I'M GETTING INTO AN EVEN BETTER SCHOOL THAN CHUO U.! EVEN IF IT TAKES AN EXTRA YEAR OF STUDYING...

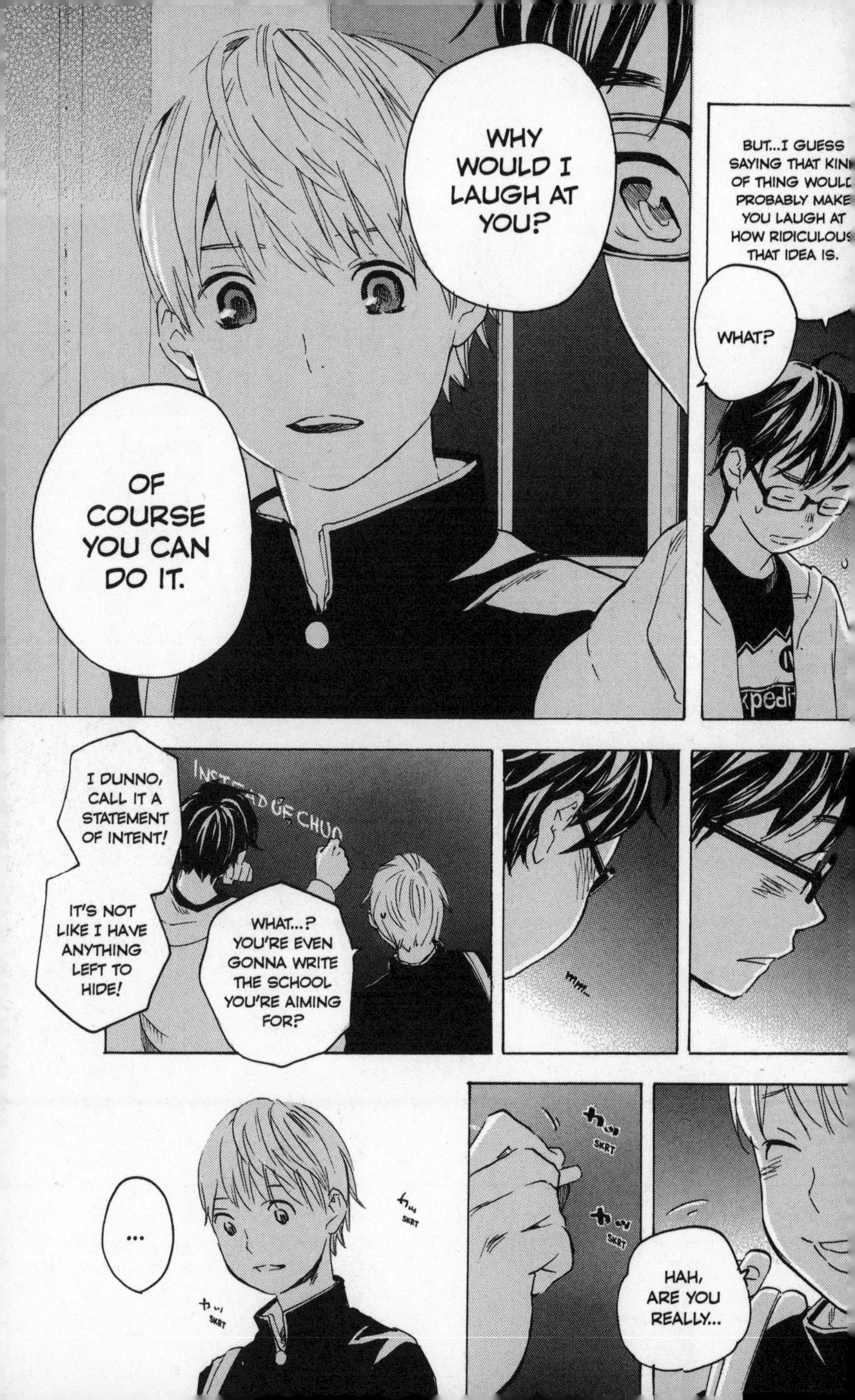
BUT...I GUESS SAYING THAT KIN OF THING WOULD PROBABLY MAKE YOU LAUGH AT HOW RIDICULOUS THAT IDEA IS.
WHAT?
WHY WOULD I LAUGH AT YOU?
OF COURSE YOU CAN DO IT.
MM...
WHAT...? YOU'RE EVEN GONNA WRITE THE SCHOOL YOU'RE AIMING FOR?
I DUNNO, CALL IT A STATEMENT OF INTENT!
IT'S NOT LIKE I HAVE ANYTHING LEFT TO HIDE!
HAH, ARE YOU REALLY...
SKRT
SKRT
SKRT
...
SKRT

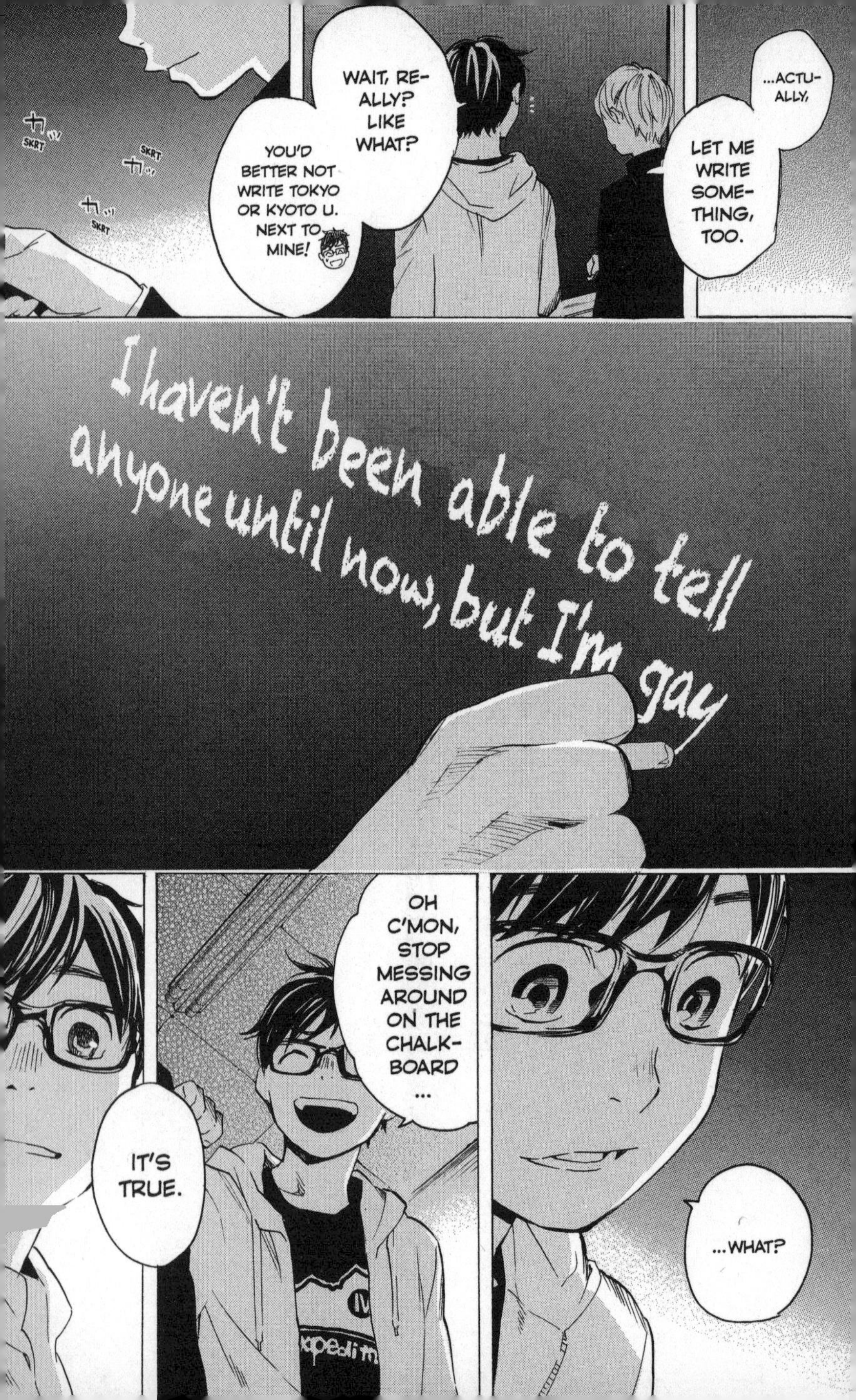
...ACTUALLY,
LET ME WRITE SOMETHING, TOO.
WAIT, REALLY? LIKE WHAT?
YOU'D BETTER NOT WRITE TOKYO OR KYOTO U. NEXT TO MINE!
カッ SKRT
カッ SKRT
カッ SKRT
I haven't been able to tell anyone until now, but I'm gay
...WHAT?
OH C'MON, STOP MESSING AROUND ON THE CHALKBOARD ...
IT'S TRUE.

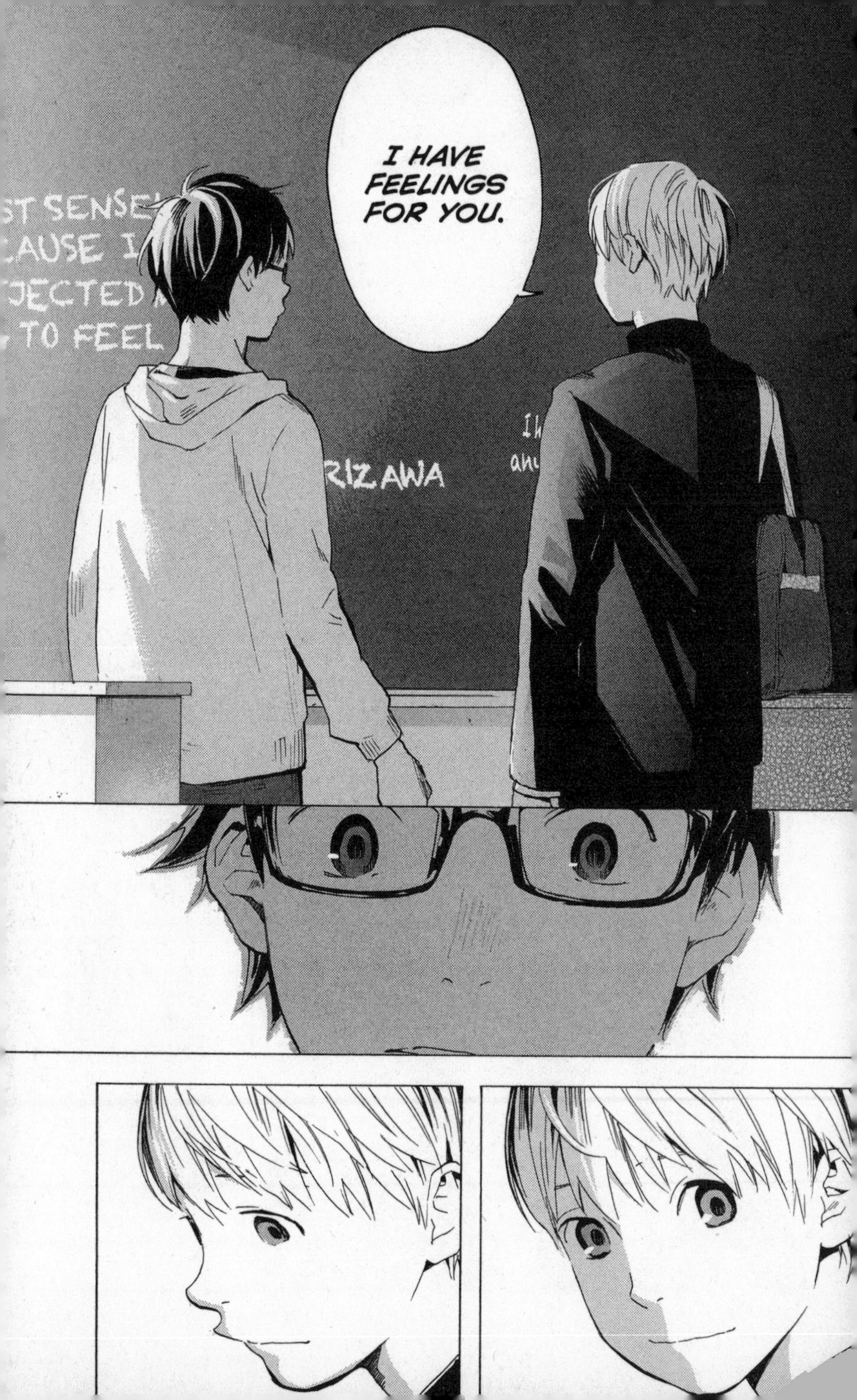
I HAVE FEELINGS FOR YOU.

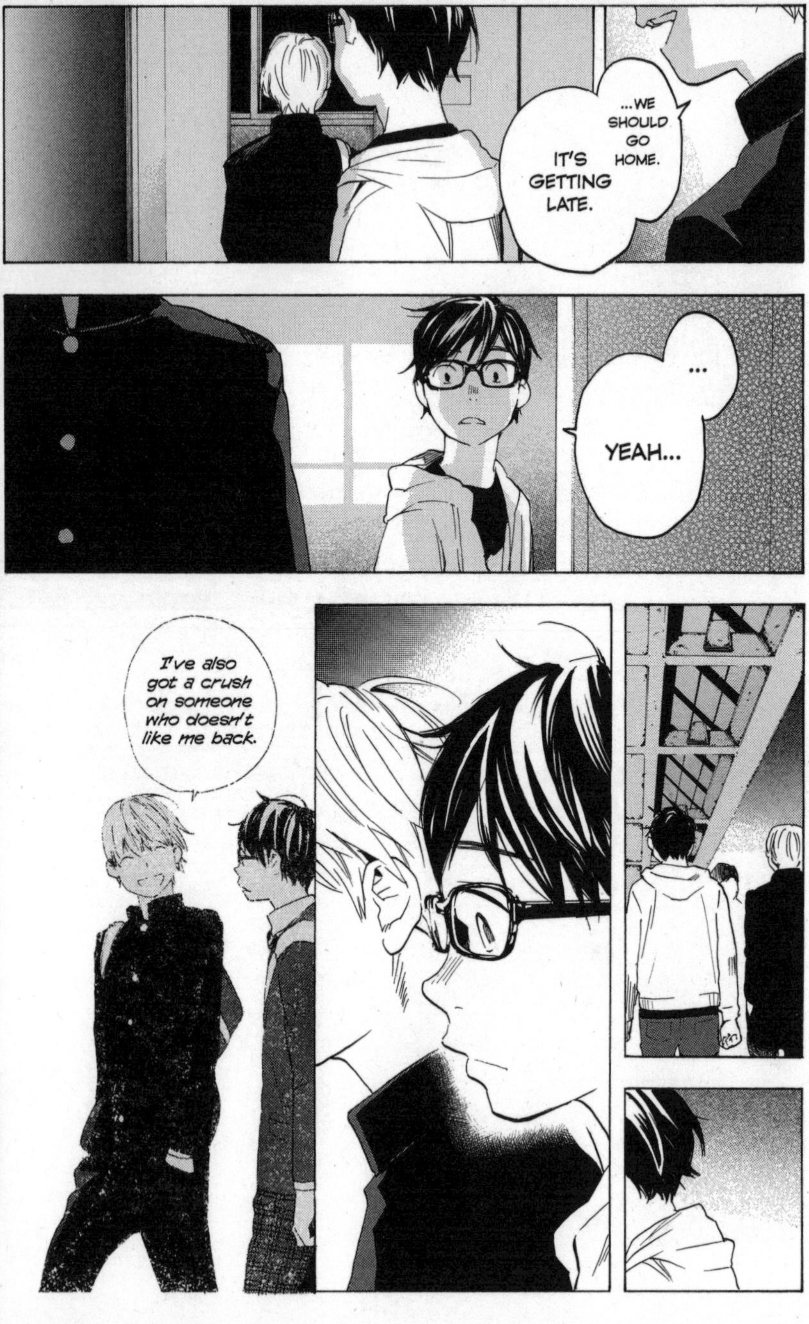
...WE SHOULD GO HOME.
IT'S GETTING LATE.
...
YEAH...
I've also got a crush on someone who doesn't like me back.

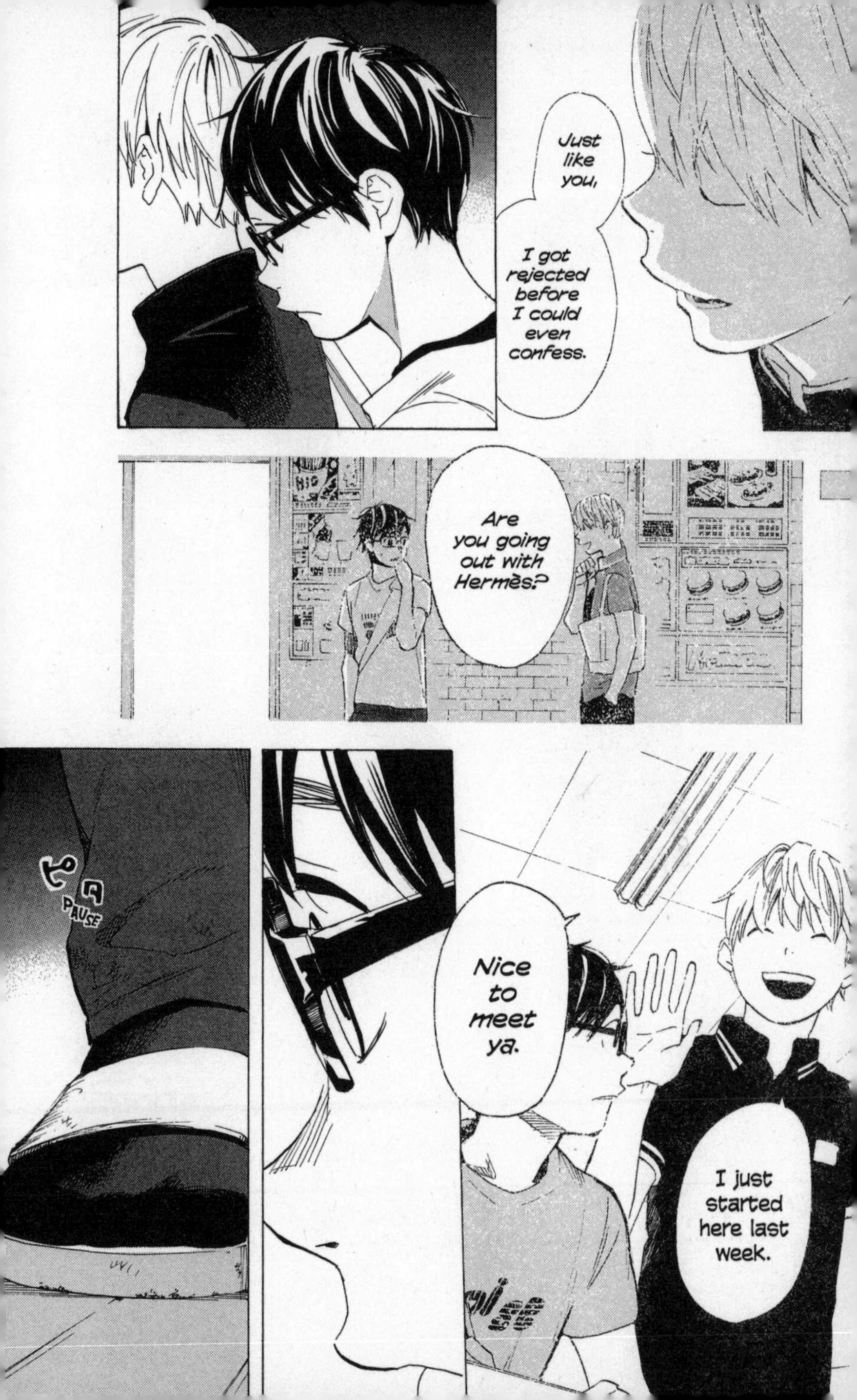
Just like you,
I got rejected before I could even confess.
Are you going out with Hermès?
Nice to meet ya.
I just started here last week.
ピク
PAUSE

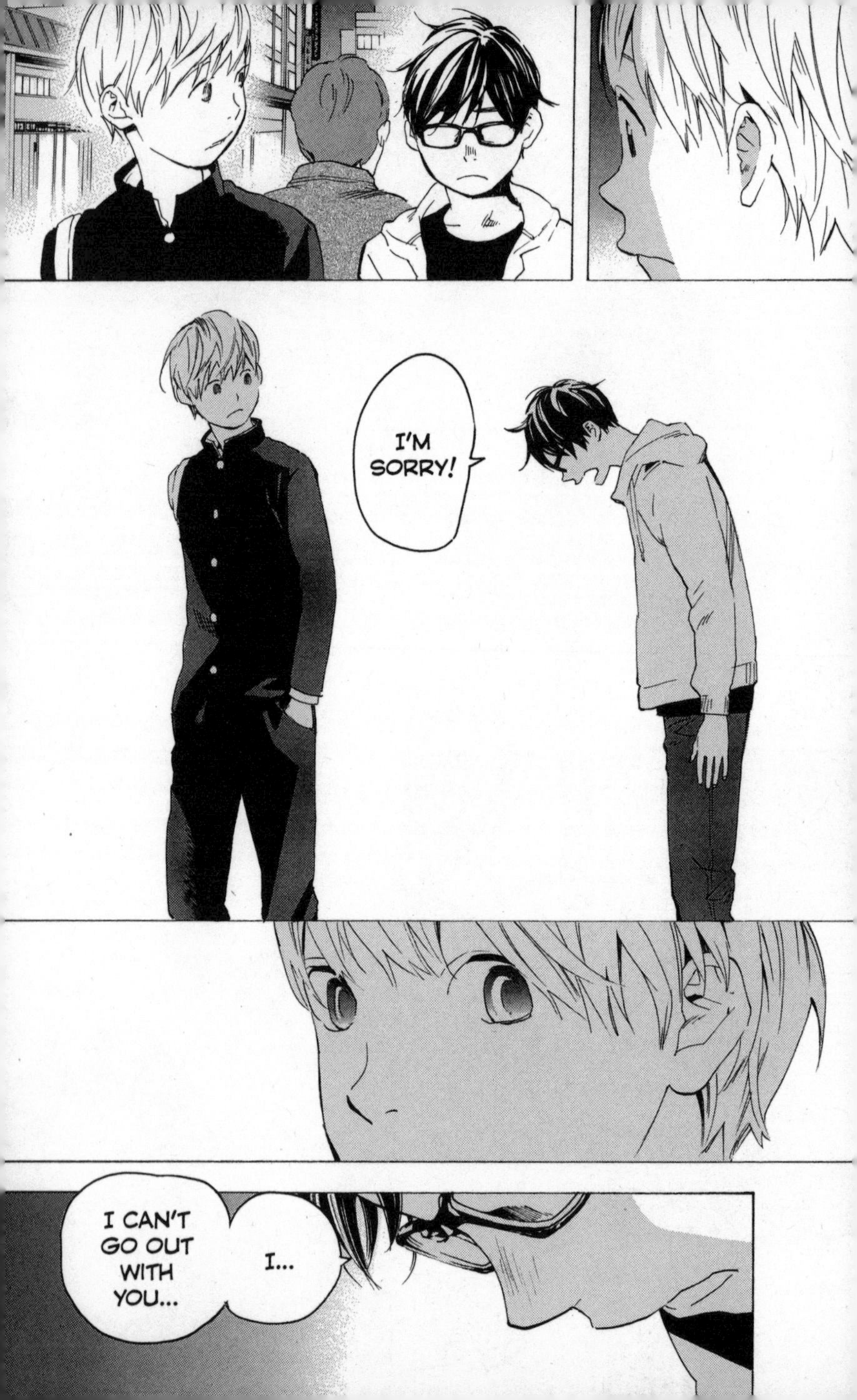
I'M SORRY!
I...
I CAN'T GO OUT WITH YOU...

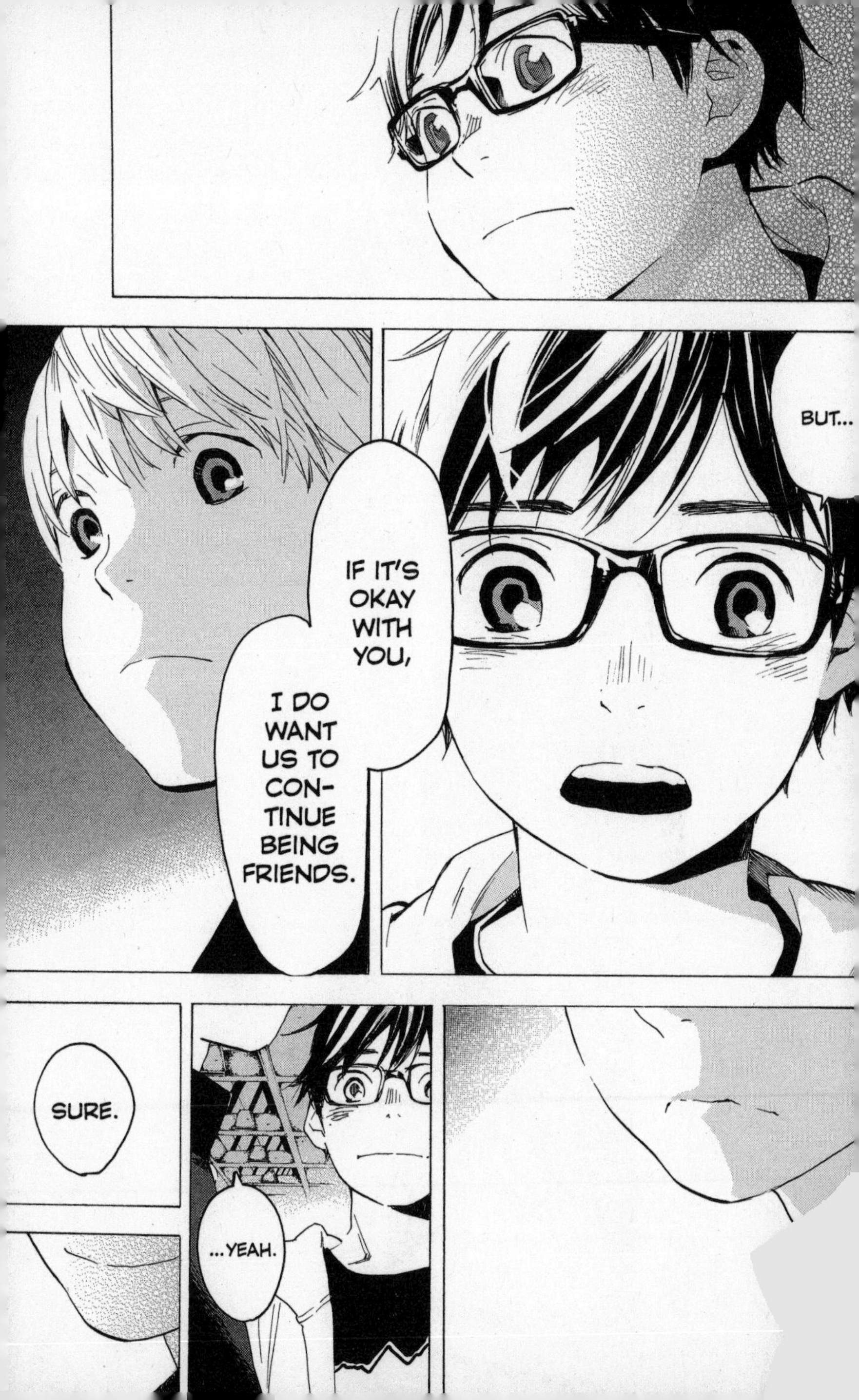
BUT...
IF IT'S OKAY WITH YOU, I DO WANT US TO CON-TINUE BEING FRIENDS.
...YEAH.
SURE.

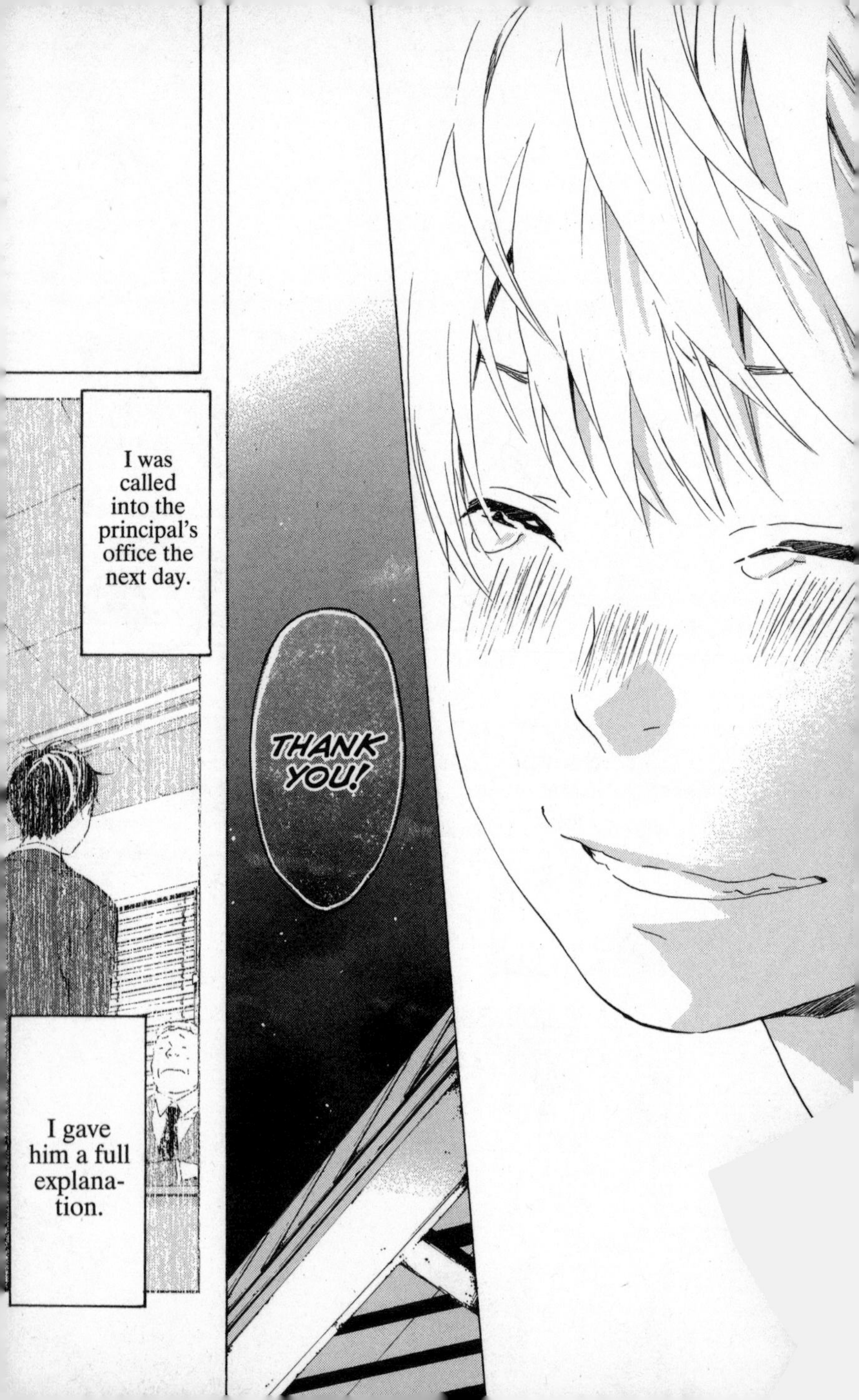
THANK YOU!
I was called into the principal's office the next day.
I gave him a full explanation.

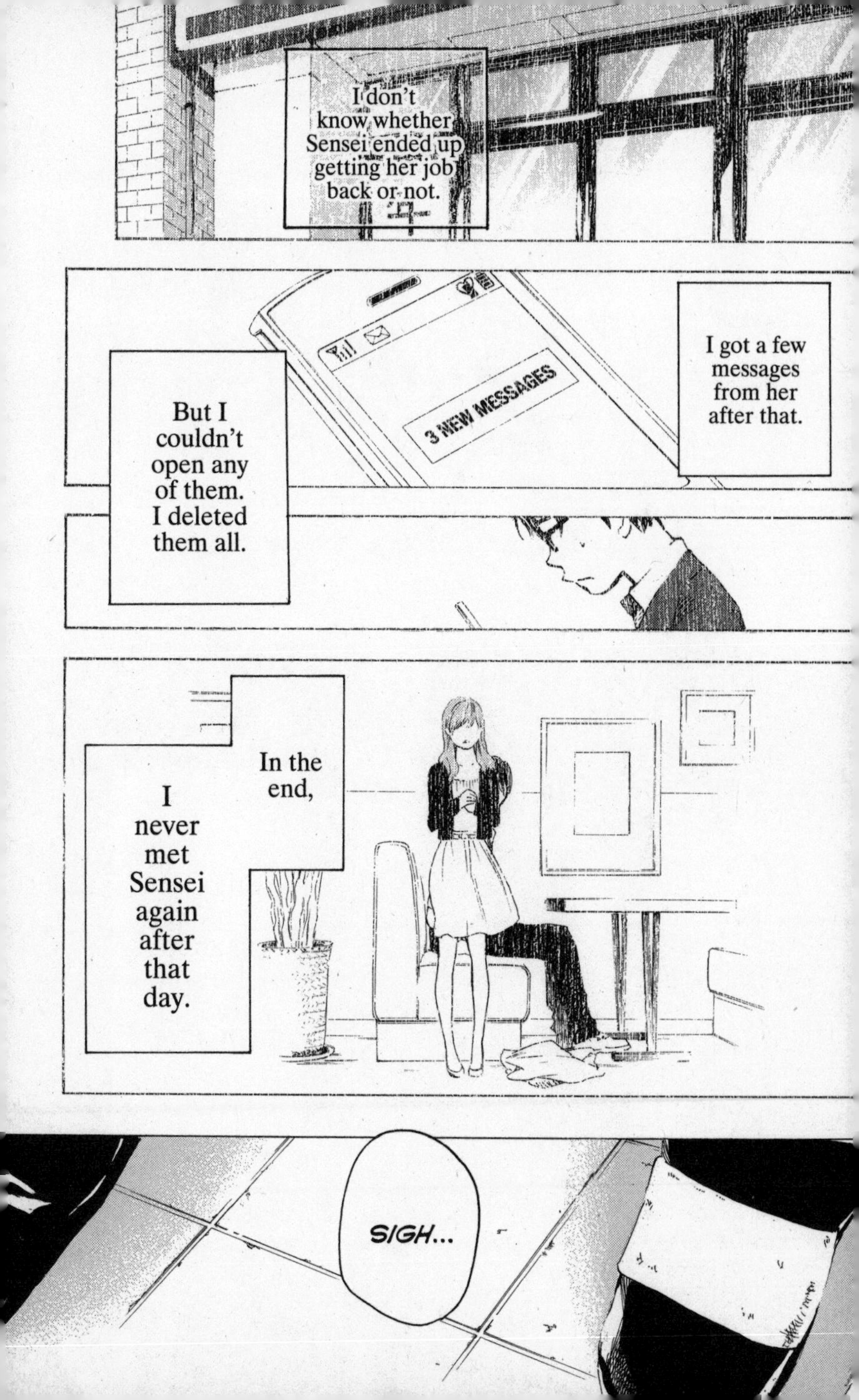
I don't know whether Sensei ended up getting her job back or not.
I got a few messages from her after that.
3 NEW MESSAGES
But I couldn't open any of them. I deleted them all.
In the end,
I never met Sensei again after that day.
SIGH...

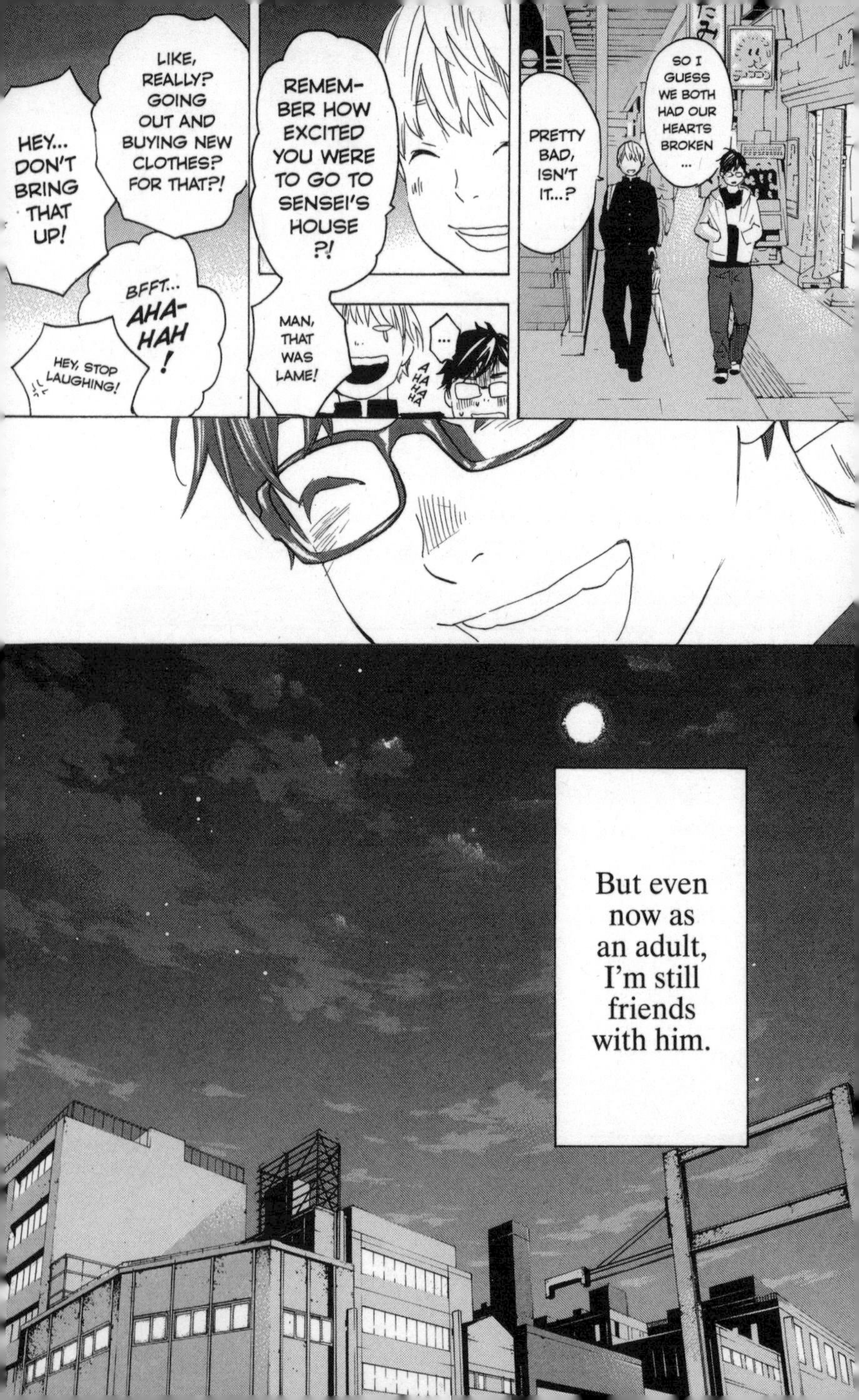
SO I GUESS WE BOTH HAD OUR HEARTS BROKEN ...
PRETTY BAD, ISN'T IT...?
REMEMBER HOW EXCITED YOU WERE TO GO TO SENSEI'S HOUSE?!
MAN, THAT WAS LAME!
...
AHAHAHA
LIKE, REALLY? GOING OUT AND BUYING NEW CLOTHES? FOR THAT?!
HEY... DON'T BRING THAT UP!
BFFT... AHA-HAH!
HEY, STOP LAUGHING!
But even now as an adult, I'm still friends with him.

Forget Me Not

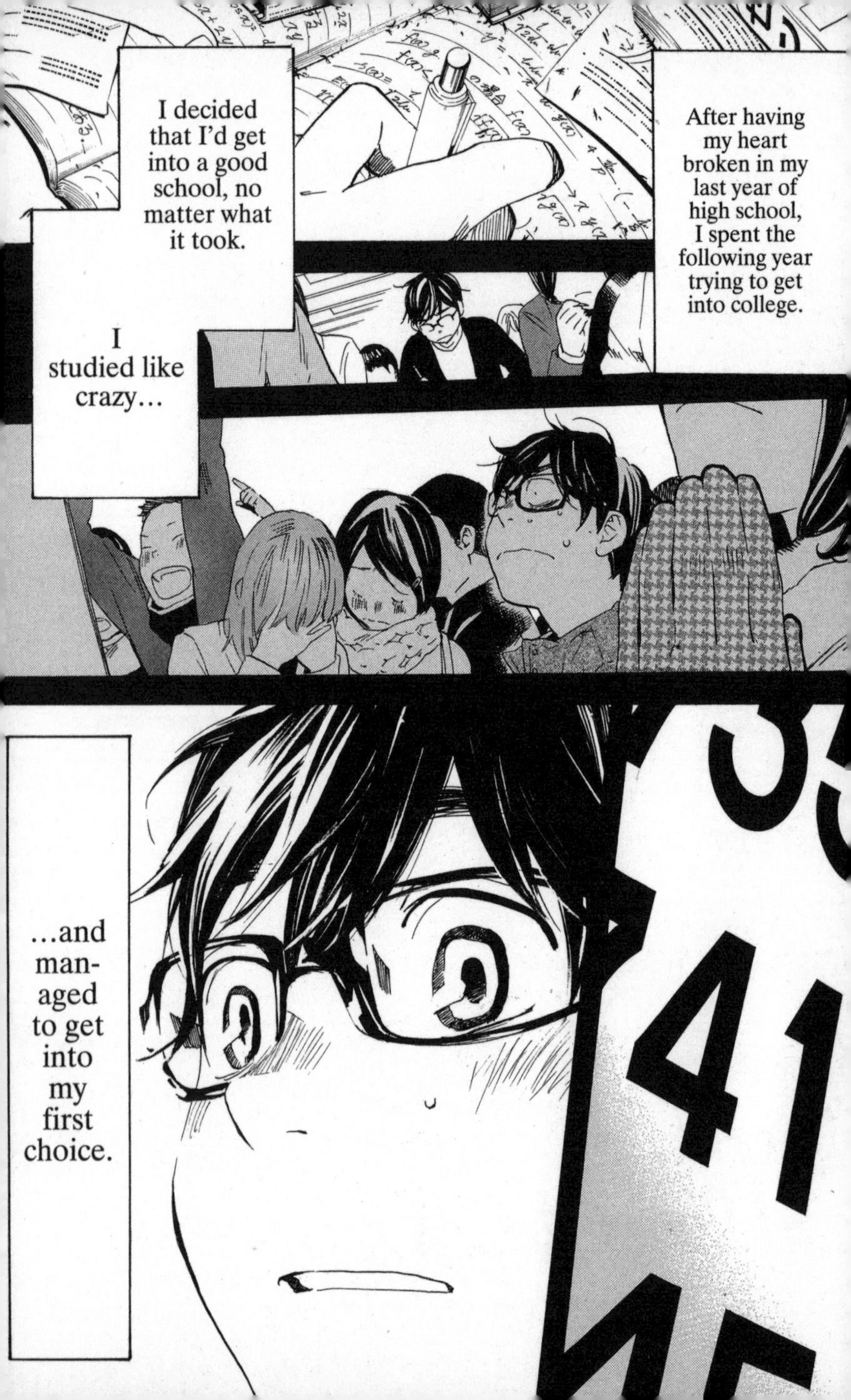
After having my heart broken in my last year of high school, I spent the following year trying to get into college.
I decided that I'd get into a good school, no matter what it took.
I studied like crazy…
…and man-aged to get into my first choice.
41

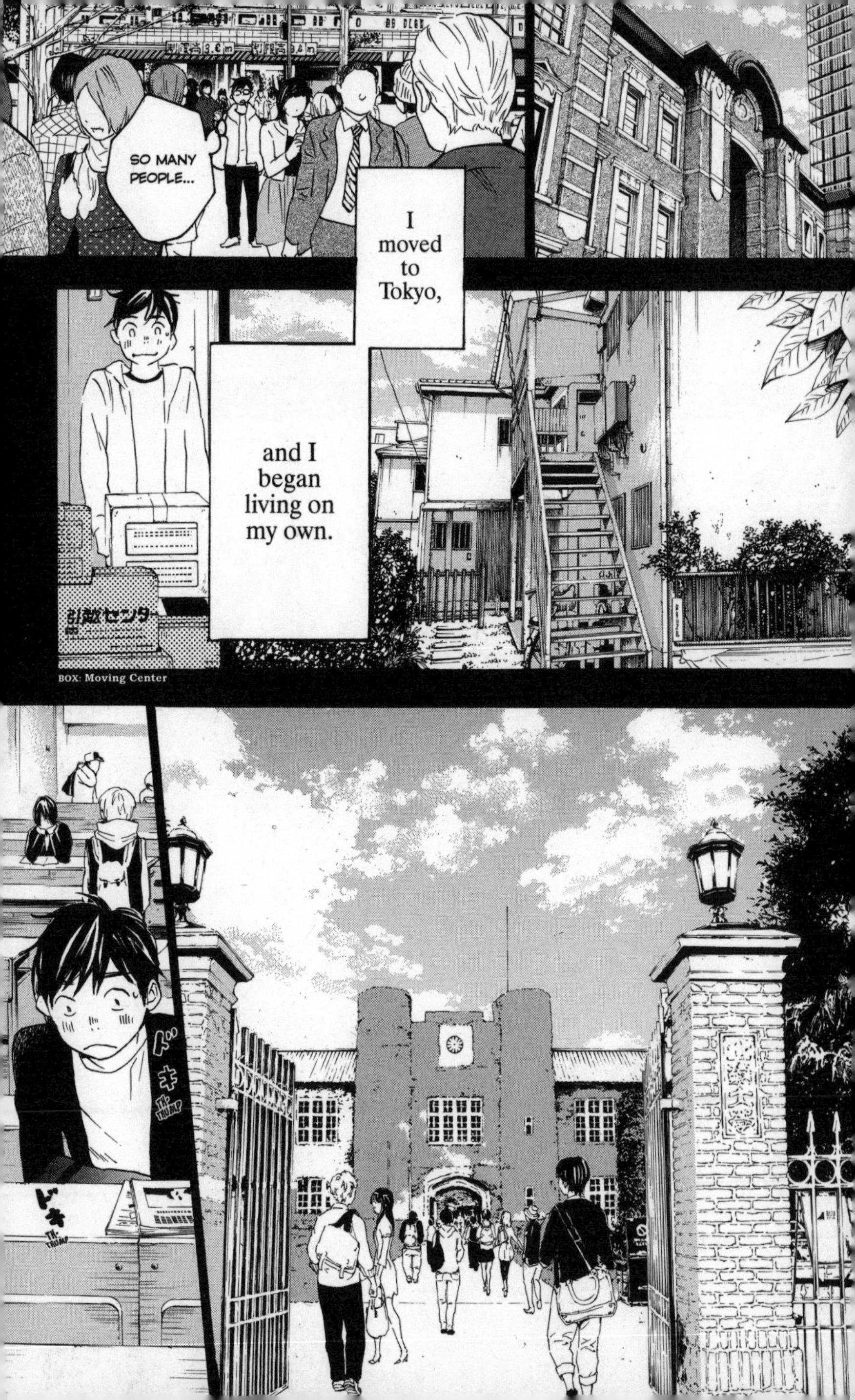
SO MANY PEOPLE...
I moved to Tokyo,
and I began living on my own.
BOX: Moving Center
TH-THUMP
TH-THUMP

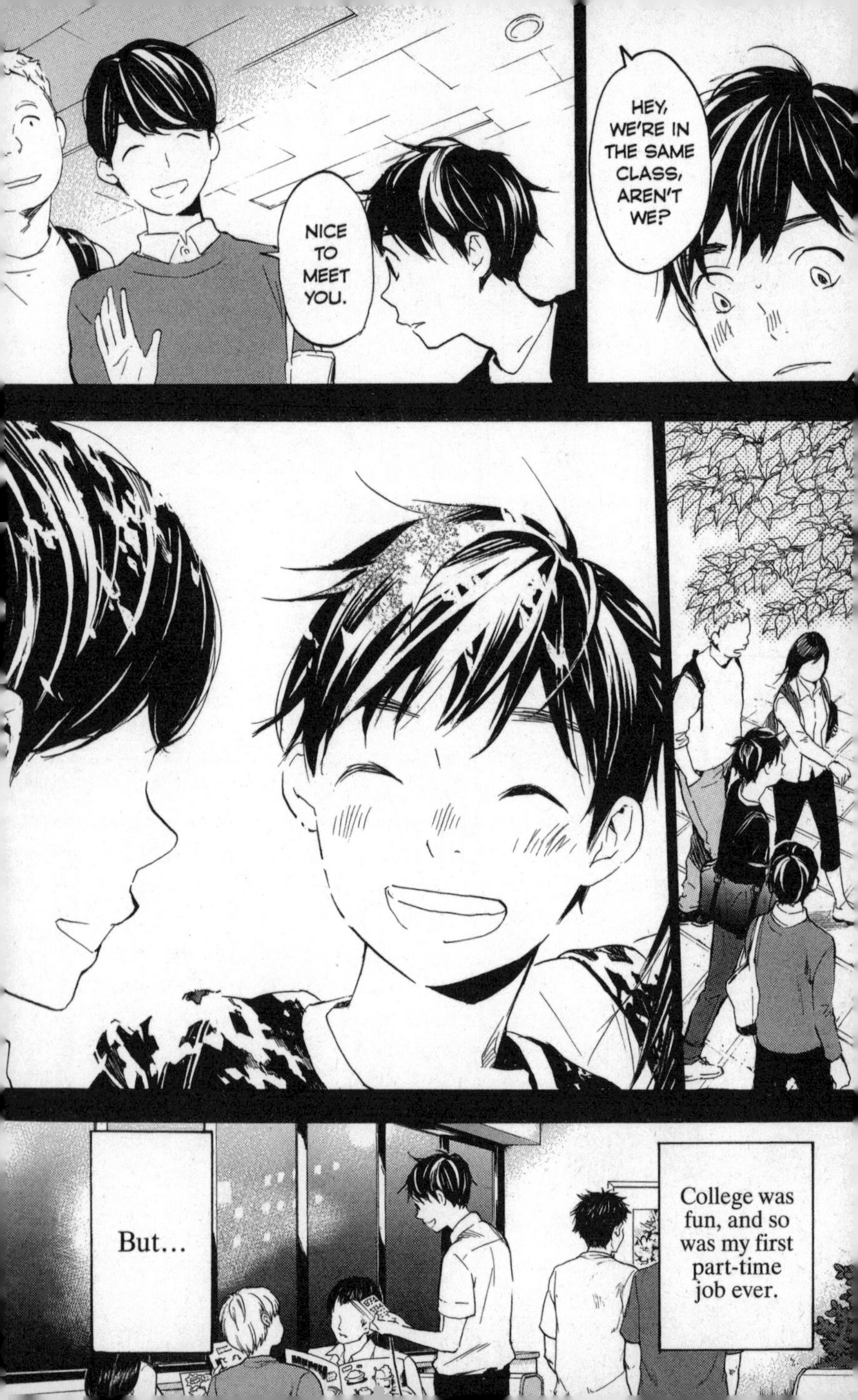
HEY, WE'RE IN THE SAME CLASS, AREN'T WE?
NICE TO MEET YOU.
College was fun, and so was my first part-time job ever.
But...

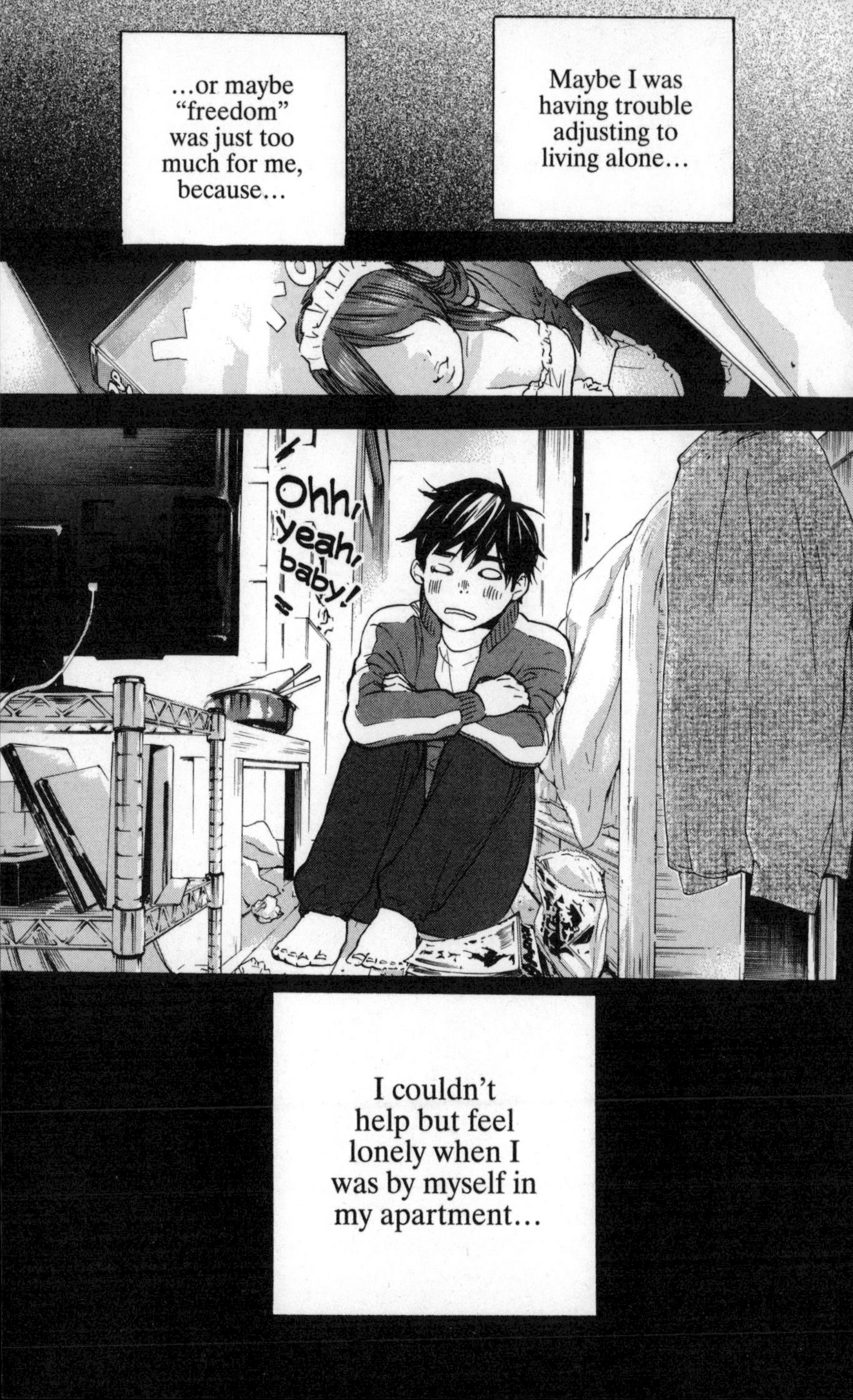
Maybe I was having trouble adjusting to living alone…
…or maybe "freedom" was just too much for me, because…
Ohh, yeah, baby!
I couldn't help but feel lonely when I was by myself in my apartment…

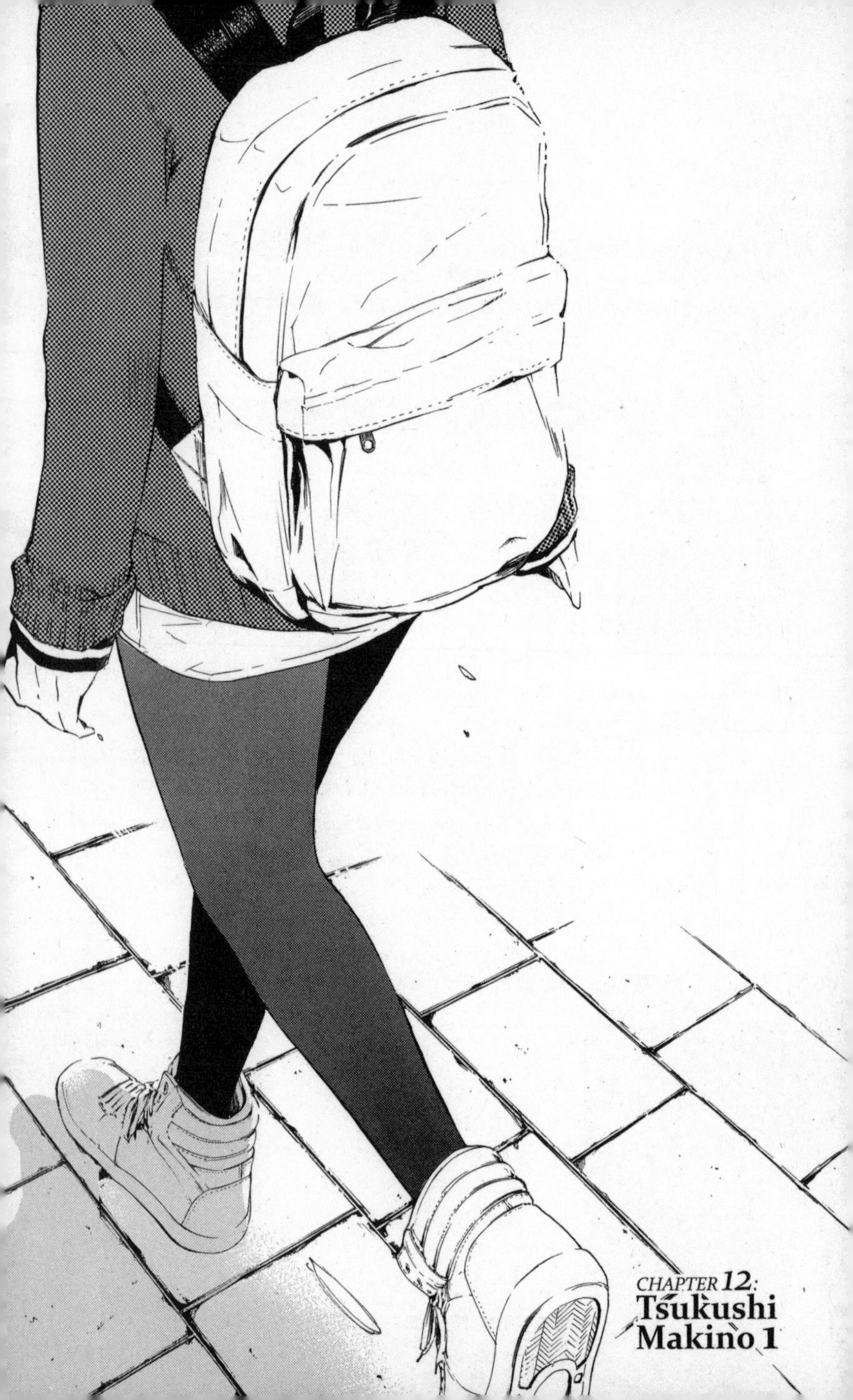
CHAPTER 12:
Tsukushi Makino 1

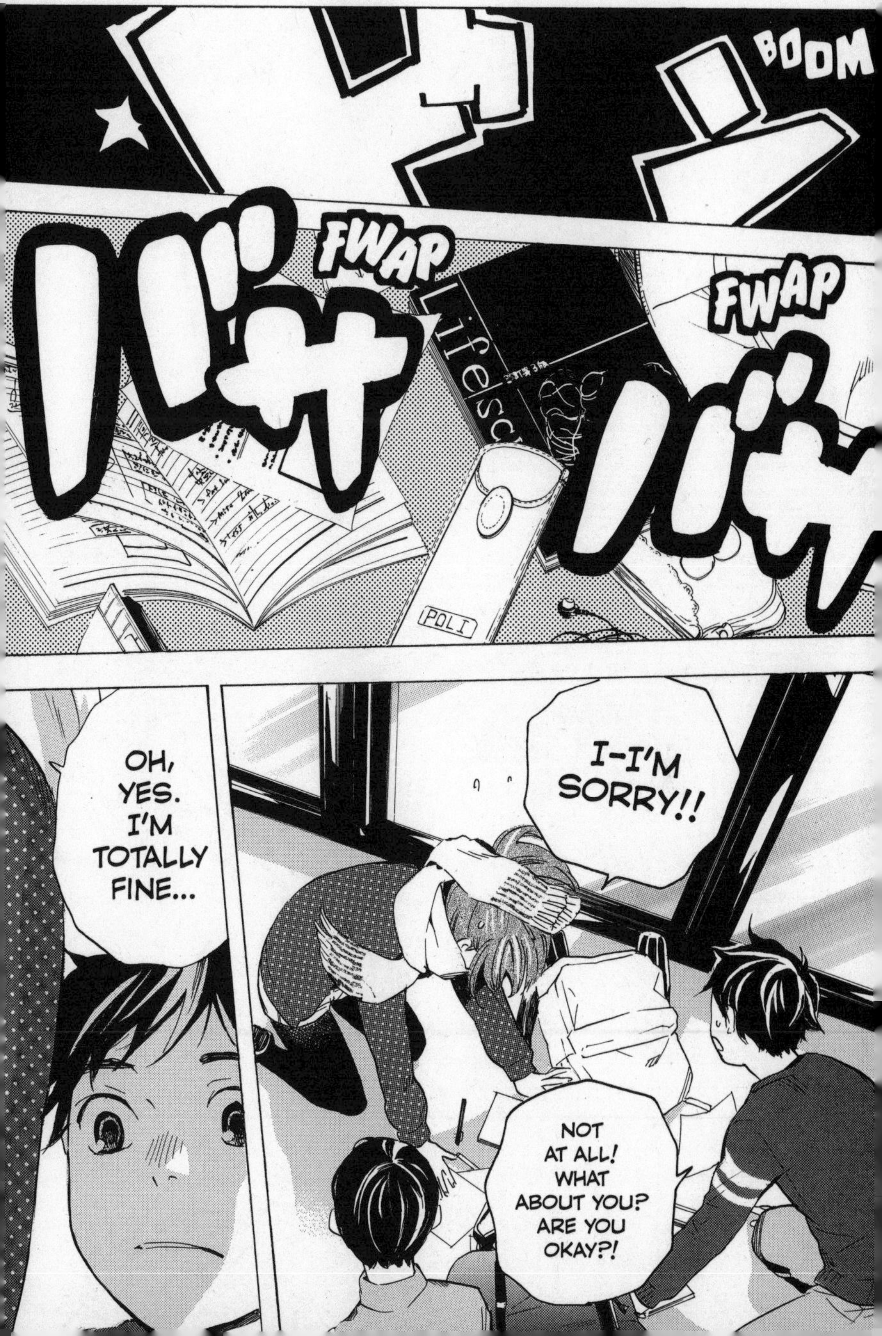
BOOM
FWAP
FWAP
POLI
I-I'M SORRY!!
NOT AT ALL! WHAT ABOUT YOU? ARE YOU OKAY?!
OH, YES. I'M TOTALLY FINE...

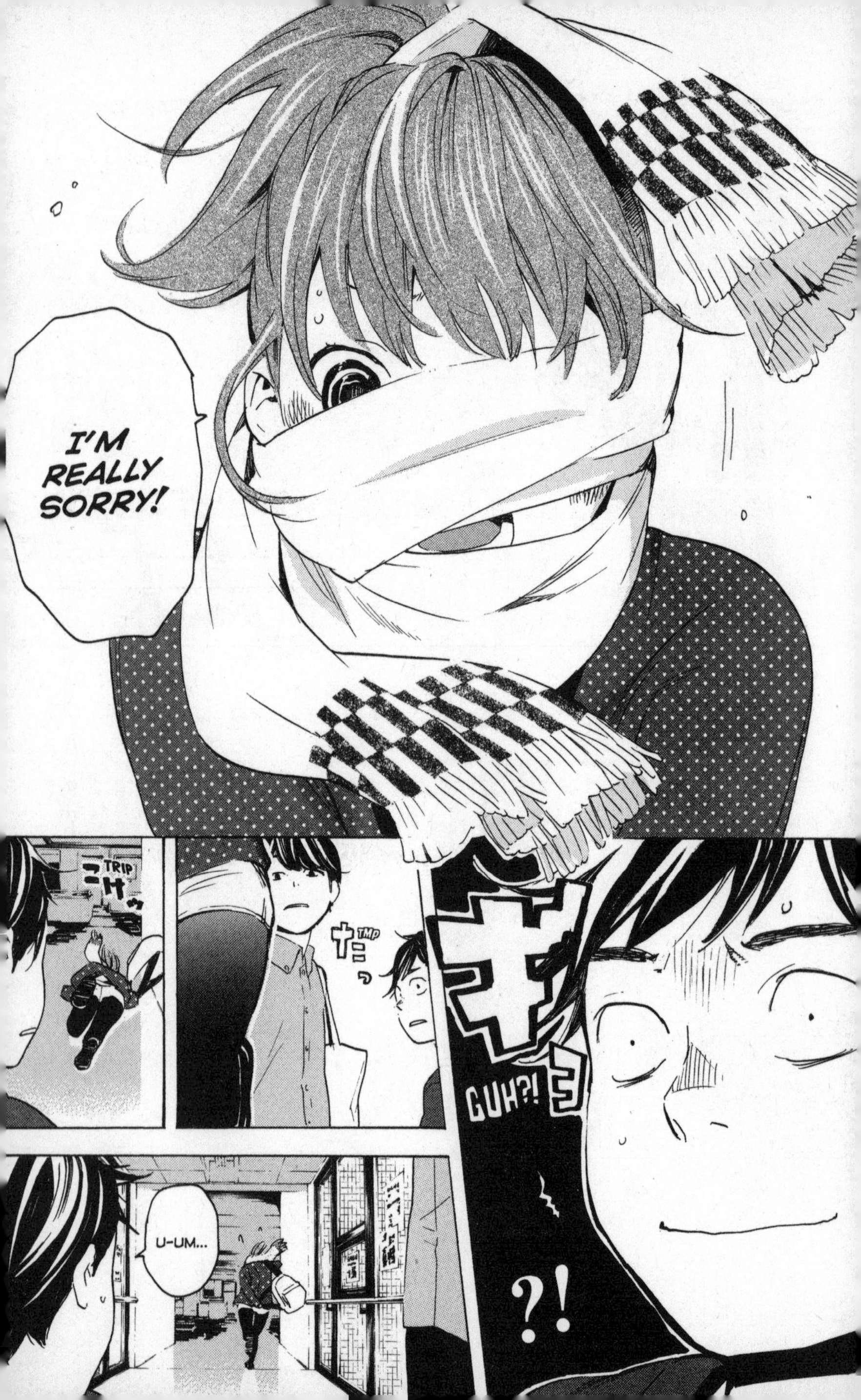
I'M REALLY SORRY!
GUH?!
?!
TMP
TRIP
U-UM...

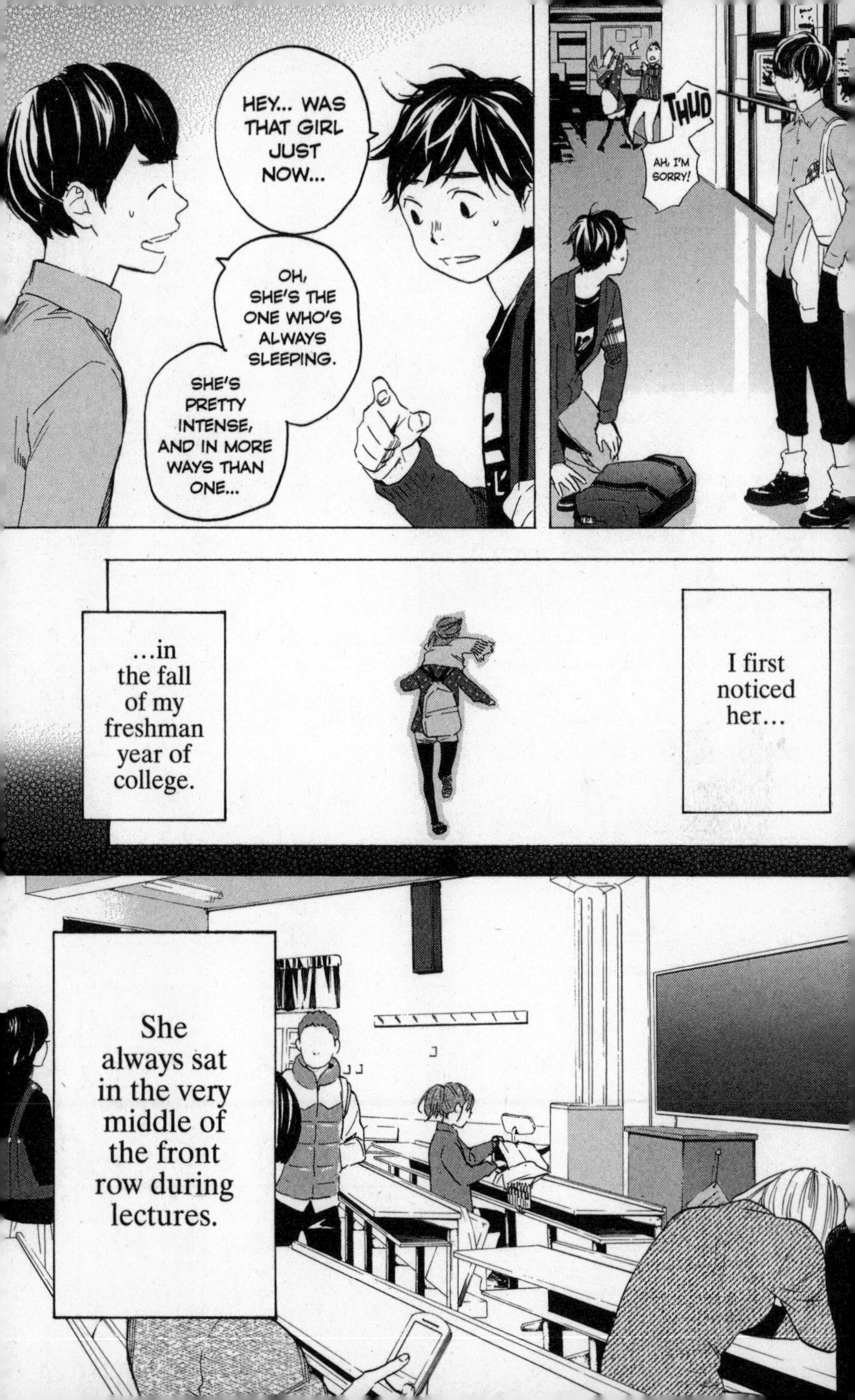
THUD
AH, I'M SORRY!
HEY... WAS THAT GIRL JUST NOW...
OH, SHE'S THE ONE WHO'S ALWAYS SLEEPING.
SHE'S PRETTY INTENSE, AND IN MORE WAYS THAN ONE...
I first noticed her…
…in the fall of my freshman year of college.
She always sat in the very middle of the front row during lectures.

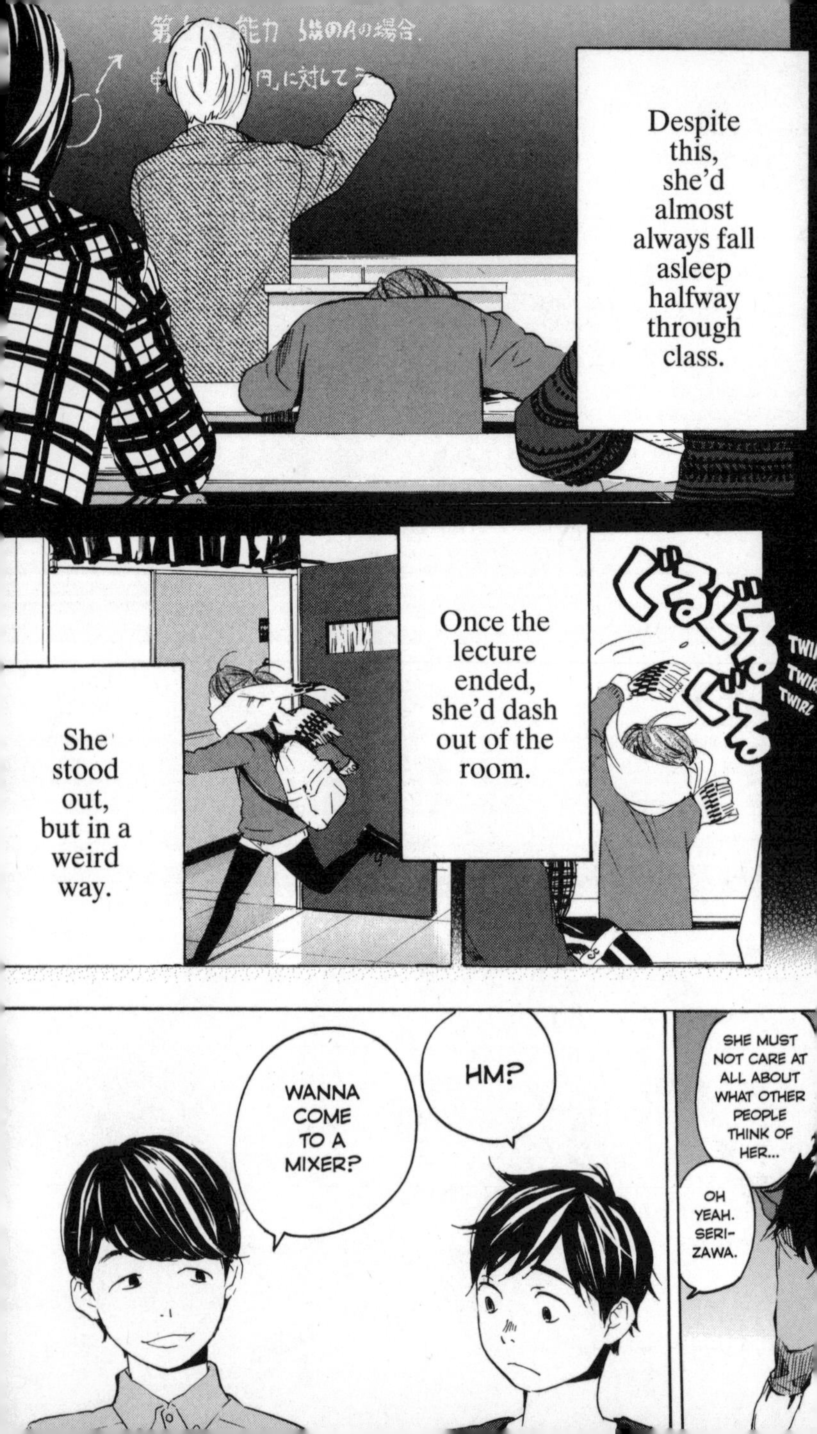
Despite this, she'd almost always fall asleep halfway through class.
ぐるぐるぐる
TWIRL
Once the lecture ended, she'd dash out of the room.
She stood out, but in a weird way.
SHE MUST NOT CARE AT ALL ABOUT WHAT OTHER PEOPLE THINK OF HER...
OH YEAH. SERI-ZAWA.
HM?
WANNA COME TO A MIXER?

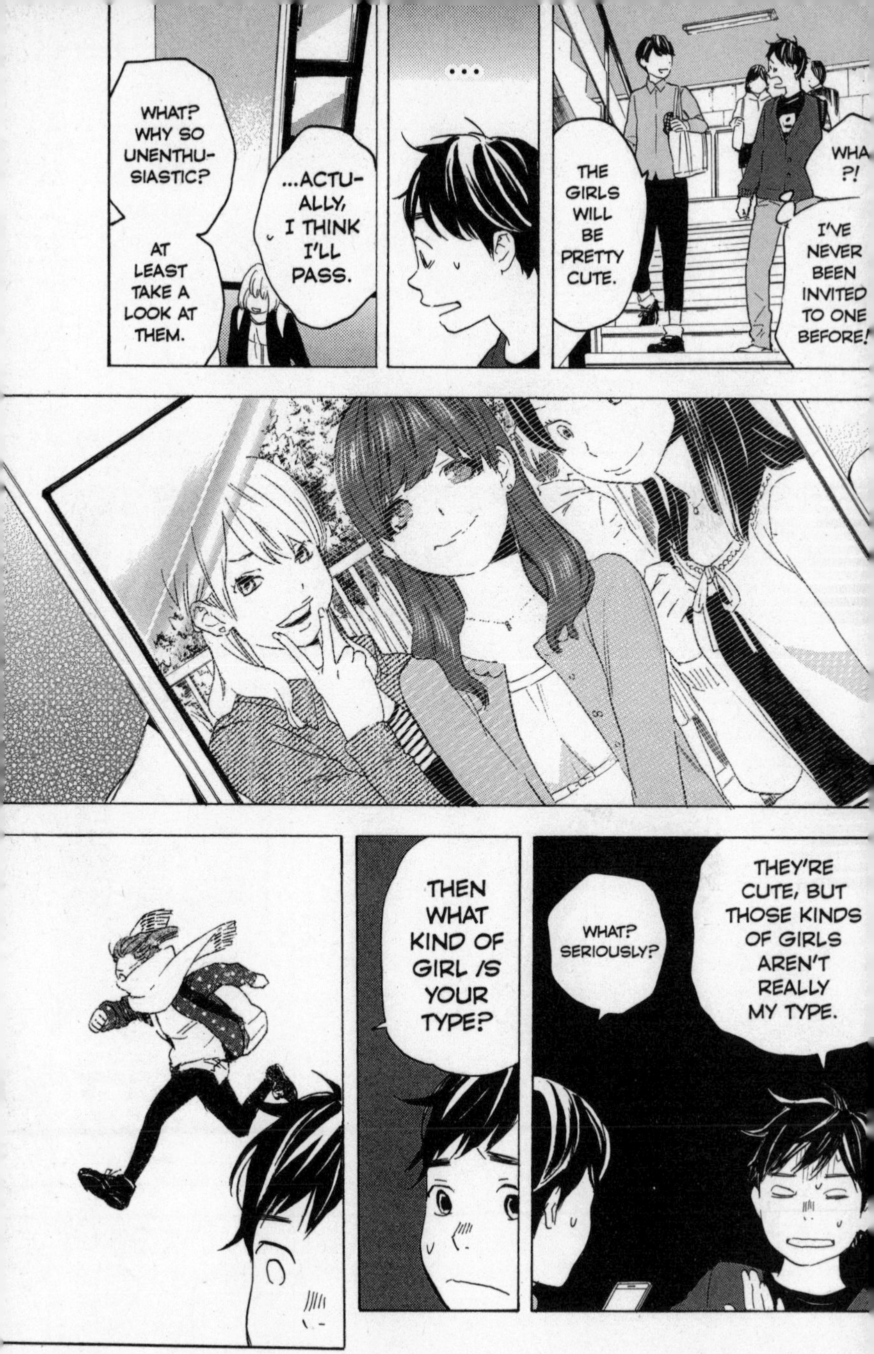
WHA ?!
I'VE NEVER BEEN INVITED TO ONE BEFORE!
THE GIRLS WILL BE PRETTY CUTE.
...
...ACTU-ALLY, I THINK I'LL PASS.
WHAT? WHY SO UNENTHU-SIASTIC?
AT LEAST TAKE A LOOK AT THEM.
THEY'RE CUTE, BUT THOSE KINDS OF GIRLS AREN'T REALLY MY TYPE.
WHAT? SERIOUSLY?
THEN WHAT KIND OF GIRL IS YOUR TYPE?

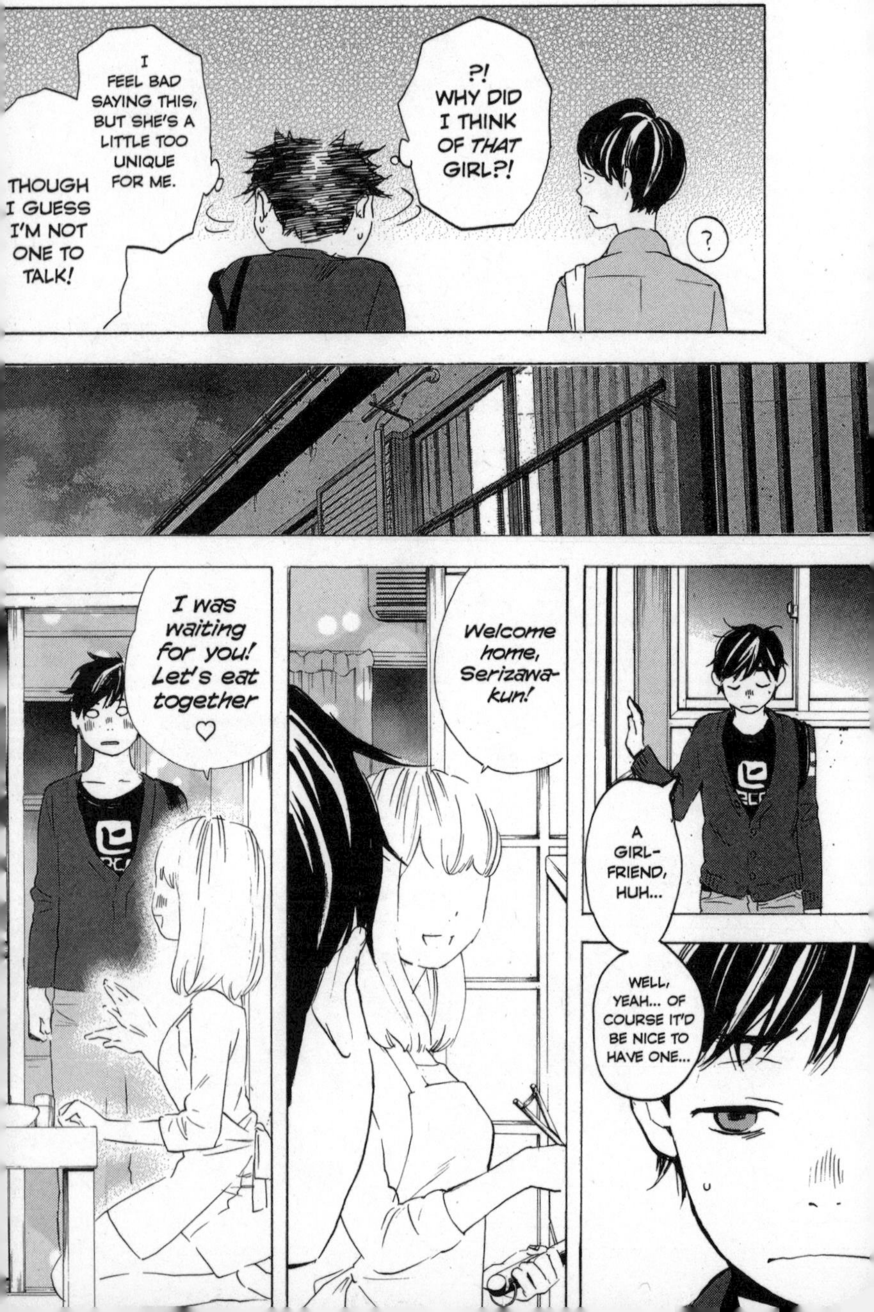
?
?! WHY DID I THINK OF *THAT* GIRL?!
I FEEL BAD SAYING THIS, BUT SHE'S A LITTLE TOO UNIQUE FOR ME.
THOUGH I GUESS I'M NOT ONE TO TALK!
A GIRL-FRIEND, HUH...
WELL, YEAH... OF COURSE IT'D BE NICE TO HAVE ONE...
Welcome home, Serizawa-kun!
I was waiting for you! Let's eat together ♡

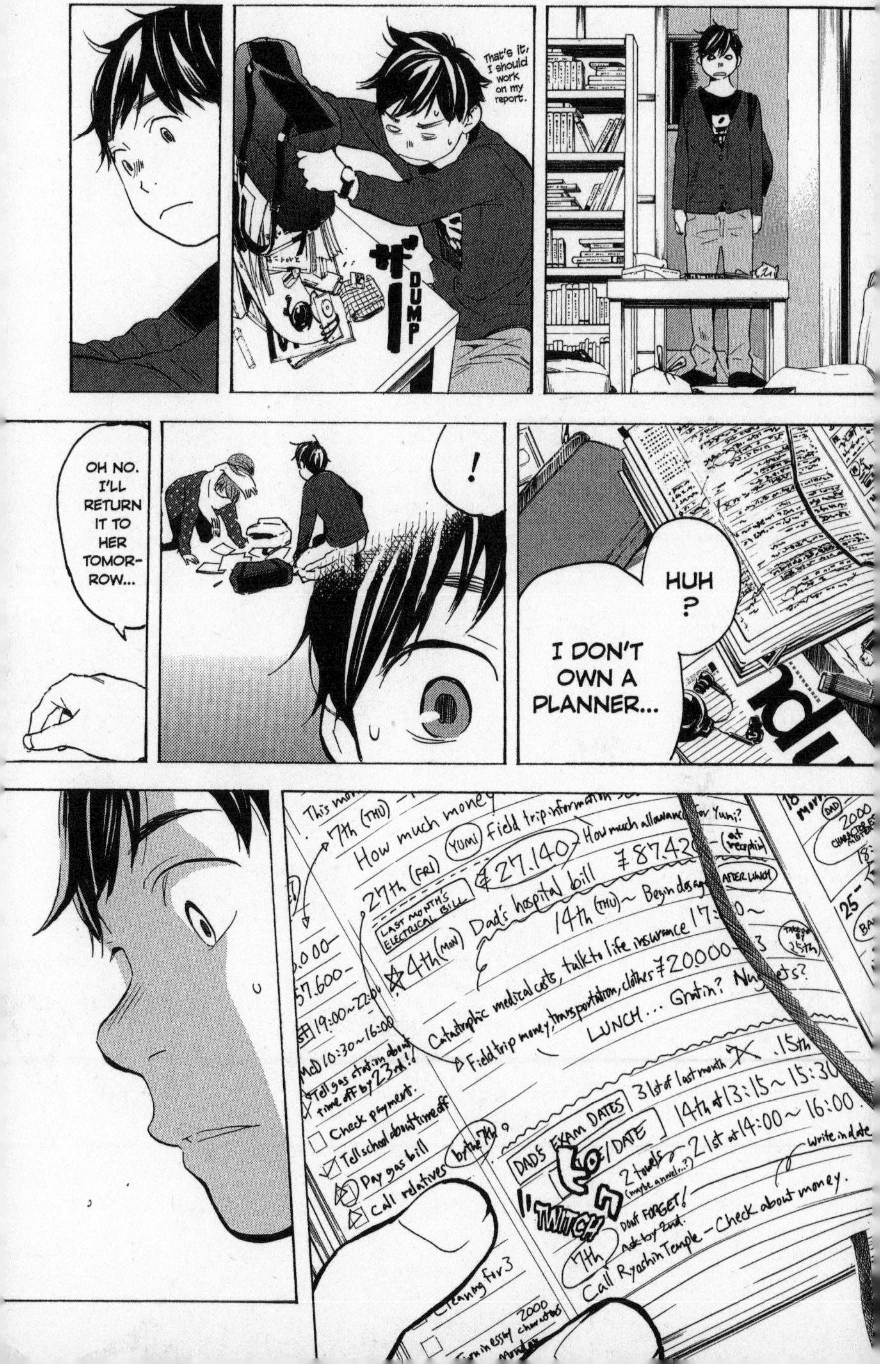
That's it, I should work on my report.
DUMP
HUH?
I DON'T OWN A PLANNER...
!
OH NO. I'LL RETURN IT TO HER TOMORROW...
7th (THU) How much money
Field trip information
How much allowance for Yumi?
27th (FRI) (YUMI) ¥27,140 ¥87,42
AFTER LUNCH
LAST MONTH'S ELECTRICAL BILL
4th (MON) Dad's hospital bill
14th (THU) ~ Begin dosage
Catastrophic medical costs, talk to life insurance
Field trip money, transportation, clothes ¥20,000
LUNCH... Gratin? Nuggets?
DAD'S EXAM DATES
31st of last month
14th at 13:15 ~ 15:30
21st at 14:00 ~ 16:00
DATE
2 towels (maybe annual...?)
Write in date
DON'T FORGET! Ask by 2nd.
Call Ryoshin Temple - Check about money.
Tell gas station about time off by 23rd!
Check payment.
Tell school about time off
Pay gas bill
Call relatives by the 7th
Cleaning fir 3
TWITCH

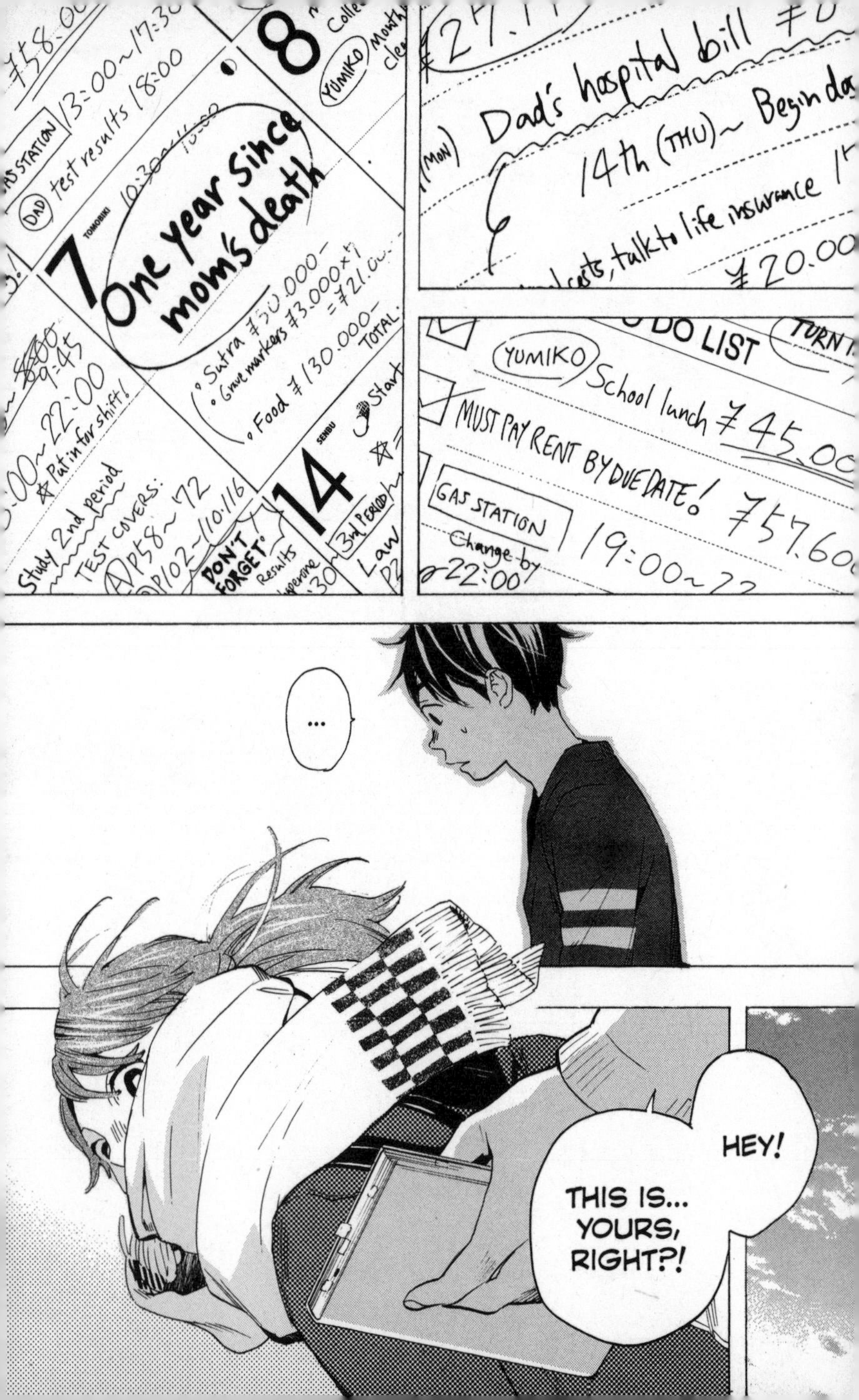
Dad's hospital bill
(MON)
14th (THU)~ Begin
talk to life insurance
DO LIST
YUMIKO
School lunch
MUST PAY RENT BY DUE DATE!
GAS STATION
19:00~
Change by 22:00
13:00~17:30
GAS STATION
DAD test results 18:00
8
YUMIKO
7
TOMOBIKI
One year since mom's death
Sutra ¥50.000–
Grave markers ¥3.000×7
Food ¥130.000–
TOTAL
9:45
22:00
Put in for shift!
Study 2nd period
TEST COVERS:
P58~72
P102~110.116
DON'T FORGET!
Results
14
SENBU
Start
3rd PERIOD
Law
...
HEY!
THIS IS... YOURS, RIGHT?!

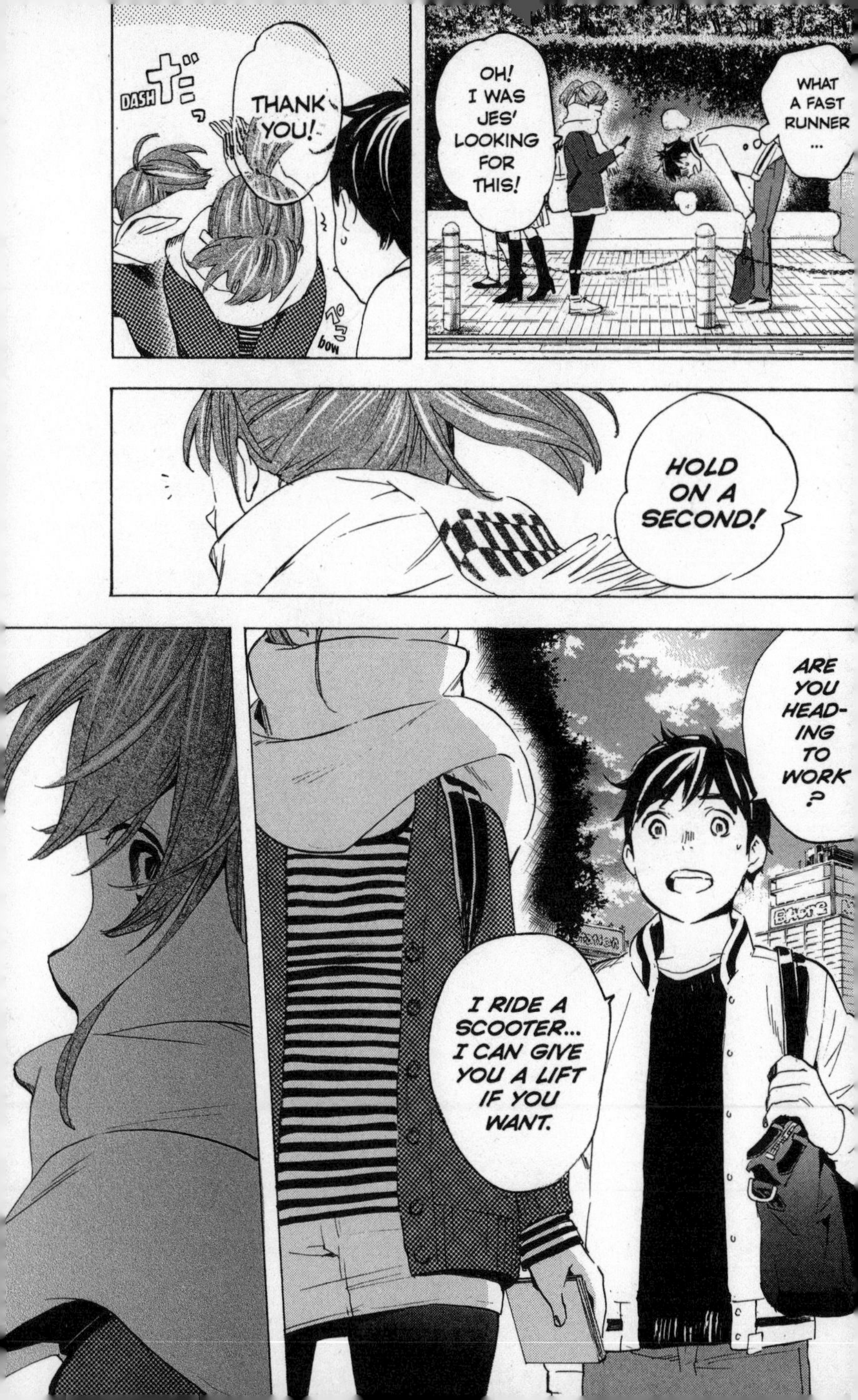
WHAT A FAST RUNNER ...
OH! I WAS JES' LOOKING FOR THIS!
THANK YOU!
DASH
bow
HOLD ON A SECOND!
ARE YOU HEADING TO WORK ?
I RIDE A SCOOTER... I CAN GIVE YOU A LIFT IF YOU WANT.

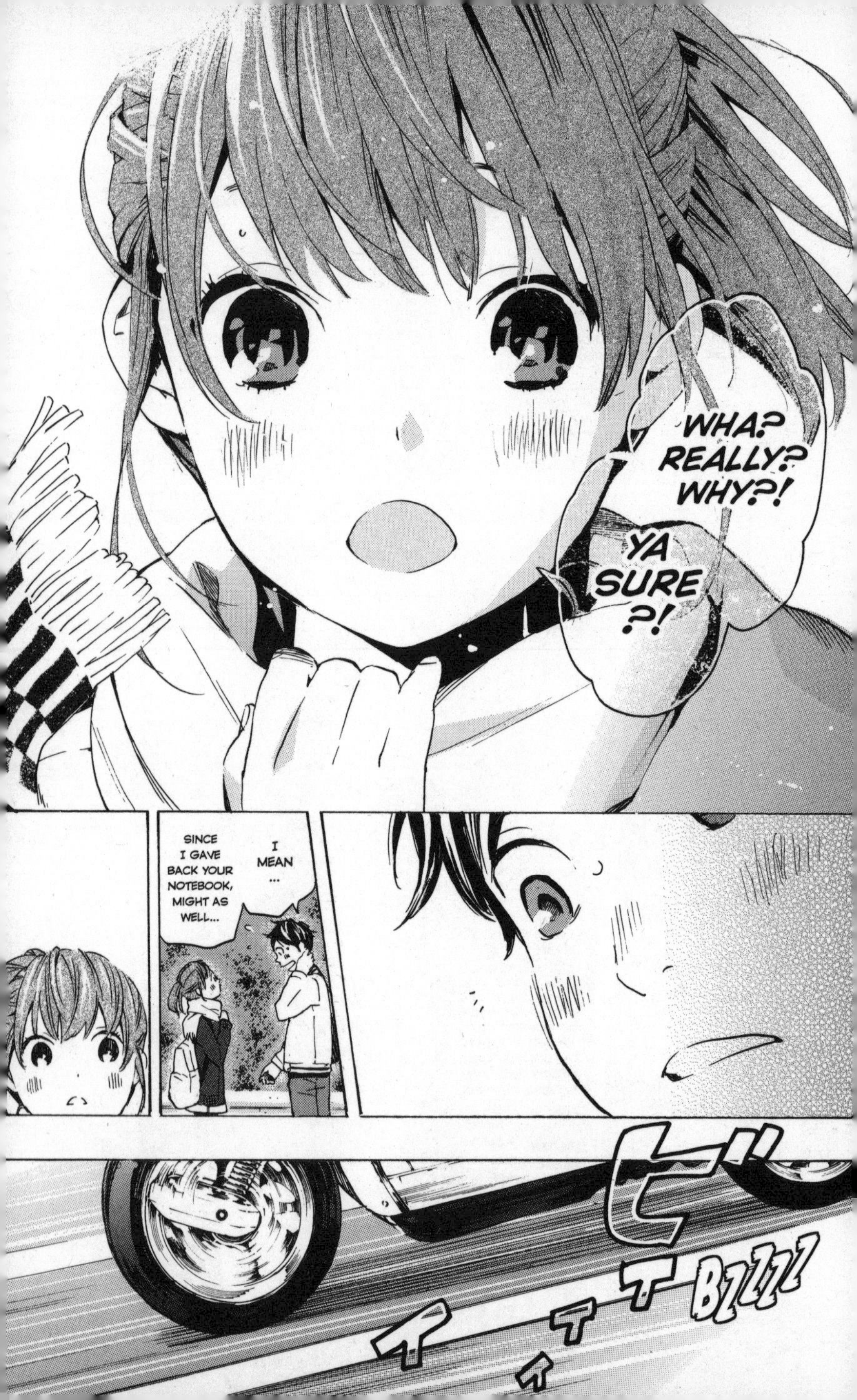
WHA? REALLY? WHY?!
YA SURE?!
I MEAN ...
SINCE I GAVE BACK YOUR NOTEBOOK, MIGHT AS WELL...
BZZZZ

NOTE: Riding a motorbike without a helmet is forbidden by Japanese traffic l

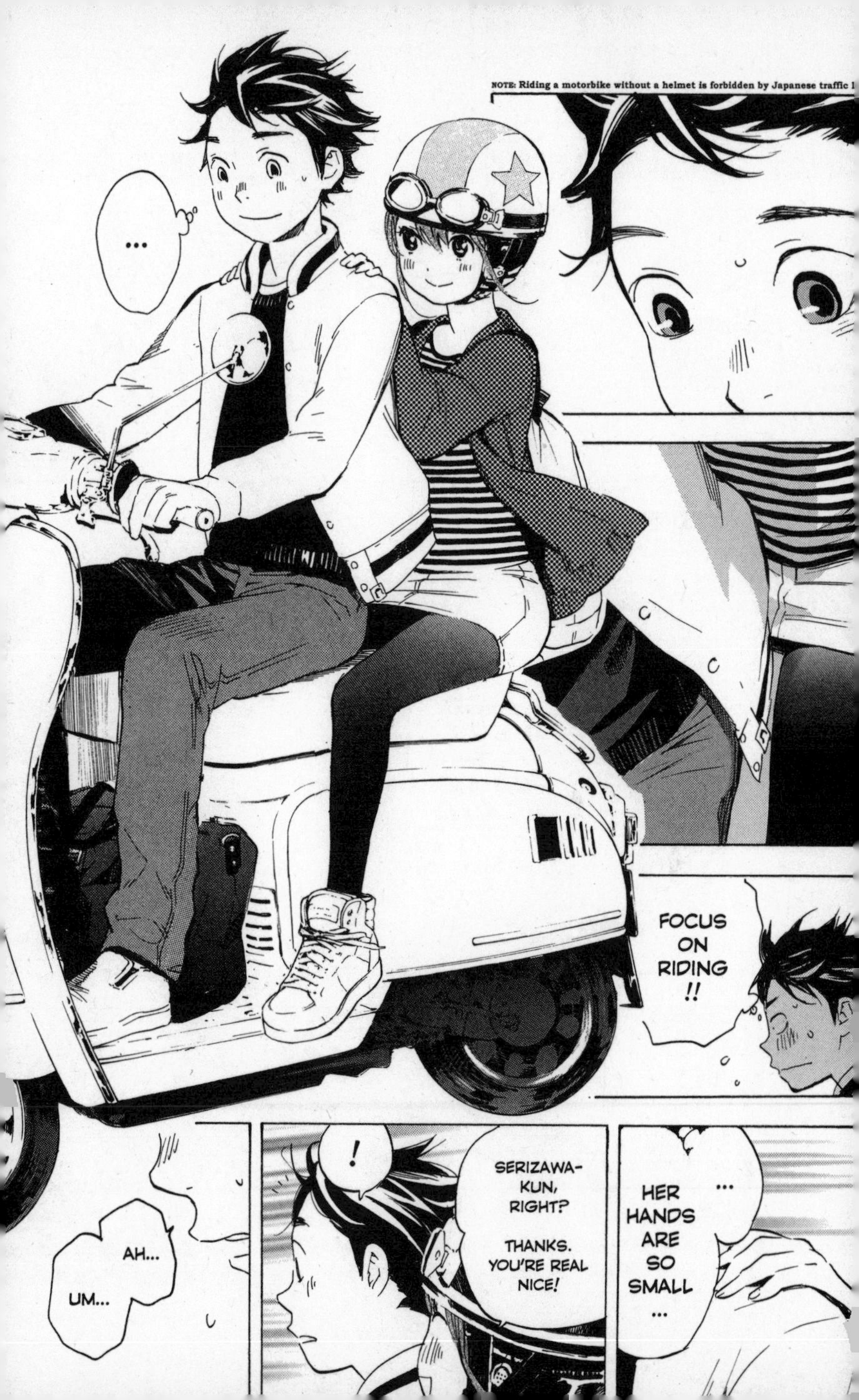
FOCUS ON RIDING !!
...
...
HER HANDS ARE SO SMALL ...
SERIZAWA-KUN, RIGHT? THANKS. YOU'RE REAL NICE!
!
AH... UM...

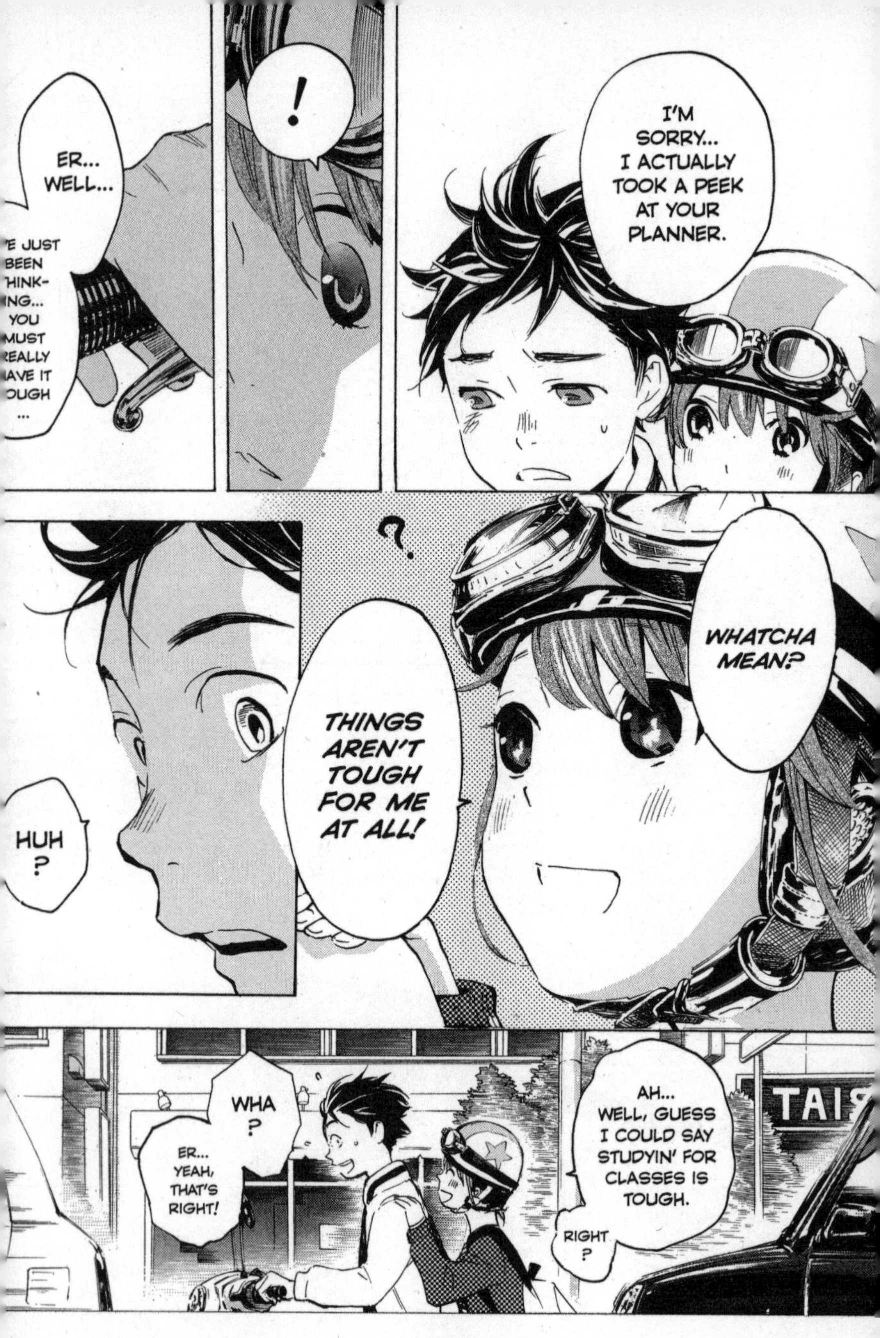
I'M SORRY... I ACTUALLY TOOK A PEEK AT YOUR PLANNER.
!
ER... WELL...
'E JUST BEEN THINK-NG... YOU MUST EALLY AVE IT OUGH ...
?
WHATCHA MEAN?
THINGS AREN'T TOUGH FOR ME AT ALL!
HUH ?
AH... WELL, GUESS I COULD SAY STUDYIN' FOR CLASSES IS TOUGH.
RIGHT ?
WHA ?
ER... YEAH, THAT'S RIGHT!

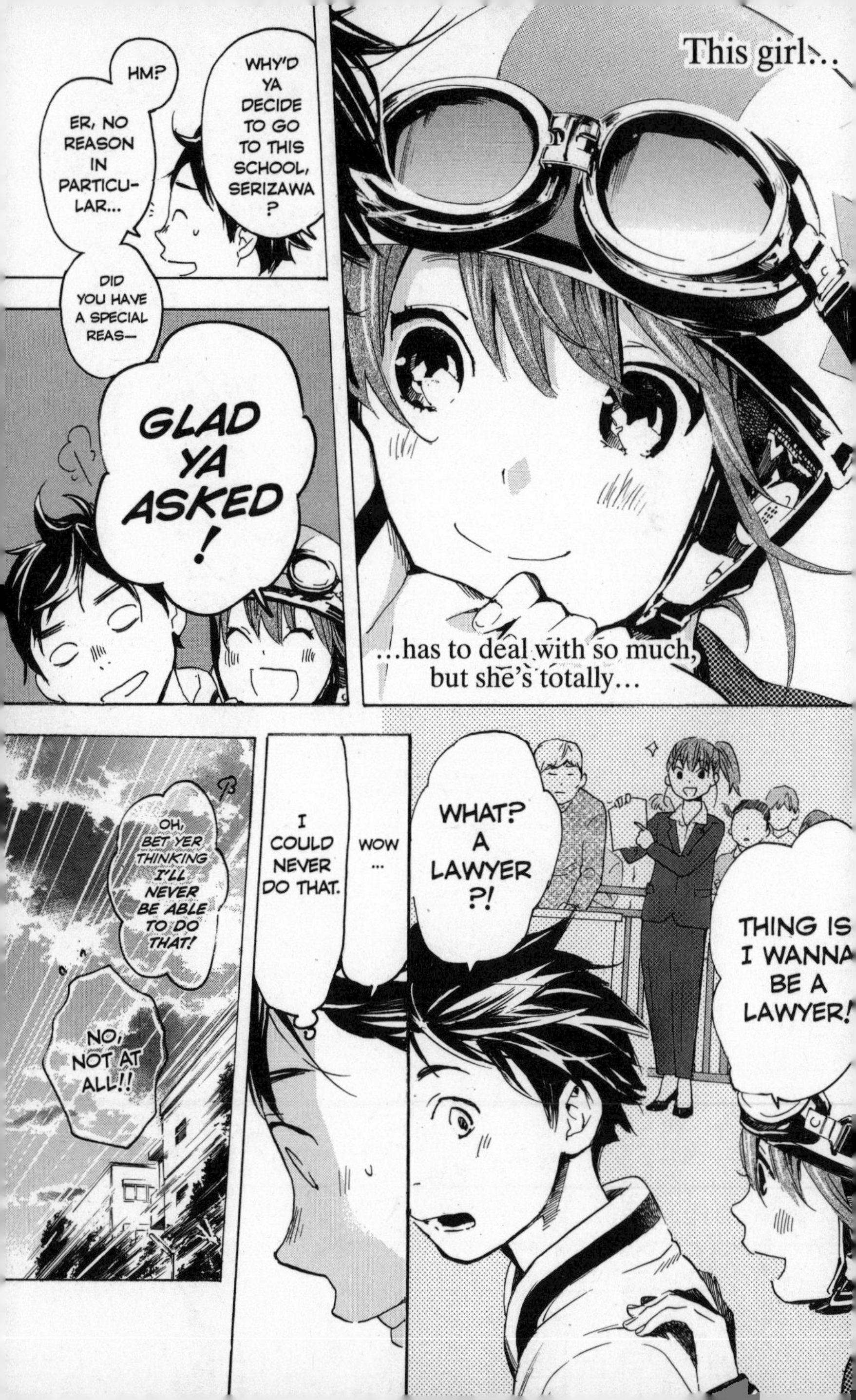
This girl...
...has to deal with so much, but she's totally...
WHY'D YA DECIDE TO GO TO THIS SCHOOL, SERIZAWA?
HM?
ER, NO REASON IN PARTICU-LAR...
DID YOU HAVE A SPECIAL REAS—
GLAD YA ASKED!
THING IS I WANNA BE A LAWYER!
WHAT? A LAWYER?!
WOW...
I COULD NEVER DO THAT.
OH, BET YER THINKING I'LL NEVER BE ABLE TO DO THAT!
NO, NOT AT ALL!!

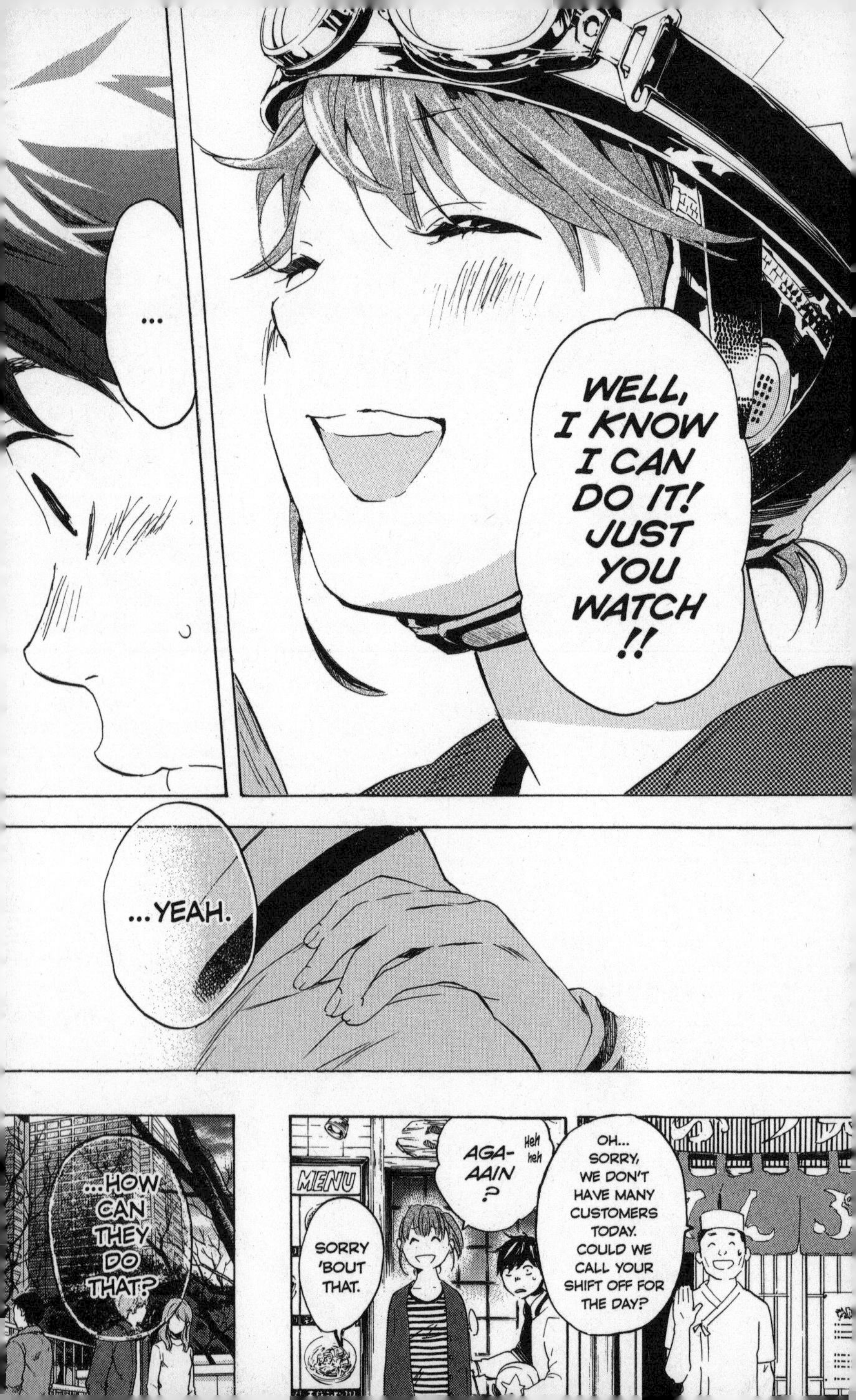
WELL, I KNOW I CAN DO IT! JUST YOU WATCH!!
...
...YEAH.
OH... SORRY, WE DON'T HAVE MANY CUSTOMERS TODAY. COULD WE CALL YOUR SHIFT OFF FOR THE DAY?
AGA-AAIN?
Heh heh
SORRY 'BOUT THAT.
MENU
...HOW CAN THEY DO THAT?

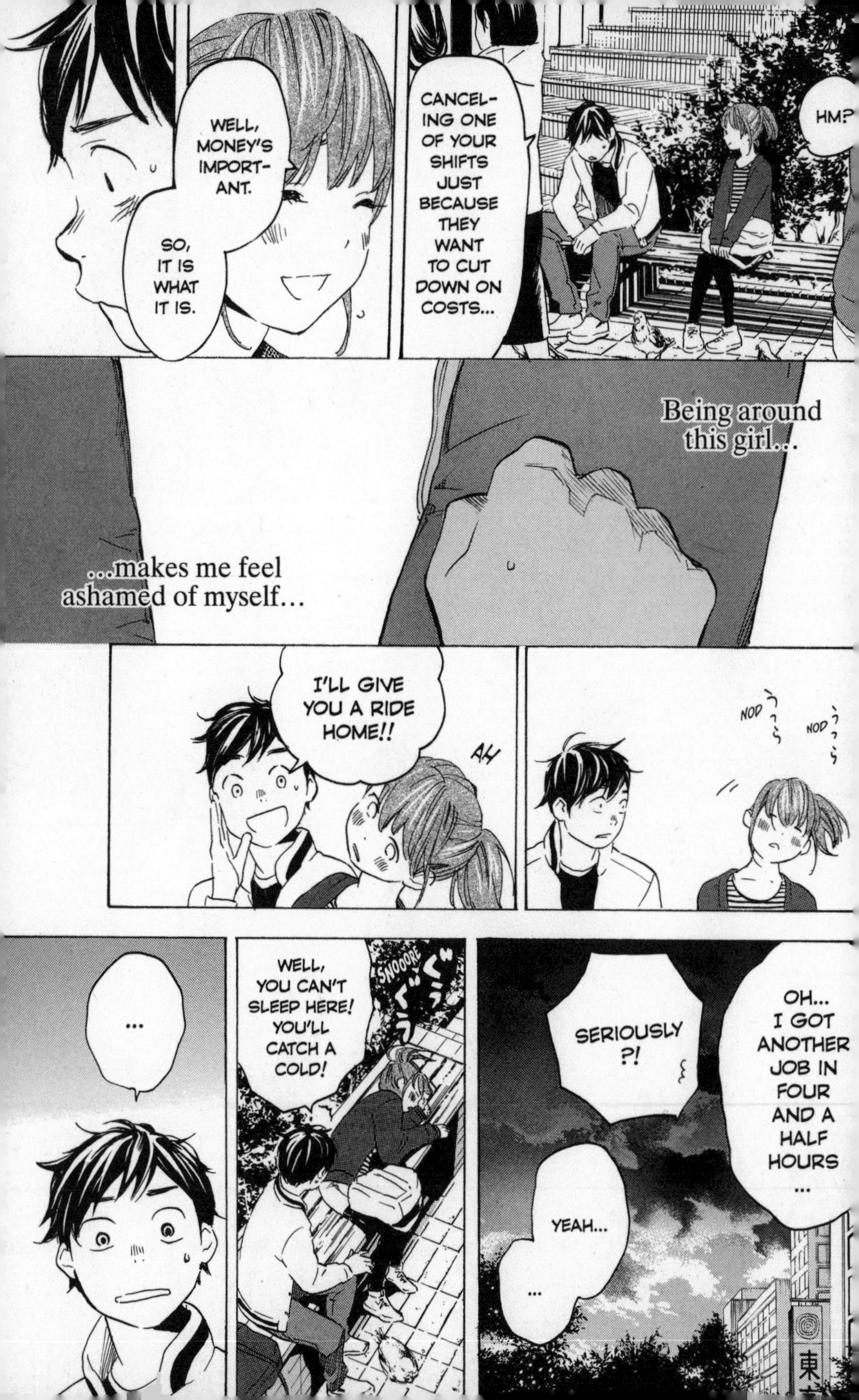
HM?
CANCEL-ING ONE OF YOUR SHIFTS JUST BECAUSE THEY WANT TO CUT DOWN ON COSTS...
WELL, MONEY'S IMPORT-ANT.
SO, IT IS WHAT IT IS.
Being around this girl...
...makes me feel ashamed of myself...
NOD
NOD
I'LL GIVE YOU A RIDE HOME!!
AH
OH... I GOT ANOTHER JOB IN FOUR AND A HALF HOURS ...
SERIOUSLY ?!
YEAH... ...
SNOOORE
WELL, YOU CAN'T SLEEP HERE! YOU'LL CATCH A COLD!
...

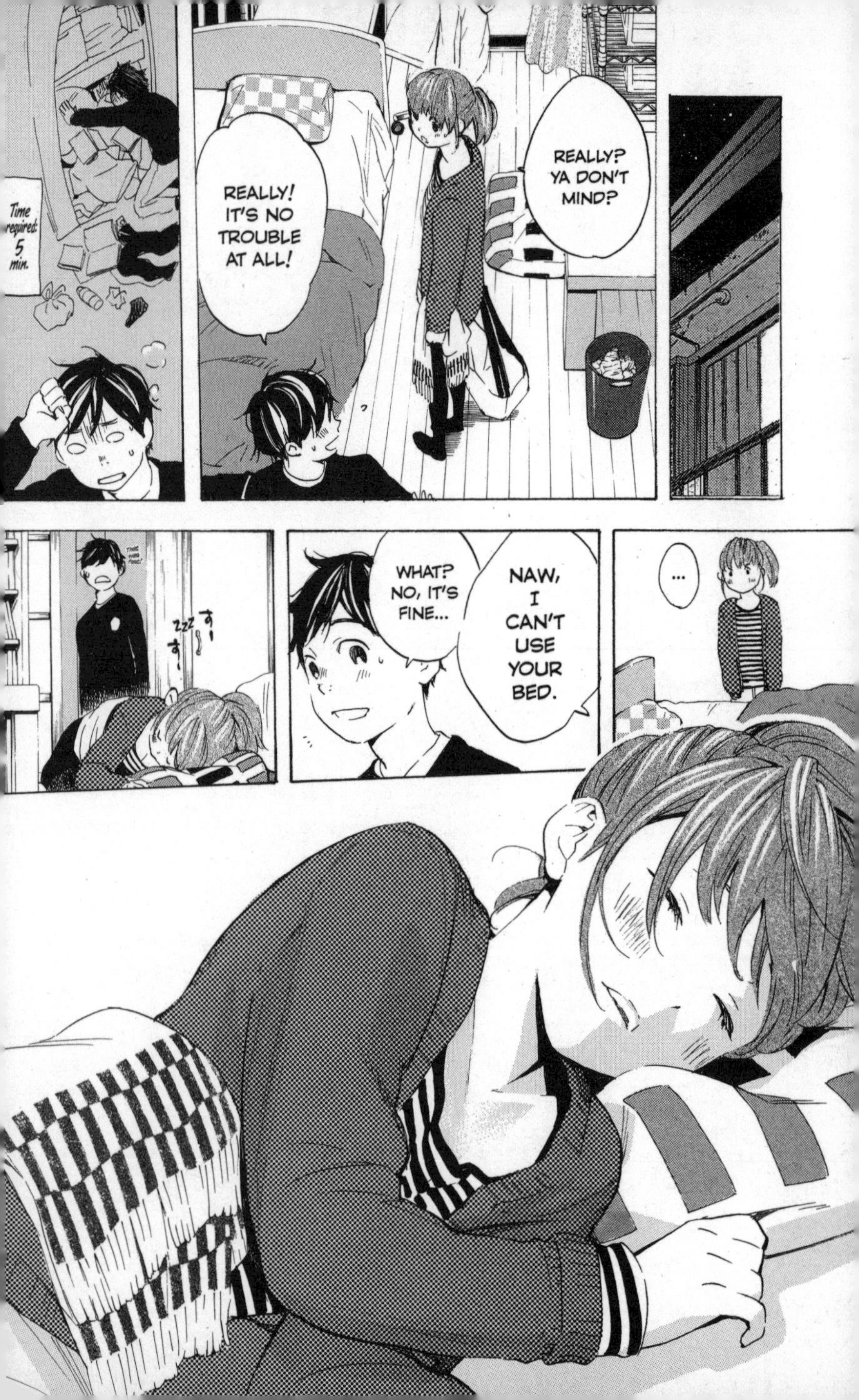
REALLY? YA DON'T MIND?
REALLY! IT'S NO TROUBLE AT ALL!
Time required: 5 min.
...
NAW, I CAN'T USE YOUR BED.
WHAT? NO, IT'S FINE...
ZZZ

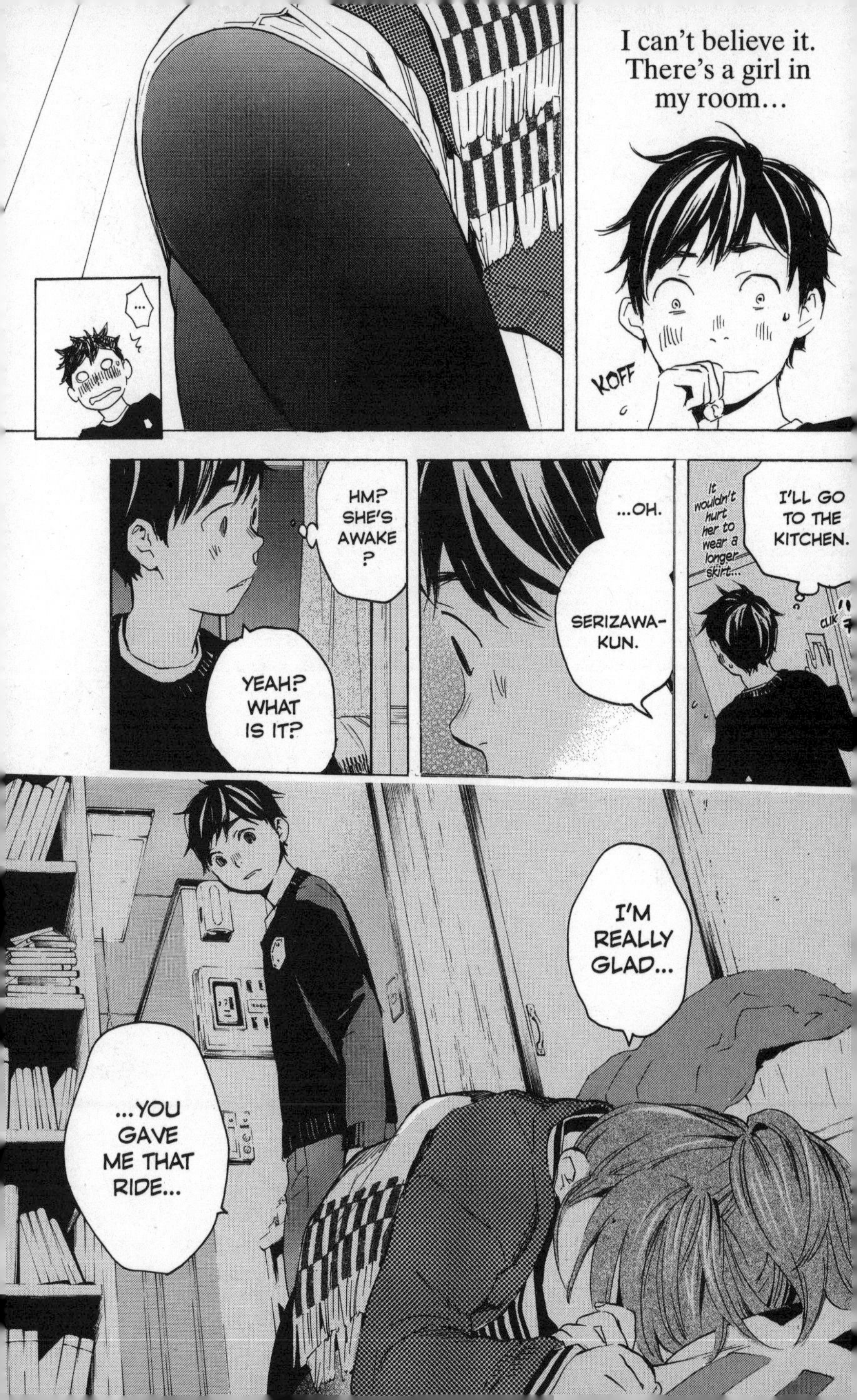
I can't believe it. There's a girl in my room…
KOFF
...
I'LL GO TO THE KITCHEN.
It wouldn't hurt her to wear a longer skirt...
CLIK
...OH.
SERIZAWA-KUN.
HM? SHE'S AWAKE?
YEAH? WHAT IS IT?
I'M REALLY GLAD...
...YOU GAVE ME THAT RIDE...

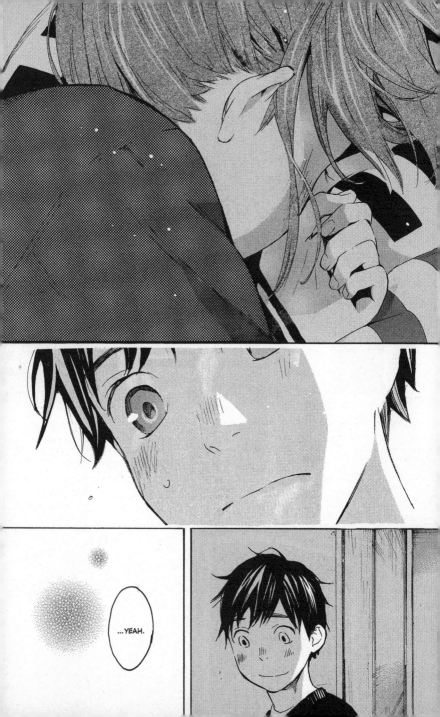

...YEAH.

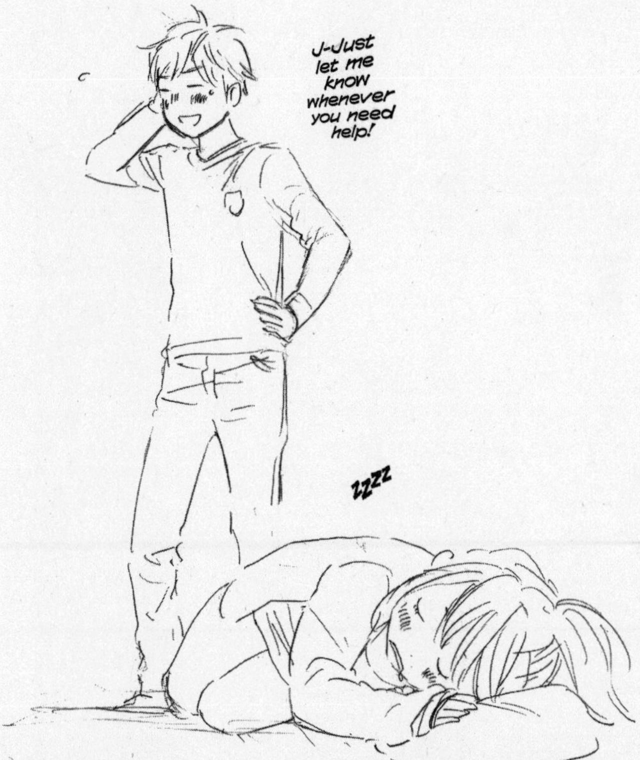
J-Just let me know whenever you need help!
zzzz

CHAPTER 13: Tsukushi Makino 2

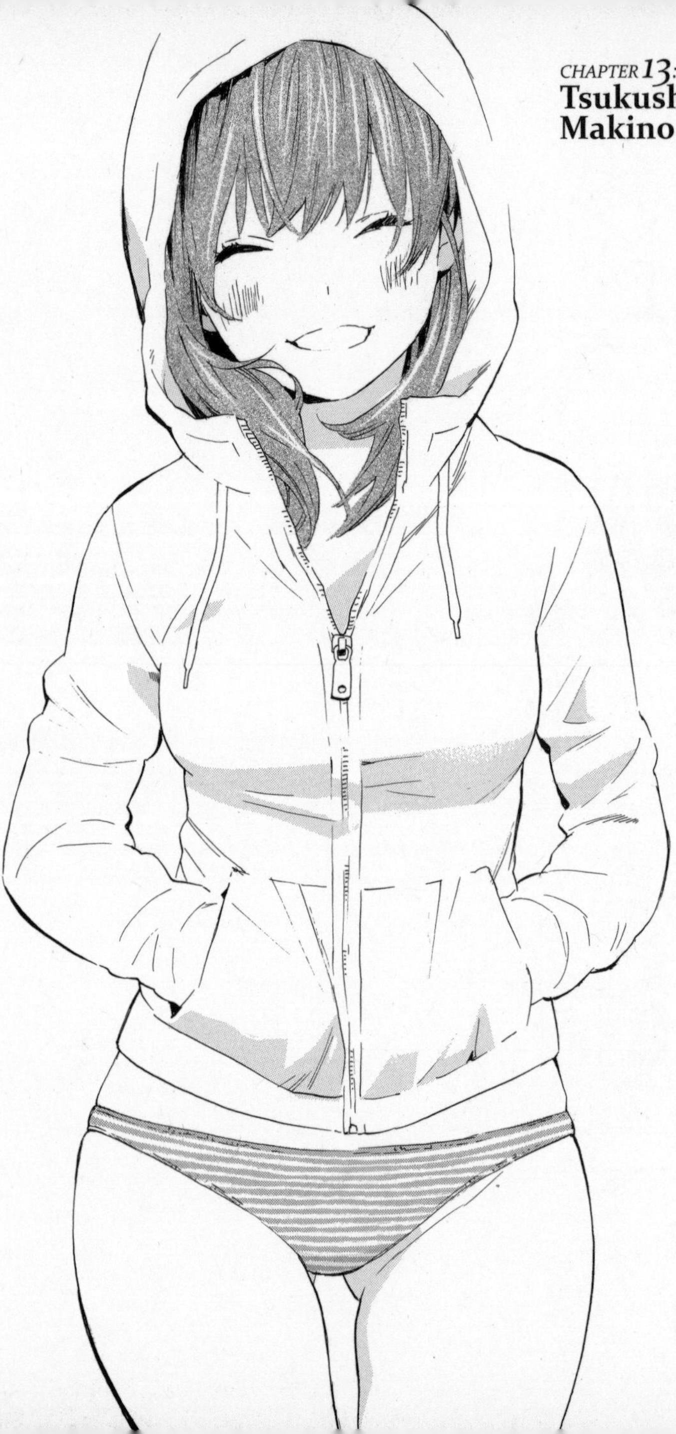

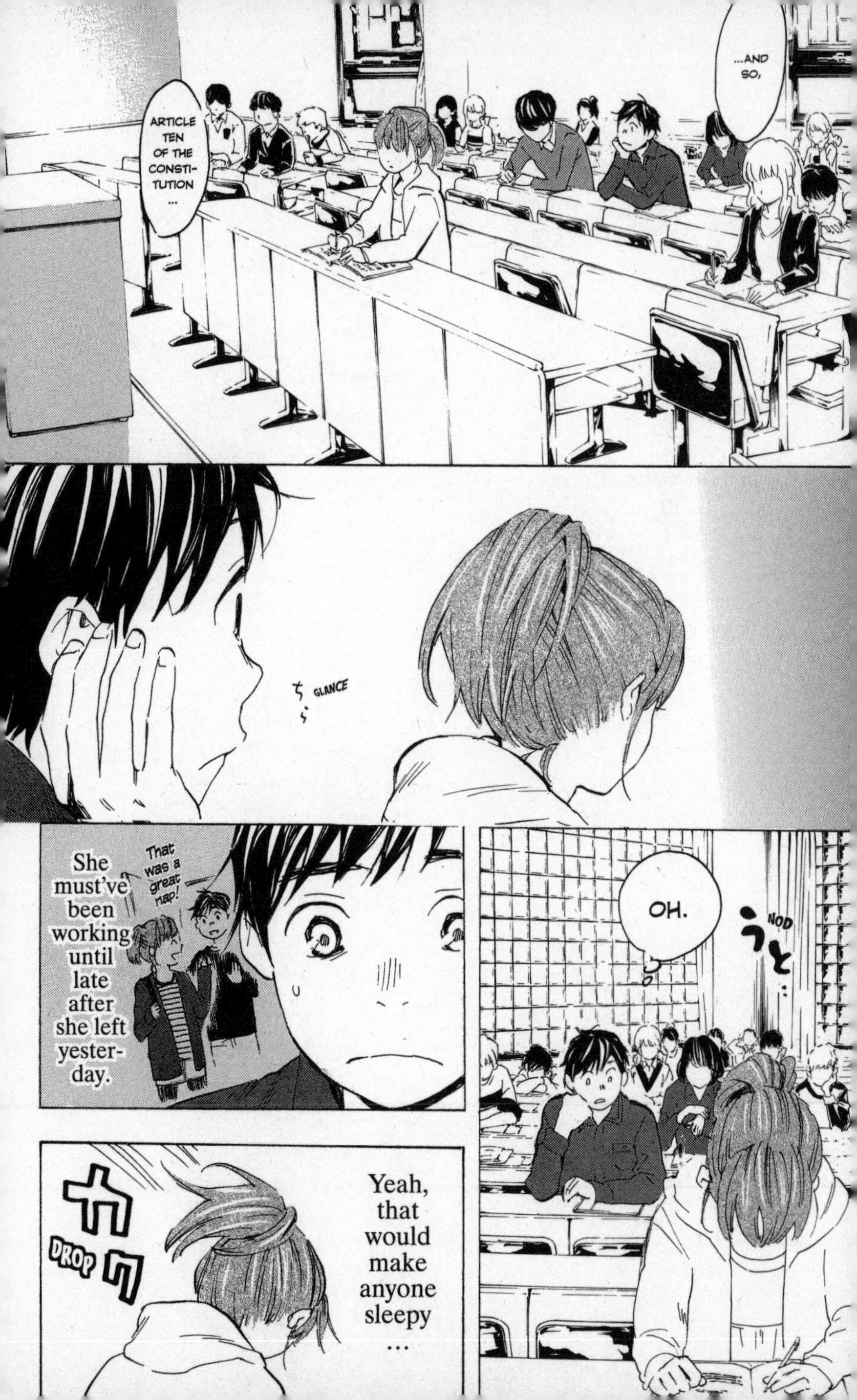
...AND SO,
ARTICLE TEN OF THE CONSTITUTION ...
ちら
GLANCE
OH.
うと
NOD
That was a great nap!
She must've been working until late after she left yesterday.
DROP
Yeah, that would make anyone sleepy ...

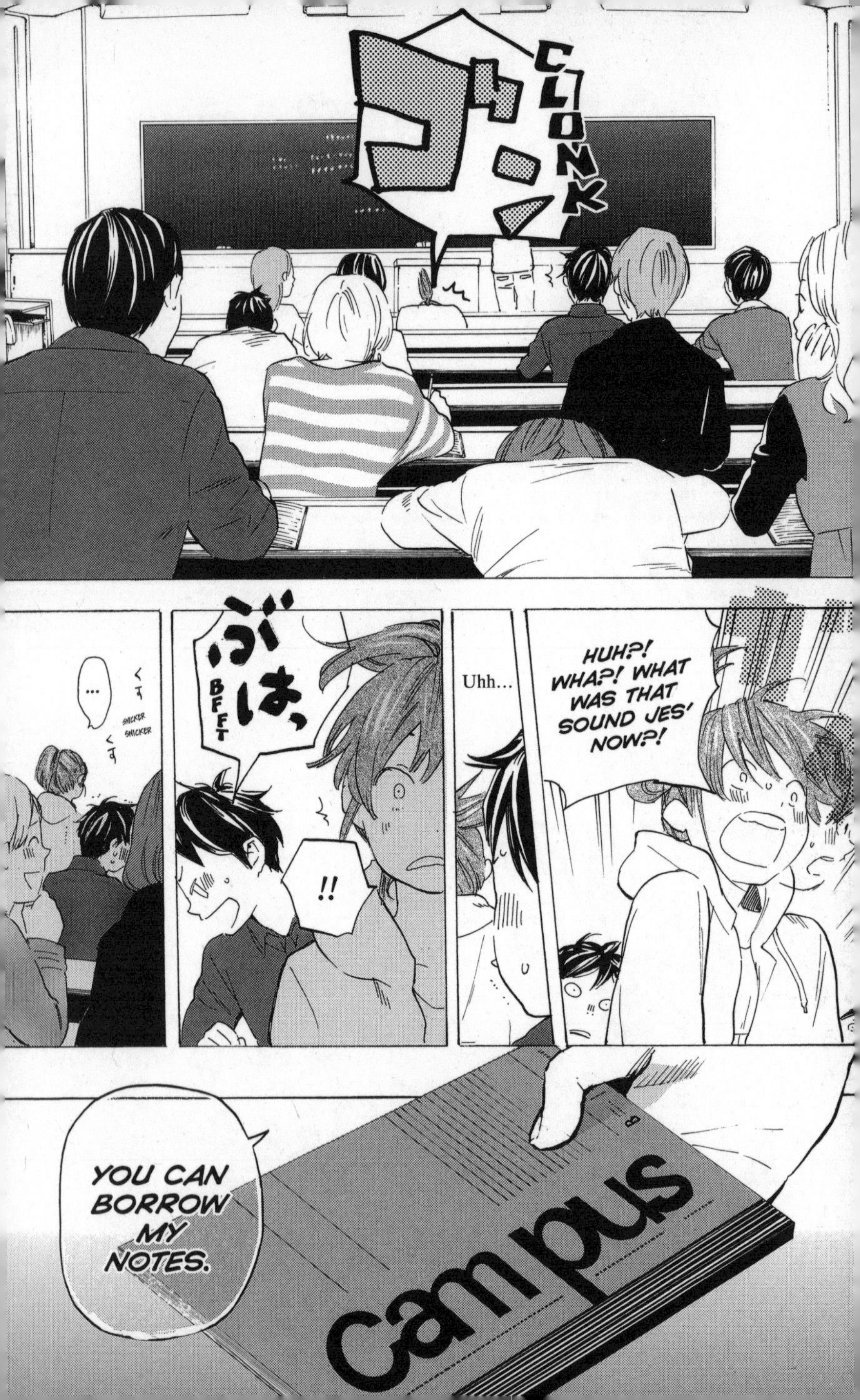
CLONK
HUH?! WHA?! WHAT WAS THAT SOUND JES' NOW?!
Uhh…
ぶは、
BFFT
!!
…
くす くす
SNICKER SNICKER
YOU CAN BORROW MY NOTES.
Campus

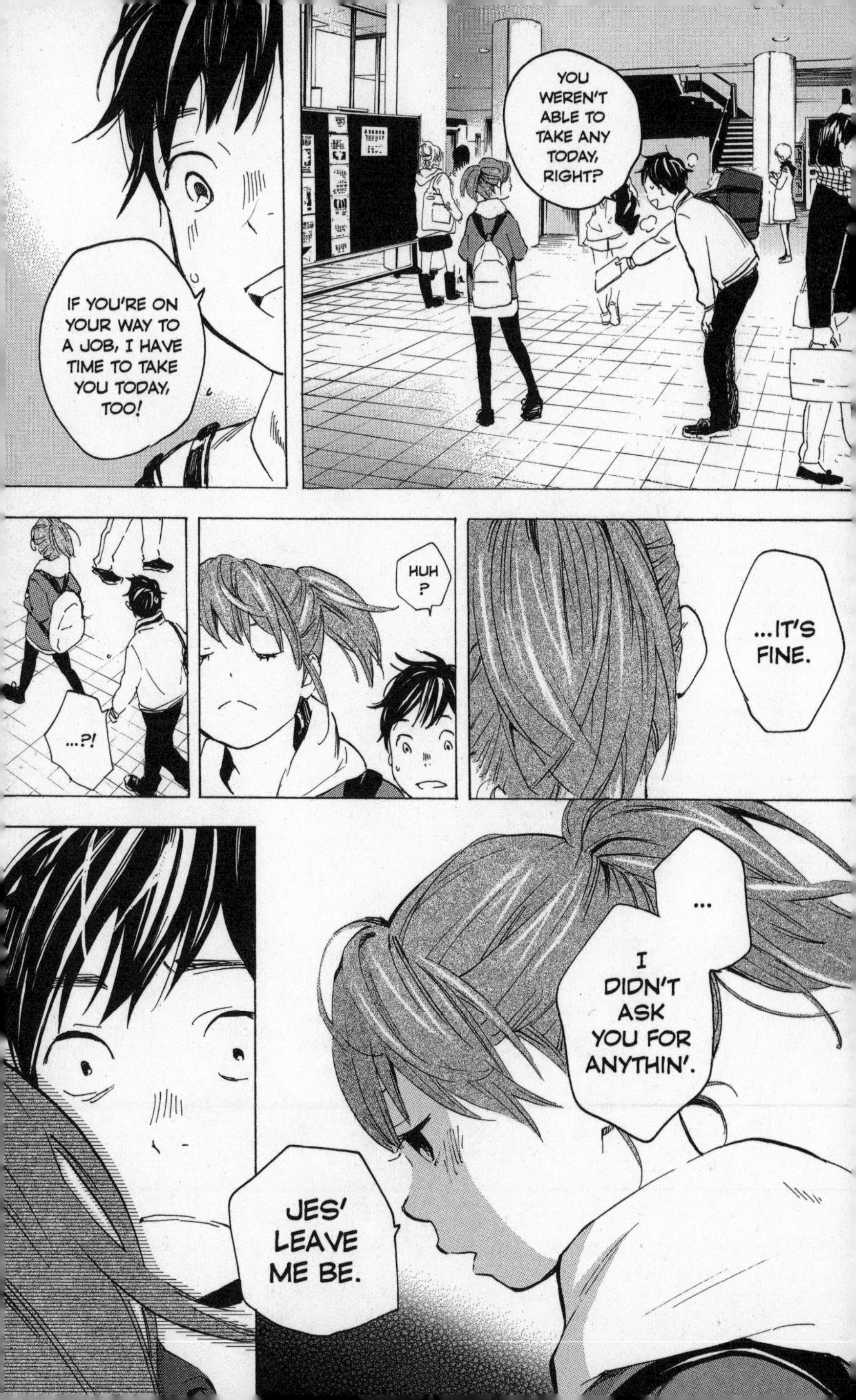
YOU WEREN'T ABLE TO TAKE ANY TODAY, RIGHT?
IF YOU'RE ON YOUR WAY TO A JOB, I HAVE TIME TO TAKE YOU TODAY, TOO!
...IT'S FINE.
HUH?
...?!
...
I DIDN'T ASK YOU FOR ANYTHIN'.
JES' LEAVE ME BE.

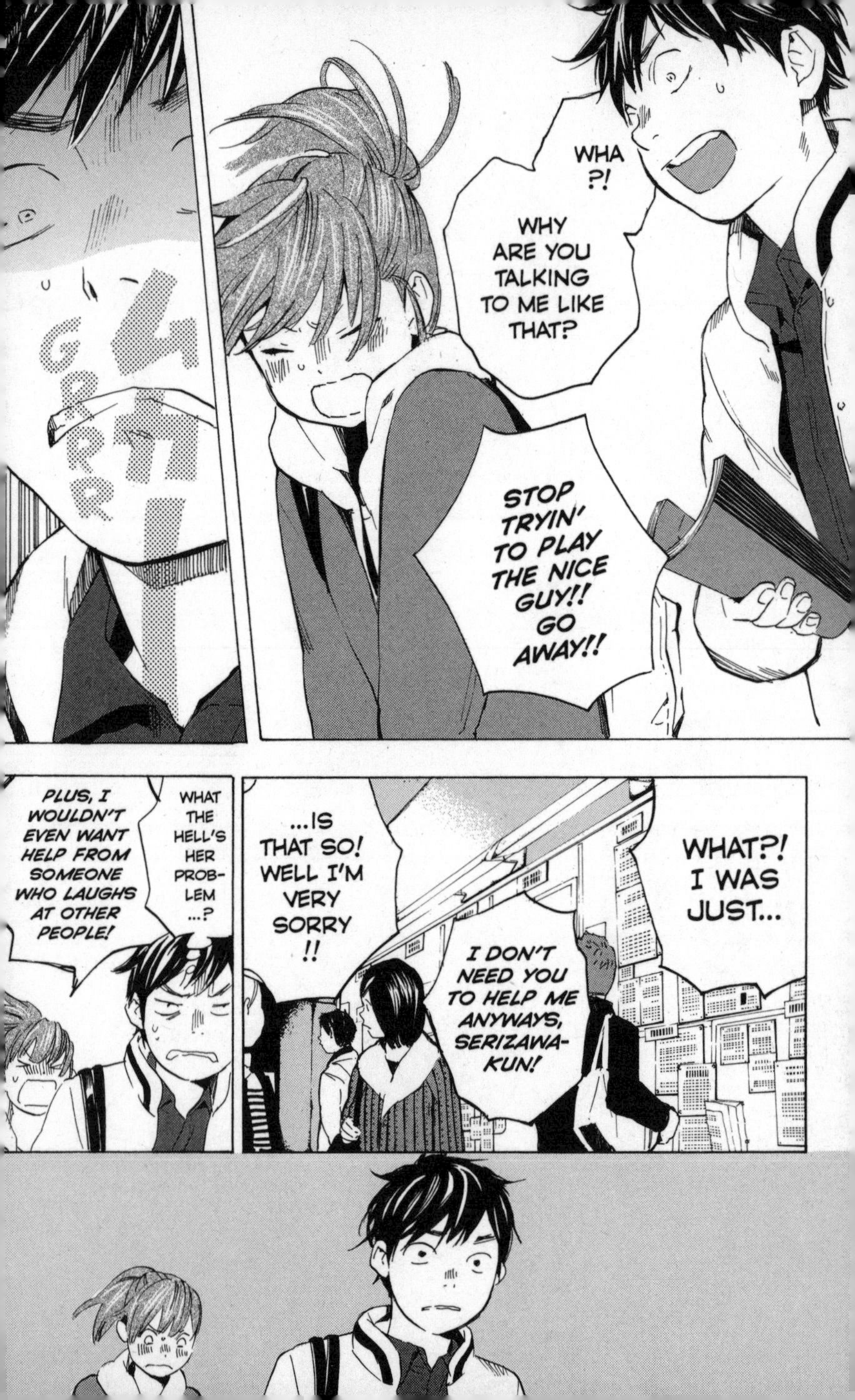
WHA ?!
WHY ARE YOU TALKING TO ME LIKE THAT?
STOP TRYIN' TO PLAY THE NICE GUY!! GO AWAY!!
GRRR
WHAT?! I WAS JUST...
I DON'T NEED YOU TO HELP ME ANYWAYS, SERIZAWA-KUN!
...IS THAT SO! WELL I'M VERY SORRY !!
WHAT THE HELL'S HER PROB-LEM ...?
PLUS, I WOULDN'T EVEN WANT HELP FROM SOMEONE WHO LAUGHS AT OTHER PEOPLE!

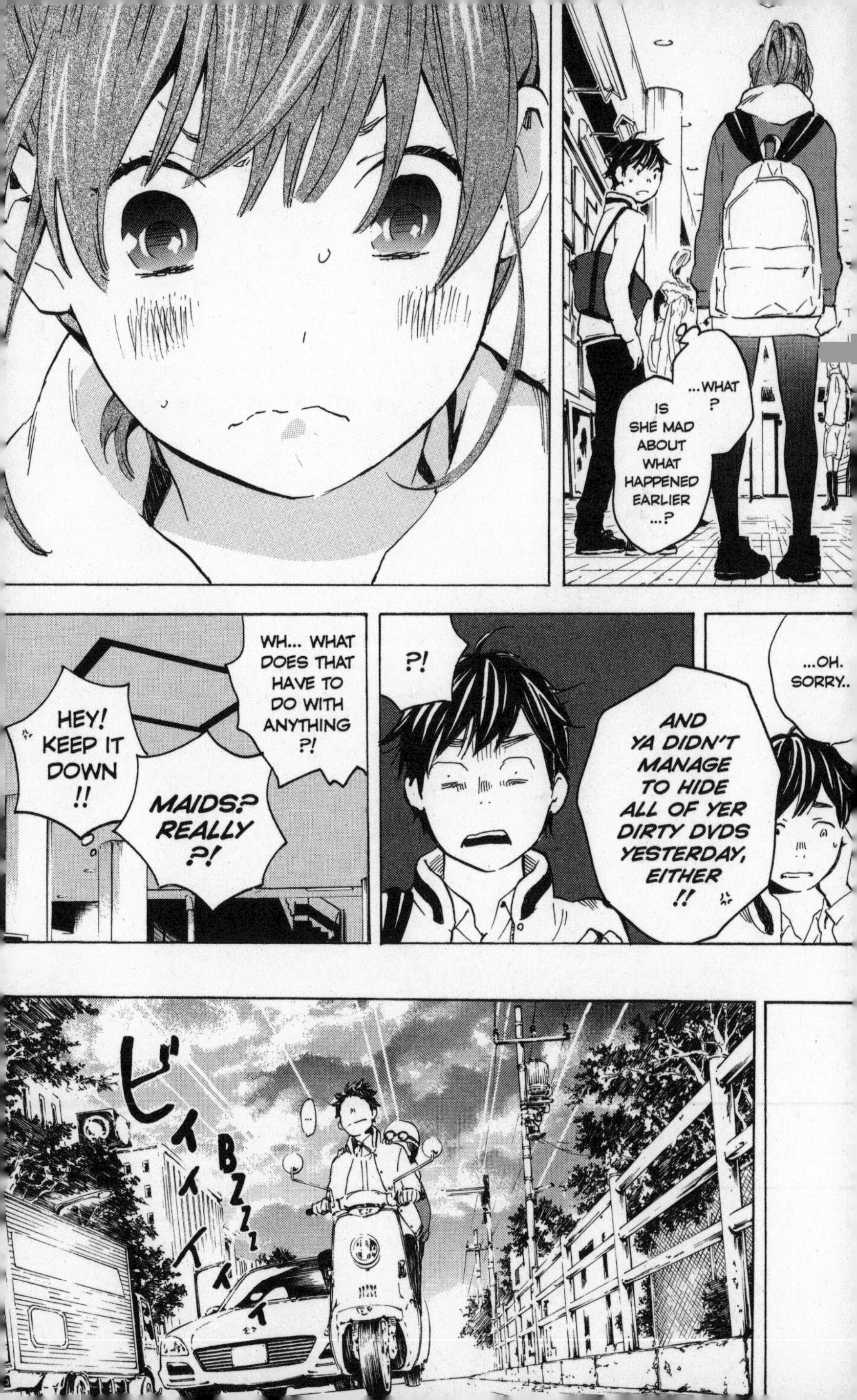
...WHAT?
IS SHE MAD ABOUT WHAT HAPPENED EARLIER...?
...OH. SORRY..
AND YA DIDN'T MANAGE TO HIDE ALL OF YER DIRTY DVDS YESTERDAY, EITHER!!
?!
WH... WHAT DOES THAT HAVE TO DO WITH ANYTHING?!
MAIDS? REALLY?!
HEY! KEEP IT DOWN!!
...
ビイイイイ
BZZZZ

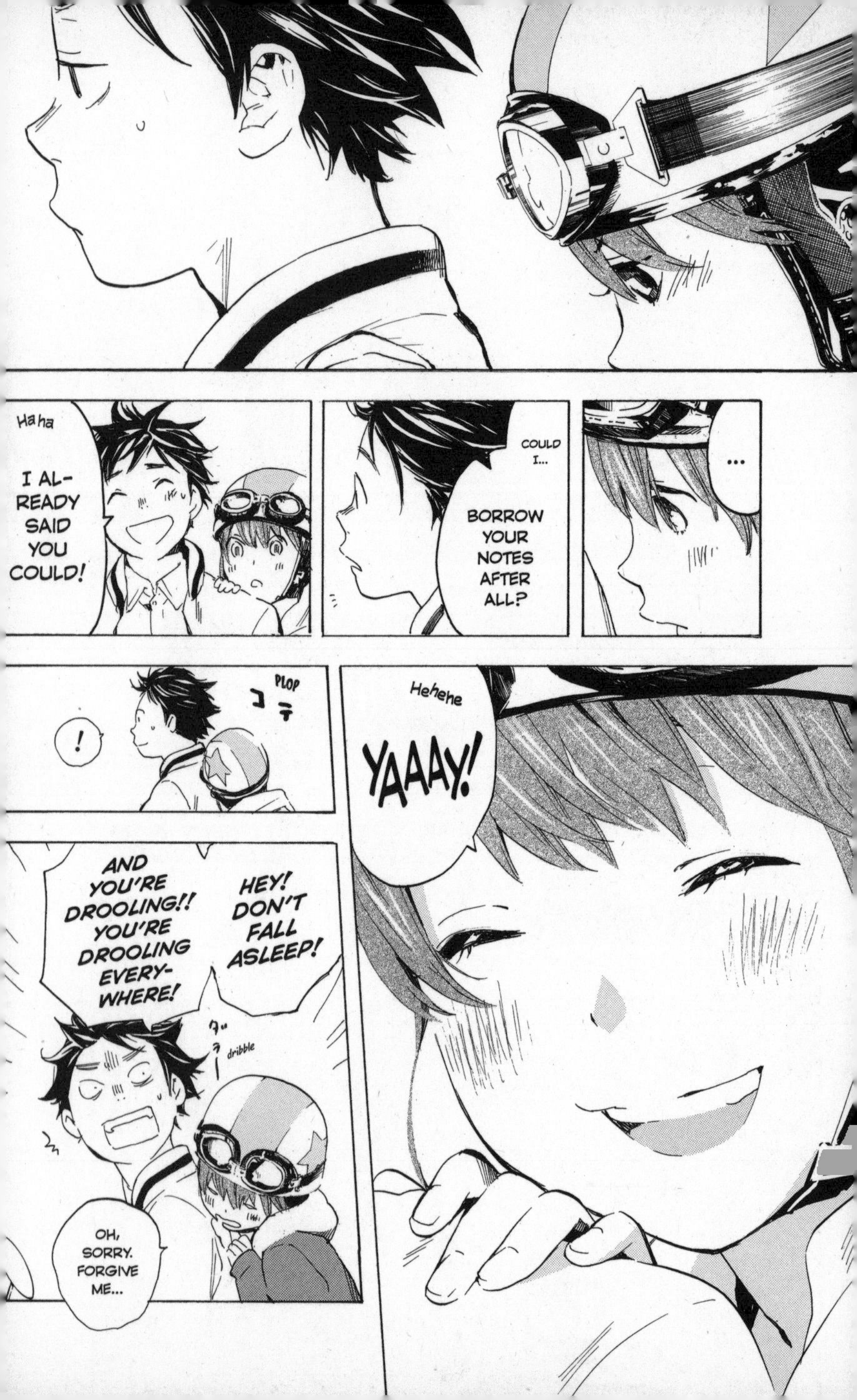
...
COULD I...
BORROW YOUR NOTES AFTER ALL?
Haha
I AL-READY SAID YOU COULD!
Hehehe
YAAAY!
!
PLOP
コテ
HEY! DON'T FALL ASLEEP!
AND YOU'RE DROOLING!! YOU'RE DROOLING EVERY-WHERE!
dribble
OH, SORRY. FORGIVE ME...

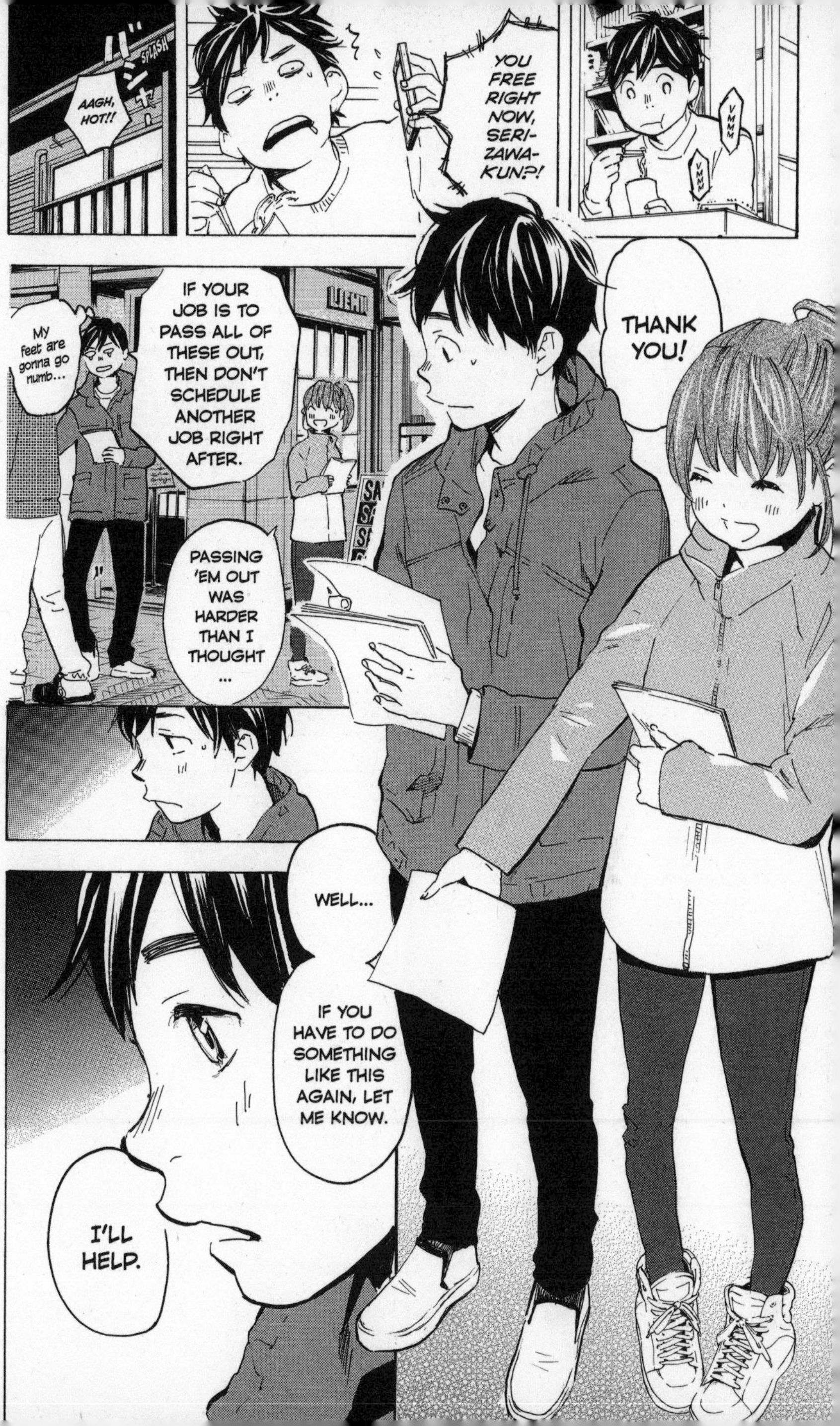
VMMM
VMMM
YOU FREE RIGHT NOW, SERI-ZAWA-KUN?!
バシャ SPLASH
AAGH, HOT!!
THANK YOU!
IF YOUR JOB IS TO PASS ALL OF THESE OUT, THEN DON'T SCHEDULE ANOTHER JOB RIGHT AFTER.
My feet are gonna go numb...
PASSING 'EM OUT WAS HARDER THAN I THOUGHT...
WELL...
IF YOU HAVE TO DO SOMETHING LIKE THIS AGAIN, LET ME KNOW.
I'LL HELP.

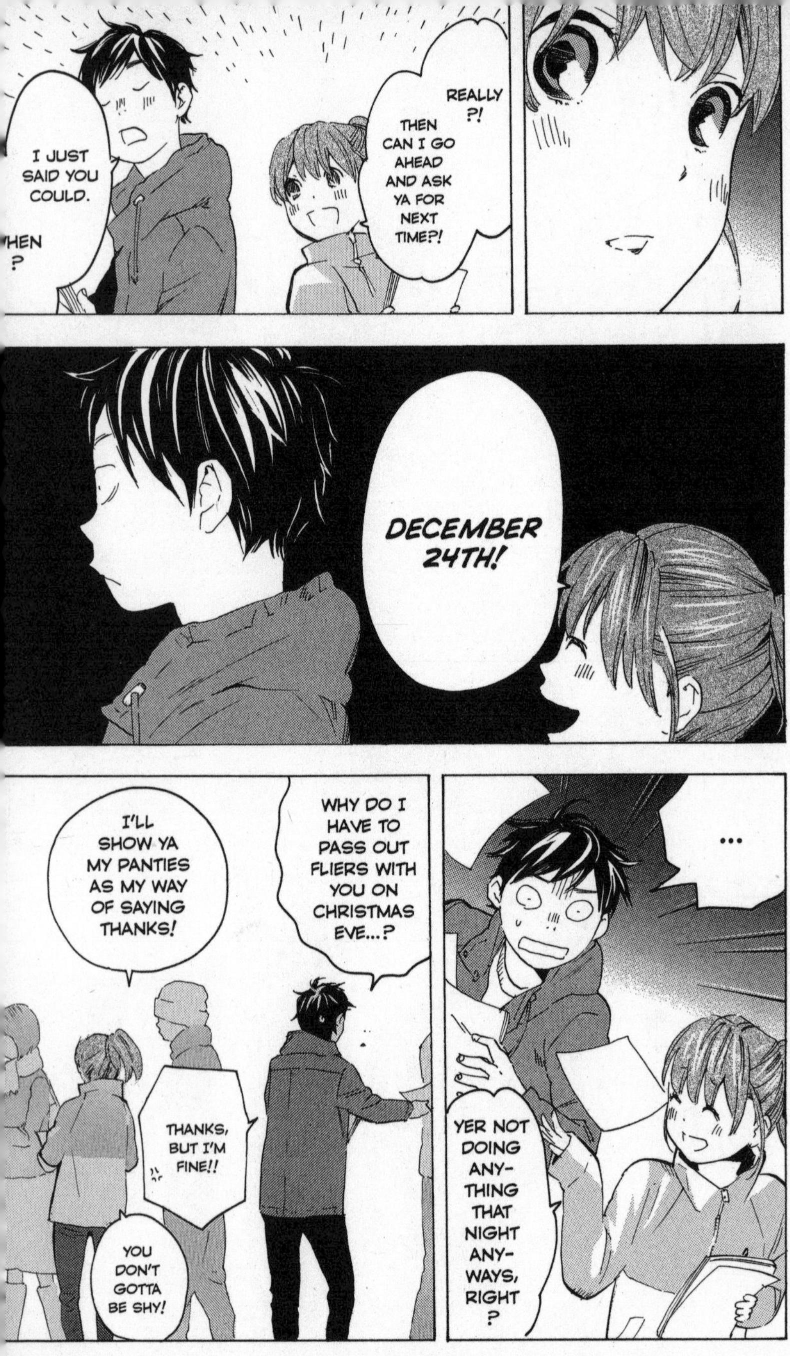
REALLY?!
THEN CAN I GO AHEAD AND ASK YA FOR NEXT TIME?!
I JUST SAID YOU COULD.
HEN ?
DECEMBER 24TH!
...
YER NOT DOING ANY-THING THAT NIGHT ANY-WAYS, RIGHT?
WHY DO I HAVE TO PASS OUT FLIERS WITH YOU ON CHRISTMAS EVE...?
I'LL SHOW YA MY PANTIES AS MY WAY OF SAYING THANKS!
THANKS, BUT I'M FINE!!
YOU DON'T GOTTA BE SHY!

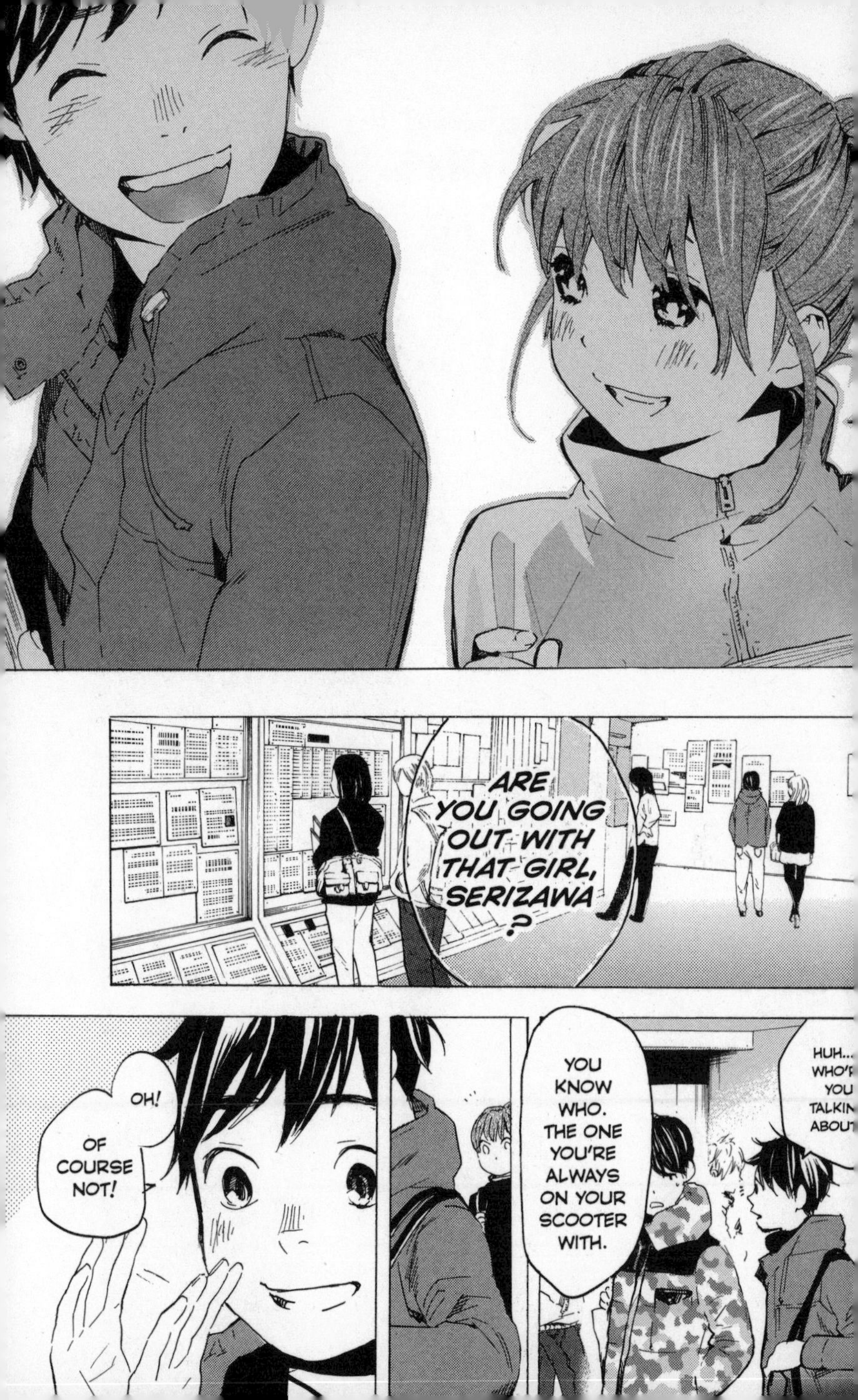
ARE YOU GOING OUT WITH THAT GIRL, SERIZAWA?
HUH... WHO'R YOU TALKIN ABOUT
YOU KNOW WHO. THE ONE YOU'RE ALWAYS ON YOUR SCOOTER WITH.
OH!
OF COURSE NOT!

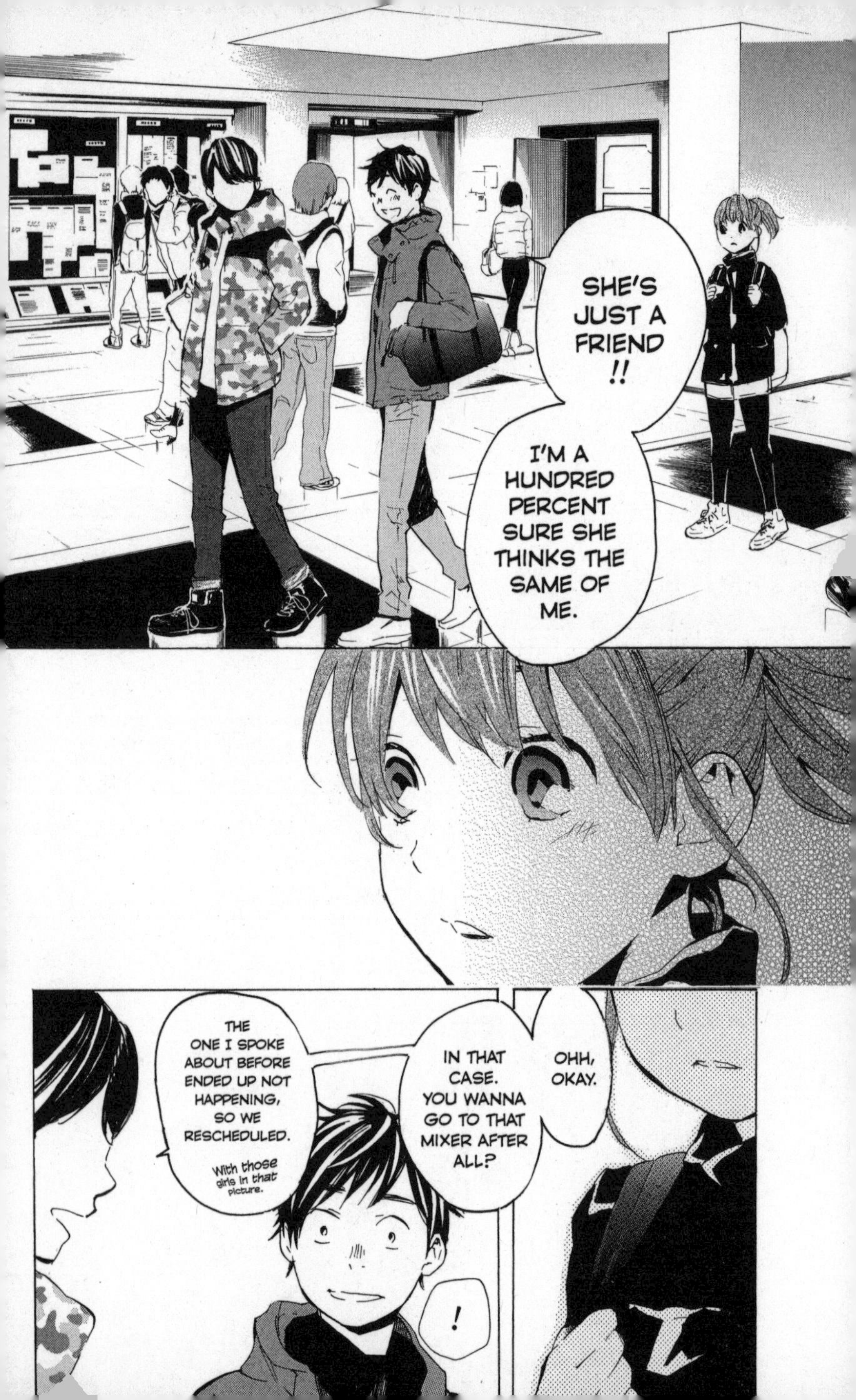
SHE'S JUST A FRIEND!!
I'M A HUNDRED PERCENT SURE SHE THINKS THE SAME OF ME.
OHH, OKAY.
IN THAT CASE. YOU WANNA GO TO THAT MIXER AFTER ALL?
THE ONE I SPOKE ABOUT BEFORE ENDED UP NOT HAPPENING, SO WE RESCHEDULED.
With those girls in that picture.
!

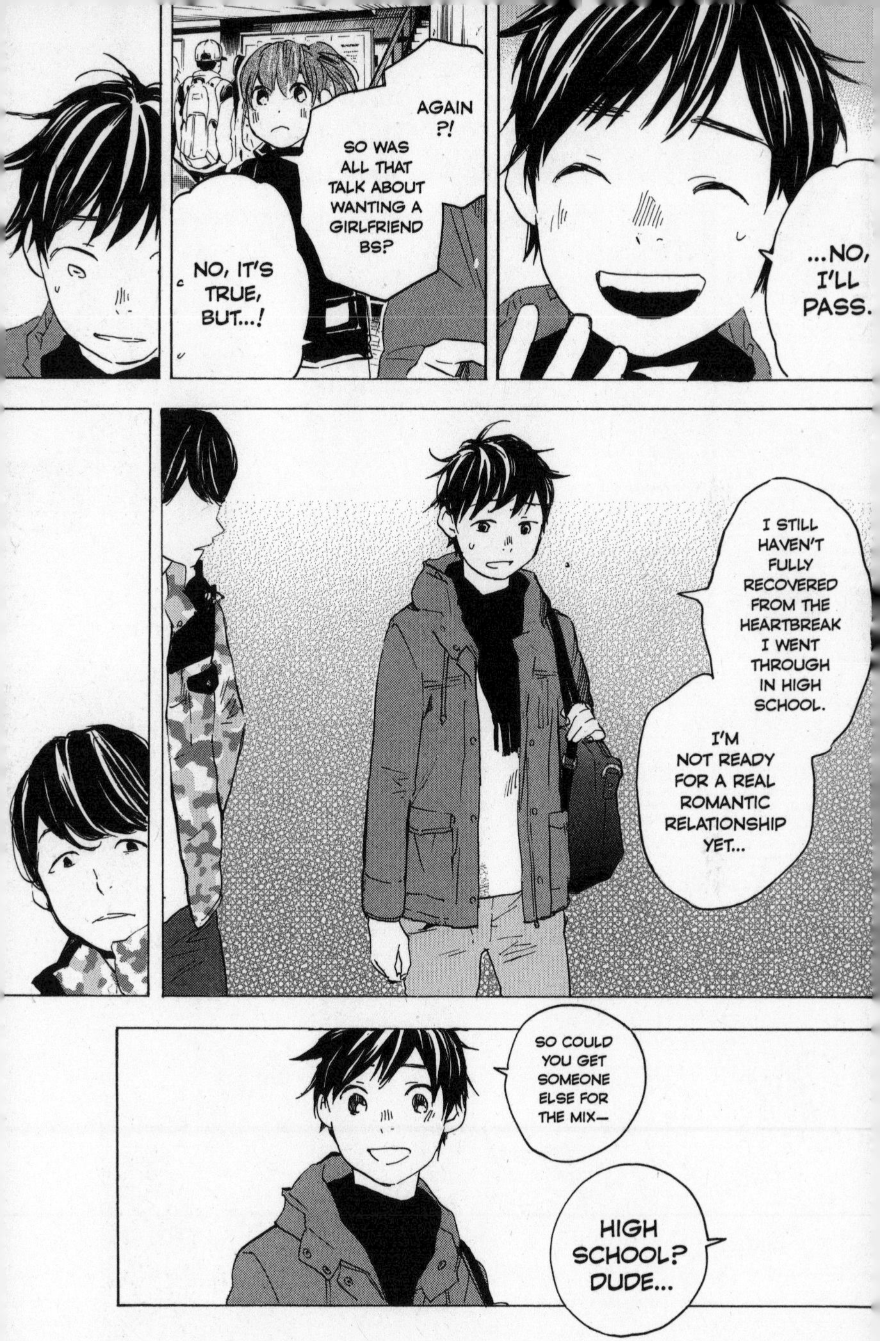
...NO, I'LL PASS.
AGAIN ?!
SO WAS ALL THAT TALK ABOUT WANTING A GIRLFRIEND BS?
NO, IT'S TRUE, BUT...!
I STILL HAVEN'T FULLY RECOVERED FROM THE HEARTBREAK I WENT THROUGH IN HIGH SCHOOL.
I'M NOT READY FOR A REAL ROMANTIC RELATIONSHIP YET...
SO COULD YOU GET SOMEONE ELSE FOR THE MIX—
HIGH SCHOOL? DUDE...

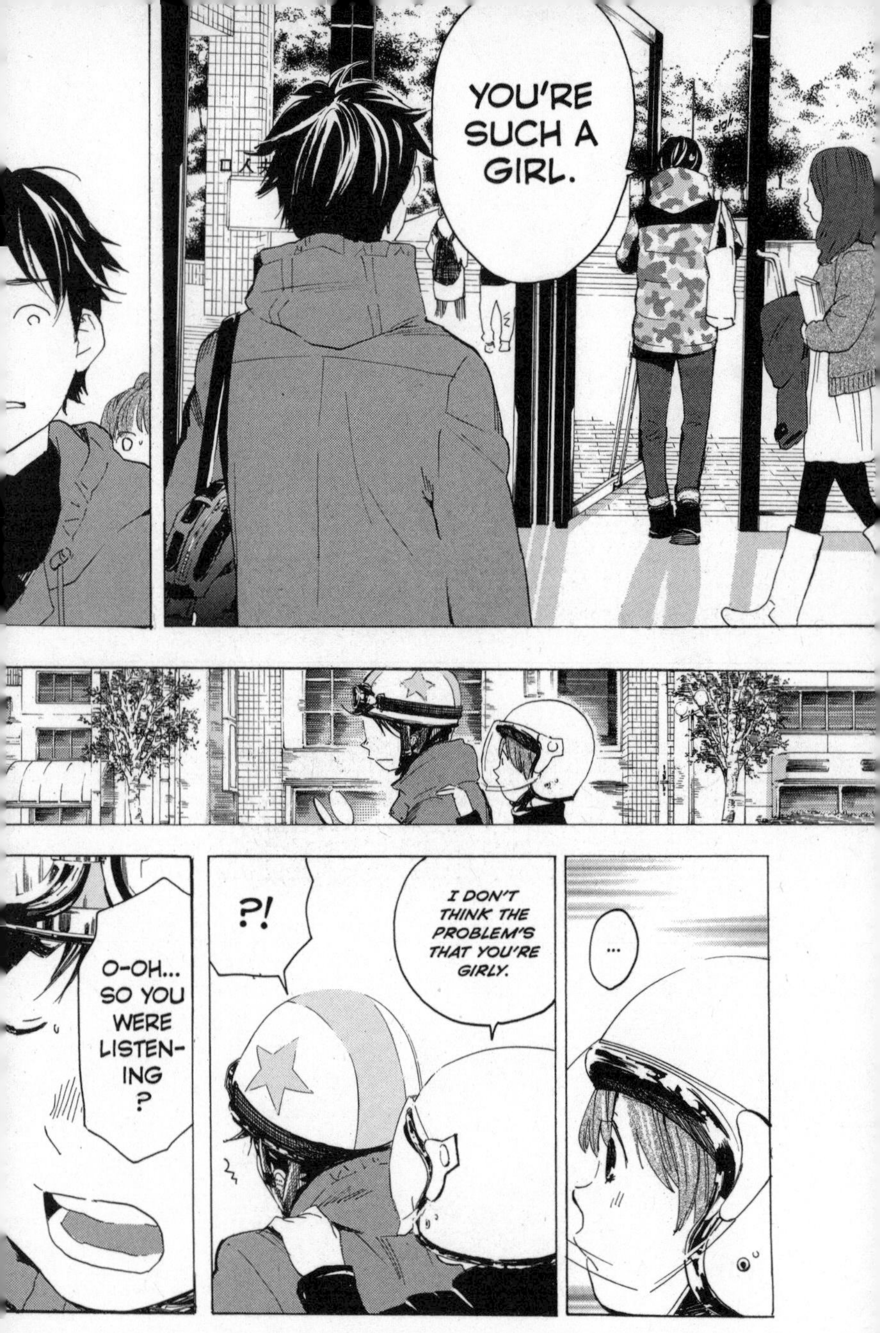
YOU'RE SUCH A GIRL.
sigh
...
I DON'T THINK THE PROBLEM'S THAT YOU'RE GIRLY.
?!
O-OH... SO YOU WERE LISTENING?

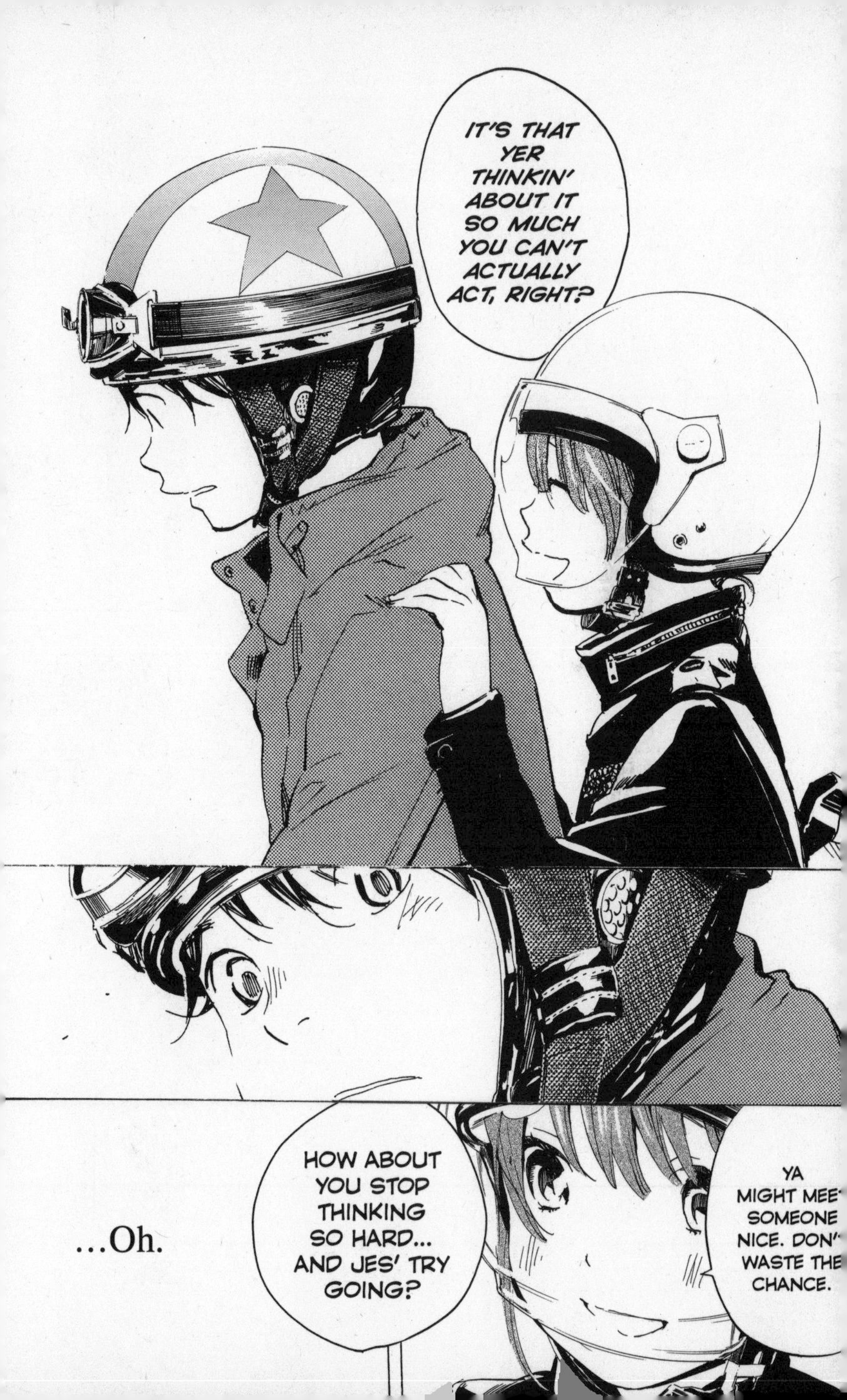
IT'S THAT YER THINKIN' ABOUT IT SO MUCH YOU CAN'T ACTUALLY ACT, RIGHT?
YA MIGHT MEE SOMEONE NICE. DON' WASTE THE CHANCE.
HOW ABOUT YOU STOP THINKING SO HARD... AND JES' TRY GOING?
...Oh.

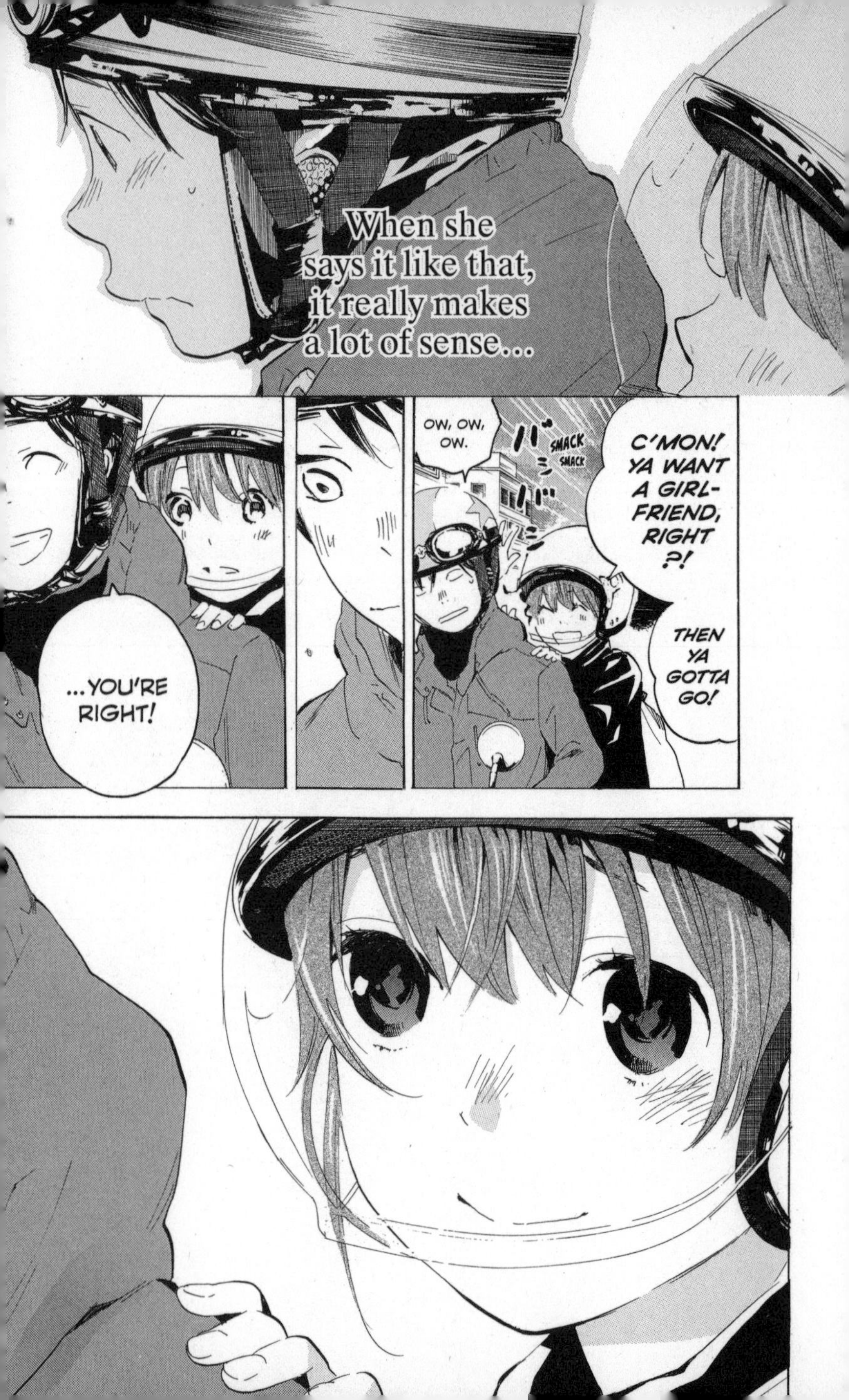
When she says it like that, it really makes a lot of sense...
C'MON! YA WANT A GIRL-FRIEND, RIGHT?!
THEN YA GOTTA GO!
SMACK
SMACK
OW, OW, OW.
...YOU'RE RIGHT!

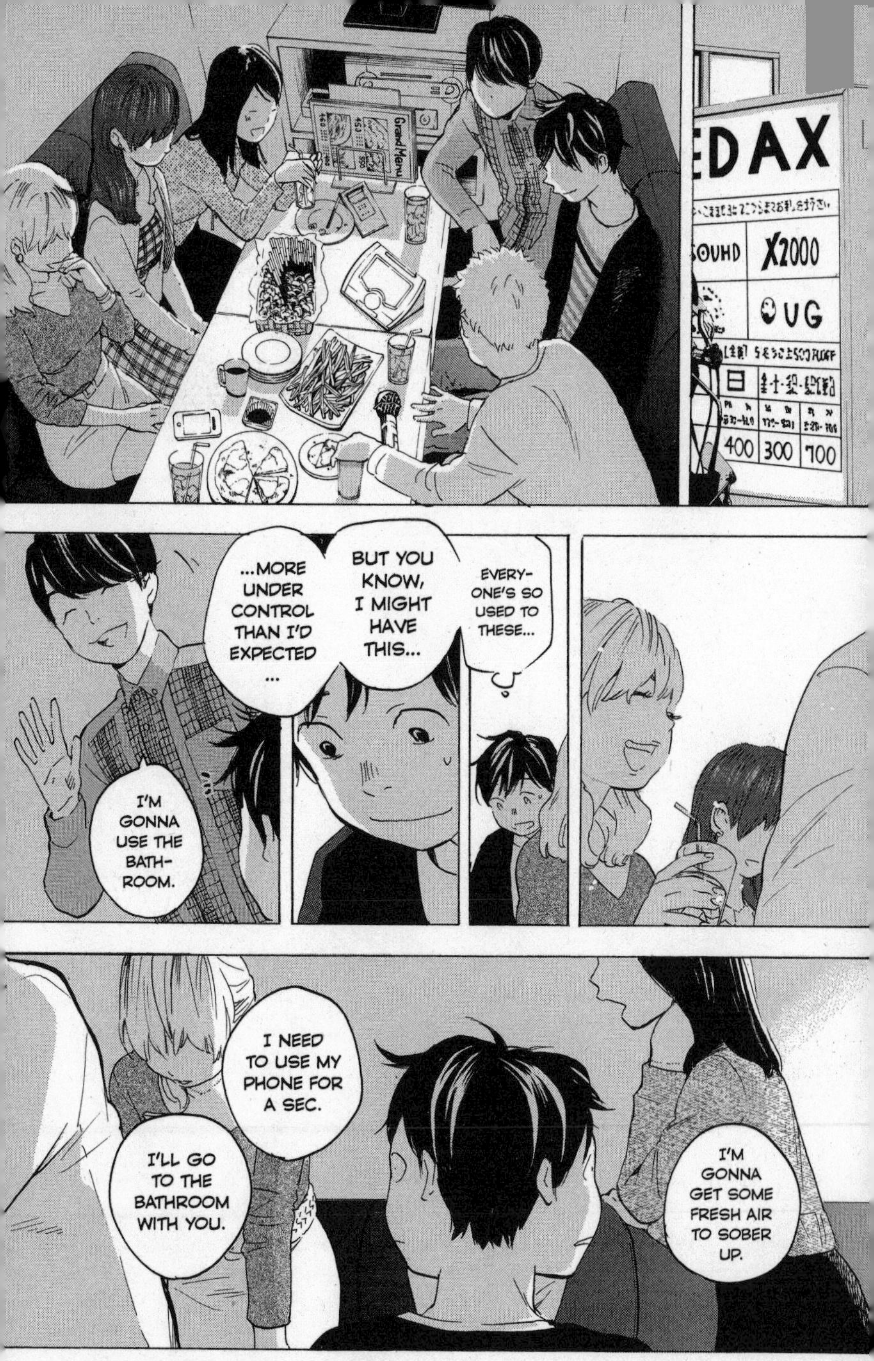
EDAX
SOUHD
X2000
UG
400 300 700
EVERY-ONE'S SO USED TO THESE...
BUT YOU KNOW, I MIGHT HAVE THIS...
...MORE UNDER CONTROL THAN I'D EXPECTED ...
I'M GONNA USE THE BATH-ROOM.
I'M GONNA GET SOME FRESH AIR TO SOBER UP.
I NEED TO USE MY PHONE FOR A SEC.
I'LL GO TO THE BATHROOM WITH YOU.

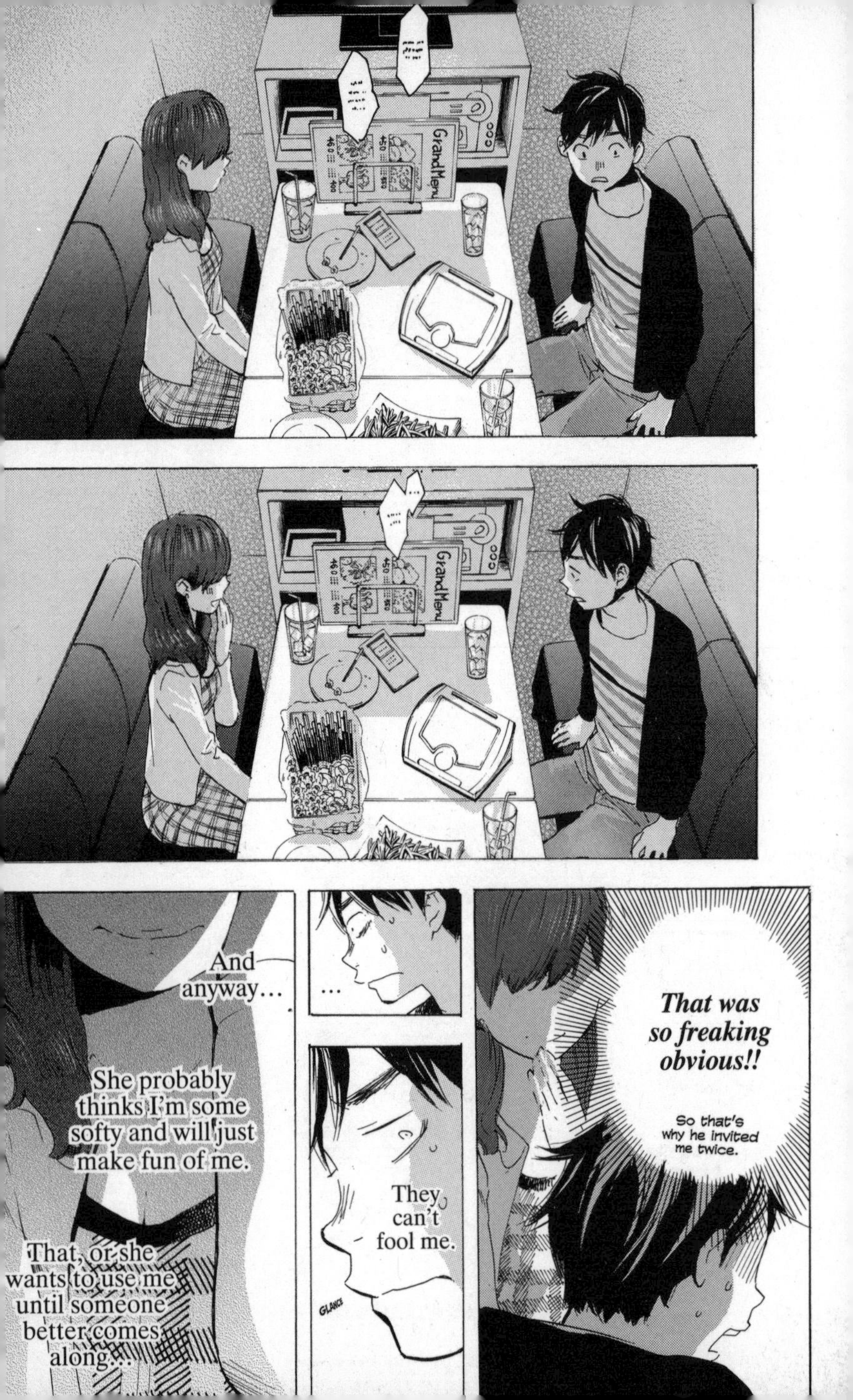
That was so freaking obvious!!
So that's why he invited me twice.
...
They can't fool me.
GLANCE
And anyway...
She probably thinks I'm some softy and will just make fun of me.
That, or she wants to use me until someone better comes along...

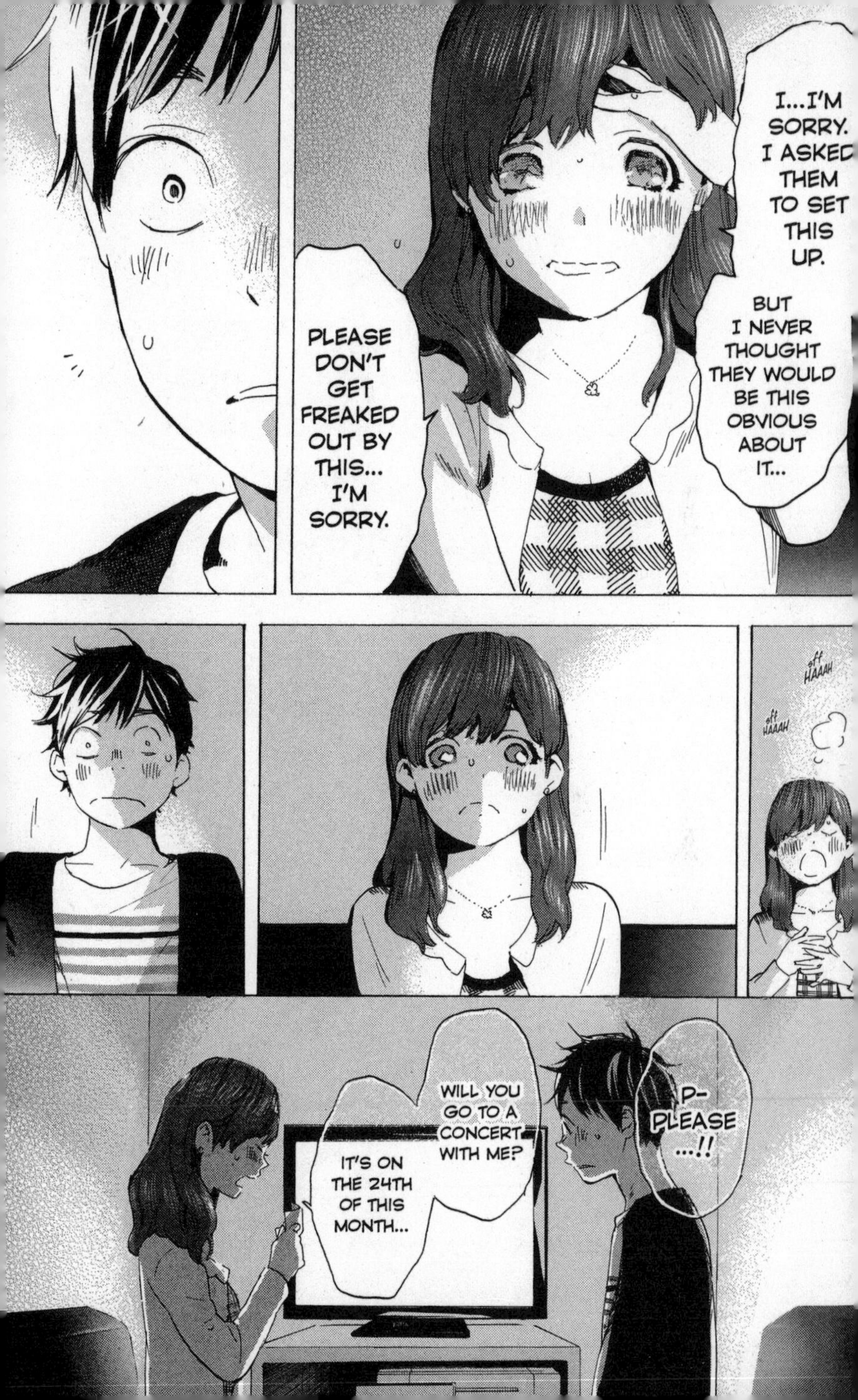
I...I'M SORRY. I ASKED THEM TO SET THIS UP.
BUT I NEVER THOUGHT THEY WOULD BE THIS OBVIOUS ABOUT IT...
PLEASE DON'T GET FREAKED OUT BY THIS... I'M SORRY.
sff HAAAH
sff HAAAH
P-PLEASE ...!!
WILL YOU GO TO A CONCERT WITH ME?
IT'S ON THE 24TH OF THIS MONTH...

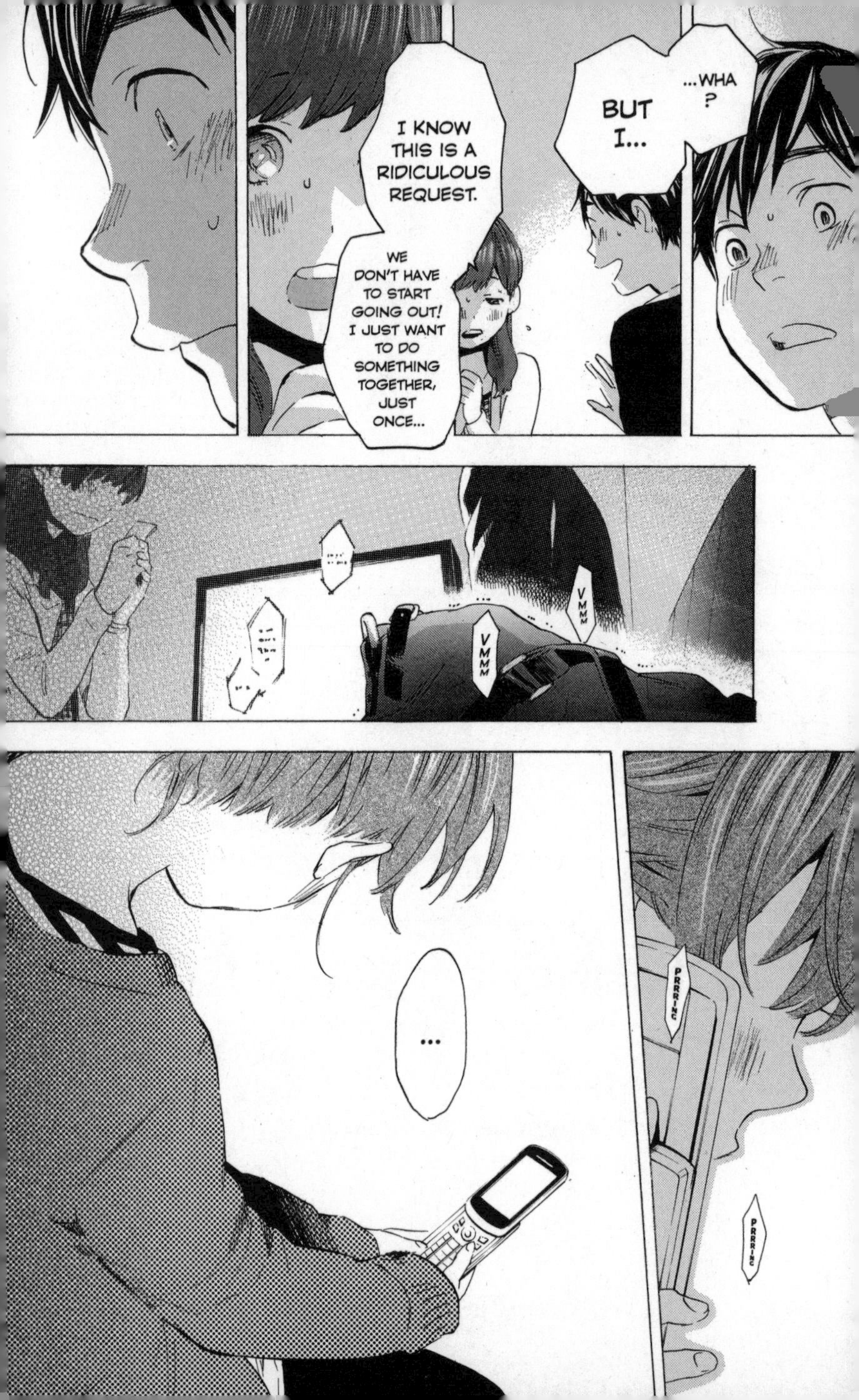
...WHA ?
BUT I...
I KNOW THIS IS A RIDICULOUS REQUEST.
WE DON'T HAVE TO START GOING OUT! I JUST WANT TO DO SOMETHING TOGETHER, JUST ONCE...
VMMM
VMMM
PRRRING
PRRRING
...

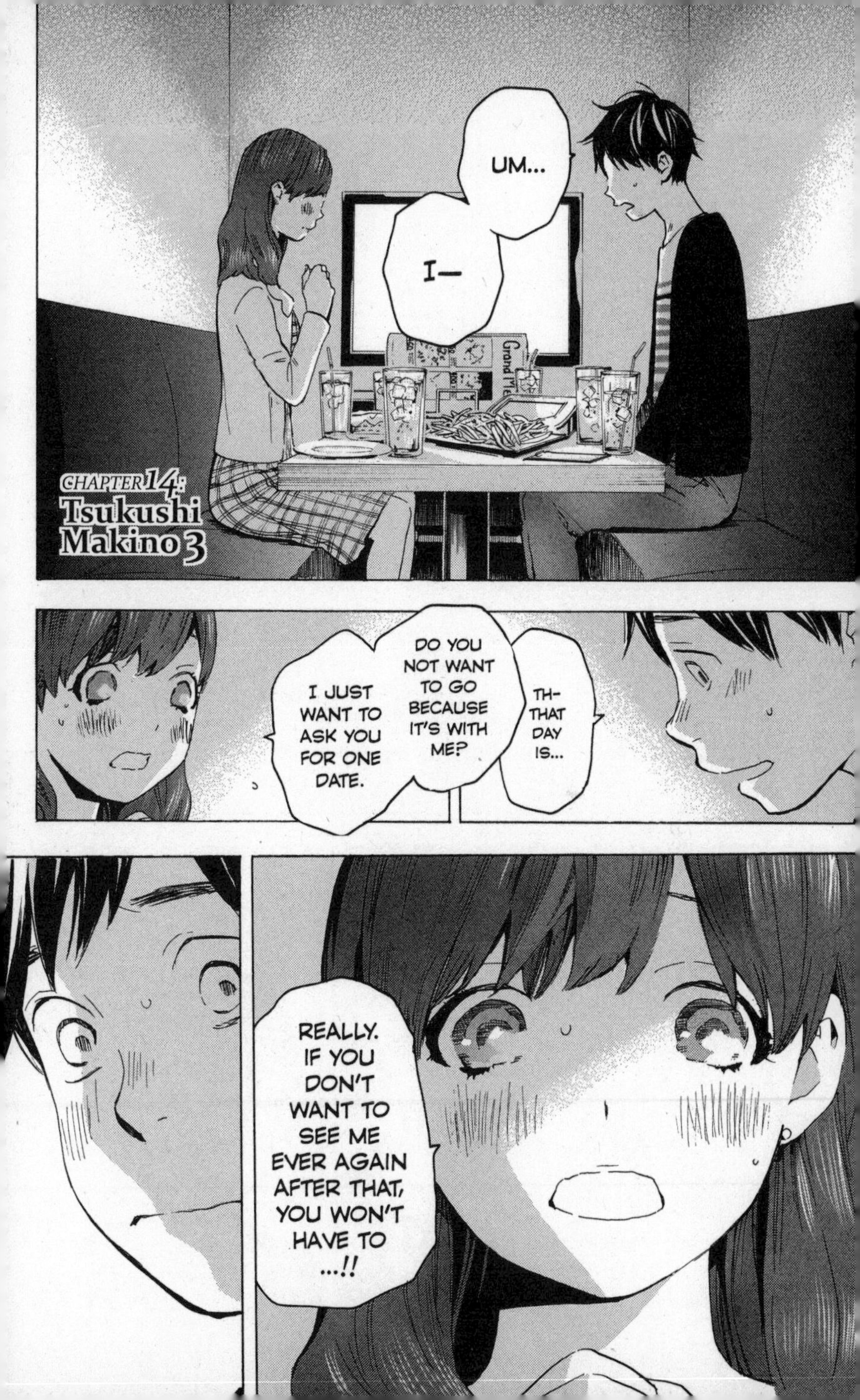
UM...
I—
CHAPTER 14: Tsukushi Makino 3
TH- THAT DAY IS...
DO YOU NOT WANT TO GO BECAUSE IT'S WITH ME?
I JUST WANT TO ASK YOU FOR ONE DATE.
REALLY. IF YOU DON'T WANT TO SEE ME EVER AGAIN AFTER THAT, YOU WON'T HAVE TO ...!!

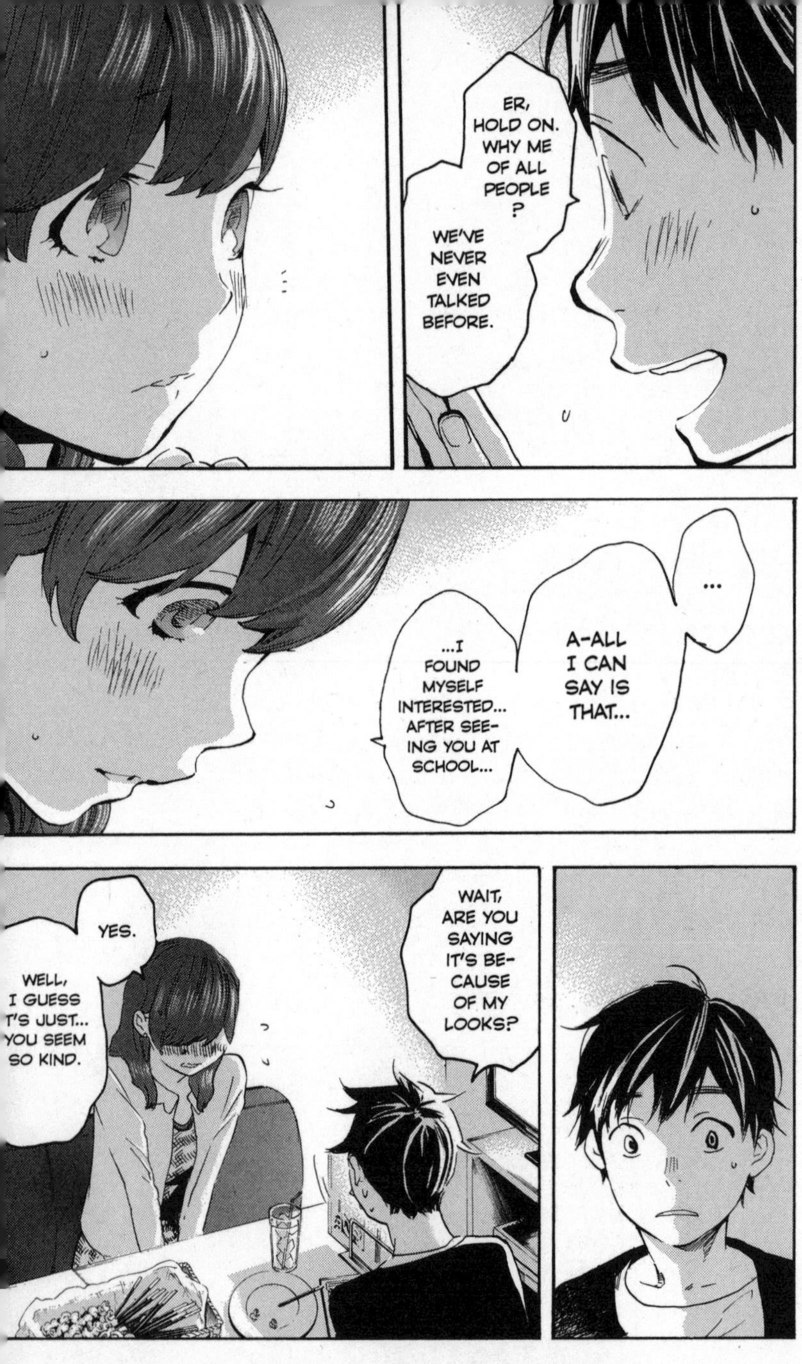
ER, HOLD ON. WHY ME OF ALL PEOPLE ?
WE'VE NEVER EVEN TALKED BEFORE.
...
A-ALL I CAN SAY IS THAT...
...I FOUND MYSELF INTERESTED... AFTER SEE-ING YOU AT SCHOOL...
WAIT, ARE YOU SAYING IT'S BE-CAUSE OF MY LOOKS?
YES.
WELL, I GUESS T'S JUST... YOU SEEM SO KIND.

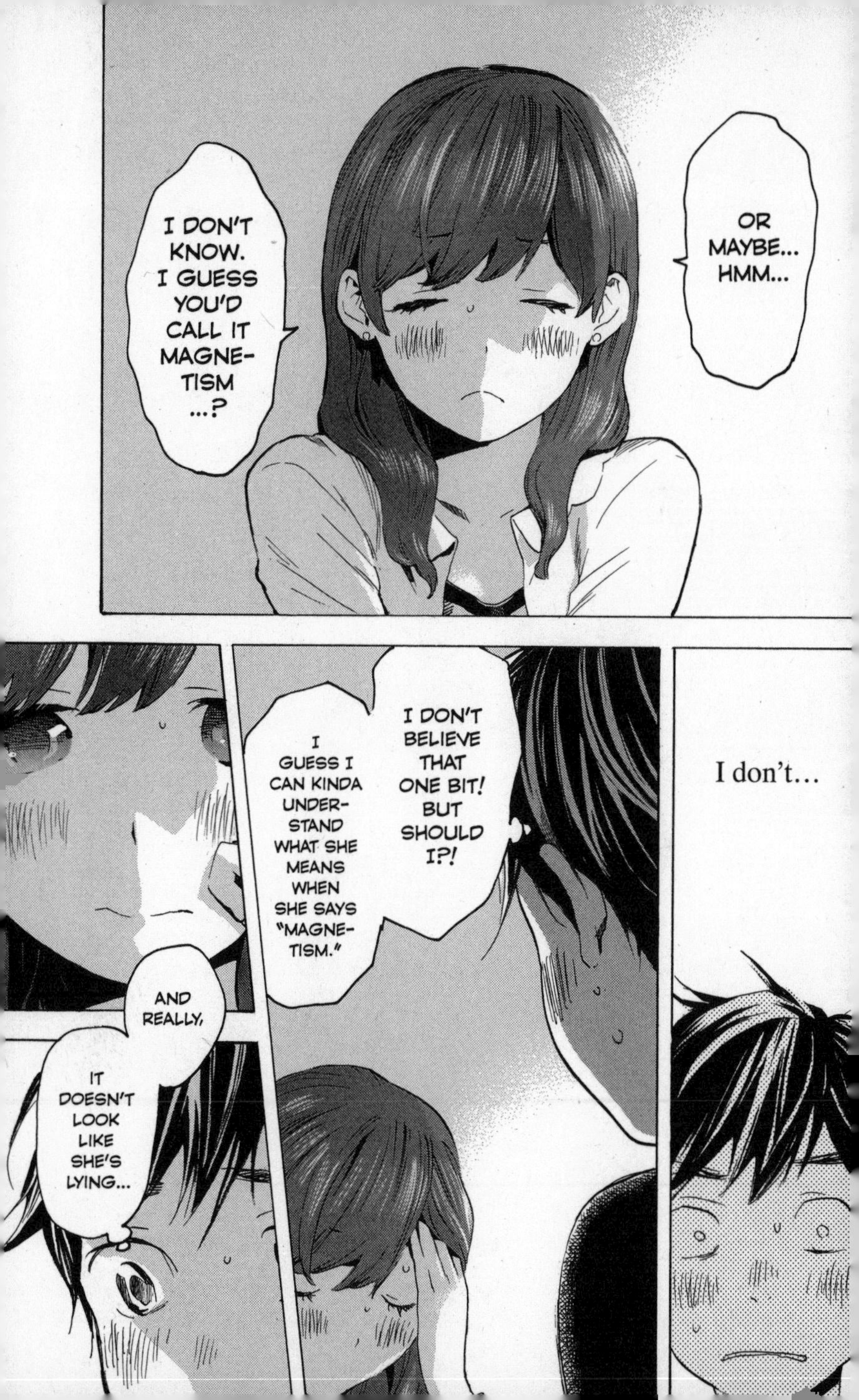
OR MAYBE... HMM...
I DON'T KNOW. I GUESS YOU'D CALL IT MAGNE-TISM ...?
I don't…
I DON'T BELIEVE THAT ONE BIT! BUT SHOULD I?!
I GUESS I CAN KINDA UNDER-STAND WHAT SHE MEANS WHEN SHE SAYS "MAGNE-TISM."
AND REALLY,
IT DOESN'T LOOK LIKE SHE'S LYING...

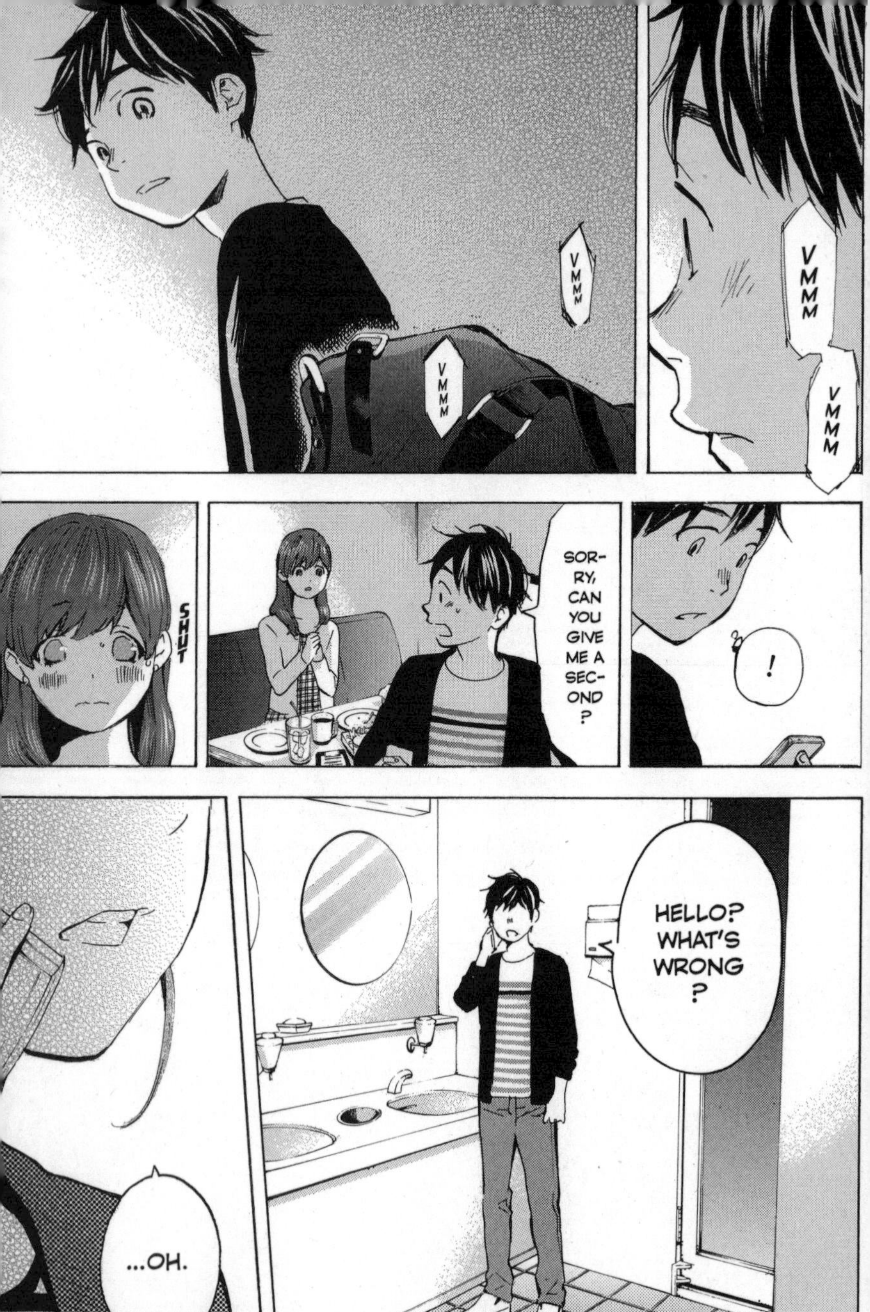
VMMM
VMMM
VMMM
VMMM
!
SORRY, CAN YOU GIVE ME A SECOND?
SHUT
HELLO? WHAT'S WRONG?
...OH.

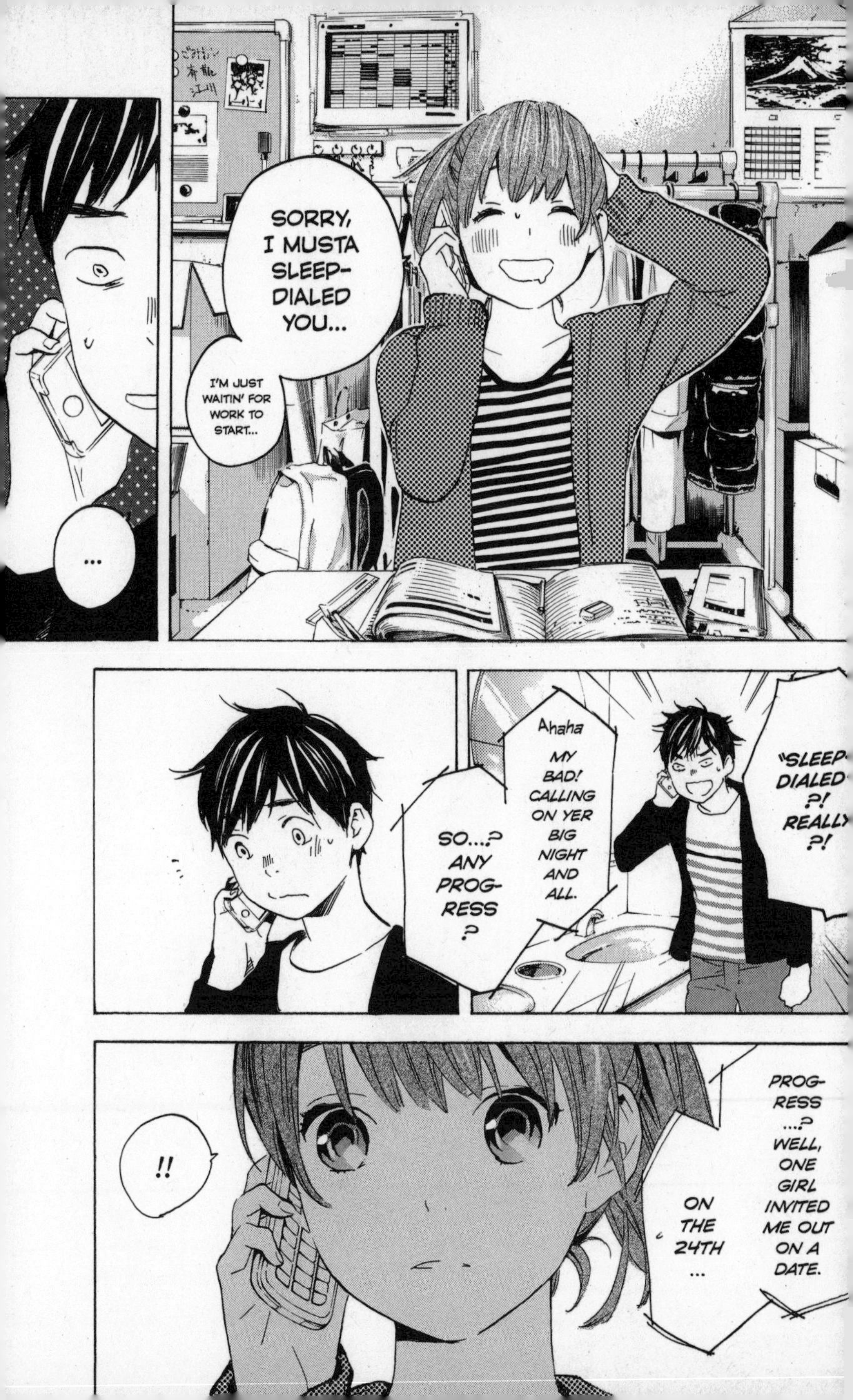
SORRY, I MUSTA SLEEP-DIALED YOU...
I'M JUST WAITIN' FOR WORK TO START...
...
"SLEEP-DIALED"?! REALLY?!
Ahaha MY BAD! CALLING ON YER BIG NIGHT AND ALL.
SO...? ANY PROG-RESS?
PROG-RESS...? WELL, ONE GIRL INVITED ME OUT ON A DATE.
ON THE 24TH...
!!

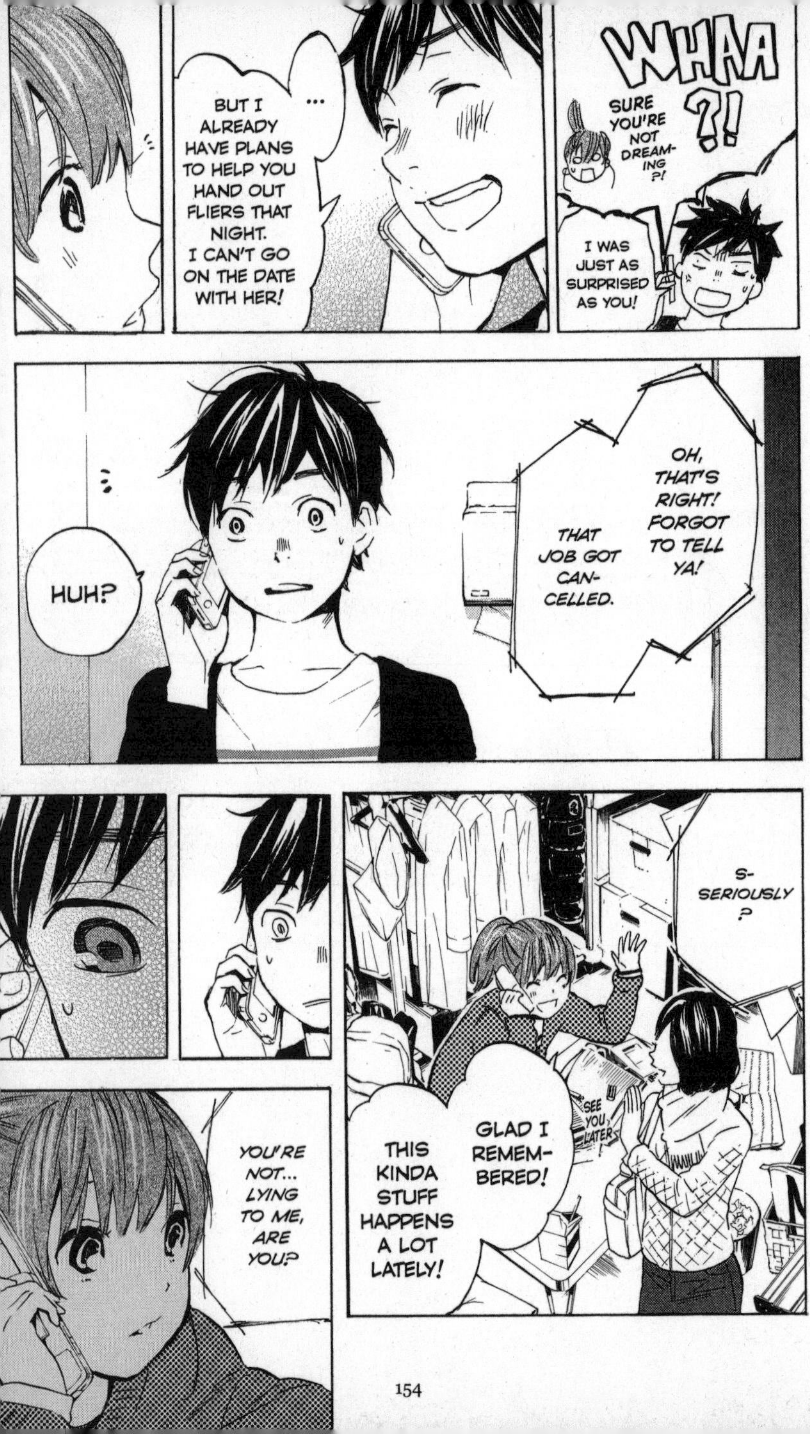
WHAA ?!
SURE YOU'RE NOT DREAMING ?!
I WAS JUST AS SURPRISED AS YOU!
...
BUT I ALREADY HAVE PLANS TO HELP YOU HAND OUT FLIERS THAT NIGHT. I CAN'T GO ON THE DATE WITH HER!
OH, THAT'S RIGHT! FORGOT TO TELL YA!
THAT JOB GOT CANCELLED.
HUH?
S-SERIOUSLY?
SEE YOU LATER!
GLAD I REMEMBERED!
THIS KINDA STUFF HAPPENS A LOT LATELY!
YOU'RE NOT... LYING TO ME, ARE YOU?

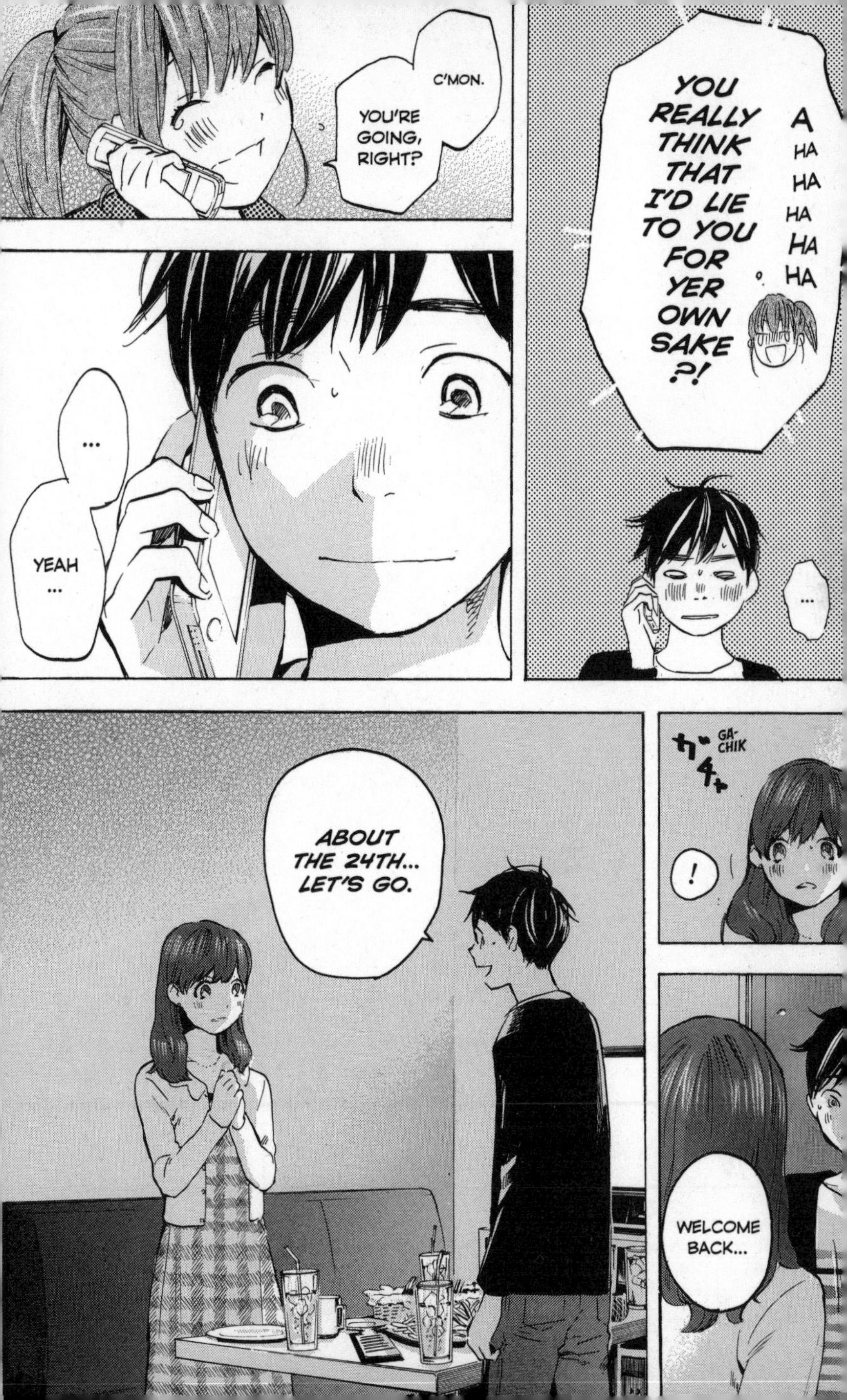
YOU REALLY THINK THAT I'D LIE TO YOU FOR YER OWN SAKE ?!
A HA HA HA HA HA
...
C'MON.
YOU'RE GOING, RIGHT?
...
YEAH ...
GA-CHIK
!
WELCOME BACK...
ABOUT THE 24TH... LET'S GO.

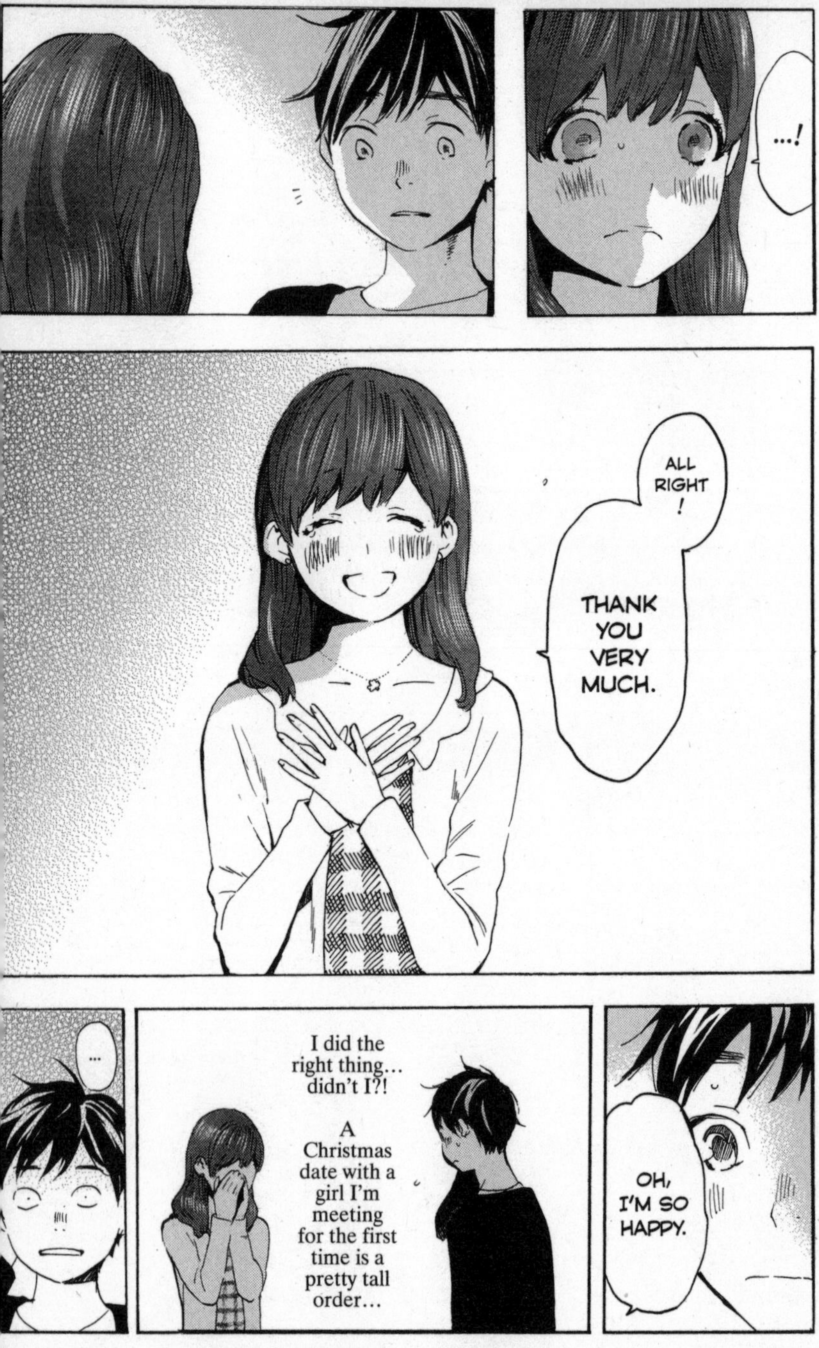
...!
ALL RIGHT!
THANK YOU VERY MUCH.
OH, I'M SO HAPPY.
I did the right thing… didn't I?!
A Christmas date with a girl I'm meeting for the first time is a pretty tall order…
...

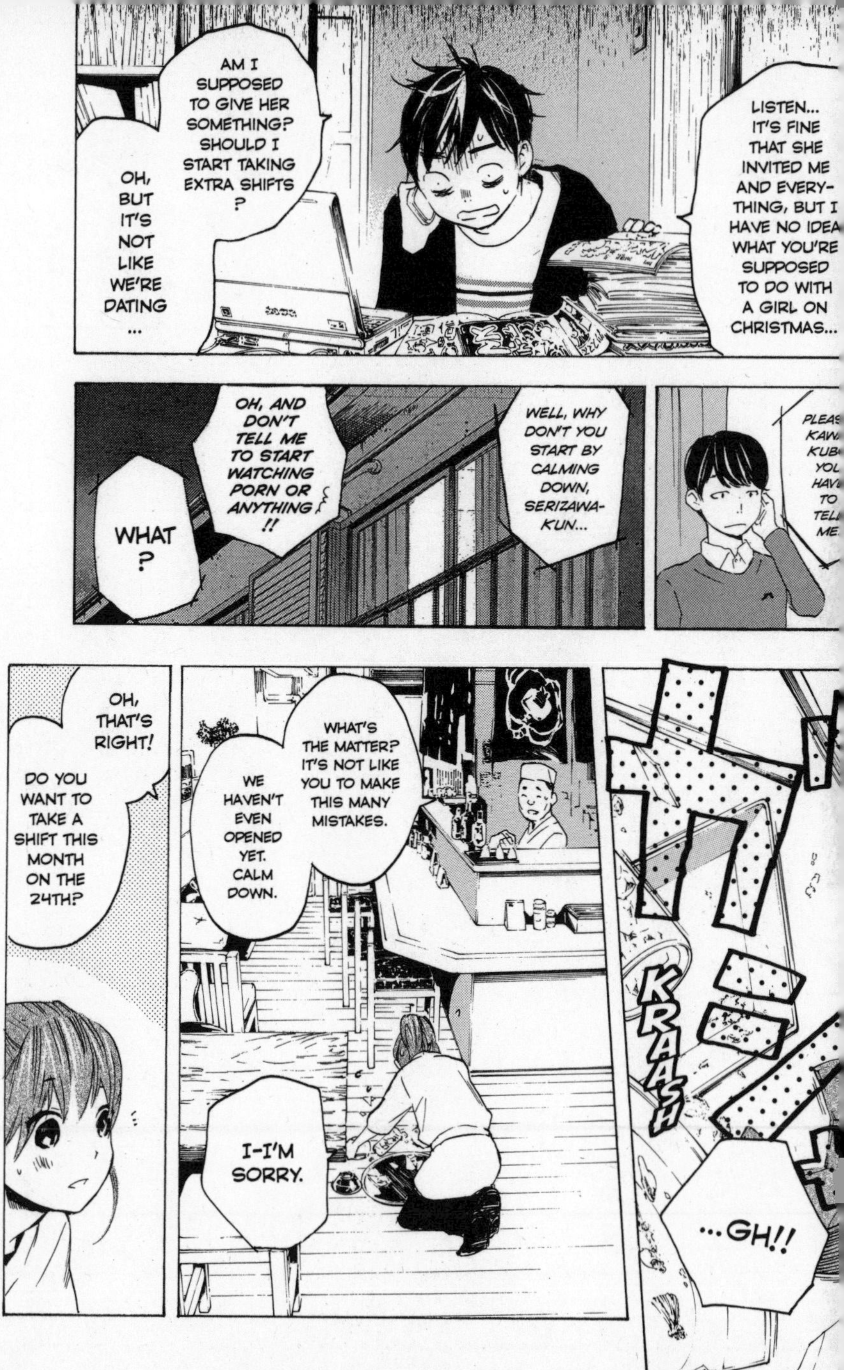
LISTEN... IT'S FINE THAT SHE INVITED ME AND EVERY-THING, BUT I HAVE NO IDEA WHAT YOU'RE SUPPOSED TO DO WITH A GIRL ON CHRISTMAS...
AM I SUPPOSED TO GIVE HER SOMETHING? SHOULD I START TAKING EXTRA SHIFTS?
OH, BUT IT'S NOT LIKE WE'RE DATING...
WELL, WHY DON'T YOU START BY CALMING DOWN, SERIZAWA-KUN...
OH, AND DON'T TELL ME TO START WATCHING PORN OR ANYTHING!!
WHAT?
KRASH
...GH!!
WHAT'S THE MATTER? IT'S NOT LIKE YOU TO MAKE THIS MANY MISTAKES.
WE HAVEN'T EVEN OPENED YET. CALM DOWN.
I-I'M SORRY.
OH, THAT'S RIGHT!
DO YOU WANT TO TAKE A SHIFT THIS MONTH ON THE 24TH?

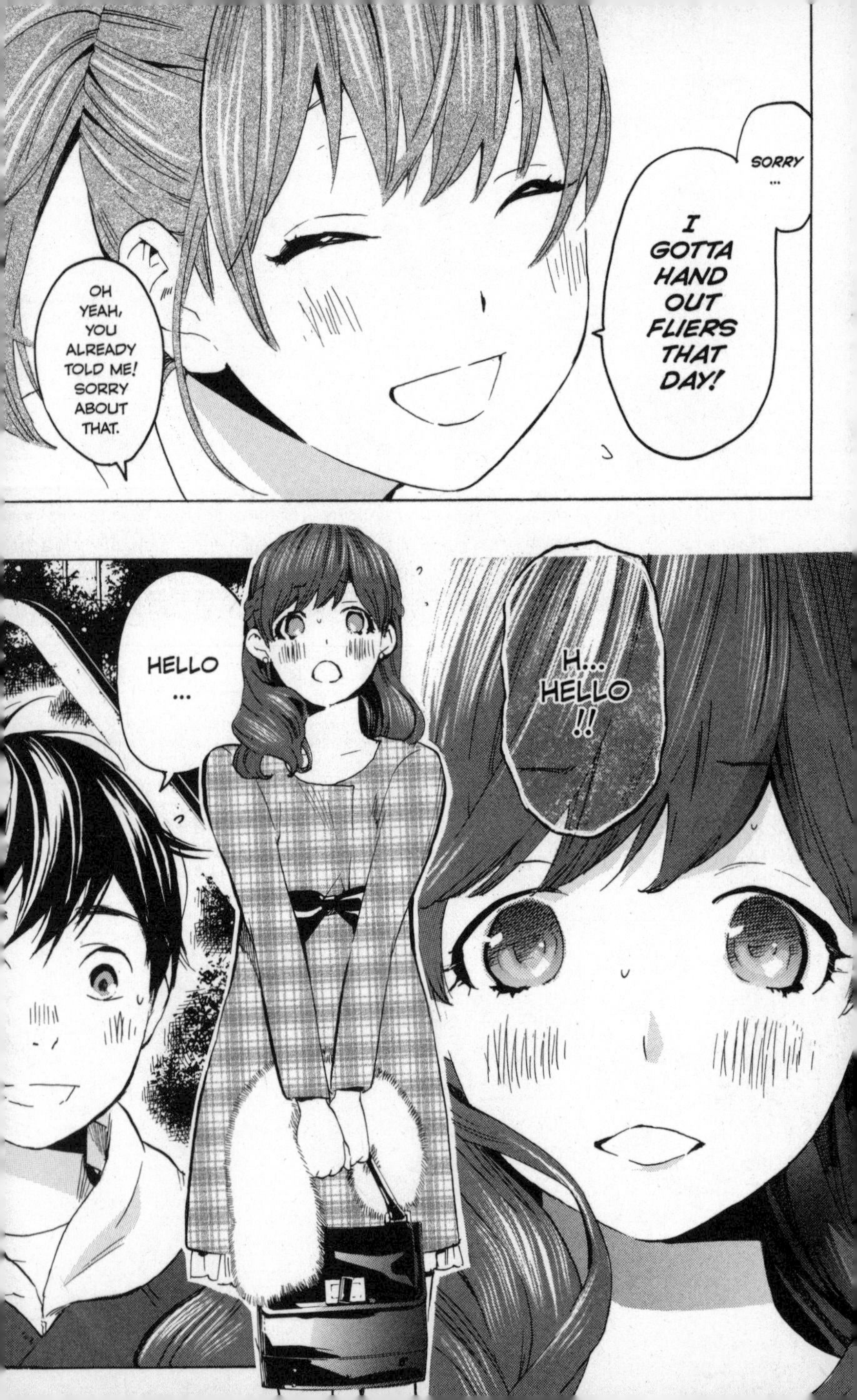
SORRY ... I GOTTA HAND OUT FLIERS THAT DAY!
OH YEAH, YOU ALREADY TOLD ME! SORRY ABOUT THAT.
H... HELLO !!
HELLO ...

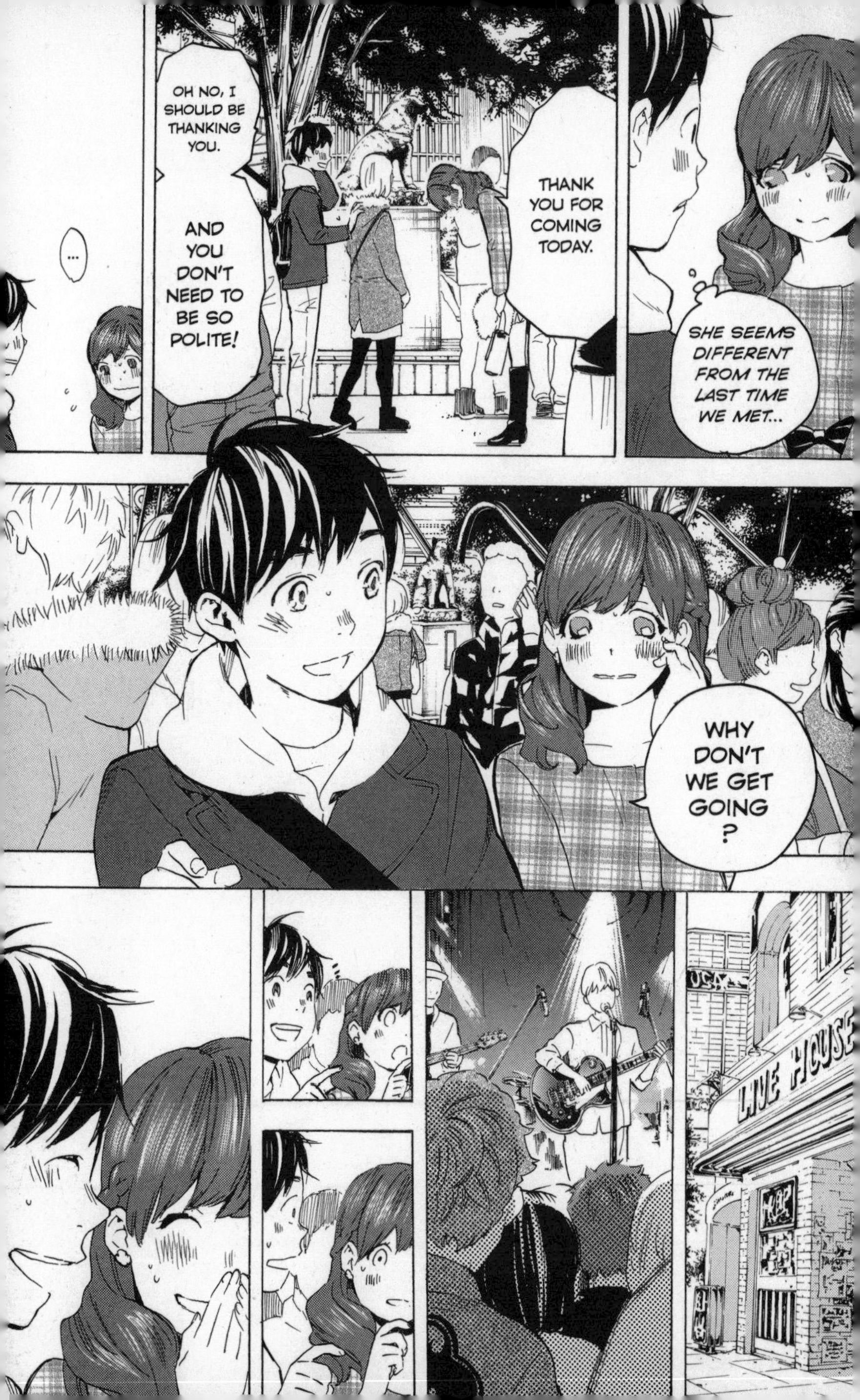
SHE SEEMS DIFFERENT FROM THE LAST TIME WE MET...
THANK YOU FOR COMING TODAY.
OH NO, I SHOULD BE THANKING YOU.
AND YOU DON'T NEED TO BE SO POLITE!
...
WHY DON'T WE GET GOING?
LIVE HOUSE

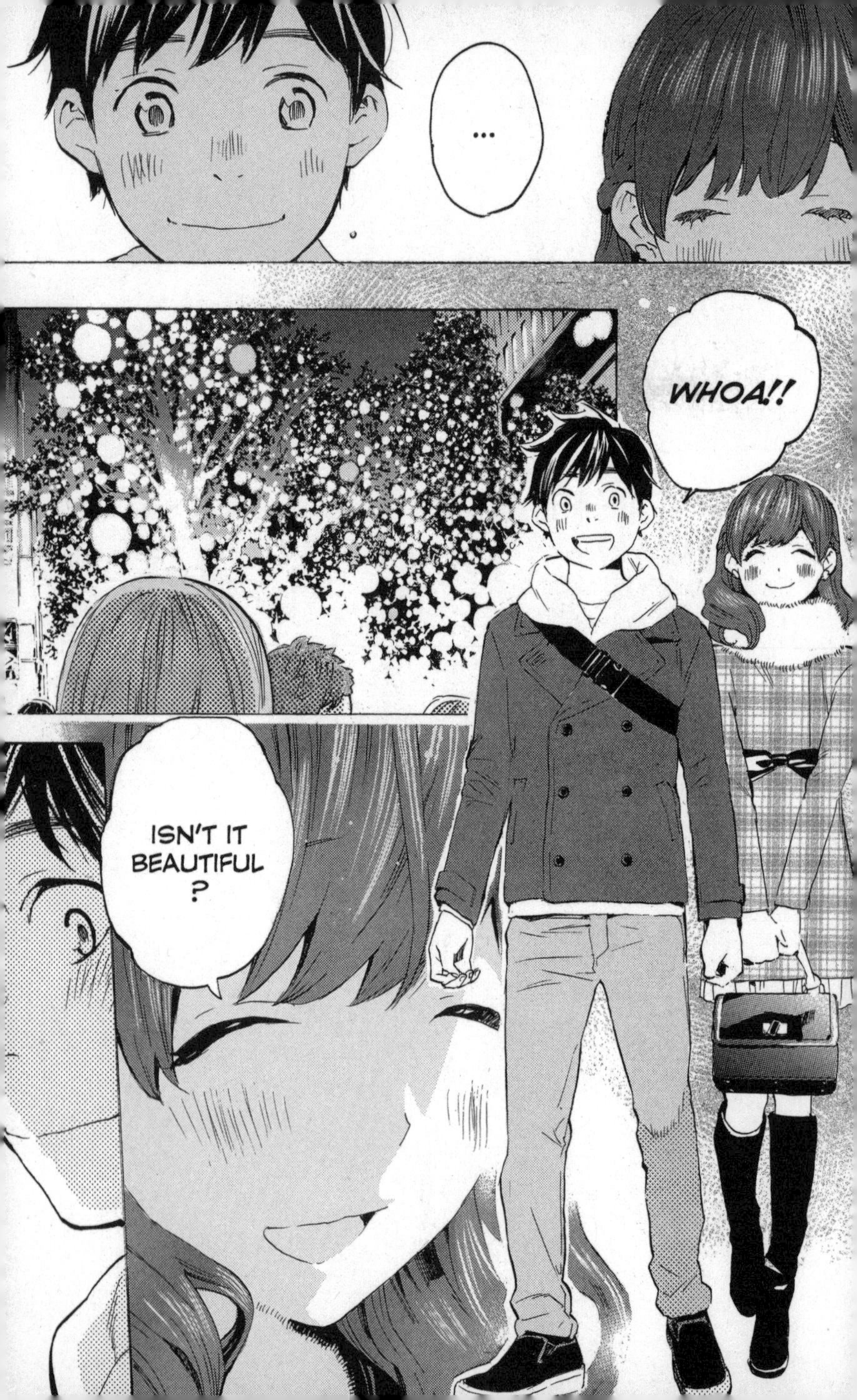
...
WHOA!!
ISN'T IT BEAUTIFUL ?

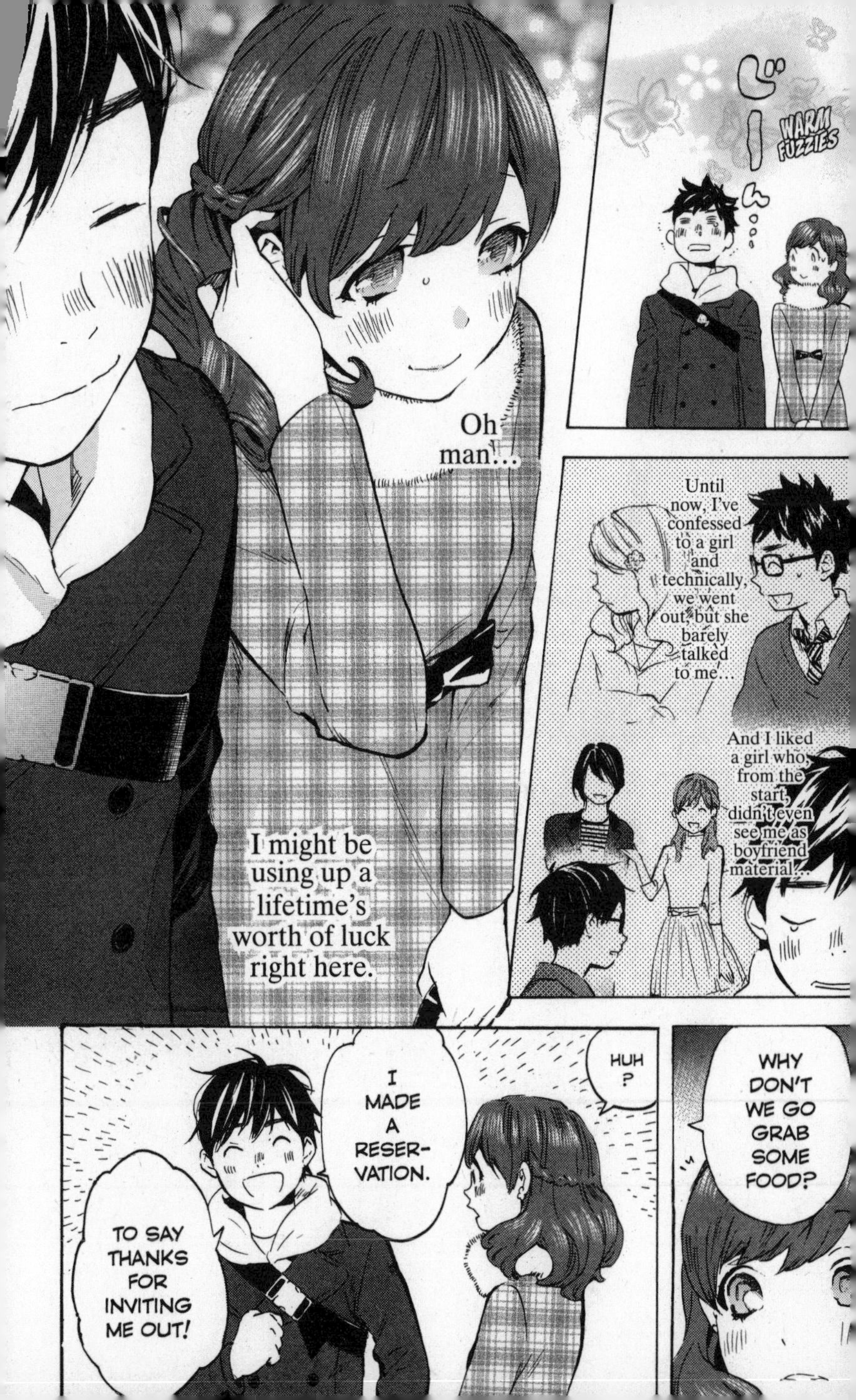
WARM FUZZIES
Until now, I've confessed to a girl and technically, we went out, but she barely talked to me...
And I liked a girl who, from the start, didn't even see me as boyfriend material...
Oh man...
I might be using up a lifetime's worth of luck right here.
WHY DON'T WE GO GRAB SOME FOOD?
HUH?
I MADE A RESER-VATION.
TO SAY THANKS FOR INVITING ME OUT!

MISTER SERIZAWA? YOUR RESERVATION IS FOR JANUARY 24TH...

God, what am I doing...?

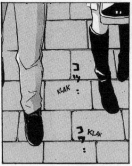

KLAK

KLAK

SORRY...

I AM SO SORRY.

OH, NO...

A-ARE YOU COLD?

I can't believe I've shown a girl such an awful time, and on Christmas..!

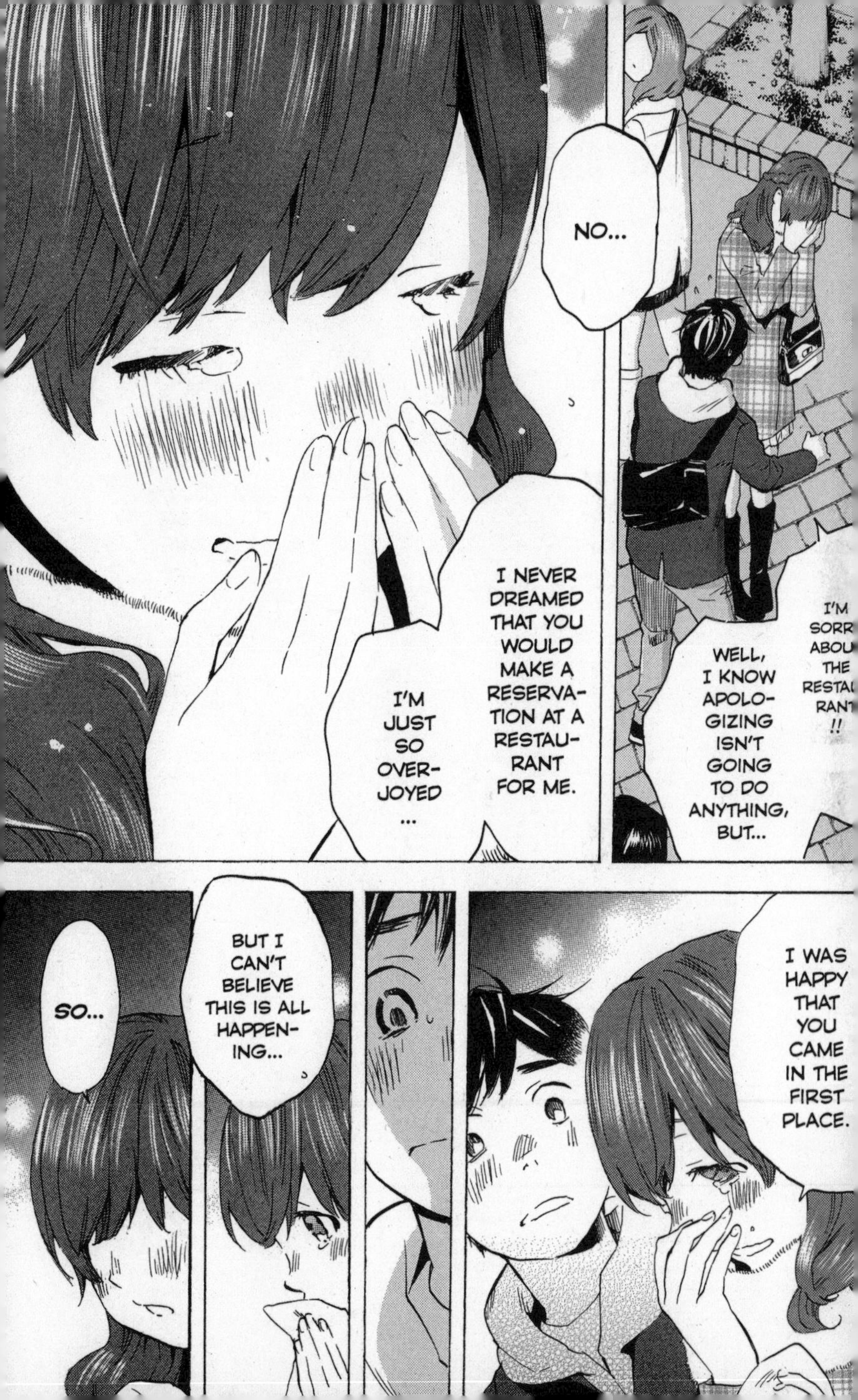
I'M SORR ABOU THE RESTA RANT !!
WELL, I KNOW APOLO-GIZING ISN'T GOING TO DO ANYTHING, BUT...
NO...
I NEVER DREAMED THAT YOU WOULD MAKE A RESERVA-TION AT A RESTAU-RANT FOR ME.
I'M JUST SO OVER-JOYED ...
I WAS HAPPY THAT YOU CAME IN THE FIRST PLACE.
BUT I CAN'T BELIEVE THIS IS ALL HAPPEN-ING...
SO...

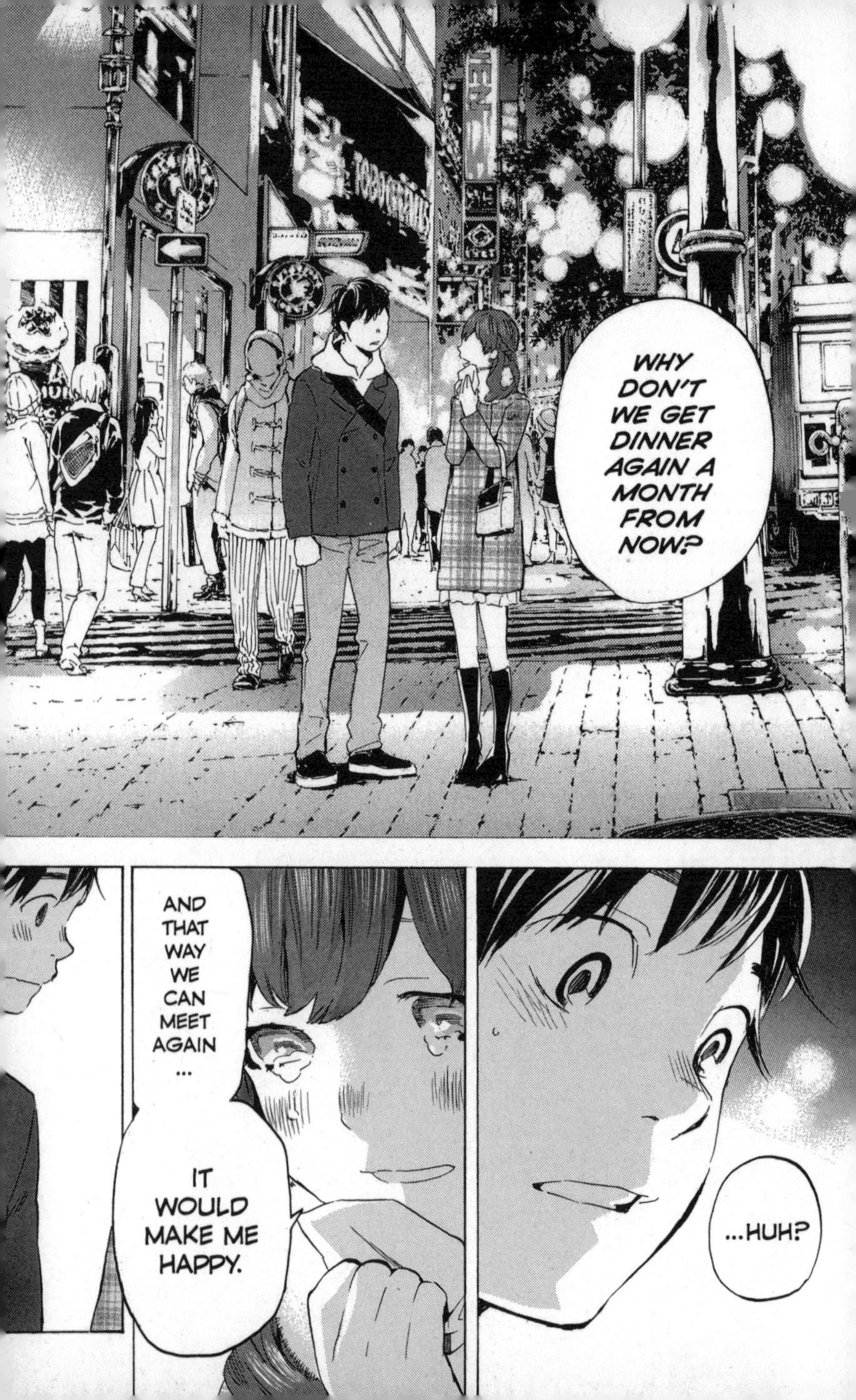
WHY DON'T WE GET DINNER AGAIN A MONTH FROM NOW?
...HUH?
AND THAT WAY WE CAN MEET AGAIN...
IT WOULD MAKE ME HAPPY.

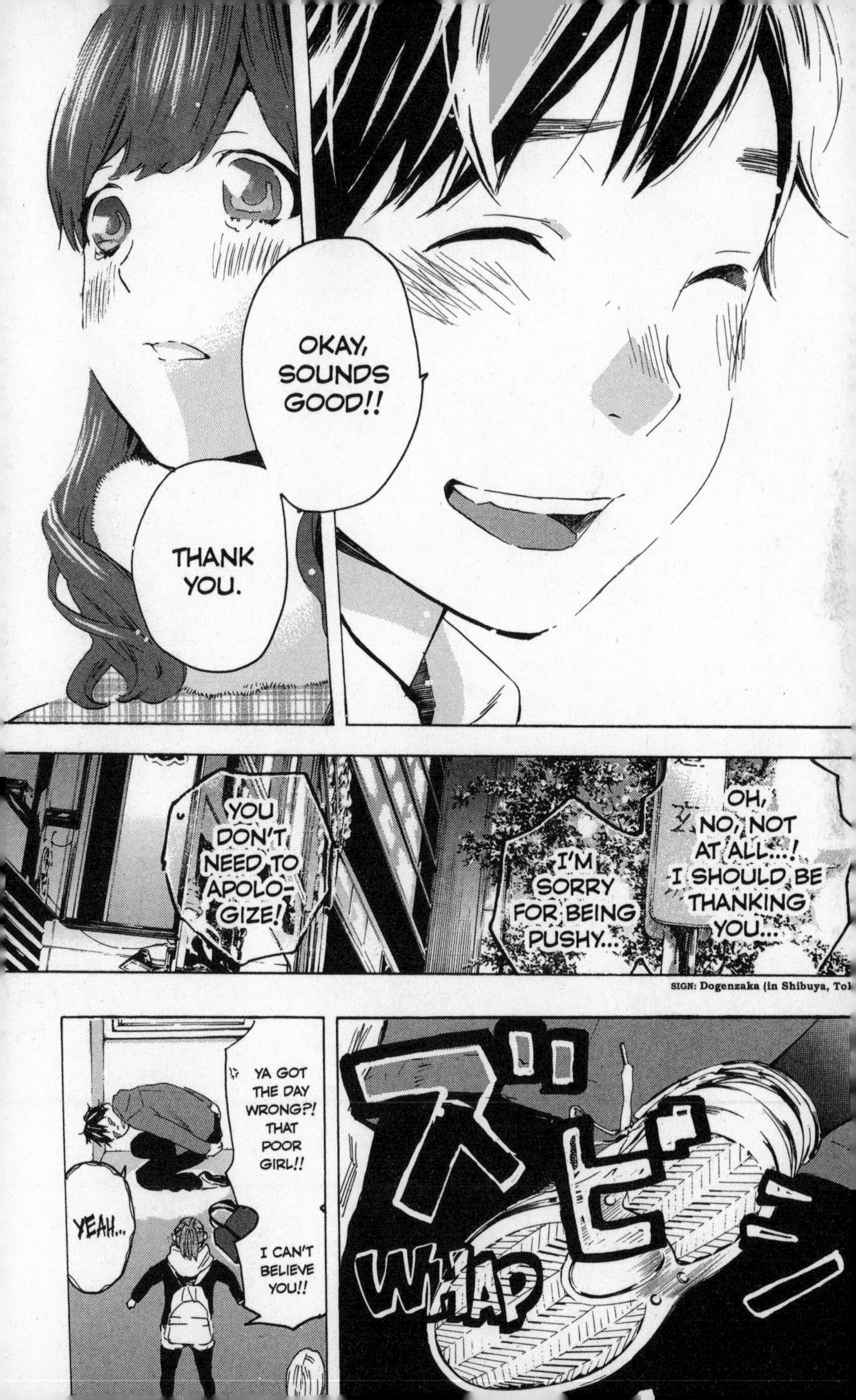
OKAY, SOUNDS GOOD!!
THANK YOU.
OH, NO, NOT AT ALL...! I SHOULD BE THANKING YOU...
I'M SORRY FOR BEING PUSHY...
YOU DON'T NEED TO APOLO-GIZE!
SIGN: Dogenzaka (in Shibuya, Tok
WHAP
YA GOT THE DAY WRONG?! THAT POOR GIRL!!
YEAH...
I CAN'T BELIEVE YOU!!

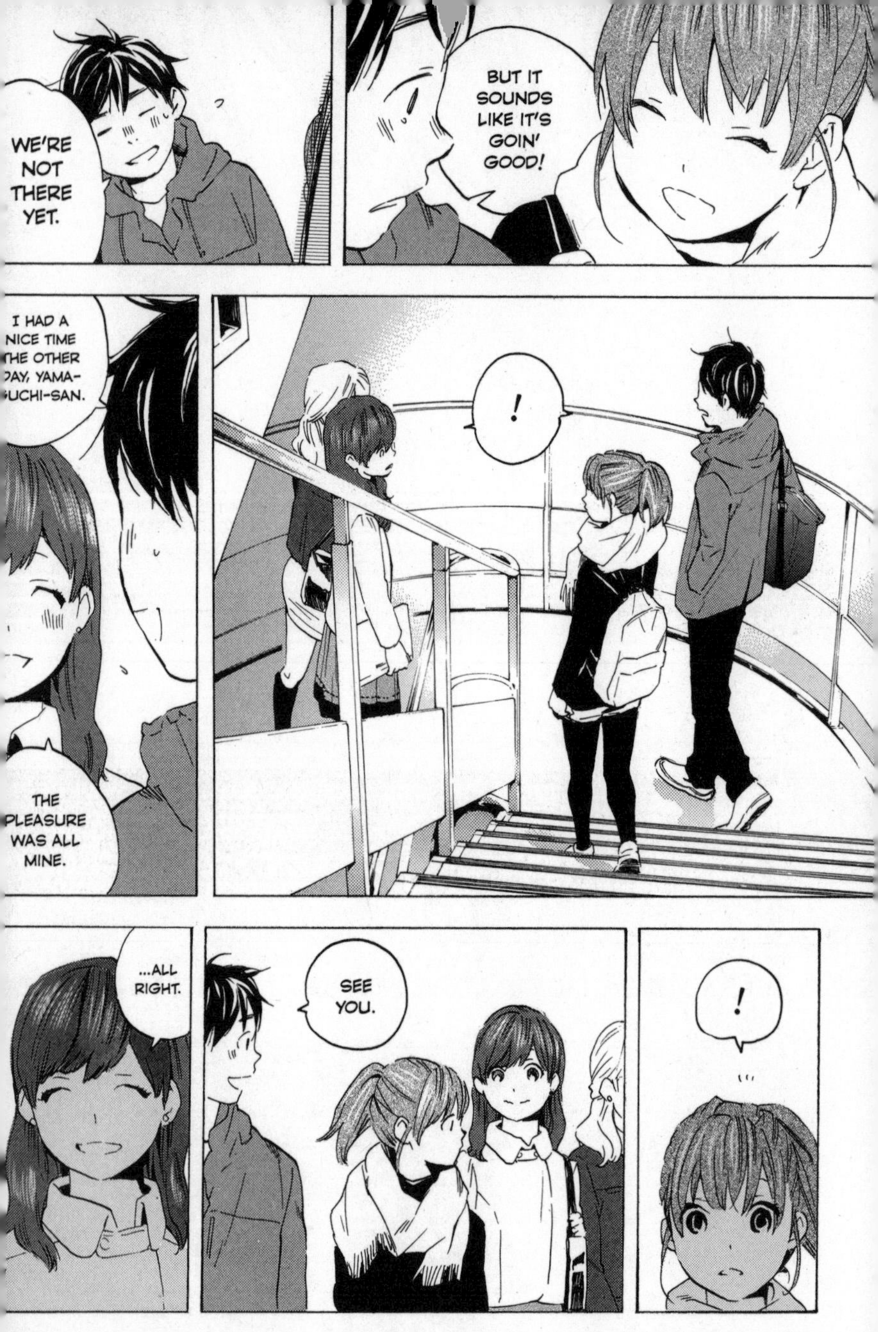
BUT IT SOUNDS LIKE IT'S GOIN' GOOD!
WE'RE NOT THERE YET.
!
I HAD A NICE TIME THE OTHER DAY, YAMAGUCHI-SAN.
THE PLEASURE WAS ALL MINE.
!
SEE YOU.
...ALL RIGHT.

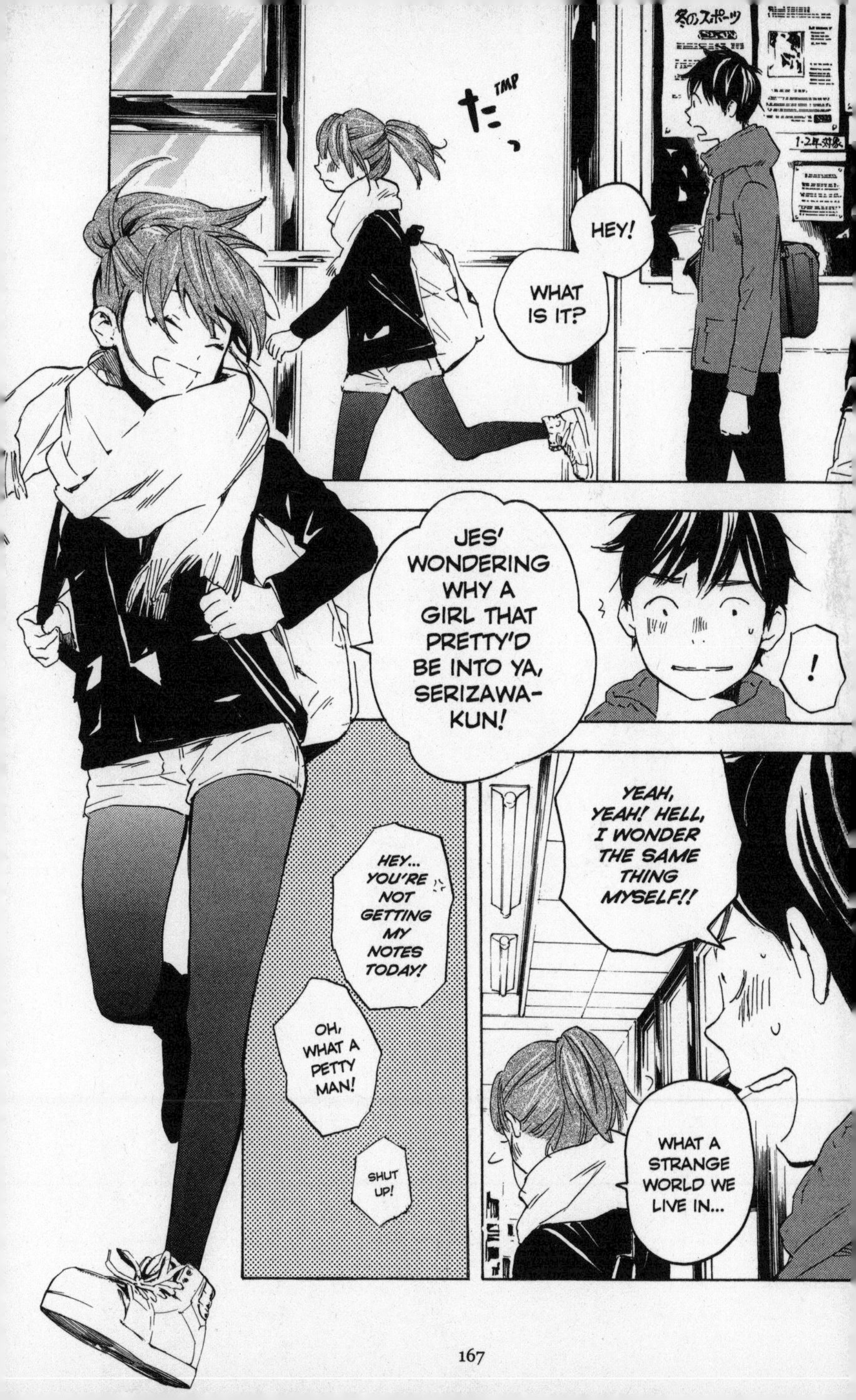
冬のスポーツ
1・2年対象
たっ
TMP
HEY!
WHAT IS IT?
!
JES' WONDERING WHY A GIRL THAT PRETTY'D BE INTO YA, SERIZAWA-KUN!
YEAH, YEAH! HELL, I WONDER THE SAME THING MYSELF!!
WHAT A STRANGE WORLD WE LIVE IN...
HEY... YOU'RE NOT GETTING MY NOTES TODAY!
OH, WHAT A PETTY MAN!
SHUT UP!

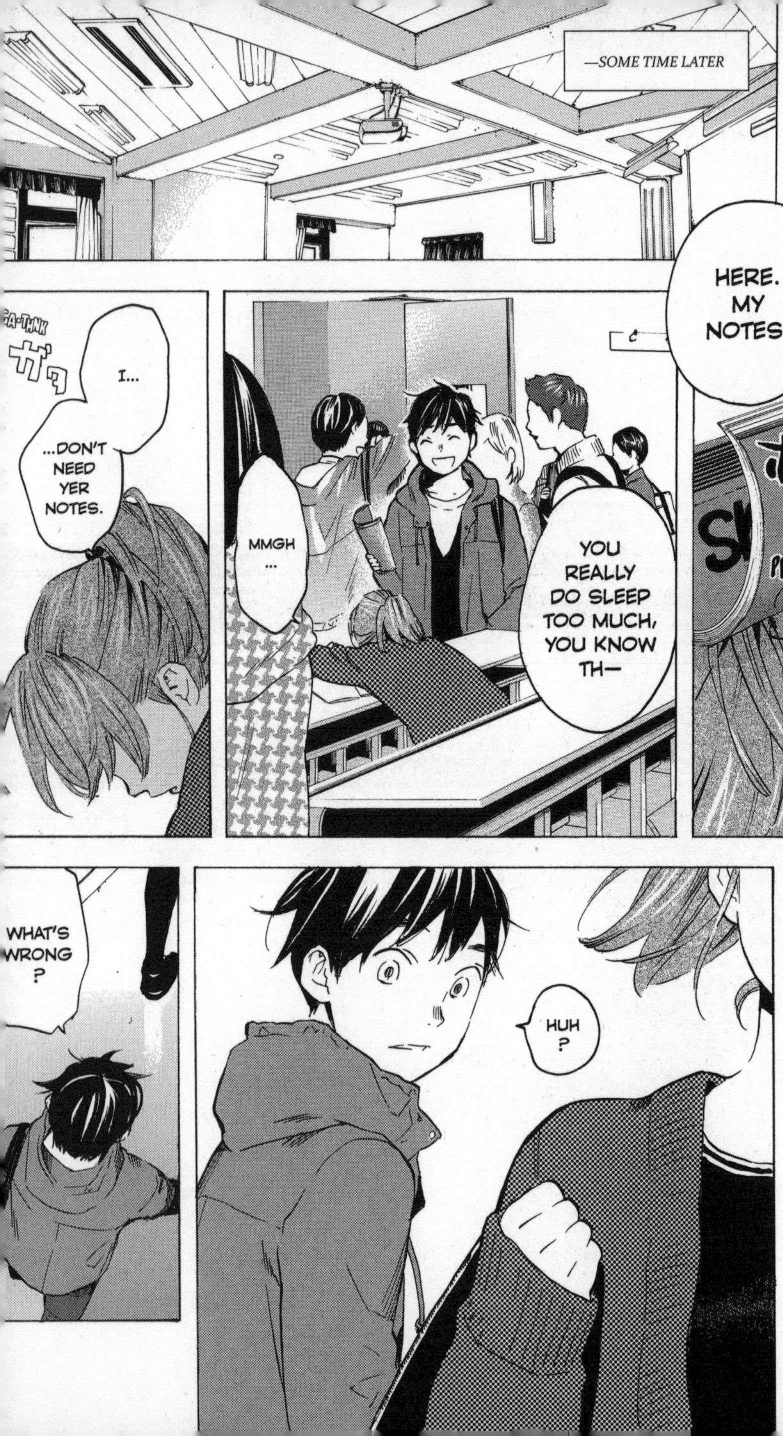
—SOME TIME LATER
HERE. MY NOTES.
ポン
PLOP
YOU REALLY DO SLEEP TOO MUCH, YOU KNOW TH—
MMGH ...
ガタ
I...
...DON'T NEED YER NOTES.
HUH?
WHAT'S WRONG?

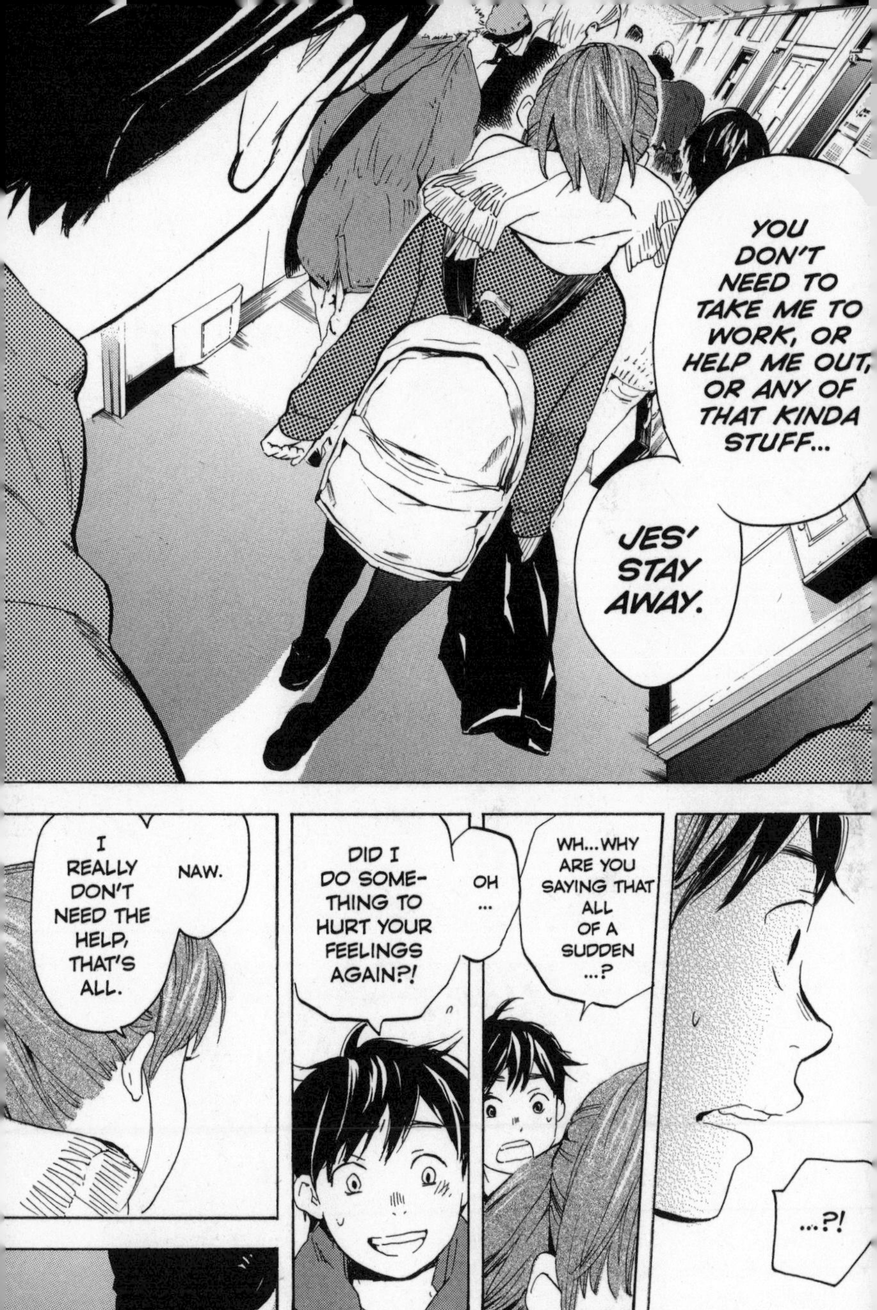
YOU DON'T NEED TO TAKE ME TO WORK, OR HELP ME OUT, OR ANY OF THAT KINDA STUFF...
JES' STAY AWAY.
...?!
WH...WHY ARE YOU SAYING THAT ALL OF A SUDDEN ...?
OH ...
DID I DO SOME-THING TO HURT YOUR FEELINGS AGAIN?!
NAW.
I REALLY DON'T NEED THE HELP, THAT'S ALL.

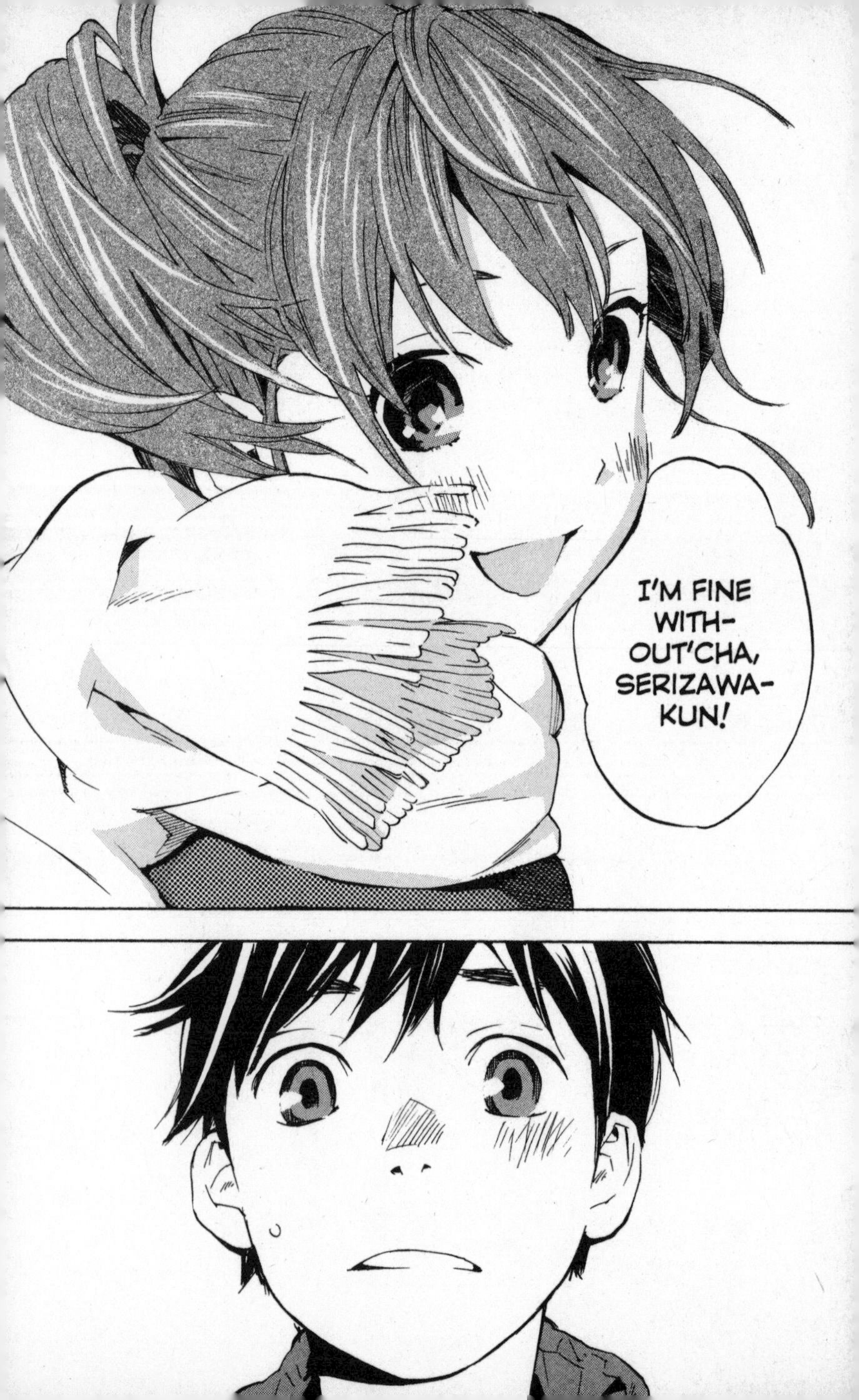
I'M FINE WITH-OUT'CHA, SERIZAWA-KUN!

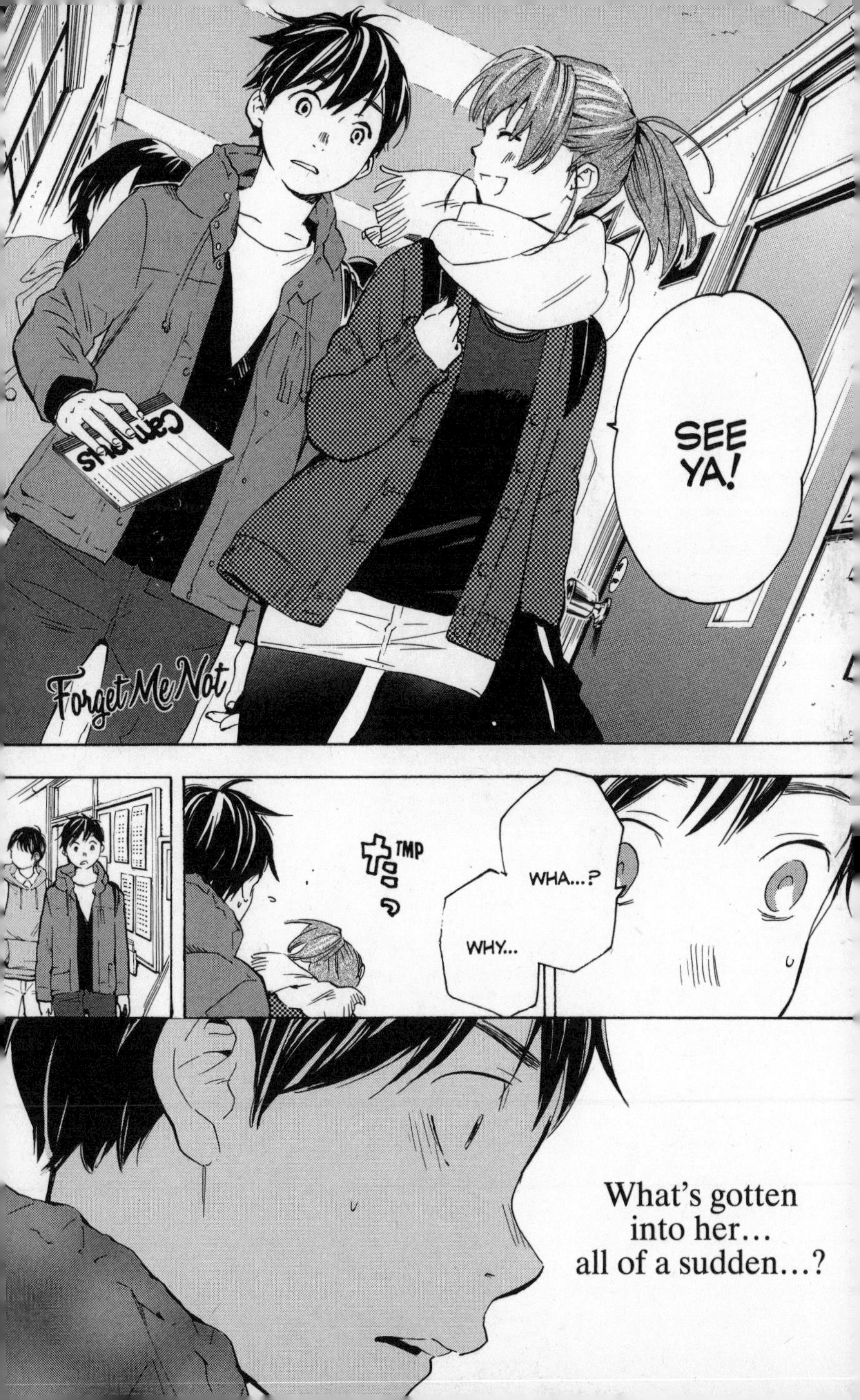
SEE YA!
Forget Me Not
WHA...?
WHY...
TMP
What's gotten into her… all of a sudden…?

CHAPTER 15:
Tsukushi Makino 4

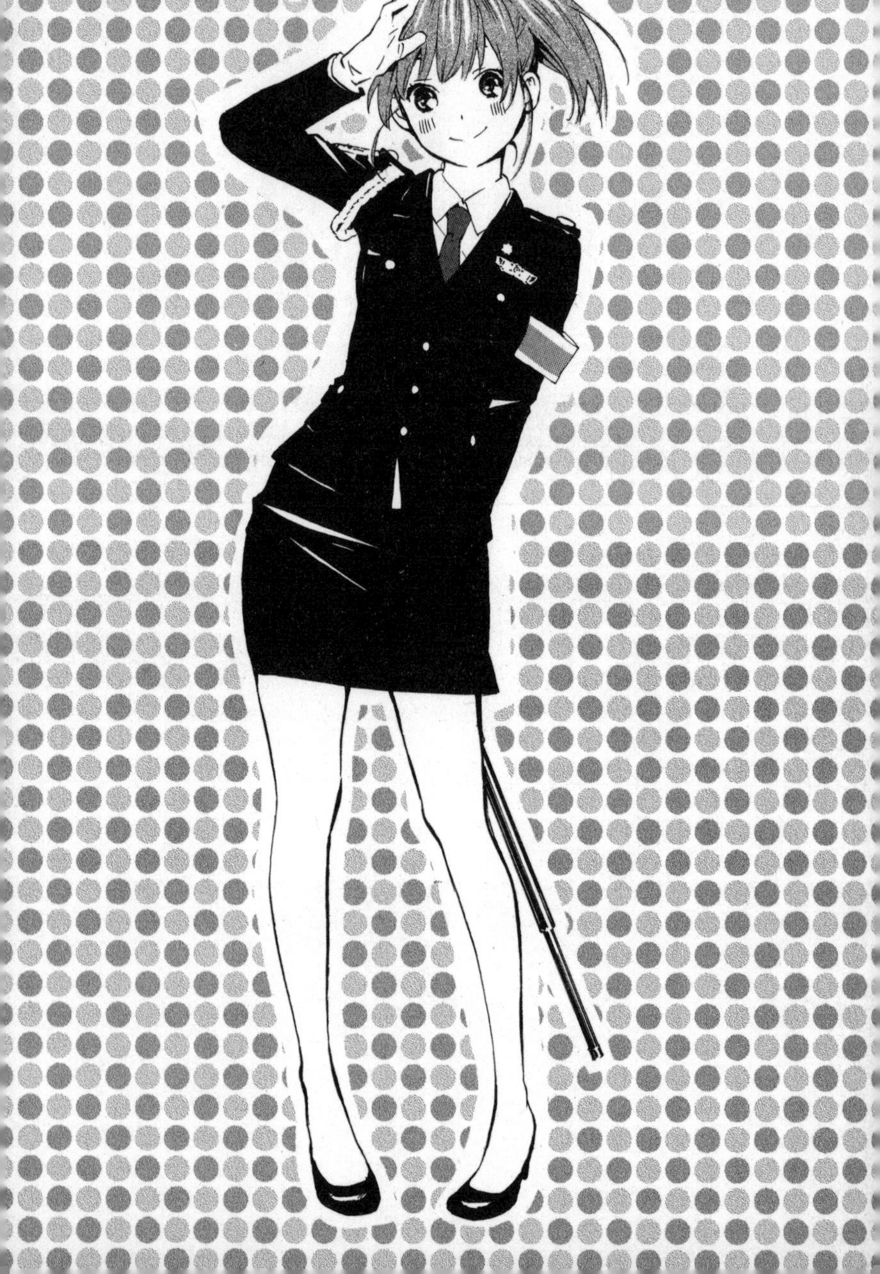

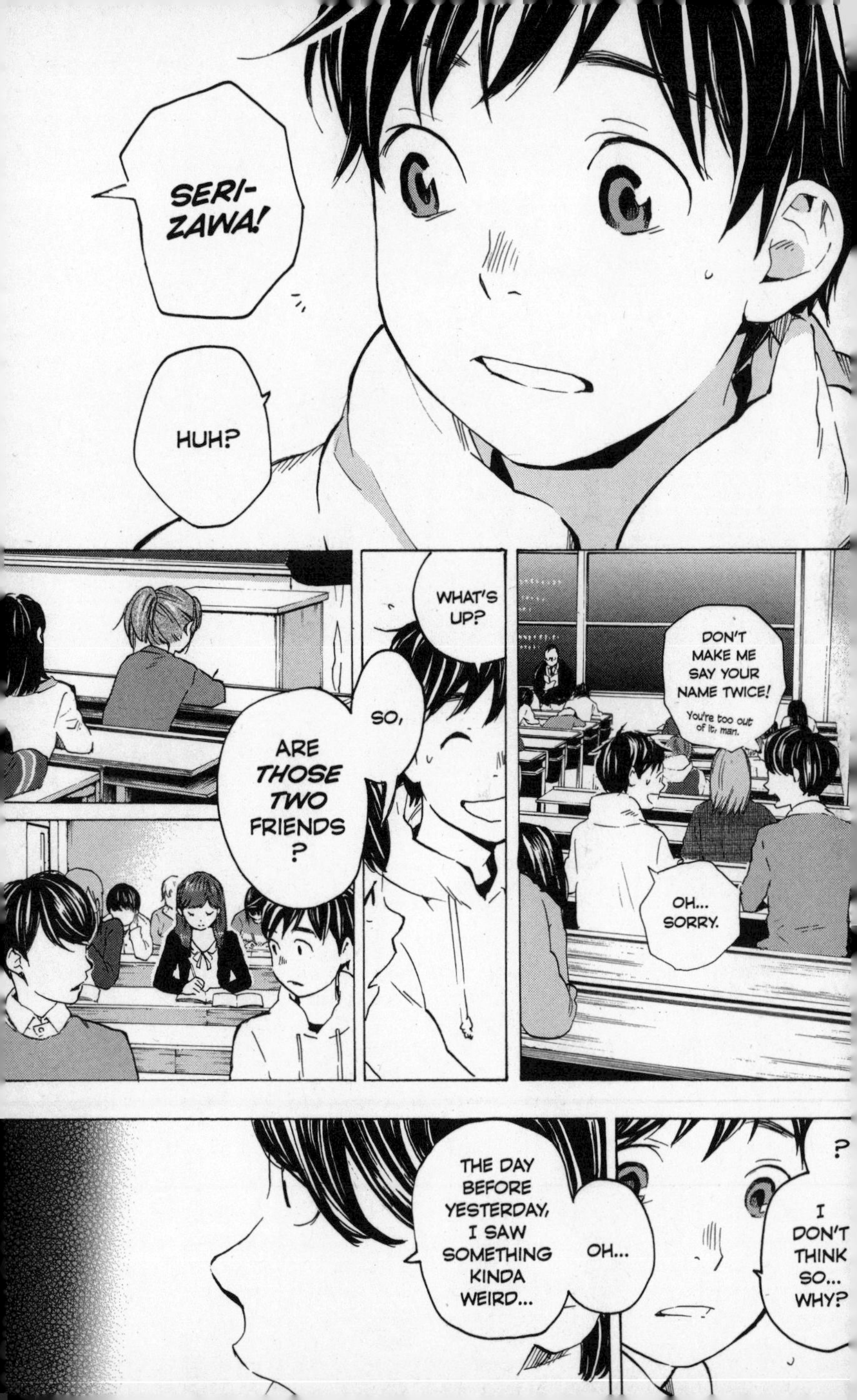
SERI-ZAWA!
HUH?
DON'T MAKE ME SAY YOUR NAME TWICE!
You're too out of it, man.
OH... SORRY.
WHAT'S UP?
SO, ARE THOSE TWO FRIENDS?
?
I DON'T THINK SO... WHY?
OH...
THE DAY BEFORE YESTERDAY, I SAW SOMETHING KINDA WEIRD...

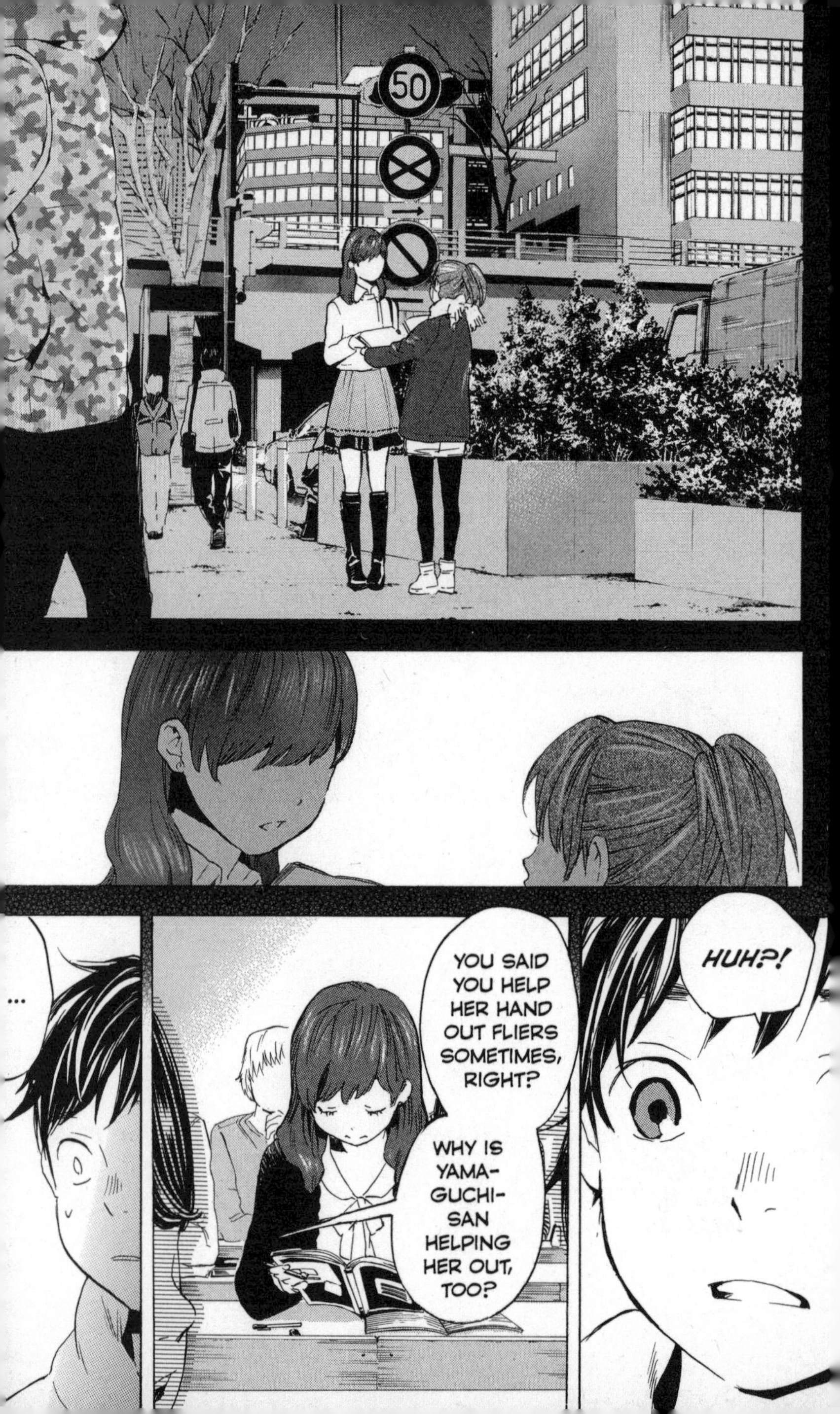
50
HUH?!
YOU SAID YOU HELP HER HAND OUT FLIERS SOMETIMES, RIGHT?
WHY IS YAMA-GUCHI-SAN HELPING HER OUT, TOO?
...

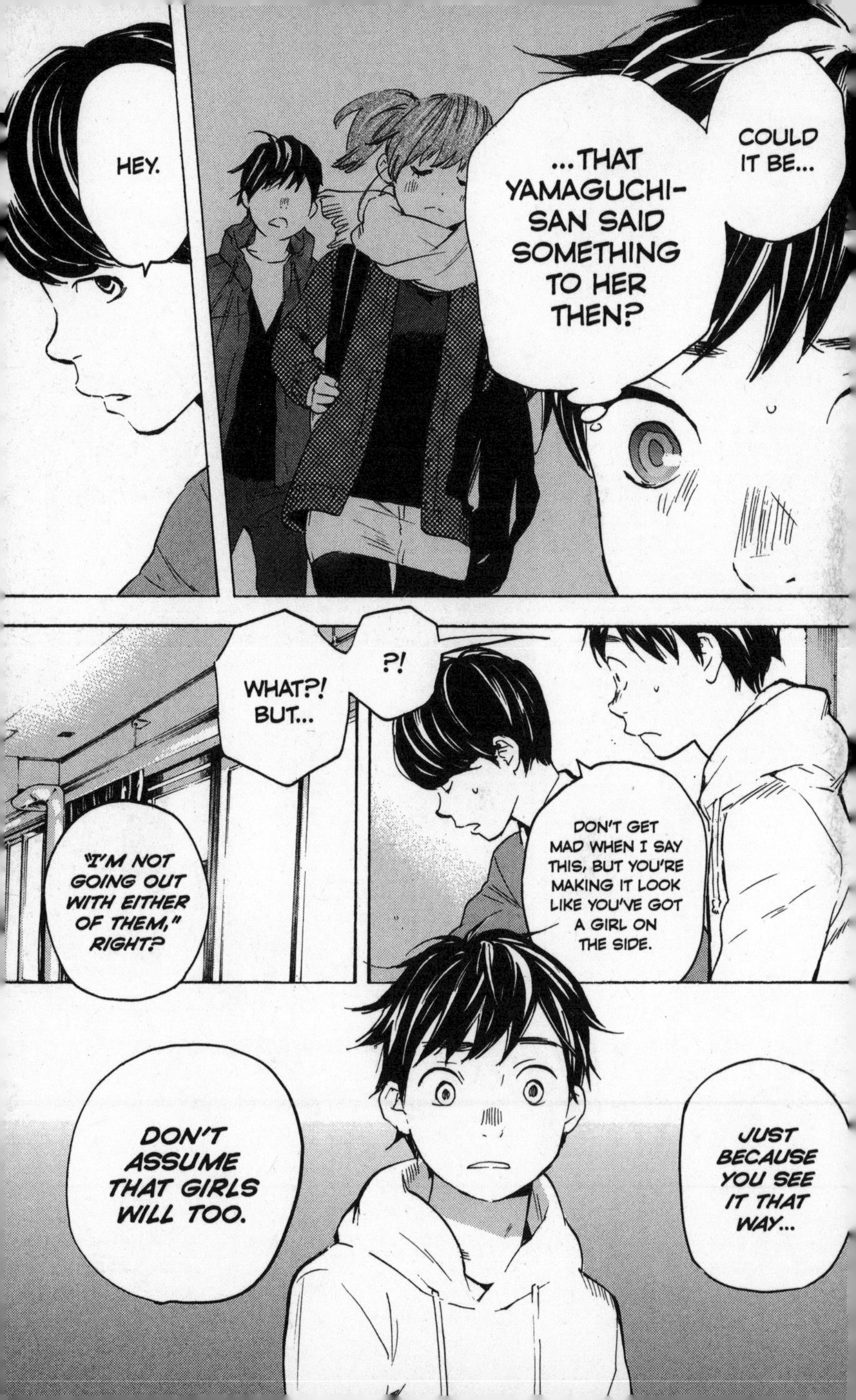
COULD IT BE...
...THAT YAMAGUCHI-SAN SAID SOMETHING TO HER THEN?
HEY.
?!
WHAT?! BUT...
DON'T GET MAD WHEN I SAY THIS, BUT YOU'RE MAKING IT LOOK LIKE YOU'VE GOT A GIRL ON THE SIDE.
"I'M NOT GOING OUT WITH EITHER OF THEM," RIGHT?
JUST BECAUSE YOU SEE IT THAT WAY...
DON'T ASSUME THAT GIRLS WILL TOO.

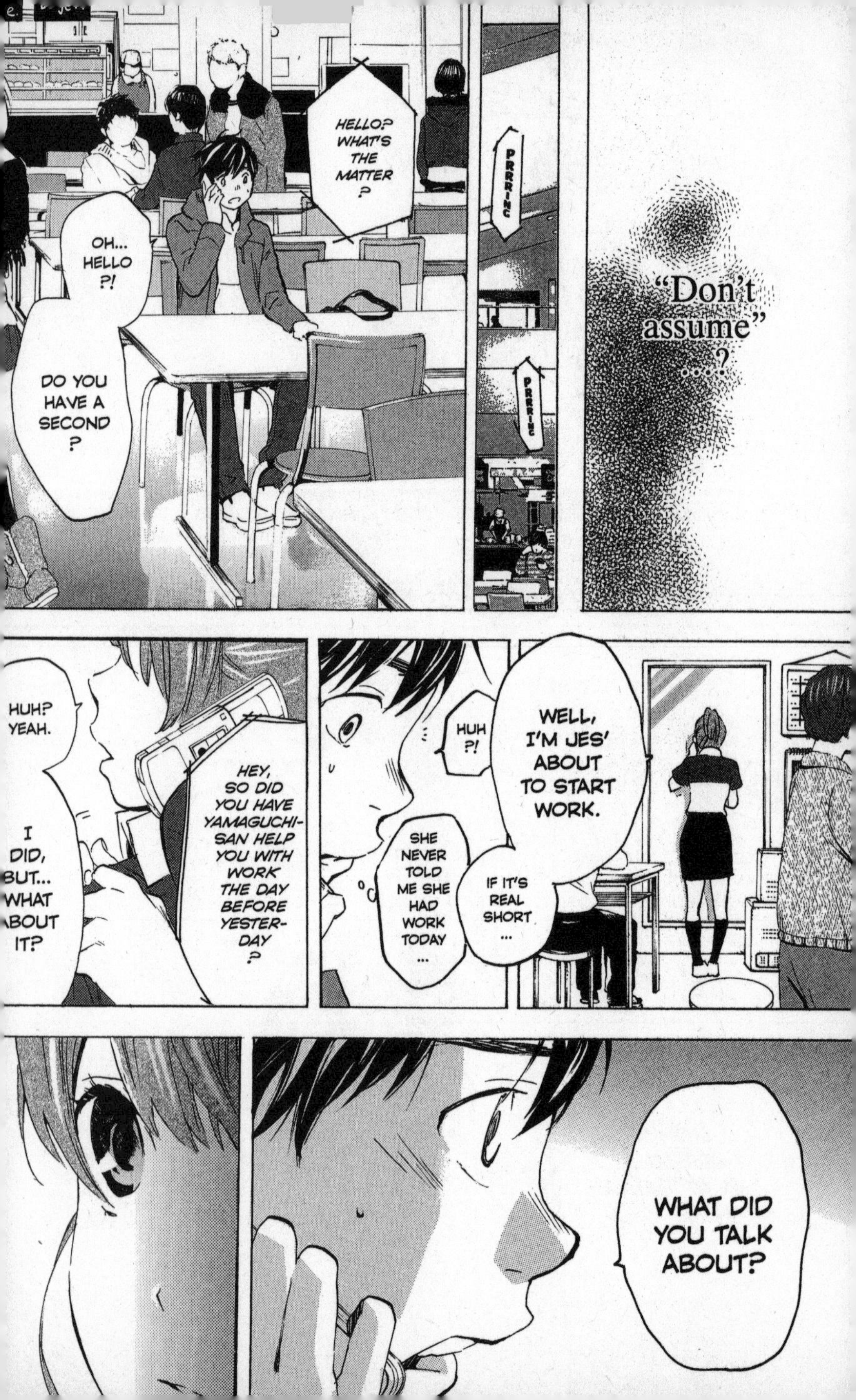

"Don't assume" ...?
PRRRING
PRRRING
HELLO? WHAT'S THE MATTER?
OH... HELLO?!
DO YOU HAVE A SECOND?
WELL, I'M JES' ABOUT TO START WORK.
IF IT'S REAL SHORT...
HUH?!
SHE NEVER TOLD ME SHE HAD WORK TODAY...
HEY, SO DID YOU HAVE YAMAGUCHI-SAN HELP YOU WITH WORK THE DAY BEFORE YESTERDAY?
HUH? YEAH.
I DID, BUT... WHAT ABOUT IT?
WHAT DID YOU TALK ABOUT?

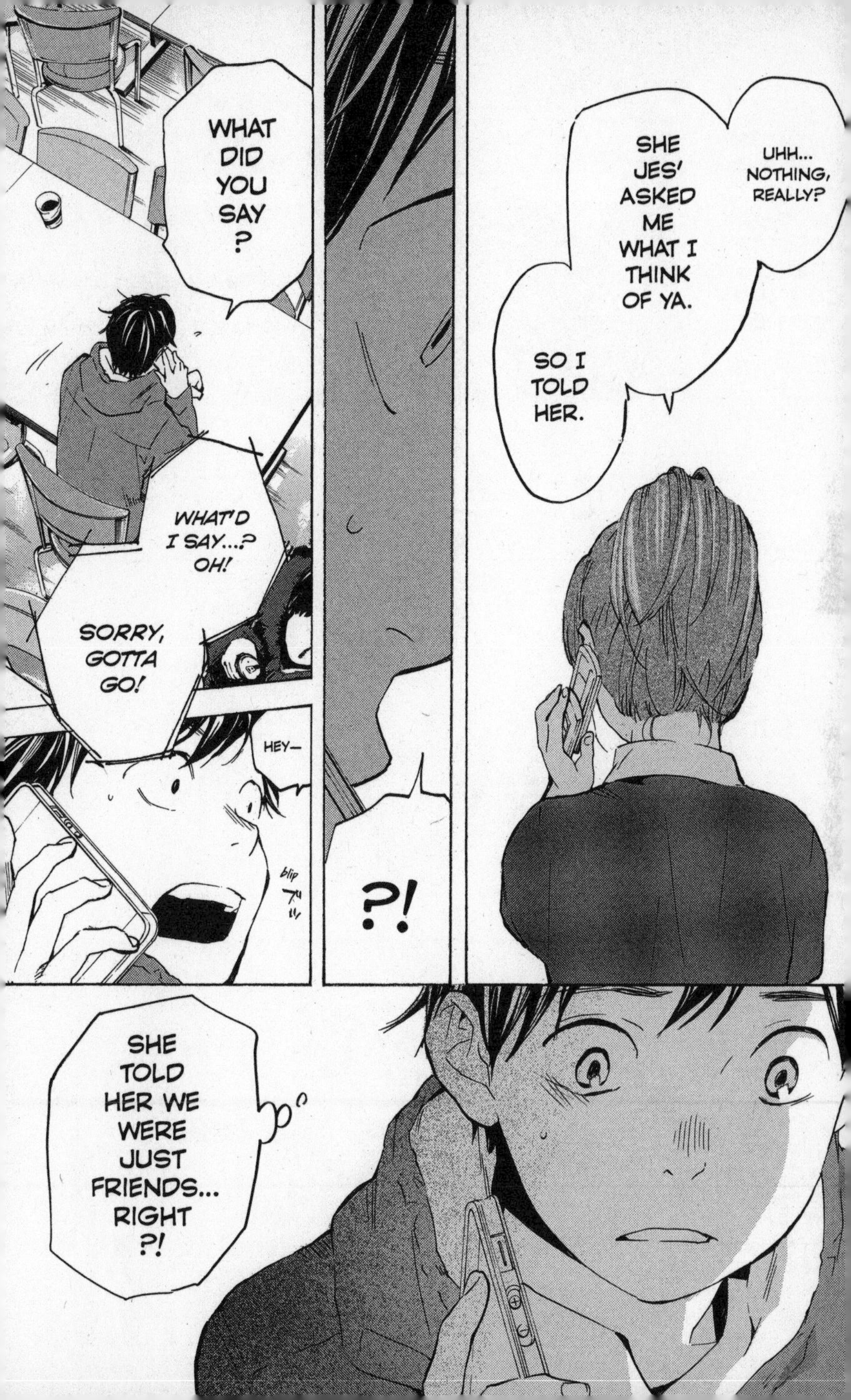
UHH... NOTHING, REALLY?
SHE JES' ASKED ME WHAT I THINK OF YA.
SO I TOLD HER.
?!
WHAT DID YOU SAY?
WHAT'D I SAY...? OH!
SORRY, GOTTA GO!
HEY—
blip
SHE TOLD HER WE WERE JUST FRIENDS... RIGHT?!

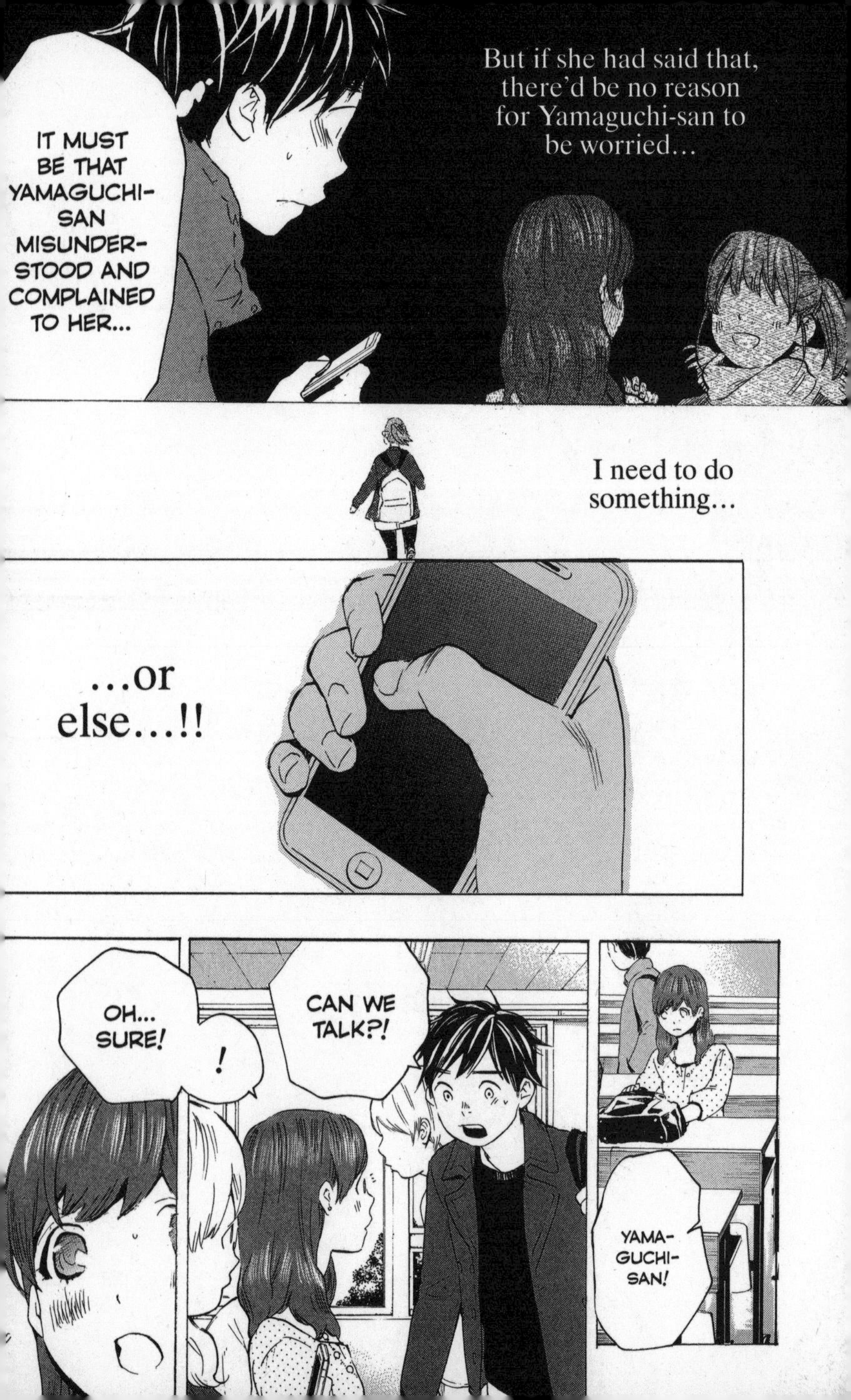

But if she had said that, there'd be no reason for Yamaguchi-san to be worried...
IT MUST BE THAT YAMAGUCHI-SAN MISUNDERSTOOD AND COMPLAINED TO HER...
I need to do something...
...or else...!!
YAMA-GUCHI-SAN!
CAN WE TALK?!
!
OH... SURE!

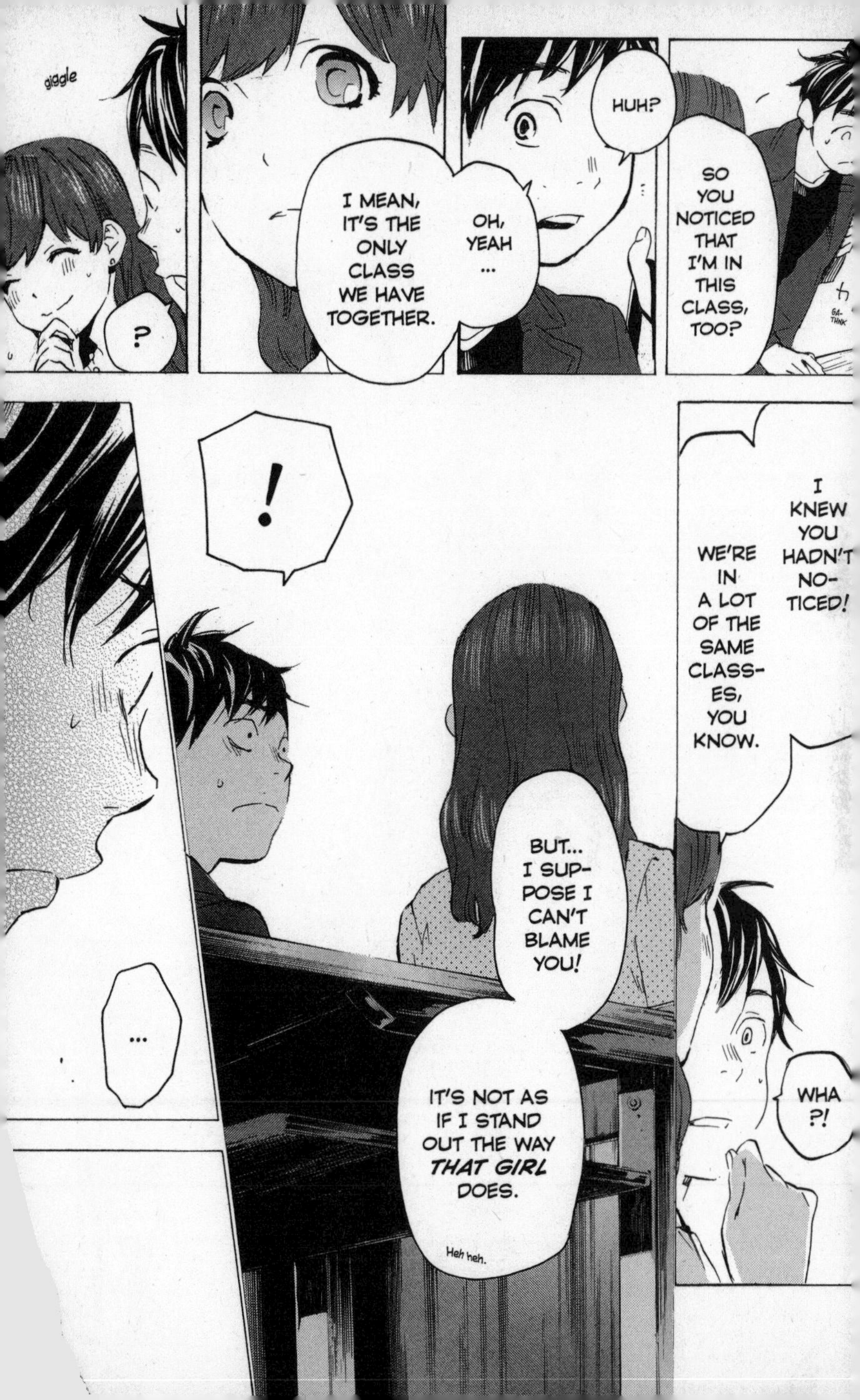
SO YOU NOTICED THAT I'M IN THIS CLASS, TOO?
GA-THNK
HUH?
OH, YEAH ...
I MEAN, IT'S THE ONLY CLASS WE HAVE TOGETHER.
giggle
?
I KNEW YOU HADN'T NOTICED!
WE'RE IN A LOT OF THE SAME CLASSES, YOU KNOW.
WHA ?!
!
BUT... I SUPPOSE I CAN'T BLAME YOU!
IT'S NOT AS IF I STAND OUT THE WAY *THAT GIRL* DOES.
Heh heh.
...

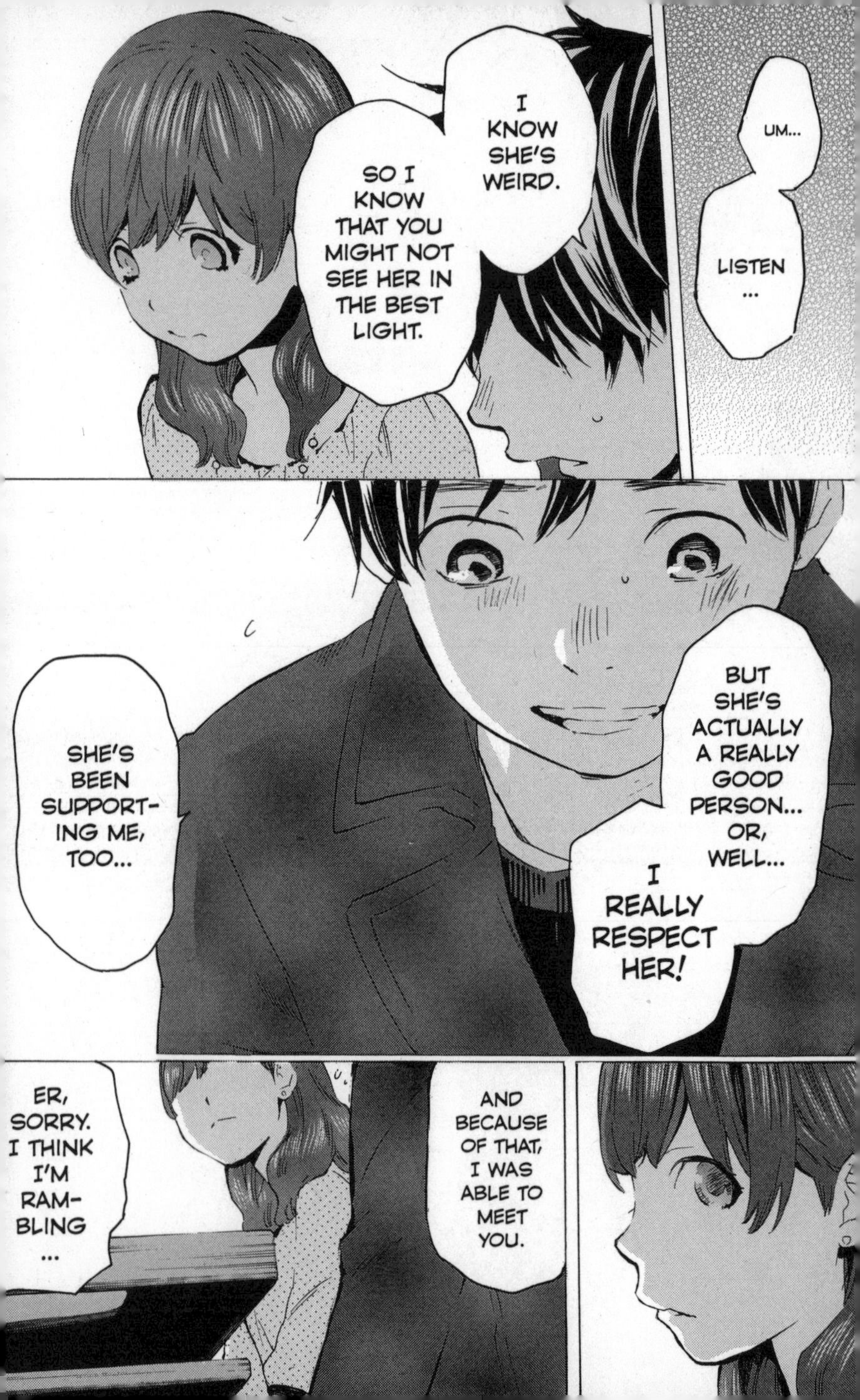
UM... LISTEN...
I KNOW SHE'S WEIRD.
SO I KNOW THAT YOU MIGHT NOT SEE HER IN THE BEST LIGHT.
BUT SHE'S ACTUALLY A REALLY GOOD PERSON... OR, WELL...
I REALLY RESPECT HER!
SHE'S BEEN SUPPORTING ME, TOO...
AND BECAUSE OF THAT, I WAS ABLE TO MEET YOU.
ER, SORRY. I THINK I'M RAMBLING...

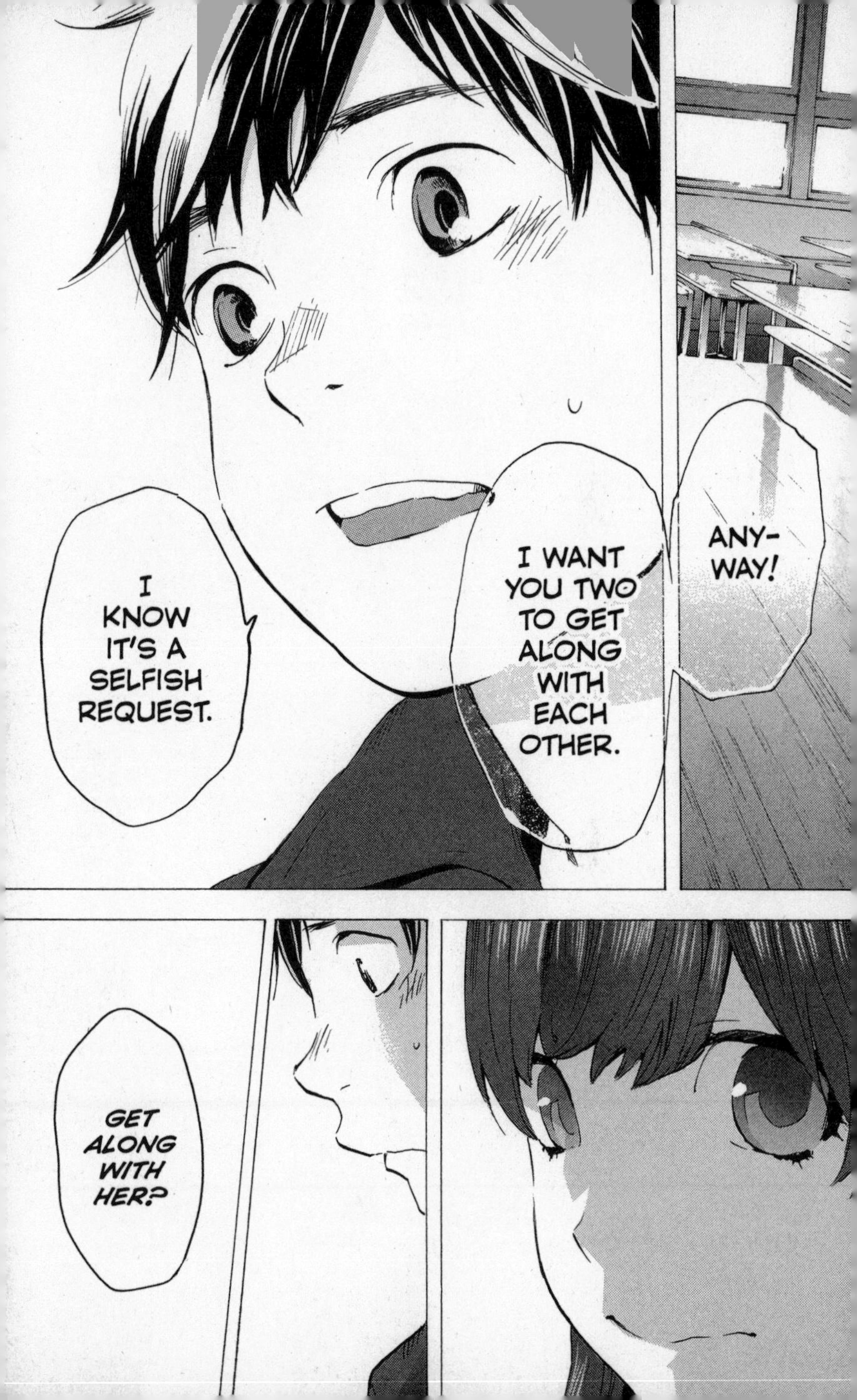
ANY-WAY!
I WANT YOU TWO TO GET ALONG WITH EACH OTHER.
I KNOW IT'S A SELFISH REQUEST.
GET ALONG WITH HER?

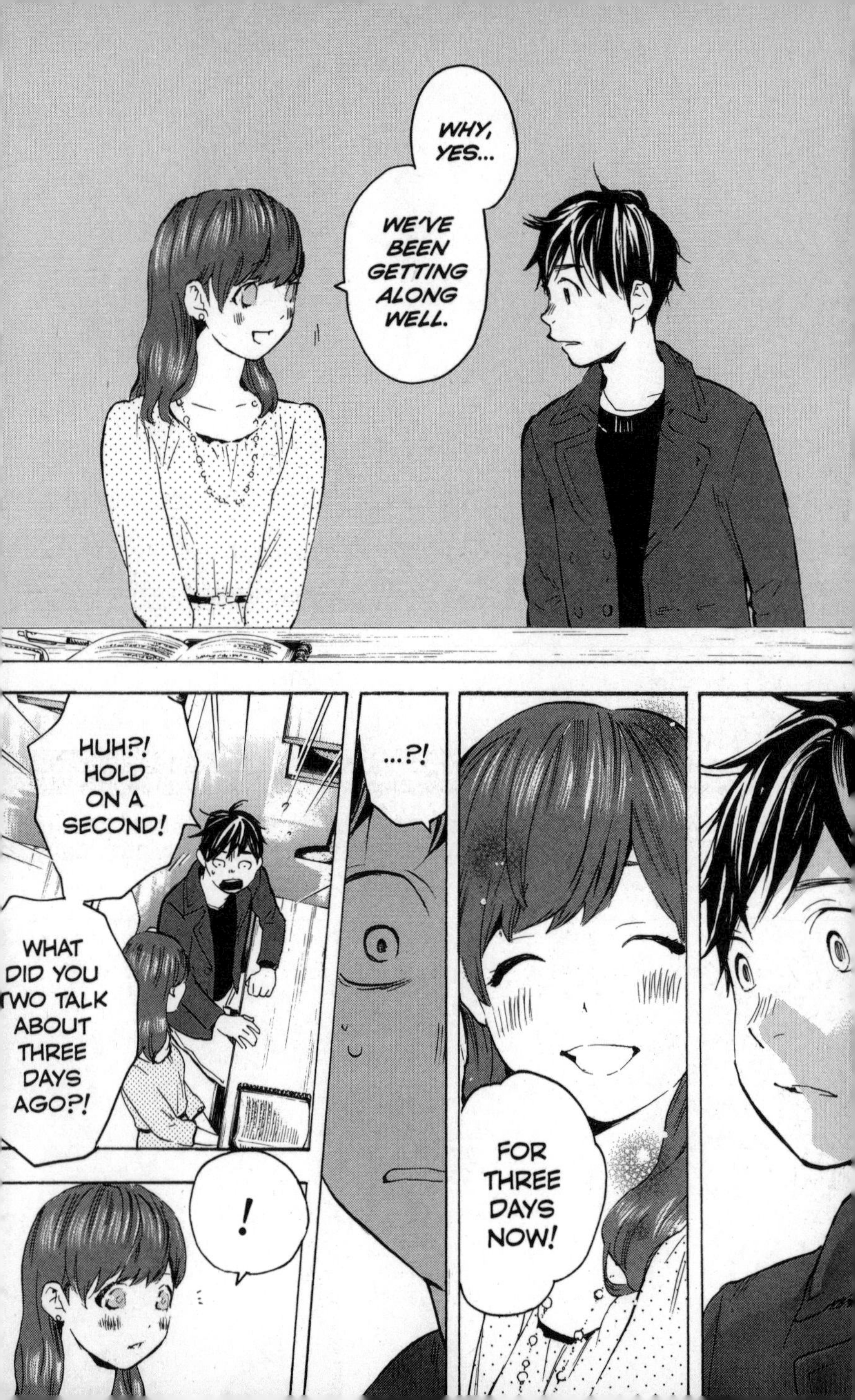
WHY, YES...
WE'VE BEEN GETTING ALONG WELL.
FOR THREE DAYS NOW!
...?!
HUH?! HOLD ON A SECOND!
WHAT DID YOU TWO TALK ABOUT THREE DAYS AGO?!
!

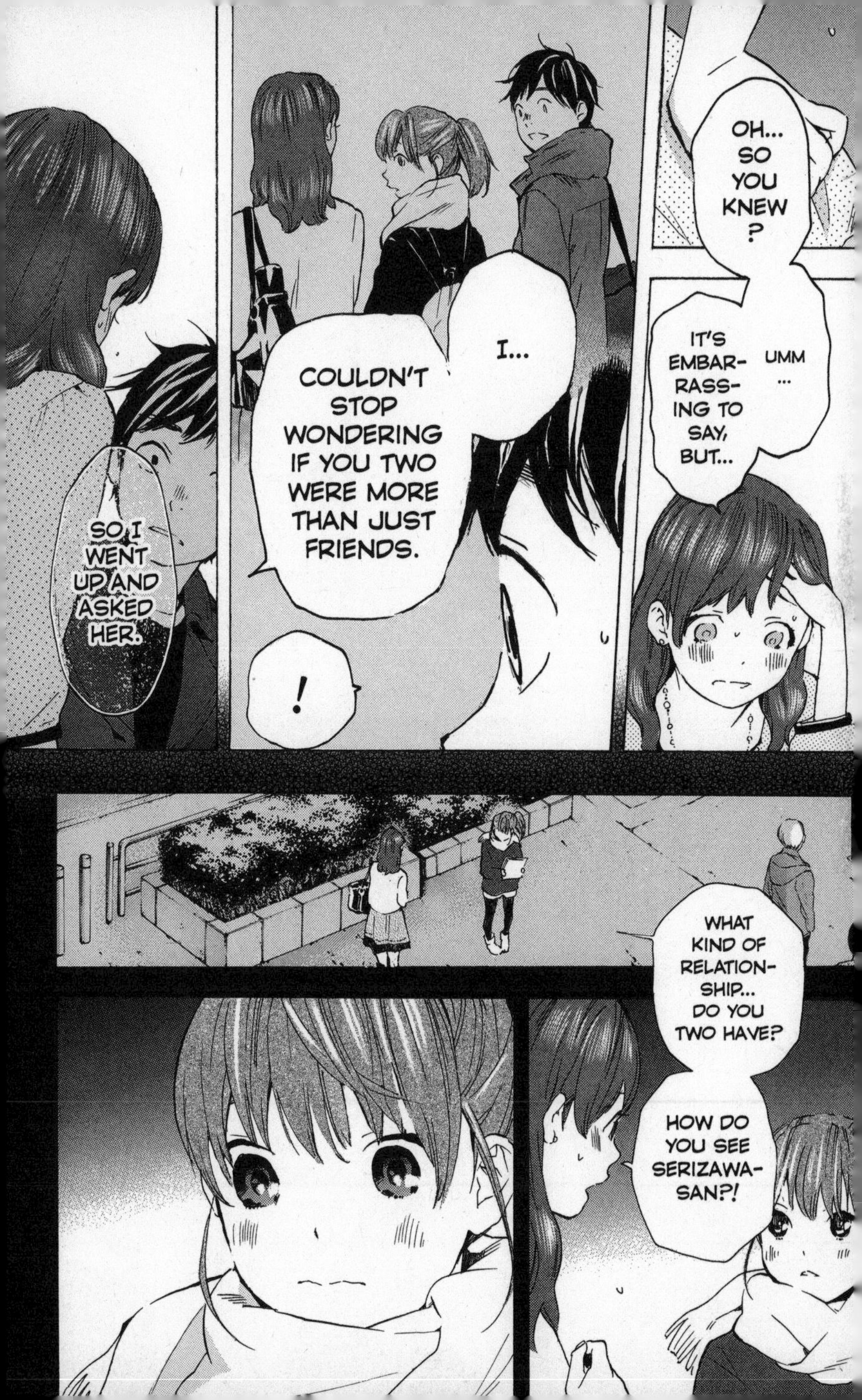
OH... SO YOU KNEW?
UMM...
IT'S EMBARRASSING TO SAY, BUT...
I...
COULDN'T STOP WONDERING IF YOU TWO WERE MORE THAN JUST FRIENDS.
!
SO I WENT UP AND ASKED HER.
WHAT KIND OF RELATIONSHIP... DO YOU TWO HAVE?
HOW DO YOU SEE SERIZAWA-SAN?!

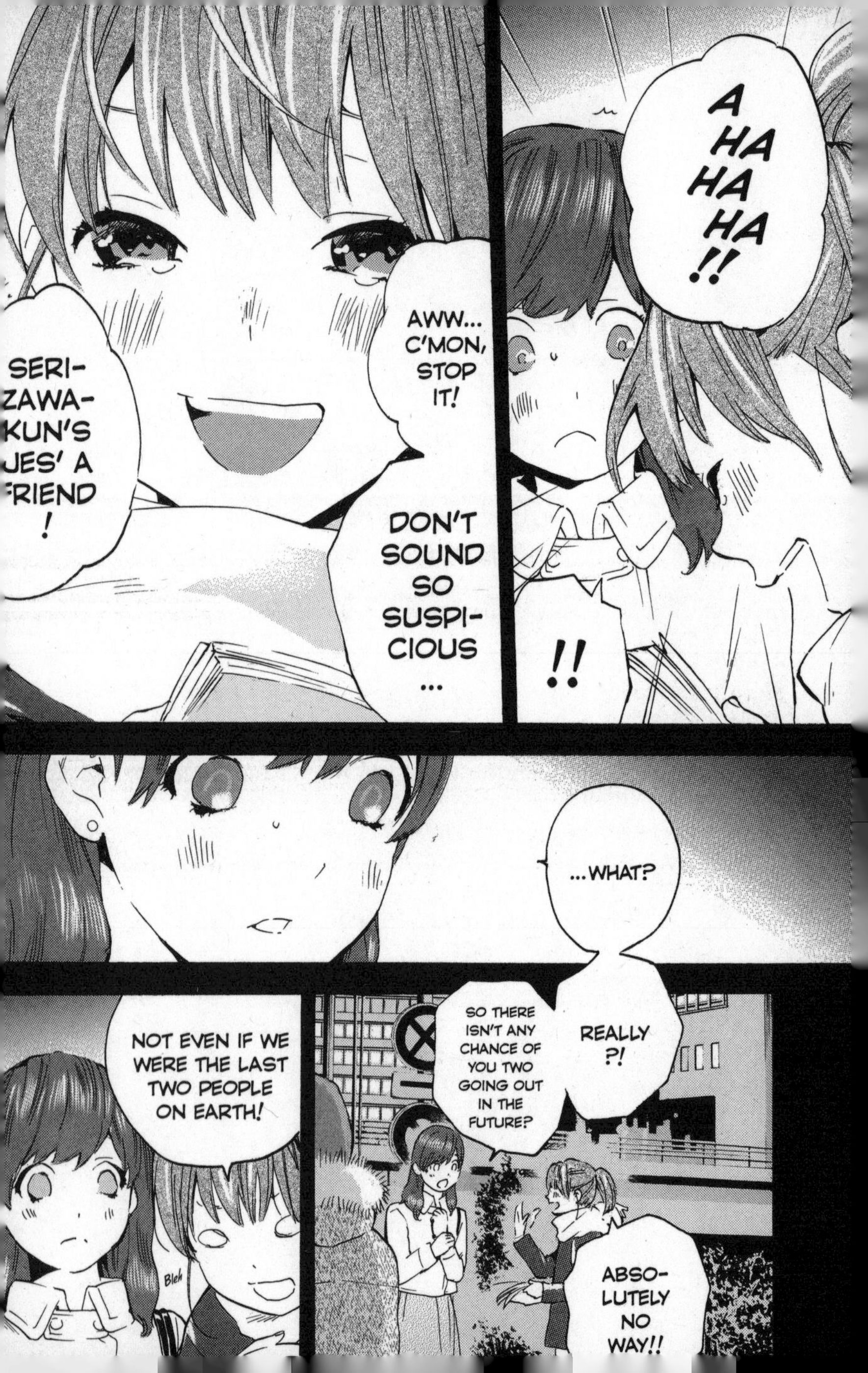
AHAHAHA!!
!!
AWW... C'MON, STOP IT!
DON'T SOUND SO SUSPICIOUS...
SERIZAWA-KUN'S JES' A FRIEND!
...WHAT?
REALLY?!
SO THERE ISN'T ANY CHANCE OF YOU TWO GOING OUT IN THE FUTURE?
ABSOLUTELY NO WAY!!
NOT EVEN IF WE WERE THE LAST TWO PEOPLE ON EARTH!
Bleh

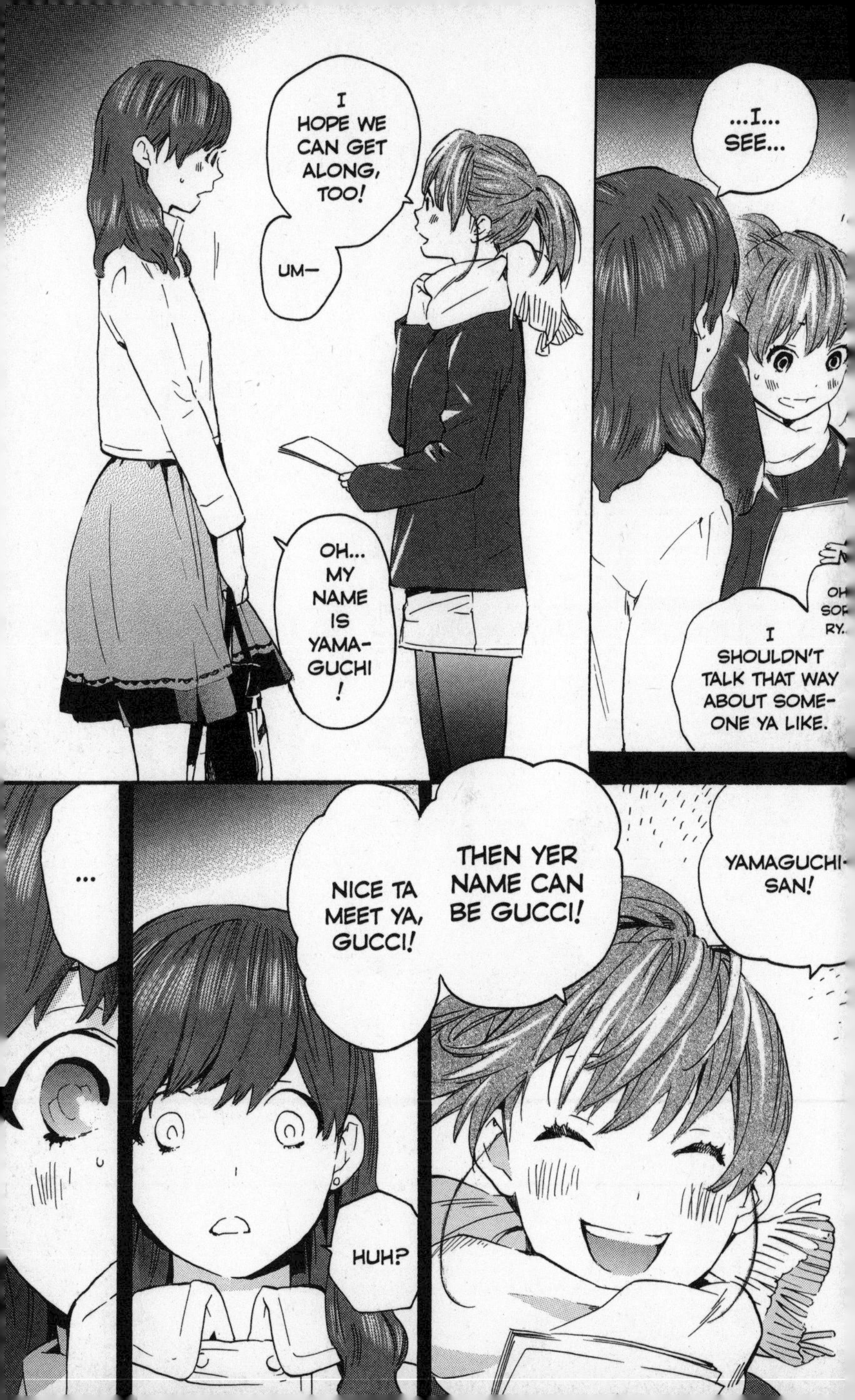
...I... SEE...
OH SORRY..
I SHOULDN'T TALK THAT WAY ABOUT SOMEONE YA LIKE.
I HOPE WE CAN GET ALONG, TOO!
UM—
OH... MY NAME IS YAMAGUCHI!
YAMAGUCHI-SAN!
THEN YER NAME CAN BE GUCCI!
NICE TA MEET YA, GUCCI!
HUH?
...

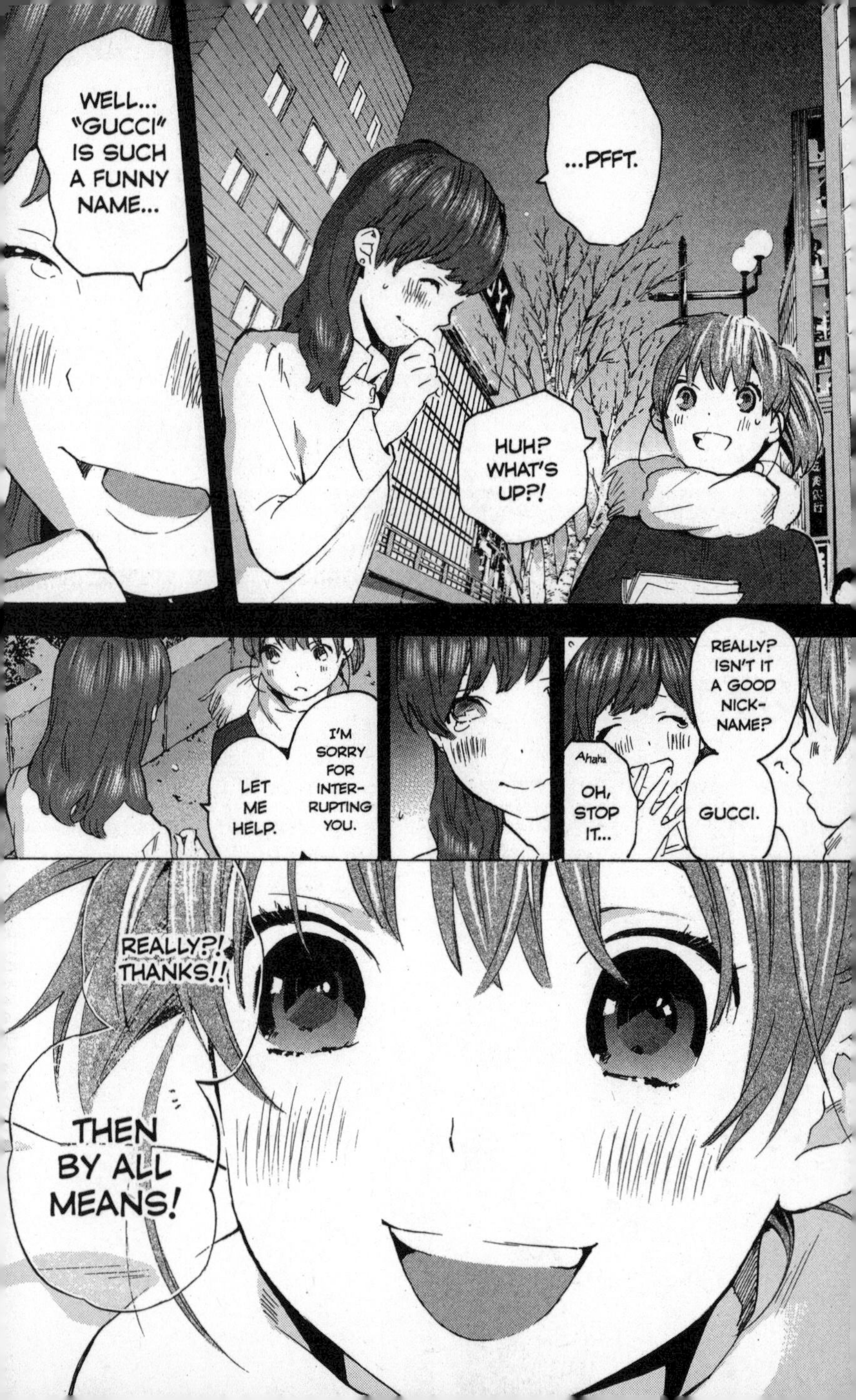
...PFFT.
HUH? WHAT'S UP?!
WELL... "GUCCI" IS SUCH A FUNNY NAME...
REALLY? ISN'T IT A GOOD NICK-NAME?
GUCCI.
Ahaha
OH, STOP IT...
I'M SORRY FOR INTER-RUPTING YOU.
LET ME HELP.
REALLY?! THANKS!!
THEN BY ALL MEANS!

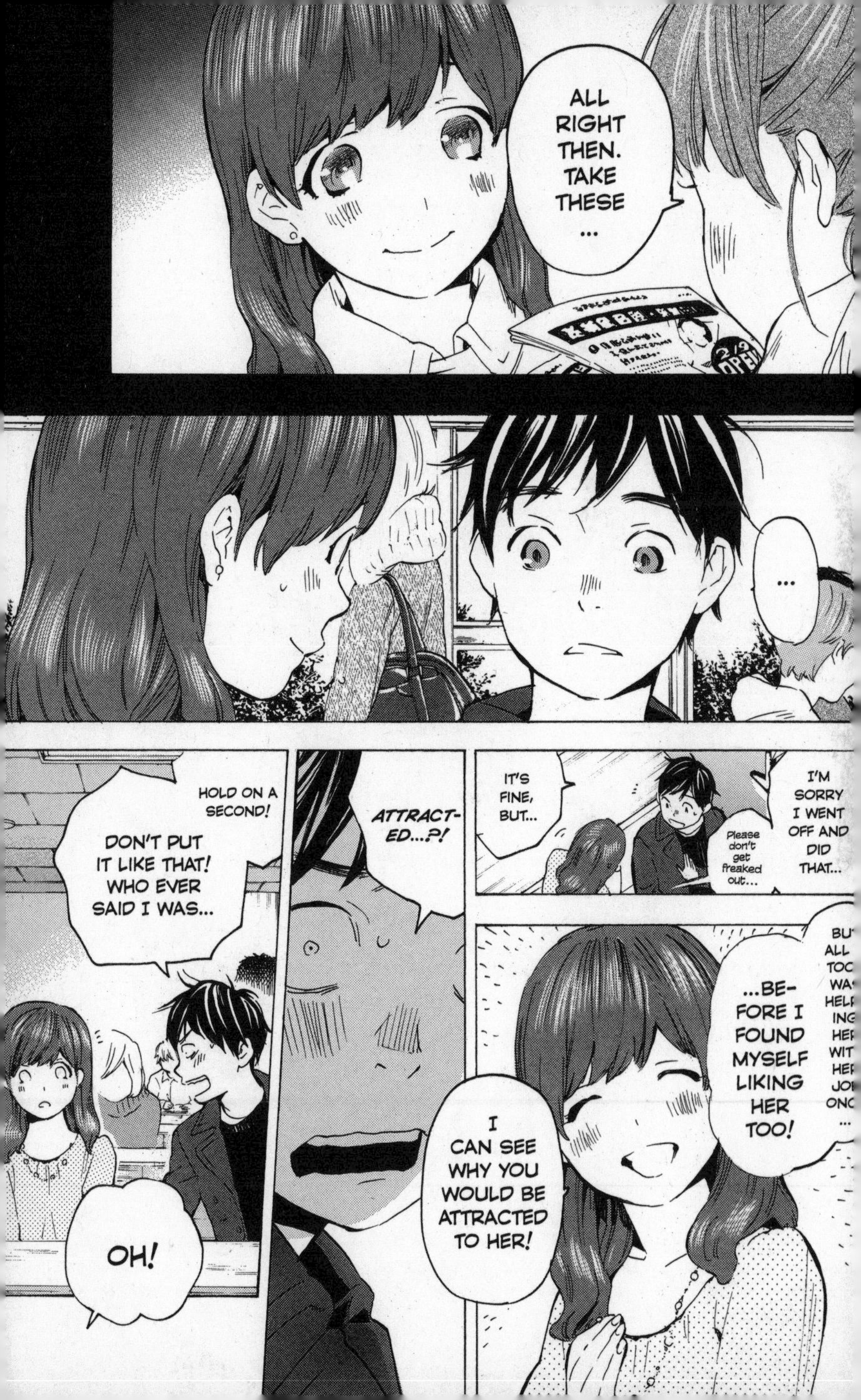
ALL RIGHT THEN. TAKE THESE...
...
I'M SORRY I WENT OFF AND DID THAT...
Please don't get freaked out...
IT'S FINE, BUT...
BU ALL TO WA HEL ING HE WIT HE JO ON ...
...BE-FORE I FOUND MYSELF LIKING HER TOO!
I CAN SEE WHY YOU WOULD BE ATTRACTED TO HER!
ATTRACT-ED...?!
HOLD ON A SECOND!
DON'T PUT IT LIKE THAT! WHO EVER SAID I WAS...
OH!

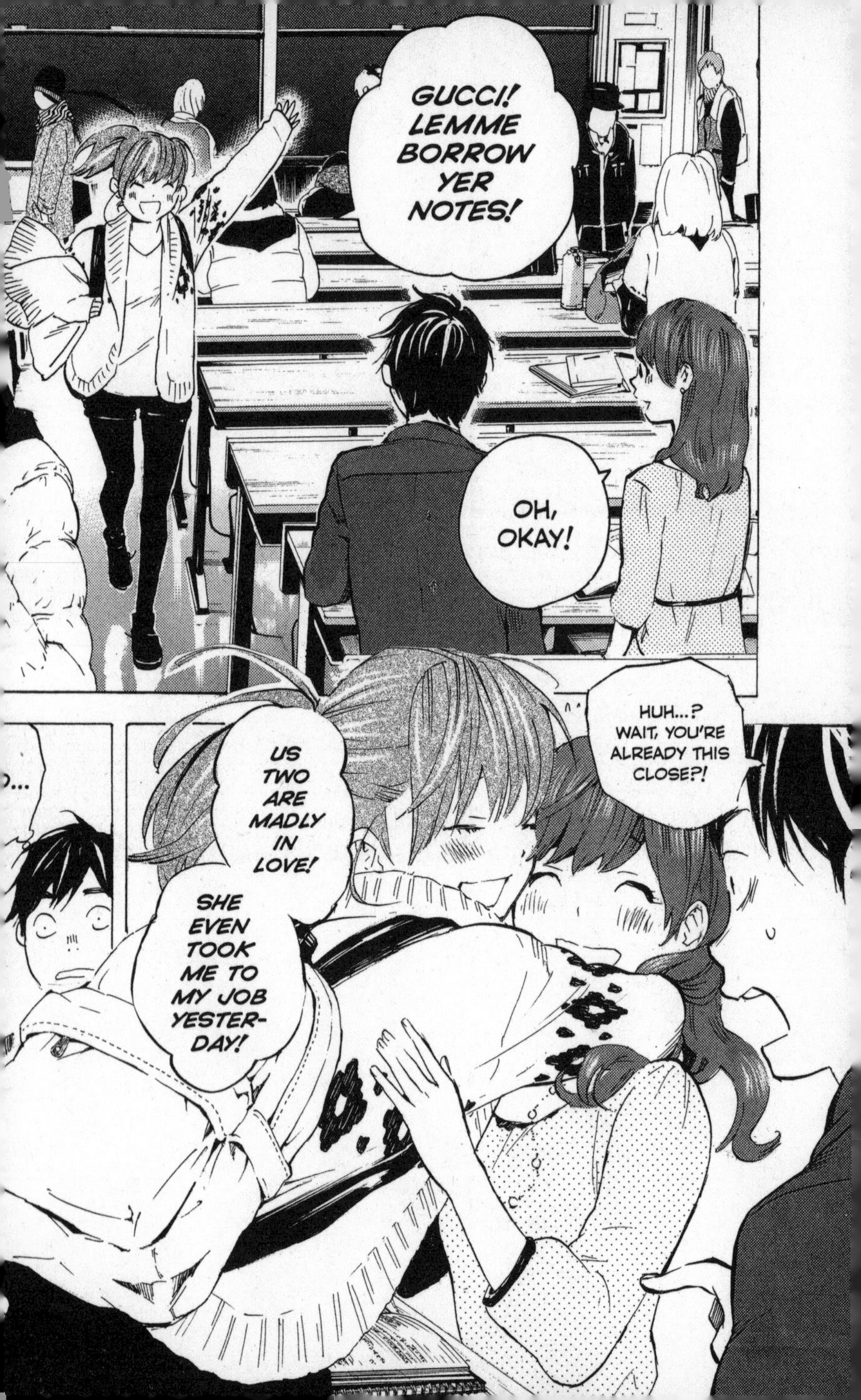
GUCCI! LEMME BORROW YER NOTES!
OH, OKAY!
HUH...? WAIT, YOU'RE ALREADY THIS CLOSE?!
US TWO ARE MADLY IN LOVE!
SHE EVEN TOOK ME TO MY JOB YESTER-DAY!

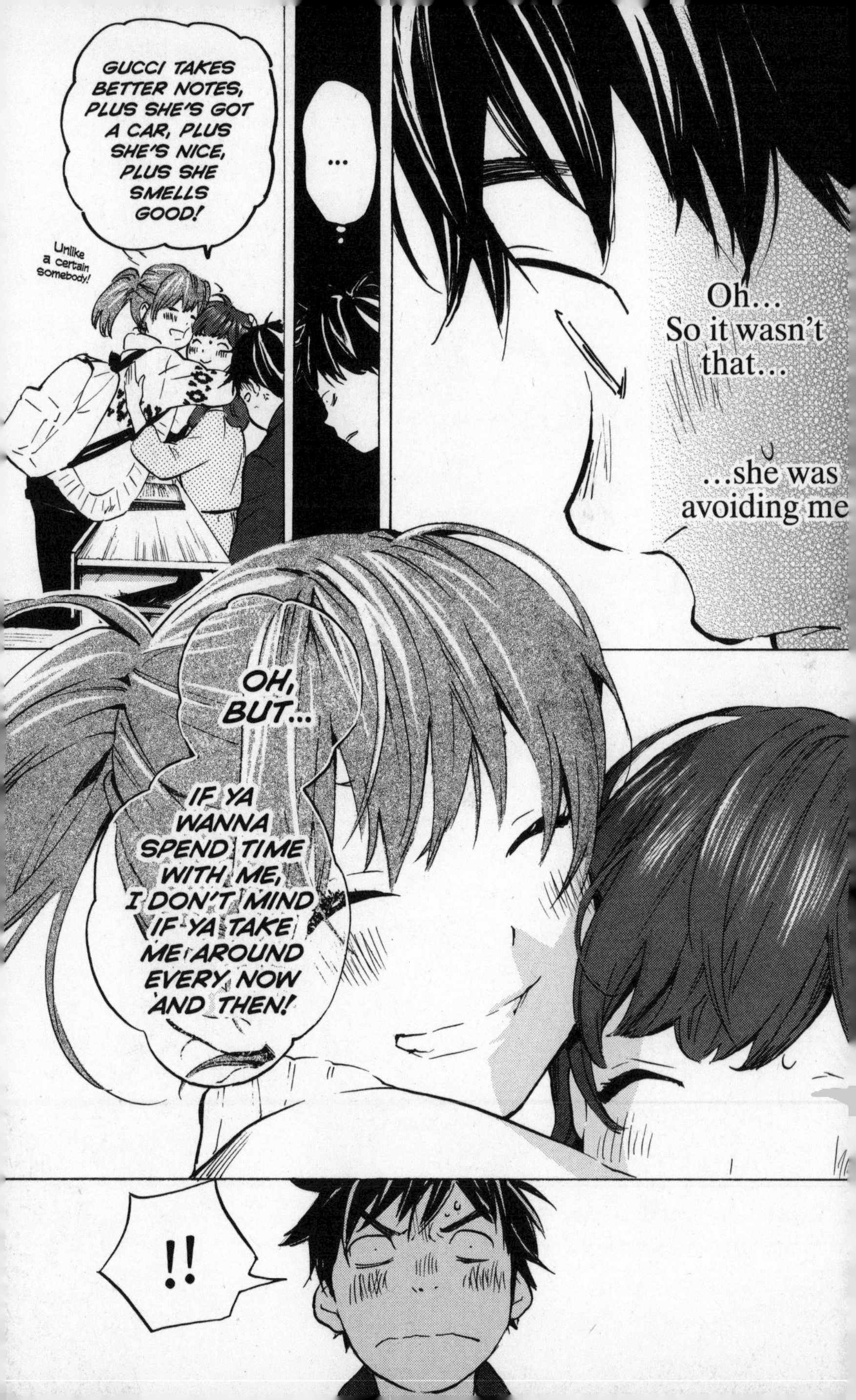

Oh… So it wasn't that…
…she was avoiding me
…
GUCCI TAKES BETTER NOTES, PLUS SHE'S GOT A CAR, PLUS SHE'S NICE, PLUS SHE SMELLS GOOD!
Unlike a certain somebody!
OH, BUT…
IF YA WANNA SPEND TIME WITH ME, I DON'T MIND IF YA TAKE ME AROUND EVERY NOW AND THEN!
!!

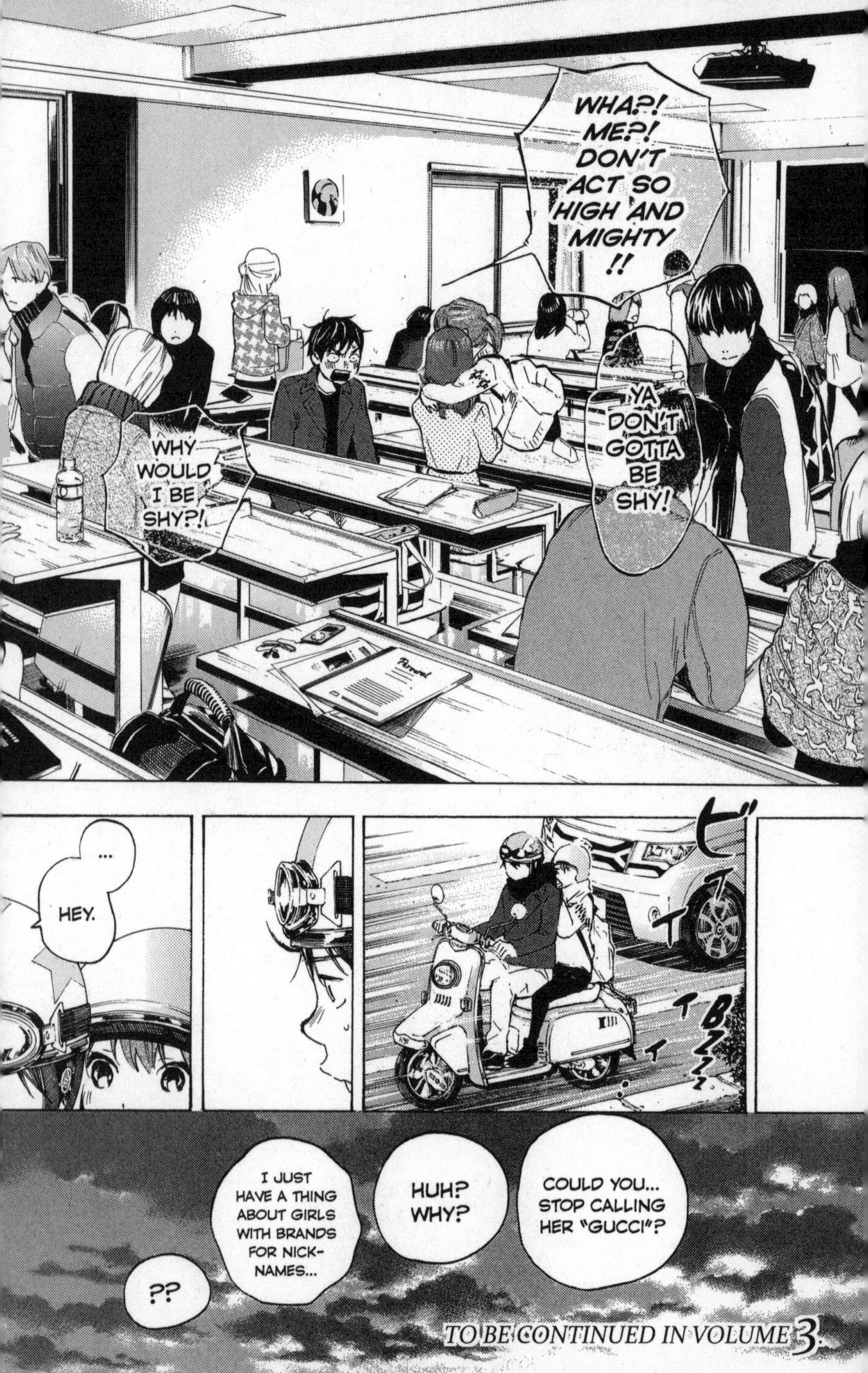
YA DON'T GOTTA BE SHY!
WHA?! ME?! DON'T ACT SO HIGH AND MIGHTY!!
WHY WOULD I BE SHY?!
BZZZ
...
HEY.
COULD YOU... STOP CALLING HER "GUCCI"?
HUH? WHY?
I JUST HAVE A THING ABOUT GIRLS WITH BRANDS FOR NICK-NAMES...
??
TO BE CONTINUED IN VOLUME 3.

Forget Me Not

— TRANSLATION NOTES —

WHEN ARE YOU GONNA DO IT? NOW! WHEN ELSE?! page 12, panel 2

This poster refers to a famous series of advertisements for Toshin High School, a major chain of college preparatory schools in Japan, that feature Osamu Hayashi, a teacher known for his catchphrase *"Itsu yaruka? Ima desho!"* ("When are you going to do it? Now, of course!")

ULFULS/GUTS DA ZE page 15, panels 1-2

Ulfuls is a popular Japanese rock band from Osaka who have enjoyed immense popularity since the 90s. The refrain for their hit single, "Guts da ze," was inspired by KC and The Sunshine Band's "That's the Way (I Like It)."

KINDAICHI page 15, panel 6

Kindaichi Case Files (Jp: Kindaichi Shonen no Jikenbo) is a long-running mystery/detective manga following the adventures of Hajime Kindaichi. Hajime is the grandson of a famous P.I. and can be easily identified by his trademark rattail.

IKUZO YOSHI page 16, panel 1

Ikuzo Yoshi is a famous singer in the Enka genre who has been active since the 1970s.

TOKYO UNIVERSITY AND KYOTO UNIVERSITY page 96, panel 2

Tokyo University and Kyoto University are commonly considered the two top universities in Japan, and are accordingly, the most competitive schools in the country.

MAKINO'S ACCENT page 119, panel 1

In Japanese, Makino has an accent from the Kyushu region (southwest Japan). There isn't really a direct equivalent to this accent in English, so non-specific, slang-like speech was used to make it clear that she doesn't speak like everyone else.

A Kodansha Comics Trade Paperback Original.

Forget Me Not volume 2 copyright © 2014 Mag Hsu & Nao Emoto
Original title "My Girls!: dedicated to those of you whom I love and hurt"
published in Taiwan 2011 by TITAN Publishing Co., Ltd.
English translation copyright © 2016 Mag Hsu & Nao Emoto

All rights reserved.

Published in the United States by Kodansha Comics,
an imprint of Kodansha USA Publishing, LLC, New York.

Publication rights for this English edition arranged through Kodansha Ltd.,
Tokyo.

First published in Japan in 2014 by Kodansha Ltd., Tokyo, as *Sore Demo
Boku Wa Kimi Ga Suki* volume 2.

ISBN 978-1-63236-281-0

Printed in the United States of America.

www.kodanshacomics.com

9 8 7 6 5 4 3 2 1

Translation: Ko Ransom
Lettering: Evan Hayden
Editing: Ajani Oloye
Kodansha Comics Edition Cover Design: Phil Balsman